THE SELF

THE SELF

BEYOND THE POSTMODERN CRISIS

Edited by

Paul C. Vitz

and

Susan M. Felch

ISI BOOKS

Wilmington, Delaware

2006

The self : beyond the postmodern crisis / edited by Paul C. Vitz and Susan M. Felch. — 1st ed. — Wilmington, Del. : ISI Books, c2006.

    p. ; cm.

    ISBN-13: 978-1-932236-86-6
    978-1-932236-03-3 (pbk.)
    ISBN-10: 1-932236-86-4
    1-932236-03-1 (pbk.)
    Includes bibliographical references and index.

    1. Self (Philosophy) 2. Identity (Philosophical concept) 3. Identity (Psychology) 4. Postmodernism. 5. Modernism(Christian theology) I. Vitz, Paul C., 1935– II. Felch, Susan M., 1951–

BD438.5 .S45 2006
126—dc22
            0603

Published in the United States by:

    ISI Books
    Intercollegiate Studies Institute.
    Post Office Box 4431
    Wilmington, DE 19807-0431

Book design by Beer Editorial and Design
Manufactured in the United States of America

TABLE OF CONTENTS

III. The Body and the Self

IV. Contemporary Society and the Self

V. College Students and the Self

VI. The Trinity and the Self

Acknowledgments

This book's genesis was a seminar held at Calvin College in Grand Rapids, Michigan, in summer 2001. There, on Calvin's delightful campus and over a five-week period, participants in the "Loss of the Self in a Postmodern Therapeutic Culture" seminar forged a new and exciting understanding of the self in spite of, or perhaps because of, the many different disciplines from which they came. These essays are the fruit of that seminar.

In all, it was a remarkable summer seminar and we owe a real debt of gratitude to those who made it possible. Anna Mae Bush cheerfully kept things running smoothly over the course of the seminar, coordinating everything from travel schedules, to housing and family needs, to the celebratory final dinner. She was aided by an excellent staff including Krista Betts Van Dyk, Kerry Schutt Nason, and Erica Schemper. We would also like to thank A. B. Chadderdon and Kara Van Drie for their competent and gracious help as the project has evolved through a follow-up conference and the publication of this book.

Neither the seminar nor the book would have been possible without the generous support of The Pew Charitable Trusts and of Calvin College's Seminar in Christian Scholarship. We are deeply grateful for this funding.

— *Paul C. Vitz and Susan M. Felch*
January 2006

Introduction: From the Modern and Postmodern Selves to the Transmodern Self

Paul C. Vitz

In the broadest sense, this book addresses the modern and postmodern selves; the crises and dilemmas that confront them; and, finally, the recapturing of the self within a new, positive framework. This is, of course, a large topic with many important dimensions, which are treated in the essays that follow. Here, however, I will present in a simple, brief way the central core issue: namely, the serious weaknesses of the modern and postmodern selves. I will then take up, again briefly, an answer to the problem; this answer will be called the "transmodern self" throughout this book.

First, a few words about vocabulary. I will use the terms "self," "person," and sometimes "identity" relatively interchangeably. I hope that any differences in the meanings of these terms will be made clear by the context. The concept of person is the largest of these notions, since person includes the totality of the body, the mind, and the spirit. The self is a subcategory, if you will, of person; self normally does not include spirit or the totality of these three terms. It is a part of them. Identity is a subcategory or component of the self. But for our purposes they will be generally interchangeable.

THE MODERN SELF

We begin with what is commonly called "the modern self." This is the familiar self, which has been around for at least a couple of centuries. Many historians place the beginning of the modern self in the period of the Renaissance and Reformation. (For a scholarly historical treatment, see Charles Taylor 1989; for an insightful summary, see Gil Bailie in this volume.) The modern self is characterized by such things as freedom and autonomy, by a strong will, and by the presumption that the self is self-created by the will, operating freely in its construction. The self is assumed to be strong, capable, and above all coherent; it is also largely conscious and heavily indebted to reason or at least reasonableness. Perhaps, as already implied, the self began in what is called the "Renaissance Man," but in recent years it has become the presumed goal or ideal of almost everyone. This is the self of self-actualization, of self-fulfillment. It has, of course, strong American roots going back to the Declaration of Independence and to the notion of the self-made man, and it was often explicitly articulated and praised by the American Transcendentalists.

The critique of the modern self has also become familiar (see Vitz 1977, 1994; Lasch 1978; Bellah et al. 1985) Three dilemmas or weaknesses are of particular concern. The first is that the modern self commonly leads to social alienation or isolation or loneliness because this self emphasizes separation: the breaking of bonds to become independent and supposedly autonomous. Second, the modern self decomposes society into isolated individuals and destroys social solidarity, neighborhoods, civic concern, and relationships of all kinds. Third, this idea of the self simply fails to understand how we, as selves or persons, are created by our personal relationships, our culture, and our language. In other words, the modern self is undergoing a crisis of intellectual legitimacy since social reality makes the whole notion of pure autonomy quite unconvincing.

THE POSTMODERN SELF

Although the term "postmodern" is hard to define, and although it contains different strands of thought, I will use it in a relatively straightforward and familiar way. By "postmodern" I mean a form of late modern or hypermodern thought and mentality. This postmodern mentality is characterized by a rejection of universal truth and objectivity and by a rejection of systematic, binding morality. In other words, for the postmodern, both truth and morality are true or good only for the individual. We have all run into this phenomenon: People say, "That's okay for you, that is your truth; this is mine" or "That's your moral system; I have mine." This particular strand of postmodernity has been traced back to Frederick Nietzsche and the notion that, as Dostoyevsky wrote, "If God does not exist, everything is permissible."

The postmodern also rejects all large theories: Marxism, socialism, libertarianism, and, of course, Christianity and other religious worldviews. It rejects all the grand narratives, all the big stories that are supposed to describe how we live, or should live.

Postmodernism also rejects the authority of the author with respect to understanding a text. Indeed, it rejects the idea that a text has an author in an authoritative sense. In some literary forms of postmodernism, theorists criticize what they would call any "privileged interpretation," any general interpretation; instead they claim that the individual reader is free to determine the interpretation just as the individual reader determines, say, truth or goodness or beauty. Not only truth and the moral life but also the meanings of the text are relativized.

This critique of general or universal interpretations by the postmodernists is actually aimed at the secular modern Enlightenment mentality. Though the postmodernist might criticize Christianity in terms of its worldview, Christianity itself is not seen as a suitable target because it is not understood as an important player in today's intellectual world. It is precisely because such theorists spend their time criticizing modernism that postmodernism is a kind of late modernism. It uses the "logic" of modernism itself to deconstruct modernity. These theorists are going after the Enlightenment understanding of objective reality, science, reason, and the other concepts that have developed from it.

Because it is primarily a critical and sometimes even nihilistic movement, I have often referred to postmodernism as "morbid modernism." Despite this relatively negative tone, postmodernism has nonetheless provided many valuable insights into the limits of reason, of science, and into the power structures that often lie behind objective systems of knowledge used in the service of goals or values that are far from objective. Much of postmodern thought, therefore, has been a kind of creative destruction. It has often served as an exposé, in the best sense of the term. And it certainly allows a much larger intellectual framework within which everyone, including Christians, can function. It provides a much bigger framework than that which existed fifty or a hundred years ago when the enlightenment rationalistic understanding of life was all that was seriously accepted. Retrospectively, the modern worldview can now be seen as a much narrower and more limited one than its adherents were willing to admit. But how does this postmodern attitude relate to the self, which is our primary topic?

Postmodern psychologists are among those who have criticized the modern self, although, as we shall see, their own constructions are not especially satisfactory. For most of us, the self has been considered a kind of unthought-about reality, intrinsically there. After all, we have magazines named after basic realities: we have *Time, Life, Money,* and we have *Self.* So these concepts should be solid. But that is not how postmodernists are thinking. For example, Kenneth Gergen (1991, 1998), one of the major critics of the self, proposes that the new self that is emerging be called the "saturated" self—a self that no longer has a coherent center. Gergen (1991) writes,

> With postmodern consciousness the last few decades begins the
> erasure of the category of self. . . . [W]e realize increasingly that
> who and what we are is not [so] much the result of our "personal

essence" . . . but how we are constructed in various social groups. The initial stages of this consciousness result in a sense of the self as a social con artist manipulating images to achieve ends. As a category of "real self" continues to recede from view, however, one acquires a pastiche-like personality. (170)

Gergen thus characterizes the contemporary self as no longer coherent and integrated. It is a self without a center, created by a huge variety of interactions with different groups and environments. Gergen notes three important characteristics of this self. The first is "polyvocality" (1998); that is, the new self has many voices. There is no longer the voice of conscience; or if there is, it is drowned out by the many other voices that we have. This polyvocality comes from the variety of people we are dealing with, from the media we are bombarded by, from the cacophony created by the new channels of information (e.g., cable television, the internet). One of the important points made by Gergen is that the older modern self is dying in large part from the effects of the new technology, which, he proposes, is causing much of the disintegration of our identity. (For specific ways in which technology is undermining the modern self, see the essays by Kent L. Norman and John Bechtold in this volume.)

Second, we are also more plastic, according to Gergen. By "plastic" he means that because we are dealing with so many different groups and worldviews, we constantly create new ways of self-presentation and self-interaction. We do not live in a reliable social environment any more. We live in a world of new groups that require not only that we accept their points of view and set up internal polyvocality, but also that we become a plastic person, with a kind of chameleon self. It is as though we are all morphing into politicians: as we try to look good to many different groups of people, we lose integrity.

For example, an article in the *New York Times* reported that a number of major corporations have an 800 number to respond to people who call in to ask questions, but the corporations were discovering that the cost of hiring young American women to answer the phones and direct inquiries was too expensive. So they off-shored this job of answering the phones to a place in southern India. And, of course, they found a fair number of young women there who could speak English well. To facilitate their work of answering Americans' questions, these women watched American television assiduously in order to understand how to speak American-ese and how to talk about different topics. All the operators also created false American identities; they had an American first and last name, an American town they lived in, American schools they had gone to. Each created an entirely new identity for this new job and new medium. I don't know what this is going to do to traditional India, to small-village Indian identity. But here we certainly have plasticity! Likewise, many people get on the Internet now and create different identities, different names, different roles and personal stories. For example, "Today I'll be a 45-year old lesbian looking for a lover." They bend genders, they create new identities, and they often have several of these "persons" going on the internet at the same time. It is this kind of plasticity that Gergen identifies.

A third characteristic of the new postmodern self is its transient nature. Obviously, high-tech media identities often do not last long. Within two or three years, perhaps, those young Indian women will have another job or will have gone on to college or gotten married—and they will have lost their old American "identity." There is a great sense of transience that flows from the new media and also from the frequent relocations in the corporate world. Even if one stays put geographically, the corporate world does not allow people much of a fixed identity within a given company because of mergers and similar corporate "morphs." One must recreate who one is. If one has lost his identity, for example, as an executive for Enron or Lucent, he must find a new way to make a living—and with the new job, a new self. It is becoming uncommon for workers or executives to spend all their working life at one company. These are all conditions causing slippage in the coherence of the self; this is the postmodern incoherence that Gergen describes as the source of the saturated self.

Another postmodern psychologist, Philip Cushman (1990, 1995), describes a different kind of self: the "empty" self. The traditional self, according to Cushman, was the self of relatively stable families and stable community life. A hundred years ago most people still lived in small towns or on farms where they had reliable traditional family lives. Everybody knew who the Smiths were: they had lived in Elmtown for three generations, maybe more. People knew one's uncles and aunts, the quirks and characteristics of one's family. Because of the stability of interpersonal relationships, there was stability to the self as well. But as we moved into the modern city, we lost that stability, and the self became empty. In the city, nobody knew who the Smiths were, they didn't know where Elmtown was, and people couldn't talk about their family: it had no meaning to other people. In this environment we began to search for a new identity. The modern identity, according to Cushman, was created by two new social institutions centered in the city. One was advertising and consumerism. Increasingly, what was meant by "image" advertising was the finding of an identity, a self, through the products one bought and the services one consumed. From the "Marlboro Man" to "I drive an Eddie Bauer jeep," we have gotten to know who we are. The logo on a Tommy Hilfiger sweatshirt tells us who we are. Do we own a barn jacket, even if we live in New York City where there is not a barn for fifty miles? (This aspect of modern identity—the consumerist self—is treated in this volume by David Burns.) In short, we get identity now through the commercial, advertising, and consumer world.

The other social institution that created modern identity, according to Cushman, was psychotherapy. Psychology gave us a self because we discovered who our family was and what our early childhood experiences were. Today, recovery groups are filled with people who can't talk about the Smiths from Elmtown but can talk about their dysfunctional family. You can talk about your inner child and how you had an alcoholic father and how your mother was a terrible enabler. Psychology gives us an identity constructed from our own, often painful, childhood and family memories. This identity is largely negative about, or critical of, the family, while at the same time it satisfies our own need to be of central importance.

Cushman claims that these two makers of the self have failed. As modernism ends, the self is shown to be increasingly empty. The problem with consumerism is that under its reign our desires—our always wanting more—are never satisfied. In fact, this is what advertising is about: keeping one permanently unhappy with one's identity and hence searching for a new product that will finally give one a truly satisfying self. Obviously, there is something very wrong with this quest, and many are beginning to become aware of it: thus, our emptiness and our knowledge of that emptiness. In addition, Cushman thinks that psychology too has become empty as a source of substantive identity. (An especially thoughtful critique of the weakness of much of the psychotherapeutic concept of self-love is given in this volume by David M. Holley.) What Cushman is saying is that the self as a modern construct has no lasting authenticity. It exists only in the way our particular society at this time in history creates who we are.

Cushman points out that one of the other forces behind the collapse of the modern self is the collapse of the modern family. It is not just technology with all its options that is creating the disintegrating self described by Gergen. Cushman and others note that one of the other determinants of this empty searching self is the social pathology in our families. The impact of divorce and of single-parent families and all kinds of blended families has marginalized the socially determined, stable self. These theorists are not talking about abstractions; rather, they are talking about two social realities that have impacted society and culture. Both technology and the proportion of people growing up with family pathologies have greatly reduced the stability of the self.

Robert Landy (1993), another postmodern psychologist, argues that there isn't any self at all. He claims that there is no such thing as a self; there are only social roles, and one plays these social roles well or not so well. Landy, who directs the drama therapy program at New York University, maintains that these roles are similar to roles in the theater. According to him, all we have are social roles. This notion is not unlike the understanding of the self in some other cultures, where people seem to have one role in one setting and another in another setting. In such cultures, the self is a collection of roles without a center. Landy admits that there is a sort of executive function that chooses among different roles, but it is not an authentic self. In fact, Landy explicitly argues that the very concept of the authentic self is inauthentic.

Implicit in all postmodern critiques is the assumption that postmodern types of changes in the self should be observable in today's culture, especially in young people. Two empirical studies that investigate this issue are found in the essays by Jim Norwine and associates, the other by Sherri B. Lantinga.

Whatever the strengths and weaknesses of these theorists, they point out that identity and the integrity of the self are for many becoming quite vague. Most of us have heard things like, "Look, I know that when we were married I promised to love you, but this is ten years later and I am a different person now, and so are you." Such statements imply that there is a weak sense of identity across a ten-year period. This loss of the integrated self is the loss of stability, not only in the individual but also in his or her relationships with others. Some theorists are beginning to worry about this loss because the morphing self calls into question the basic idea of a contract. How can one make a contract if one becomes a different person every few years? After all, if one has changed his signature, or his name, or even his sex, is he the same person? These questions raise serious issues about personal stability.

In sum, there are major problems with both the modern and postmodern self:

1. The modern self by emphasizing autonomy and separation has ignored the importance of interpersonal relationships, especially those early in life, in the formation of the self.

2. The objective validity of the self as rooted in the body has been ignored. (This is a major weakness of *both* the modern and postmodern positions.)

3. The modern self has no systematic intellectual rationale, instead it recognizes only total individual autonomy. (This weakness is exploited by postmodern critics.)

4. Finally, modern theorists of the self had little understanding of the formation of the adult social self within a cultural and historical context. (This is the major basis of the postmodern critique.)

The Transmodern Person

As an answer to the modern and postmodern problem, we should consider an alternative understanding of the person, one that has been emerging since the 1990s. I use the term "transmodern" to describe this new vision of the person and perhaps the new historical mentality that will follow the postmodern period (Vitz 1995a, 1995b, 1998). Transmodern means a new understanding that *transforms* the modern and also *transcends* it. This new approach does not reject most modern contributions but transforms their meaning. Moreover, the new meaning is often of a higher, transcendent nature—sometimes explicitly theological or spiritual but always with an emphasis on higher meaning. With respect to the person, the theoretical writers have been primarily theologians and philosophers, but their ideas are directly relevant to psychology, as will be shown here, and in due time these ideas may dramatically affect the culture in general. In part, the significance of this approach comes from the fact that these theorists articulate an understanding of the person that is intimately connected with the Judeo-Christian tradition; this approach therefore speaks to a core tradition of Western culture.

The empirical evidence for a new understanding of the self, however, is coming from contemporary cognitive psychology and neuroscience. Many researchers in these fields seem unaware of the broader implications of what they are doing, although a few are venturing into explanatory theories. William Hurlbut, whose integration of science and spiritual anthropology is included in this volume, asks the question: How does the self originate and develop over time?

The importance of the human body has been ignored in theories of the self (problem no. 2 above). It is now clear that there is a self that might be called the visual and perceptual self. Sometimes it is called the *ecological* self. Specifically, as the human infant looks around and somewhat later moves around in the world, he or she is clearly aware of a spatial or perceptual world in which it is in the center. This center of awareness is nonverbal, and this early sense of individuality or self is also biological, that is, rooted in perceptual experience and hence in the body; it is not, however, distinctly human because probably most of the higher animals have a similar invariant centering.

A second aspect of the bodily self that emerges is the *proprioceptive* self. This term acknowledges that I know where I am in space because I feel my body directly. I know I am at this desk, I am sitting, I can feel the cues of sitting, and so on. These internal kinesthetic or proprioceptive cues allow me to know where I am in space, and I've known this spatial center since I was an infant. This center also gives an invariant center for the identity of a person. (For more on the body-based self, see my essay as well as that by Glenn Weaver in this volume.)

Another important early understanding that develops in the infant at about the same time is the beginning of the interpersonal self (problem no. 1). Even before speech has begun, the infant and the mother (or mother figure) begin interacting in a way that is protoconversational. One of them makes certain sounds or responses, and then waits, and the other laughs and responds, and this interaction continues often for many minutes. It is very much like adult interaction but relies on body communication (plus speech from the mother but not yet comprehensible by the infant), though the mood or affect in the speech seems to be understood by infants very early. Somewhat later, early interpersonal relationships involving speech and social interaction with the mother, then the father and other family members, develop. Although these relationships, which are strongly internalized, are unique to each child, they also share common features across societies. These early relationships are part of a central self that is thus neither arbitrary nor later capable of much change. (For outstanding treatments of the interpersonal nature of self in the work of Girard and Bakhtin, see the essays by Gil Bailie and Caryl Emerson in this volume. Karen Coats's essay discusses the central relevance of love to self-formation; and Bert H. Hodges presents the importance of interpersonal relationships to self-formation.)

In short, it is now becoming clear that the self has an origin in the body and in early interpersonal relationships that are unique in particulars to each individual and yet have much in common with people everywhere.

The third problem mentioned is that the modern self has lacked any systematic intellectual rationale. Historically, the self or person was defined as "an individual substance of a rational nature" (Boethius). This expression meant reason operating in a body. However, over time, the term "substance" lost its clear meaning, and as a result Western philosophers increasingly ignored the body. A person or self became a kind of disembodied individual rationality. In philosophy and psychology, we ended up with the concept of the autonomous self.

The extreme emphasis on such ideas as independence, will, freedom, and autonomy by modern Western philosophies was no doubt supported by the neglect of the body. After all, the body puts limits on such interpretations.

Historically, the last major philosopher to emphasize the body and realism was Thomas Aquinas. However, many have interpreted Aquinas as failing to appreciate and recognize the importance of relationships as central to the notion of the person. A significant neo-Thomist response to this problem has been published by Norris Clarke (1998) who argues that relationship was always at least an implicit part of the Thomist understanding of person or substance. In any case, Clarke has explicitly remedied the situation by developing a systematic Thomist description of a person as a rational or intellectual substance-in-relationship. By this formulation, a firm philosophical grounding of a person as a body-in-relationship with others is now available (see 13–24).

An even larger, richer theoretical rationale comes from a biblical understanding of person or self. In particular, from Genesis it is clear that a person is made from matter, that is, has a body; in addition, some persons are male and others female in body. It is equally clear from the Judeo-Christian Scriptures that humans are created for interpersonal relationship—both with God and with other human beings.

In the last few decades, a new Christian rationale for the importance of relationships to the nature of person has emerged out of trinitarian theology. Thomas Torrance (1983, 1985) is an example from the Protestant perspective. Concurrently, Joseph Ratzinger (Pope Benedict XVI, 1970, 1990) and Karol Wojtyla (Pope John Paul II 1979; see also Connor's translation and interpretation [1992] of Wojtyla) have provided a similar Catholic trinitarian interpretation of person. Finally, the Eastern Orthodox theologian John Zizioulas (1985) has developed yet another similar and highly supportive trinitarian understanding of person as involving relationships. This is a remarkable confluence of interpretations. (In this collection there are two such trinitarian interpretations: one by Mark Lowery and another by Steve Stratton.)

Finally, we must address the fourth problem, the cultural critique of the postmodernists. Here again, a biblical understanding of person provides an answer. The two great commandments to love God and to love others clearly identify love as at the core of relationship and provide a cultural and historically invariant way to express the self or person. Loving God and loving others are the two universal coordinates—one vertical, one horizontal. They are applicable to all people at all times as guidelines for forming and expressing one's self and one's identity. However, these general rules are worked out in specific detail very differently from culture to culture and from one historical period to another. Thus, these two commandments, which speak to Christian and Jew alike (indeed probably to all theists), allow an invariant authentic core person or self to exist, along with the valid insights of the postmodern relativists who identify the many masks and roles that they have, often rightly, shown that we wear.

THE SOLUTION TO THE MODERN/POSTMODERN SELF/PERSON

In this volume, the authors will take up the challenge of proposing a solution to the modern and postmodern dilemma of the self. The solution will be developed from various perspectives, as summarized below.

PART 1: THE THEOLOGICAL RATIONALE

God is a person. Human beings are made in the image of God and therefore are also persons. As persons, we are made from earth and have bodies as do other animals. Explicitly, humans are made male and female in body (and this is good). As humans we are made for relationships with others. Adam for Eve, Eve for Adam, and both for relationship with God. The particular relationship humans are made for is love, which is understood as self-giving. This follows from the great commandments to love God and others. It also follows explicitly from trinitarian theology since God is three persons in a mutually self-giving loving relationship, and we are made in that image. (All of this is developed much more fully in the various writings on the theology of the body and the theology of the Trinity.)

PART 2: THE PHILOSOPHICAL RATIONALE

From a Thomist or Neothomist perspective, the human being is a rational substance in relationship. Thus both substance and relationship are primordial properties of the person. "All being, therefore, is by its very nature as being dyadic, with an 'introverted,' or *in-itself* dimension, as substance, and an 'extroverted' or *towards-others* dimension, as related through actions. . . . To be is to be *substance-in-relation*" (Clarke 1998, 15–17).

PART 3: THE PSYCHOLOGICAL RATIONALE

The visual-acoustic proprioceptive self, derived from bodily sensations and perceptions, is formed very early in life and sets up a core bodily based self similar to that of other human beings but specific to each person because of individual bodily and environmental differences for each child. Early language experience also establishes an early foundational self; early language constructs an interpersonal and even social-cultural self as well. Other early relationships especially with the mother as conceptualized by psychoanalyists (e.g., Object-relations theorists) and by those who study early attachment (e.g., Bowlby) make it equally clear that we are formed as selves/persons in interpersonal relationships.

PART 4: THE NEUROLOGICAL RATIONALE

Neurological evidence is clear that the human being is highly conditioned by the body. This evidence is substantial and widely understood as strongly conditioning each person's self. In addition, early relationships such as mother-child bonding are well known to have a neurological/biological basis, for instance oxytosin. Thus, we are biologically based in our bodies and in relationships that release chemicals cementing interpersonal bonds.

PART 5: THE CULTURAL RATIONALE

At the higher level of the social or cultural self, it is quite true that today's dramatic new communication technologies combined with family and cultural disintegration have done much to undermine the stability of the person or self. Nevertheless, the core of the person as previously described remains unchanged, and personal self-disintegration or incoherence is a form of suffering. The answer to this condition requires some culturally and historically invariant framework for maintaining an integrated, stable self. The two great commandments—love God and love others—provide such a framework while allowing the specifics of how to respond to these commands to vary with a person's culture and historical period.

I. New Theorists of the Self

1

The Imitative Self: The Contribution of René Girard

Gil Bailie

If there is a scripture passage that can be considered the bed-rock of biblical anthropology, it must surely be Gen. 1:27, where we are told that God created human beings in his own image and likeness. What are we to make of this charming piece of folklore? Surely it is one of the biblical passages most suited to demythologization of the Bultmannian variety. What serious biblical scholar, armed with the knowledge of the priestly authorship and sacerdotal biases of this text, would dare to regard it as anthropologically decisive? Even those who retain a deferential atti-tude toward Scripture, conceding its quaint anthropomorphism, might not think it strong enough to function as the fulcrum of biblical anthropology. How often does it happen, however, that the very texts we treat with smil-ing condescension turn out to be vastly more significant than those that accommodate themselves more readily to our existing prejudices and worldviews.

On the other hand, the historical nature of biblical revelation is such that the truth embedded in this ancient Scripture can be expected to release itself in response, not to idle curiosity or exegetical manipulation, but to the emergence of legitimate historical or existential situations that throw us back upon it with humility. We who face these new situations call upon biblical resources for facing them, not with Bultmann's exegetically pre-sumptuous but biblically timid approach, but rather with his appreciation for the "continual vitality which, thanks to the force of its original thrust, enables faith to dominate ever new historical situations by embracing them" (noted in Lubac 1986, 249).

THE MIMETIC SELF

What can be said of a creature who is made in the image and likeness of another? Surely this: that this creature can only fulfill its destiny by becoming like someone else. So counterinstinctual and counterintuitive is such a thing, that the likelihood of this creature actually fulfilling such a destiny would be slim, indeed, unless the creature were somehow endowed with a desire to do so, a desire equally counterinstinctual and counterintuitive, a desire to be itself by becoming like someone else. If we really are made in the image and likeness of God, such a desire, dangerously fickle though it might be, could well function, after a kind of Dantean purification of itself, as the key to our sanctification.

But what a strange creature this would be, one endowed with a desire to fulfill its own unique destiny by modeling its life on another. Can any such creature be found? René Girard, the Andrew B. Hammond Professor in French Language, Literature, and Civilization, Emeritus at Stanford University, thinks he has found such a creature. In fact, he thinks he *is* one. Over the course of the last thirty years, Girard has insisted that the decisive feature of human existence is the central role played in human affairs by what he calls *mimetic desire*, the ineradicable impulse to desire what one sees another desiring, to fashion one's own desire on the model of another's desire, in short, to imitate. In books and articles too numerous to catalog, Girard has demonstrated the irreducible centrality of mimetic desire in human affairs, and in the course of demonstrating this he discovered something he never dreamed of discovering at the outset, namely, the anthropological centrality and historical singularity of the Christian revelation. Most of what I have to say is indebted to Girard.

So, let's begin with the hypothesis that Genesis is right, we are made in the image and likeness of God. But which god? For there are, as St. Paul tells us in First Corinthians, "many 'gods' and many 'lords'." (Biblical quotations are taken from the New American Bible.)

During summer 2001, the pop music idol Madonna launched a worldwide tour, which almost instantly sold out. The *New York Times* reported that on the day of the first New York performance the $125 seats were being scalped for $700. Susan Saulny (2001), the *Times*' reporter covering the opening night enthusiasm of Madonna's devotees, wrote:

> There are, apparently, an infinite number of ways to show love for Madonna.
>
> An unimaginative but nonetheless sincere fan might wear a T-shirt emblazoned with her likeness. A very good fan might slip into a kilt, in tribute to her fondness for things Scottish, or wear a rhinestone necklace and rubber bracelets, à la the original Material Girl. A great fan will dye black hair blond, squeeze a man's foot into a pair of high-heeled boots, and declare Madonna the icon of our age.

But someone who has totally given himself over to Madonna, the pop artist of a thousand incarnations, will do all of these things at once. His name is Bobby Tuttle.

"This is the event of the century," Mr. Tuttle, who is 24, proclaimed last night to a crowd of believers eagerly waiting to enter Madison Square Garden, where Madonna was set to take the stage at 8 p.m. for the first of five sold-out performances. (6)

The best commentary on the devotion of the most enthusiastic Madonna fans, and especially on those like Mr. Tuttle who have totally given themselves over to Madonna, is a sentence from Girard's *Deceit, Desire, and the Novel*: "There is not one element of this distorted mysticism," he writes, "which does not have its luminous counterpart in Christian truth" (1965, 61). Which brings me to the central point of this essay, an ancient anticipation of the one just quoted from Girard. It comes from the second century theologian Tertullian. It is this: "The soul is naturally Christian."

Desire, Girard tells us, is always "the desire to be another." Whether one is squeezing a man's foot into a Madonnaesque pair of high-heeled boots or imitating the selflessness of Christ, our deepest and defining impulse is to adopt as our own the attributes of another. "Choice always involves choosing a model," Girard writes, "and true freedom lies in the basic choice between a human and a divine model" (1965, 58). To which I might add—revealing my own religious sensibilities—that since even our imitation of a divine model will inevitably involve the mediation of intermediary human models, Mr. Tuttle's ontological prognosis might be greatly improved if he were to fall under the spell of another Madonna. For nothing better encapsulates the spirit of Christian existence than the utterance placed into the mouth of Jesus' mother by the evangelist Luke: "Behold the handmaid of the Lord, be it done unto me according to Thy word."

NUPTIAL TRUTH

To claim, however, that true freedom lies in choosing a proper model, is to raise this question: What *is* the nature of truth? Postmodernists are not terribly convincing when they say that they want to know the answer to this question, but that's because they continue to rely on modern skepticism without treating it, in a truly postmodern fashion, skeptically. The single greatest cultural contribution of postmodernity is that it eliminates the presumption of intellectual neutrality that modernity automatically associated with skeptical rationalism. By calling this presumption of neutrality into question, postmodernity makes a great breakthrough possible.

It shows, not that all truth is socially constructed, but that the uniquely human act of bearing witness to the truth is always a moral as well as an intellectual or empirical or noetic act.

As ludicrous and dangerous as the Nietzschean perspectival understanding of truth is—that there is no truth, only *your* truth and *my* truth and "*Ted Turner's* truth" and "*Noam Chomsky's* truth"—as ludicrous and dangerous as this idea is, might it not lead us to a rediscovery of the mystery of Christian truth, a mystery that has tended to be lost on those imbued exclusively with modernist epistemological preconceptions. I'm thinking, for instance, of the *nuptial* understanding of truth, that truth which will set one free, the kind of truth about which the Gospel is concerned and has a great deal to say and which awaits a *yes* on the part of its potential recipient. The etymological origin of the English word *truth* is the Old English word *treowth*, from which comes the word *troth*, suggesting a hidden covenantal understanding of truth. There may be reason to hope that in countering, as we must, the dangerous and cockeyed notions about truth circulating today under the postmodern banner we may discover a lost mystery.

The assumption that all truth is socially constructed is intimately linked to its postmodern corollary: the socially constructed (and deconstructed) self. These issues come together as well in quite different ways in Christian thought, and in responding to the postmodern challenge, Christians may well surprise themselves. For there seems to me a tremendous potential in the postmodern assumption that the self is an artificial social construct. The assumption is naïve and it usually harbors hidden agendas, but if we took it seriously it might help awaken Christians to the fact that something at least as shocking lies at the heart of Christian personhood. In a very real sense, at the burning center of Christianity is a person who emphatically insists that he exists only to bear witness to another person, a person whose life is therefore iconic in the extreme, an icon of the invisible God, the God, moreover, in whose image and likeness Genesis tells us we are made. If postmodernity is setting up questions to which Christianity has answers, then rediscovering those answers may do both postmodernity and Christianity a world of good.

THE INVISIBLE SELF

"As one casts out to sea in the contemporary world," writes Kenneth J. Gergen (1991), describing the postmodern psychological predicament, "modernist moorings are slowly left behind."

It becomes increasingly difficult to recall precisely to what core essence one must remain true. The ideal of authenticity frays about the edges; the meaning of sincerity slowly lapses into indeterminacy. And with this sea change, the guilt of self-violation also recedes. As the guilt and sense of superficiality recede from view, one is simultaneously readied for the emergence of a pastiche personality. The pastiche personality is a social chameleon, constantly borrowing bits and pieces of identity from whatever sources are available and constructing them as useful or desirable in a given situation. (150)

Gergen's observation of the postmodern psychological situation is marvelously perceptive, though his cheerfully naive assumption that "if one avoids looking back to locate a true and enduring self" the situation can be "properly managed" is considerably less useful. Given the growing pharmacological arsenal for anesthetizing "the guilt of self-violation," it would be naïve to suggest that it cannot be done, but it would be even more naïve to overlook the spiritual price to be paid for doing so. Modern psychology emerged, and put its stamp on the twentieth century, precisely because an increasing number of people were unable to manage properly the psychological house of mirrors Gergen so well describes. Symptoms of the psychological distress associated with this problem emerged centuries earlier, at the dawn of the modern age, and the spiritual and cultural shifts that gave rise to these symptoms are older still. The most obvious fact about the postmodern crisis of the self is that it is a historical phenomenon. With Professor Gergen's sketch of what he calls the "pastiche personality" fresh in our minds, we can perhaps detect its early manifestations in a few texts dating from the early seventeenth century.

A passage that bears remarkable likeness to Gergen's appears in Shakespeare's *Antony and Cleopatra*. Tellingly, it occurs at the onset of Antony's great crisis in act 4 of the play.

With both his erotic desires and his political ambitions in ruins, Antony asks his attendant, not coincidentally named Eros, whether he, Antony, is still visible. To which Eros answers, "Ay, noble lord." But Antony, his ontological substantiality draining away, cannot be persuaded by such perfunctory reassurances. He proceeds to relate his psychological predicament:

Sometime we see a cloud that's dragonish,
A vapor sometime like a bear or lion,
A towered citadel, a pendent rock,
A forked mountain, or blue promontory

With trees upon't that nod unto the world
And mock our eyes with air . . .
That which is now a horse, even with a thought
The rack dislimns and makes it indistinct
As water is in water.
My good knave Eros, now thy captain is
Even such a body. Here I am Antony,
Yet cannot hold this visible shape, my knave. (4.14.2–14)

Shakespeare's Antony is suffering from precisely the sort of self-dissolution about which Gergen remains so sanguine. Chameleon-like, Antony has begun to take on the form of whatever exerts an influence on him, but he is unable to regard the unraveling of his identity with Gergen's serenity. An exploration of the roots of Antony's ontological predicament, its origin in mimetic desire and the passions it awakens, would take us too far afield. Suffice it to say that his psychological disintegration was the reason for, and not the result of, the erotic and political misadventures that preceded it, the final collapse of which coincided with his eventual recognition of his plight. In the image of his curse we can see the portraiture of ours, for the crisis that is now looming was preceded and prepared for by decades of political and sexual hysteria, in the aftermath of which many are, like Antony, "borrowing bits and pieces of identity from whatever sources are available."

MISPLACED MIMETIC DESIRE

Antony and Cleopatra was probably first performed in 1607. Two years earlier in Spain, Cervantes had published part 1 of *Don Quixote*, and, as an actor was declaiming Antony's lines in London, Cervantes was at work on the second part of his novel, which was published in 1615. Cervantes' masterpiece is the story of a man suffering a milder form of the same spiritual and psychological crisis into which Shakespeare's Antony was slipping. The protagonist of Cervantes' novel is a man responding to a deep desire to imitate another. His predicament is less grave than Antony's for the simple reason that he has managed to keep one single model before him throughout his life, the fictional hero of contemporary novels of chivalry, Amadis of Gaul. Yet, like Shakespeare's Antony, the man from La Mancha has a moment of truth at which he awakes, not to a cloud that was dragonish, but to windmills and remorse.

After a life spent emulating his model, on his deathbed Don Quixote belatedly comes to his senses. Like Antony, he mumbles about misty shadows and the loss of his identity. He says to those attending to him in his extremity:

> My judgment is now clear and free from the misty shadows of ig-
> norance with which my ill-starred and continuous reading of those
> detestable books of chivalry had obscured it. Now I know their
> absurdities and their deceits, and the only thing that grieves me is
> that this discovery has come too late, and leaves me no time to
> make amends by reading other books, which might enlighten my
> soul. . . . Now I am the enemy of Amadis of Gaul and of all the
> infinite brood of his progeny. Now all profane histories of knight
> errantry are odious to me. I know my folly now, and the peril I have
> incurred from reading them. Now, by God's mercy, I have learnt
> from my own bitter experience and I abominate them. (935–36)

Realizing that his life has been misspent slavishly imitating a model whose escapades were unworthy of such devotion, Don Quixote doesn't renounce imitation, as his modern heirs would, rather he bemoans the fact that his imminent death leaves him so little time to make amends for having read and imitated certain books by reading and imitating certain *other* books, those that might enlighten his soul. Don Quixote, or rather Cervantes, realizes that imitation is an unavoidable fact in human life, the crucial choice being whom one takes as a model. He sees the folly of having modeled his life on novels about chivalrous knights rather than on the lives of the saints, which is surely what Cervantes means by books that enlighten the soul. Don Quixote's deathbed conversion consisted of his realization that he had imitated the wrong model. His response was to want to imitate the right ones.

In this, Cervantes writes in the great tradition of Dante, who, on finding himself lost in the dark wood, turns from jousting at the political and philosophical windmills of fourteenth century Florence to new models that enlighten his soul, Virgil, Beatrice, and Bernard. Like Don Quixote, the pilgrim Dante had fallen into error by imitating the wrong models and his conversion would consist, not in renouncing imitation—the modern move par excellence—but in finding the right models.

The paradigmatic conversion stories in the Gospel—Peter hearing the cock crow and Saul hearing Christ call him a persecutor on the Road to Damascus—are analogous in many ways to the moments of illumination which left Shakespeare's Antony and Cervantes' Don Quixote, and the pilgrim Dante reeling. This is no mere coincidence. For the psychological perils from which Antony, Quixote, and Dante suffered are symptomatic of a vast anthropological shift set in motion by the Gospel, and specifically the revelation of the cross that is at the heart of the Gospel. Those able to share fully in the social solidarity generated by religiously sanctioned collective violence enjoy real psychological benefits—a sense of cultural identity, of moral rectitude, and of intense camaraderie—albeit at the expense of those on whom their unanimous contempt or violence falls. By revealing the innocence of the victim and the madness of the victimizing crowd, however, the Gospel disrupts the procedure upon which humans have depended for both social solidarity and psychological poise since the birth of culture itself. In societies that have fallen under Christian influence, the mechanism for periodically reinforcing psychological and social identity grows weak and attenuated. The social and psychological impulses that give rise to these rituals of cultural rejuvenation—what we today call the scapegoating mechanism—nevertheless retain considerable residual power. So even as the Gospel continues to deprive this mechanism of the religious and moral privileges it enjoyed in the past, the crisis that accompanies its demise paradoxically inclines those caught up in it to resort again to the mechanism.

The truth of the cross is not only, however, an exposé about the role of sacred violence in cultural life; it is also the truth about the origin of the passions that lead inevitably to the violence and endow it with religious meaning. It is the truth about mimetic desire. Few may understand this link between sacred violence and mimetic desire, but the affinity between them is such that a culture's aversion to the truth about the former will always be accompanied by a corresponding aversion to the truth about the latter. Both conventional cultural forces ("the world") and deeply embedded psychological reflexes ("the flesh") will, in a crisis-ridden world, collaborate to ward off or marginalize the Gospel's moral and cultural influence. So, as evidence of the truth of mimetic desire emerges, we can safely predict that cultural forces will be awakened in opposition. It is not surprising, therefore, that at almost the same time that Shakespeare and Cervantes were issuing their literary warnings about the approaching mimetic crisis in the West, a philosophical effort was being launched which would have the effect of thwarting the revelation for which Shakespeare and Cervantes served as heralds. As the role of mimetic desire in human affairs became visible in such literary works, modernity's great philosophical recoiling from that revelation was launched.

DESCARTES' MIMETIC DENIAL

Both Shakespeare and Cervantes died in 1616. During the Dutch winter of 1628, René Descartes ensconced himself in a little garret for the purpose of clearing *his* head of some "misty shadows of ignorance." The difference between his response and that of his literary contemporaries may help us understand the modern and postmodern predicament. At the beginning of his *Third Meditation*, Descartes (1968) describes the physical surroundings that most suited his purpose: "The onset of winter held me up in quarters in which, finding no company to distract me, and having, fortunately, no cares or passions to disturb me, I spent the whole day shut up in a room heated by an enclosed stove, where I had complete leisure to meditate on my own thoughts" (35).

This passage may tell us more about the Cartesian revolution than Descartes' elaborate philosophical justifications for it. It indicates where the problem lies for Descartes. It lies in other people. The ideal setting for Cartesian thought is not just solitude in, say, the time-honored monastic sense—that is to say, being alone with God in prayer and being silently present to others in work and worship. No, Descartes' solitude was cloistered isolation set up to wall him off from mimetic suggestion. If he is to have reliable thoughts of *his own*, the "cares" and "passions" aroused in him by the presence of others must be extinguished. Sartre's "hell is other people" is still more than three centuries down the road, but Descartes has taken the first steps on that road, not because he is a misanthrope, but because he realizes how inevitably influenced by each other we humans are and he sees in this not the possibility of a covenant community, the communion of saints, but simply an obstacle to his quest for certitude and autonomy.

For Descartes, the only thing about which he harbored no doubts was that the person harboring the doubts existed, and this was the starting point of his philosophical revolution. For Descartes, the doubting mind *is* the thinking mind; to think is to doubt and to doubt is to exist as an independent being. I am skeptical, therefore I exist. The most important thing about Descartes' methodological skepticism is that it is radically individualistic. *I* am skeptical, therefore *I* exist. If Christian faith is always covenantal, Cartesian skepticism is always individualistic. Christian faith is intensely personal, but it is emphatically not individualistic. The Christian being is an ecclesial being. Faith grows by exposure to faith. The Cartesian quest for certainty, on the other hand, is the quest for *unmediated* knowledge, knowledge that one acquires by eliminating the mimetic influence of others, avoiding (or trying to) the epistemological corruption such an influence might have. Wariness about mimetic influence is certainly a legitimate concern, but mimetic desire is what makes humanity what it is, a creature made in the image and likeness of an Other and endowed with a deep-seated and irrevocable desire to fulfill itself by falling under the influence of another.

One could as well live without oxygen as eliminate the mediating influence of others, and Descartes' efforts to do so anticipate the desperate self-referentiality of the modern self and its wistful efforts to experience its own ever-elusive authenticity.

Descartes represents himself as ensconced for six days in an isolated Dutch garret where he communes only with his own thoughts, but at length the elimination of the physical presence of others seems not to be sufficient. He must redouble his efforts to insure that it is, in fact, *his own thoughts* on which he is meditating. He writes: "I will now close my eyes, I will plug my ears, I will turn aside all my senses . . . in this way, concerned only with myself, looking only at what is inside me, I will try, little by little, to know myself, and to become more familiar to myself" (quoted in Zweig 1968, 121).

According to Charles Taylor (1989), it is here that we can glimpse most clearly "Descartes' decisive moment of inspiration" (157). William Temple (1940) was more emphatic; he called Descartes' withdrawal into himself "the most disastrous moment in the history of Europe" (57). Concentrating only on him*self*, looking only at what is *inside* him*self*, straining to know him*self*, Descartes has made the inward turn, and in doing so has set out to systematically eliminate mimetic influence of others.

The psychological crisis faced by Cervantes' Don Quixote is rooted in his susceptibility to the mimetic influence of the model under whose spell he fell. Realizing how foolish he had been, Quixote wanted to amend his ways by imitating better mimetic models. Descartes' solution to this dilemma was to eliminate imitation altogether. This may be the defining gesture of modernity: some move made to eliminate mimetic influence or to try to show how impervious one is to it. Like postmodernists, Descartes was raising the question of truth, of what could be said to be true, of what could not be successfully challenged by naysayers. His answer finally was this: his own thought, *cogito, ergo sum*, a banal and ultimately idolatrous parody of the biblical "I AM who Am," an abandonment of biblical anthropology. It was only a matter of time before Nietzsche, brooding in *his* dark garret, hatched the Cartesian egg, and launched the postmodern era by declaring that the only truth possible is radically individualized truth, *my* truth, ontologically insulated from the gainsaying of others. From Descartes' quest for unmediated certainty to the solipsistic disintegration of truth in Nietzsche, what's at work is the fear of mediation, the fear of mimetic desire with all its messiness and muddle, which is, at bottom, the fear of Christian truth.

Remember, if you will, the post-Easter scene of Jesus appearing for the second time to the disciples, this time with Thomas the Twin (often called doubting Thomas) present among them, and saying to Thomas, "Blessed are those who have not seen but who believe" (John 20:27). When Jesus says "blessed are those," he isn't saying they are blessed because they manage to overcome or stoically accept the handicap of having not seen. Rather he is saying that it is *better* to receive the truth through the testimony of others, to receive it by way of human mediation, than it is to receive it any other way. He is saying that by receiving the truth from the hands of others we enter more fully into the great trinitarian mystery of mutuality that is the mystery of God par excellence, the very purpose of biblical revelation. Blessed are those who have not seen and yet believe on the testimony and living example of others. A Christian is someone who has met a Christian. Mediation is how it works. Faith begets faith, and in the process persons are ontologically engaged, brought to life, by the grace of God resurrected. In the quest for philosophical certitude, Descartes renounced the mimetic mediation that plays such a pivotal role in the transmission of Christian truth. Whereas what we might call Quixotic disillusionment led to the search for good mimetic models, Cartesian disillusionment led to a flight from imitation, fear of the influence of others, and the dreary autonomy of the modern self.

For all his epochal philosophical significance, and despite its promulgator's determination to insulate himself from the mimetic influence of others, Descartes' revolution had a long prehistory. "In his desire to portray his thought as originating *ab ovo*," writes Michael Allen Gillespie, Descartes "goes to considerable lengths to conceal his sources" (1996, 29). Of course, the task of concealing influences was to become endemic in the modern world, in order to insulate the myth of autonomy against the mimetic facts of life. In going to considerable lengths to conceal his sources, Descartes was simply foreshadowing the plight his spiritual heirs would suffer as the truth of mimetic influence relentlessly undermines the public demonstrations of autonomy designed to keep this truth from intruding.

For Descartes, nevertheless, there were influences aplenty, and arguably the greatest of them is the influence of Augustine. As Paulos Mar Gregorios (1992) reminds us, Descartes begins where Augustine began, with doubt as the only thing that could not be doubted.

> In Augustine's fertile mind arose the idea that only one thing was certain, namely that everything was uncertain. So he latched on to that as his starting point, namely that he was doubting everything, except the fact that he was doubting. That, he thought, was not to be doubted: the indubitable existence of the doubting and the doubter. I, the doubter, exist—that much was self-evident to Au-

> gustine. Descartes, who had studied with the Jesuits and knew his
> Augustine, made a slight change and got to his *cogito, ergo sum*: I
> think therefore I exist. (90–91)

Descartes' "slight change," like Chesterton's concept of a small mistake in doctrine, was the beginning of a massive repudiation of Christian
anthropology. The depth and seriousness of Descartes' doctrinal commitments have been long argued, but it was his anthropological miscalcula-
tion, not his creedal eccentricities, that made his revolution so problematic.
Whatever the content of Descartes' Christian faith, the point is that creedal
orthodoxy, alone, cannot offset the danger posed by faulty anthropological presuppositions. It is in light of this fact that another of Augustine's
influences on Descartes looms far larger than the methodological doubt
with which they both begin their reflections.

AUGUSTINE'S INWARD SELF

Augustine is widely acknowledged as the father of Western Christianity,
and his writings are a treasure trove of Christian faith. Not only, however,
does Augustine represent the Cartesian revolution in embryo, but, more
importantly, he is the source of the very notion of the "inner self" which
was its major presupposition (see Cary 2000 and Taylor 1989). One could
argue that, from the moment when he first saw Ambrose reading silently,
Augustine did more to encourage authentic Christian interiority than anyone in the early church. But it was not the influence of Ambrose that was to
become problematic; rather it was the influence of the Neoplatonists, whom
he was reading with great enthusiasm during and for years after his Christian conversion.

"By the Platonic books I was admonished to return into myself," Augustine tells us in the *Confessions*" (1991, 123). Throughout his life, the
Platonic influence was there, especially that of the Neoplatonist philosopher Plotinus. What Augustine finds in Plotinus are things like this: "How
can one behold this extraordinary beauty which remains in the inner sanctum and will not come outside to be seen by the profane? Let him who can
arise and come into the inside, leaving the sight of the eyes outside and not
turning back to corporeal beauties" (quoted in Cary 2000, 37). The Cartesian revolution began as though in strict conformance to this admonition,
and Augustine almost surely served as its unwitting Christian mediator.

If William Temple thinks Descartes' radical self-referentiality is "the
most disastrous moment in the history of Europe," Hans Urs von Balthasar,
who in other respects acknowledges Augustine's greatness, is equally un-

equivocal. "At the time of his conversion in Milan," von Balthasar writes, "Augustine was assiduously practicing Neoplatonic self-absorption" (1986, 261). According to Phillip Cary, however, this Neoplatonic influence remained throughout Augustine's life. "The story of Augustine's intellectual development does not begin with Platonism and end with Christianity," Cary writes, "but rather [it] introduces us to a distinctive brand of Christian Platonism in the making" (2000, 35).

Charles Taylor quotes a line from Augustine which he suggests is paradigmatic of his thought: "Do not go outward; return within yourself," Augustine writes, "in the inward man dwells truth" (quoted in Taylor 1989, 129). "Augustine," Taylor insists, "is always calling us within" (1989, 129). Can one imagine Christ calling for such an inward turn? Shut the door and pray, yes, but turn your back on corporeal beauties in favor of an inner sanctum? I don't think so. How far from Christian orthodoxy Augustine's quest for truth "within" was, Cary observes, "can be measured by noting that it stands in obvious conflict with the belief that we are brought to blessedness by the death of Christ or the resurrection of the body" (2000, 103).

So commonplace has the notion of turning inward become, however, that Augustine's descendants—meaning, Western culture in its entirety— would appeal to the metaphor of inwardness without recognizing either its metaphorical limits, its doctrinal peculiarity, or its anthropological dubiousness. If, in responding to the postmodern challenge, we are forced to clarify some of the muddle into which we have fallen in the modern era, we will need to free ourselves, in the words of Karl Rahner, from "the Neoplatonic habits of thought which have held us in bondage for two thousand years" (1962, 28). And in some respects at least, the anthropology of the modern self, now being challenged by the postmodernists, is the fruit of precisely that bondage.

Notwithstanding the need to disentangle Augustine's theology from the Neoplatonic presuppositions in which it is so often embedded, the *Confessions* show us a man of prayer, a man whose Neoplatonist reflexes inspired him to "turn inward," but who, nevertheless, understood that turn to be part and parcel of a turn toward a genuinely transcendent God to whom he poured out his heart. Let it be a lesson to us all; an inadvertent doctrinal eccentricity can worm its way into cultural presuppositions, infecting the lived experience of countless lives for centuries.

ROUSSEAU'S AUTONOMOUS INDIVIDUAL

When, toward the end of the eighteenth century, Jean-Jacques Rousseau wrote his *Confessions*, it presented to the world, not the God in whom Augustine assured his readers they could find rest, but an immensely restless man desperately trying to appear self-possessed and at peace. The first words of Rousseau's *Confessions* are these:

> I have resolved on an enterprise which has *no precedent*, and which, once complete, will have *no imitator*. My purpose is to *display* to my kind a portrait in every way true to nature, and the man I shall portray will be *myself*. Simply myself. I know my own heart and understand my fellow man. But I am made unlike any one I have ever met; I will even venture to say that *I am like no one in the whole world*. I may be no better, but at least I am *different*. (1953, 17; emphasis added)

In an observation that fairly sums up the history in the West of the "autonomous individual," of whom Rousseau was the most famous exemplar, René Girard has written: "Imitative desire wants nothing more than to be free from imitation. Complete self-sufficiency is its ultimate idol" (1993, 9). Rousseau was eager to impress others with the fact that he had no need to impress them. He desperately needed the attention of others and just as desperately needed to believe that he had no such need. He was the first to realize how much social adulation could be aroused by a convincing demonstration of one's complete disinterest in it.

If we read the opening lines of Rousseau's *Confessions* against the backdrop of Descartes' *cogito*, we see another effort to avert attention from what Girard calls mimetic desire, the elimination of which is tantamount to the rejection of Christian anthropology. Rousseau begins his *Confessions*, not with a prayer, but with an assertion, and what he asserts is precisely the repudiation of mimesis. His enterprise has no precedent and it will remain inimitable. Rousseau is like no one else in the world. He is different. Of course, the claim that he has no predecessors is odd, even comically odd, in light of the fact he has chosen as the title of his autobiography the title Augustine used for his. Rousseau's claim that he will have no imitator has a comic dimension as well, in light of the fact that in short order he became the most imitated man in Europe, the model of individuality. His genius may well have been in realizing the seductive power of autonomy on public display, something he systematically performed for the benefit of his rapt European audience. The very use of the word display in these opening lines of his *Confessions* must not go unremarked. Unlike Descartes, who took great pains to isolate himself from the mimetic contagion of others, Rousseau, concerned less with epistemological than with psychological verisimilitude, hit upon another strategy. In fact, it was the direct opposite of Descartes' solution, and for that reason just as dubious. Rousseau would be alone *in public*, a curious but fascinating inversion of monasticism's solidarity in solitude. It all depended, of course, on Rousseau's dramatization of his aloneness and aloofness. If Don Quixote imitated the fictional Amadis of Gaul, Rousseau imitated the fictionalized Jean-Jacques Rousseau. Sartre would later aptly call this self-imitation "bad faith," and Rousseau was its grand propagator. As Leo Braudy puts it: Rousseau's political views "emphasize the primitive freedom of human beings, but in his own autobiography, and in his life, he shows how dependent that freedom is on the observation of others" (1986, 376–77).

The man who would have no imitators had legions of them, each infected with the mimetic dilemma that Rousseau personified: how to get others to notice how disinterested one is in whether they notice or not; how to attract enough social attention to make up for the diminution of what Henri de Lubac (1958) calls "ontological density," the waning of which, de Lubac argues, is the salient feature of our age. Before turning to the Christian tradition for clarification of these matters, let us look at a few of Rousseau's more amusing descendants.

The novel as a literary genre is coterminous with modernity. It catalogs the modern predicament. The first novel was Cervantes' *Don Quixote*, and I now want to turn to my personal choice for the hotly disputed distinction of being the last novel, namely, Virginia Woolf's *The Waves*. (By "last" I don't necessarily mean the last in a strictly chronological sense.)

One of the characters in Virginia Woolf's novel is a man named Bernard who fancies himself a writer, even at times a romantic poet, even though he can rarely put two sentences together. His notebooks are full of scribblings he hopes one day to use in a great literary work, though his actual literary output is miniscule. He waits for the romantic mood to overtake him, for it is that which, he feels, will transform him from the colorless scribe that he is into the dashing romantic poet he imagines himself to be. The essence of Bernard's romantic illusion, of course, is a Rousseauesque notion of unique individuality, a life so sublimely disinterested in what others think that others would surely think of little else. This is the salvation for which Bernard is searching, or rather waiting, for he can only hope to be seized by the passionate impulses that will rise up from *within* him and turn him into that rare and admirable creature, a romantic poet. On one occasion, lightning strikes, or at least seems to, and suddenly he is disposed to pour his passionate heart onto the page.

> . . . all is propitious. I am now in the mood. I can write the letter
> straight off which I have begun ever so many times. I have just come
> in; I have flung down my hat and my stick; I am writing the first
> thing that comes into my head without troubling to put the paper
> straight. It is going to be a brilliant sketch which, she must think,
> was written without pause, without an erasure. Look how unformed
> the letters are—there is a careless blot. All must be sacrificed to
> speed and carelessness. I will write a quick, running, small hand,
> exaggerating the down stroke of the "y" and crossing the "t" thus—
> with a dash. . . . . I must seem to her (this is very important) to be
> passing from thing to thing with the greatest ease in the world. . . .
> It is the speed, the hot, molten effect, the lava flow of sentence into
> sentence that I need. Who am I thinking of? Byron of course. I am,
> in some ways, like Byron. Perhaps a sip of Byron will help to put
> me in the vein. Let me read a page. . . . (Woolf 1959, 78–79)

Spontaneity, carefully exhibited to others, advertises one's autonomy.
It demonstrates that one isn't imitating anyone. Our world is full of these
little autonomy-plays, the contemporary analogue, I suppose, for medieval
morality plays. For those who have eyes to see, they demonstrate the lack
of what they aim to advertise. Just as the effort to appear sincere is always
insincere, and the desire to be humble often rooted in pride, so the effort to
demonstrate one's spontaneity is symptomatic of one's lack of it. Woolf's
Bernard labored mightily to feign a spontaneity he was never able to actually experience. Here he takes great pains to demonstrate his spontaneity—by not bothering to put the paper straight, scribbling in an almost
illegible hand, crossing the "t" thus with a dash—all this meticulous attention to detail in order to convince the letter's recipient how oblivious to
detail he was. Our world is today full of performances easily as entertain-
ing as Bernard's, and equally symptomatic of today's spiritual and psychological crisis.

Suddenly withering from the realization of his dependence on a model,
Bernard slinks over to the bookshelf and picks up his copy of Byron, drinking in its heady romanticism in hopes of returning to his labored effort to
be "spontaneous." Here is the modern self struggling against the facts of
mimetic desire to see itself as pure spontaneity, to think of its desire as
essentially autonomous. Bernard suffers his little recurring letdown only to
return to the very romantic illusion that was its source. His gesture of getting up and going to the bookshelf was the right gesture; it's just that when
he got there he picked up the wrong book. If only Don Quixote had longer
to live, he tells us, his trip to the bookshelf would have been more produc-

tive, for he would have chosen other books, with other models. What Virginia Woolf's account of this scene shows us is nothing less than that, as Tertullian put it in the second century, the soul is naturally Christian.

Meanwhile, Virginia Woolf has more to teach us. Bernard, we soon discover, like so many postmodernists, had already made quite a few trips to the bookshelf, and he has yet to pick up the right book, or even read the ones he has picked up profitably. So desperate is he for mimetic suggestion about who he is and how he is to live that he has gone from one literary idol to the next, and the cumulative effect is beginning to take its toll. He is a late modern on the threshold of the shocking postmodern discovery that he has become a "pastiche personality." "I changed and changed," Bernard writes, "was Hamlet, was Shelley, was the hero, whose name I now forget, of a novel by Dostoevsky; was for a whole term, incredibly, Napoleon; but was Byron chiefly" (Woolf 1959, 249).

A Christian has a far greater pool of possible models than did Virginia Woolf's Bernard, for the humblest person in a breadline (or a traffic jam) can serve, unwittingly in most cases, as an exemplar of Christian charity, kindness, or selflessness. But the real difference between Bernard's fickle psychological promiscuity and Christian mediation is that what the Christian emulates in his or her model is precisely the model's *Imitatio Christi*. In other words, those for whom Christ is the *ultimate* model will be aided by the mediation of countless *penultimate* ones, both professing Christians and virtuous nonbelievers. With Christ as the transcendent model, however, this plethora of human exemplars will not have the decentering and destabilizing effect it had on Bernard, and that it is having on millions of people today who are being tossed on a sea of mimetic influences without the ballast required to stay on course. The conspicuously modern hope that with arduous enough acts of introspection "the self" could acquire this ballast on its own is precisely the hope the postmodernists have called into question, and that Virginia Woolf parodies in her novel.

Faced with this psychological instability, one can relieve the symptoms, as Rousseau did, by infecting others with the disease. One can perform one's hysteria for onlookers; one can become, in the words of the *New York Times* reporter, a "pop artist of a thousand incarnations." Instead of performing little "autonomy plays" for so limited an audience—the woman Bernard imagined himself to be courting—one can perform an even more histrionic version of the same masquerade for a larger audience, attracting thereby a greater quantum of the social attention that serves, temporarily, as a substitute for genuine ontological density.

FROM PERSON TO SELF

The disappearance of such density is marked by the word *self,* which comes from the Greek term *autos,* as of course does the word *autonomy.* The prevailing Western notion of "individuality" is rooted in precisely the gesture of disidentification with which the individual distinguishes himself from others.

The notion of the person, however, as it took shape in European cultures, involved the confluence of a number of influences—Christian efforts to understand the Second Person of the Trinity paramount among them. But its etymological history begins earlier. Its most remote appearance occurs in connection with ancient Etruscan ritual, as that religious ritual was beginning to evolve into performance drama. Masks worn in quasi-ritual dramatic performances served both to amplify the voice and set aside for the duration of the drama the human identity of the ritual performer. The ritual veneration of the goddess Persephone required a liturgical performer to *speak through a mask* of the goddess, and the name for the mask, *phersu,* was derived from the goddess's name. The Etruscans influenced Roman theater, and the Romans, in adopting the Etruscan term, fused it with the Latin verb for "speaking through"—the verb: *personare,* the noun form of which is *persona.* So the term for mask came into Roman usage as *persona,* which at first indicated the actor's mask, but eventually came to refer to any *personage* playing a role, whether on stage or in cultural life.

The Greeks, for their part, used the word *prosopon* for the mask the actor wore on stage, and it was also via this reference to the actor wearing a mask that the Greek idea of the person first appears, suggesting, some have thought, an intriguing affinity between these two concepts: mask and person. The apparent superficiality of the term was one of the issues in contention during the theological debates of the fourth and fifth centuries, the debates that led to the formulation of the doctrine of the Trinity. The Eastern fathers resisted the use of the term *person* precisely because it still carried the superficial connotation of a social "role" without serious ontological status.

A solution was finally found, which according to John Zizioulas amounted to "a philosophical landmark, a revolution in Greek philosophy" (1985, 36). It was to equate the Greek word *hypostasis* and the Latin word *persona.* In other words, to interpret personhood in hypostatic terms. By a kind of etymological adoption, the theologically insignificant word *persona* was thereby infused with the theological riches of the term *hypostasis.* Perhaps the best way to convey the deeper implications of this remarkable concept is with two words: icon and sacrament.

In pondering the mystery of the Christ, the early Council fathers—anticipating the Second Vatican Council's insistence that "only in the mystery of the incarnate Word does the mystery of man take on light"—were compelled by the mystery of the incarnate Word to discover the hypostatic mystery of personhood itself, a discovery that, in the words of Dennis Edwards, "gave a radically new weight to the idea of person" (1997, 77). "The revolution of the person," writes Paul Evdokimov, "is the event of Christianity," and human desire is simply "the inborn nostalgia to become a 'person'" (1985, 53).

The person, in the original Christian sense of the term, is always iconic, while the self, the secular simulation of the person, is inevitably idolatrous. The person, as Christianity understands the term, is never the one who comes in his own name, even though "this world" would be happy to believe him if he did. Nor is the uniquely Christian form of personhood to be regarded as a concession to a regrettable mimetic propensity in fallen creatures, for Jesus' own personhood was as defined by his trinitarian consubstantiality with the Father as Christian personhood is defined by the *Imitatio Christi*. In John's Gospel, Jesus says: "The words that I say to you I do not speak on my own; but the Father who dwells in me does his works. Believe me that I am in the Father and the Father is in me" (John 14:10–11). This is God's incarnate Word, in whose image and likeness humans are made, revealing to us the intersubjective mystery of personhood—the personhood of God no less than the mysterious personhood to which we have access in Christ. Unique as it is, Christ's intimacy with the Father was "not something to be grasped at," rather it is something he offers freely to others, so that, as Paul says "we might receive adoption as children," an adoption that comes about when God sends "the Spirit of his Son into our hearts, crying, 'Abba! Father!'" (Gal. 4:5, 6). And so each of the "Persons" of the Trinity plays a "role" in the gift of personhood to humanity. And so it is that the Gospel evokes at the most profound level precisely the "interdividuality" whose anthropological validity René Girard has confirmed.

But what are we to make of the theatrical origin of the concept of the person? asks John Zizioulas. Why were the concepts of the theatrical "mask" and the human person affiliated so readily and felt to be so easily compatible? Was it an etymological accident? Was it pure coincidence? "What connection does the actor's mask have with the human person?" Zizioulas asks (31). Answering his own question, he says, "It is precisely in the theater that man strives to become a 'person'" (32). In "speaking through" the mask of another, the actor dispossesses himself of his "own self" in order to be possessed by the other. As a result of his mask, Zizioulas writes that "the

actor, but properly also the spectator—has acquired a certain taste of freedom, a certain specific 'hypostasis,' a certain identity, which the rational
and moral harmony of the world in which he lives denies him. . . . [A]s a
result of the mask he has become a person, albeit for a brief period, and has
learned what it is to exist as a free, unique and unrepeatable entity" (33).

Of course, the "hypostasis" the actor is able to briefly experience is
the hypostasis that figured so decisively in the development of both the
doctrine of the Trinity and the doctrine of the divinity of Christ. The early
controversies that led to these doctrines were finally resolved by the recognition on the part of the Church fathers of the hypostatic nature of the
person, a recognition that made it possible for the doctrines of the Trinity
and the Incarnation to begin their triumphant theological journey through
history.

TOWARD CHRISTIAN PERSONHOOD

In light of the etymological and historical affinity between the actor and
the person, it is worth noting that the man who served for many—inside
and outside the Roman communion—as an icon of Christian faith, morally dominating the world stage for nearly three decades, was an actor, play-
wright, and director as a young man. John Paul II's first important book
was titled *The Acting Person*. To echo Zizioulas, is this mere coincidence?
There is, Gabriel Marcel reminds us, a passage in Scripture that can apply
to the actor on the stage, namely, "Ye are not your own." The actor, Marcel
says, "can only find himself if he is prepared to lose himself. Thus, pursuing his vocation, he can provide us, through his unusual life, with a metaphor of human life as it aims toward its supernatural goal" (quoted in von
Balthasar 1988, 10).

Even more to the point of the present reflection is Hermann Bahr's
suggestion that the actor "presents us directly with the ultimate mystery of
human nature," and that what the actor represents "is the absolute opposite of all hysteria" (quoted in von Balthasar 1988, 10–11). In contrast to
the "individual" and the hysteric (who is an individual whose private rituals of disidentification have become flamboyant enough to attract clinical
attention), the actor willingly identifies with the other to whose mimetic
influence he actively submits in accord with his professional responsibilities—becoming in this regard like the "little child" in the Gospel, who, hum-
bling himself, accepts his appointed role in the unfolding drama of salvation. Were an actor to submit with the same attentiveness and self-
abandonment to the one who said "whoever has seen me has seen the Father"—the one referred to in the Letter to the Hebrews as the "icon of the

living God"—he would enter the company of the Christian mystics. His *Imitatio Christi* would consist of imitating the single animating desire of Jesus, which was simply to do the will of his heavenly Father. Inasmuch as the Father calls us each by name and gives us each a mission, the Father's will for each of us is utterly unique. So, in sharp contrast to all other forms of mimetic submission, the *Imitatio Christi* leads, not to hackneyed sameness, but to utter uniqueness.

Christian personhood is inseparable from the role a Christian is assigned in the drama of salvation history, a drama of which no Christian is permitted to become a mere spectator, lest he be robbed of his true Christian identity. We are called and sent. Obedience is our freedom. "In His will is our peace," the souls in paradise told Dante. In following Christ, we do that which we cannot help but do: we imitate; we let Christ speak through us (*personare*); we "put on Christ." "Vicariousness is not something esoteric," writes Lucien Richard, "rather, it is the fundamental principle of all personal life" (1997, 176).

As the truth about the mimetic nature of human subjectivity continues to undergo its gradual paracletic self-disclosure, we will gradually come to realize, as Paul Evdokimov put it, that "man can make of himself an 'icon of God,' or he can become a demonical grimace, an ape of God" (1985, 57). Or, as René Girard (1996) has put it: "Both Jesus and Satan are teachers of imitation and imitators themselves, imitators of God the Father. This means that human beings always imitate God, either through Jesus or through Satan. They seek God indirectly through the human models they imitate" (215).

A Christian is someone who has met a Christian. A person, in the fullest Christian sense, is someone who is in the presence of person—in fact, in thought, or in prayer. The mystery of our identity is mediated to us, the question is who is the mediator? Amadis of Gaul or Francis of Assisi, Lord Byron or the Lord of Glory, the pop artist of a thousand incarnations or the incarnate Word.

Kenneth Schmitz reminds us that our task as Christians is "to transmute the metal of self by a kind of spiritual alchemy into the gold of personhood." But then he wonders, wistfully perhaps, "Can such a call to spiritual personhood be made today in such a way that it might be heard?" (1986, 203–4). If Evdokimov is right about the revolution of the person being *the* event of Christianity, and about desire being an inborn longing to become a person, then there is no more urgent question than the one Schmitz asks. Can the call to personhood be heard today? The answer is yes, if we make it intelligible and anthropologically sound—and spiritually and psychologically gratifying.

2

Building a Responsive Self in a Post-Relativistic World:

The Contribution of Mikhail Bakhtin

Caryl Emerson

The title of this chapter is a tall order, and to give some shape to it, I will organize my comments around several paradoxes. The Russian literary critic and philosopher of culture, Mikhail Bakhtin (1895–1975), was an obscure provincial thinker during most of his life; he is now a world-famous name. So famous, in fact, that his ideas have become clichés. Many of us wince outright upon hearing the word "dialogue," "carnival," "the grotesque body," "polyphony," "heteroglossia," or "unfinalizability" applied to something we love. All too often, it seems, those fashionable catchwords are no more than jargon lowered down on an unsuspecting text, not to elucidate its message or its author but merely to lend an up-to-date theoretical gloss to the voice of the critic. Do those terms mean anything precise? Did they ever?

Bakhtin has paid the familiar price for his success. Like Nietzsche and Freud before him, he was a wonderfully inventive thinker with a gift for devising powerful binaries and vigorous, colorful metaphors. The accessible upper layers of his thought caught on. His hypotheses became dogma, his ruminations—often culled from private notebooks never prepared by their author for publication—became statements of principle. A "Bakhtin Boom" ensued, during which masses of his writings were translated without context, in the chaotic order in which they were discovered, both prepared and unprepared for print. An industry grew up around his word that was part scholarship, part rumor, and part hype. (As one of the earliest translators, I have been in the Bakhtin industry for thirty years and can attest that there is a lot still circulating that ought to be weeded out, but his words themselves are too good to give up.) Errors of fact are not the worse thing, however; all translations make mistakes and famous people will always generate myth. More troubling is that Bakhtin voluntarily mythologized and mystified himself, faking portions of his curriculum vitae, borrowing stretches of other scholars' texts (largely German) and incorporating them into his own without credit, spreading legends he knew were untrue. It is not for us to cast stones self-righteously at survivors of Stalinist Russia. More serious than biographical and textological obfuscation, I believe, is the fate of his ideas, their "cultural residue," as it were, now that the stormy front of the Bakhtin Boom has passed.

For Bakhtin is now a classic, which means he has become an adjective. "Bakhtinian" exists alongside Freudian, Aristotelian, Heideggerian. In the *Collected Works of Bakhtin* now being published in Moscow, hundreds of pages of commentary explicate the extant texts. A Bakhtin Centre has been functioning for a decade in Sheffield, England; a dozen international conferences devoted to Bakhtin's thought have taken place around the world since the early 1980s; four journals publish exclusively on Bakhtinian themes. With all that concentrated attention by so many full-time scholars, Bakhtin's legacy has indeed become richer, clearer, its own sources better understood. But the academic industry around a thinker is something separate from the "cultural residue," the reputation at large. That, I think, is in less good shape. Bakhtin's terms, universally applied, have tended to become limp and banal. Removed from their unfree Russian context and inserted into overly free Western cultures, they lose their cutting edge. What is "dialogue," after all, except an excuse to keep talking, to give everyone his say, to enjoy the process of self-expression so much that the actual product of talk (the decision, the vote, the policy with its often awful ethical implications) fades from view and from public memory—a frequent complaint about our noisy and distracted American democracy? And what about carnival and grotesque bodies? These ideas might have been daring in prudish, regimented, socialist-realist Russia of the 1930s and '40s, where according to official posters all workers' bodies were covered up head to toe and all workers worked joyously all the time. But in America, with its endless uncensored chatter, its public fascination with private lives, its unembarrassed consumerism and quest for constant entertainment—what does carnival give us, except a stamp of approval on the messy, the rebelliously individualistic, the heterogeneous, the marvelously diverse: all those traits that already define us?

I suggest that one of the reasons Bakhtin "caught on" with us was that his ideas and values, so shockingly bold within their own Soviet-Stalinist context, happened to fit quite comfortably with habits and priorities in the West. Knowing Bakhtin allowed us to go on being ourselves while also feeling new, cosmopolitan, "theorized," in touch with the philosophy of continental Europe. As I hope to show in the course of this essay, exactly such "easy belonging," seeking what feels like home, is what Bakhtin strove hard to discredit, in principle and in the practice of his own life—a life lived as an Orthodox Christian in an atheistic state, as an apolitical loner in a hyperpoliticized, collectivist society. Indeed, his central teaching might well turn out to be: "How might I *not* comfortably belong, how might I remain on the outside, but always in a creative way?" Dialogue, carnival, polyphony, and unfinalizability all contribute to this outsiderly project. At its base lie three intersecting models of personality, devised and revised by Bakhtin over his long life. *Which* version of Bakhtin's teaching you ultimately find most congenial depends largely on which of his three models of selfhood you prefer. All three insist that once you establish an identity, you set to work testing it, refining it, or otherwise getting out of it; all posit a self that is responsive rather than essentialist. But each is responsive to a different type of stimulus, paces itself in a different way, deals with its residue differently, and tests us for a different set of strengths.

These three models of selfhood are the *dialogic*, the *carnival*, and the far less famous (although arguably the most profound) *architectonic* self. All are theologically inflected. None, strictly speaking, is "therapeutic"— in the sense that it is designed to make us feel better by enhancing our self-confidence, by bringing us immediate relief, or by making it easier to get through the day. On the contrary, properly understood, each model imposes severe obligations. Each also takes for granted that we would sooner sacrifice ourselves (or what might intuitively be called our "immediate interests") than impose such sacrifice on others. Finally, each model insists on the virtues of *being outside of* and *different from* that which you love. According to Bakhtin, one gains an identity only across a boundary. Which is to say, you know others by being non-coincident with them, and know yourself when your view of yourself comes not from within but from somewhere else. In Bakhtin's opinion, it takes a minimum of two consciousnesses to guarantee an authentic image of any given self—and he would go further: any attempt to "enact an event with only one participant" is doomed to failure (Felch and Contino 2001, 220).

One can detect here the omnipresence of an attentive personal God in Bakhtin's cosmos, as in the Russian Orthodox cosmos generally. (It is noteworthy that although the Russian language has words for loneliness, it has no native word for privacy, nor for aloneness as a positive, sought-after value. One simply cannot be ontologically alone in a Russian Orthodox world.) A caring, spiritually astute aura embraces all Bakhtin's selfhood scenarios. Within this basic similarity, however, each model observes its own optimal ratio between inner and outer. To get a handle on these dynamics, we must consider Bakhtin's more basic working vocabulary, the units he posited as building blocks of human personality.

BAKHTIN'S MODEL OF THE PSYCHE

In the early 1920s, Bakhtin devised a tripartite model of the human psyche. This tripartite structure had nothing in common with Sigmund Freud's famous, thrillingly pagan medieval-hydraulic model of id, ego, and super-ego, which at the time was causing such a stir in Central and Eastern Europe. However, Bakhtin's model did recall, faintly, the Holy Trinity. Each of us, Bakhtin posited, has two fundamental sensitivities co-existing within our minds: a sense of inside and outside. The first sensation he calls the *I-for-myself* (how I look and feel from inside to my own consciousness). The second he calls the *I-for-the-other* (how I look from outside to someone else). Although both perspectives are real, only the latter is palpably concrete and articulate. *I-for-myself* is the realm of potential: unrealized alternatives, inchoate hope and despair, unnamed anxieties, unformed dreams. This *I-for-myself* is constantly in flux, dissatisfied with any given act because it knows that every actually-realized thing could have been (and usually should have been) different and better. Since my *I-for-myself* is deep inside itself, far from the boundaries, it doesn't have a mouth and eyes of its own, since those organs are conduits to the outside. Thus it is unreliable as a source of stories that would explain myself to my self. Whatever images and words I have, I receive through the *I-for-the-other*. That entity is still my "I," of course, in the sense that I am innerly aware of it, but it does not originate with me; it is a composite of what others see me as, project on to me, and what I then incorporate into my self-image. These projections can be kindly or cruel, true or false, but I am helpless to ignore them completely because they are the only firm data I have on myself. They provide me with my terms. Every day, I put my self together out of bits of "finished surface" that others perceive and project on to me. Bakhtin insists that in matters of identity and self-worth, we always work with others' views of us. By the same token, of course, all others must work with my view of them; thus *I-for-the-other* has a flip side, the *other-for-me*. But in both cases, impressions, images, and intonations must cross the boundary between one consciousness and another before identity as such is registered. Identity doesn't belong to individuals, but to the boundary between them: it is concrete, historical, and inevitably shared.

Some interesting implications of this selfhood model are worth mentioning. First, if we are to enrich our options and increase our self-confidence, it clearly behooves us *not* to sit inside some echo chamber, collecting praise (it is this frightened habit that traditionally makes tyrants so very vulnerable, once cracks in their tyranny begin to appear) but rather, we should seek out the most varied possible feedback on our outer selves. We should surround ourselves with as many different types of people as possible, and absorb their reactions to us open-mindedly and with gratitude. Bakhtin would have been a severe and skeptical critic of "group identity politics," with its practice—happily much less widespread now than two decades ago—of "studying oneself": women in women's studies, blacks in black studies, Hispanics in Hispanic studies, a reflex grounded in the conviction that "it takes one to know one," and that the best route to self-knowledge is to cluster with people who look and act pretty much like you. Just the opposite is required, Bakhtin would insist; the more you reinforce what you were merely "born as," the narrower your reflexes and options become, the more fatally are you tied to a single image or word, and the rich diverse language you need in order to deal with the contingency of the world will begin to die out.

And what—one might justifiably ask—about those "different others" who react to you with hatred and prejudice? Who would like not to listen to you or to enrich your options but, say, to kill you? Must we absorb their reactions too, for the sake of our greater literacy and flexibility? This charge has been leveled frequently at Bakhtin, and he is serene in the face of it. He was an apolitical man. He was a man, moreover, who, like his great compatriots Leo Tolstoy and Fyodor Dostoevsky, saw the ideal responsive self embodied in the person and personal courage of Jesus Christ. Bakhtin did not deny the evil of the world. But he was convinced that only love was aesthetically and ethically productive. He did not, apparently, find questions of hatred, rejection, or undeserved violence theoretically interesting.

This recommendation, to embrace as many different *others-for-me* as possible and thus to guarantee a rich, inventive, diverse, and unthreatenable self, has a large-scale cultural equivalent as well. But here matters get complicated. Bakhtin, who is always scrupulously aware of contexts and their unrepeatable complexity, will not permit any of us to rest for long inside any secure identity. Nothing of importance happens inside; everything, he insists, happens on, near, or just beyond one's own borders. Implicit in this conviction is some challenging advice on how to behave in foreign contexts and foreign cultures. What does it mean to empathize or "identify" with the other? How should we strive to "fit in"? In 1970 Bakhtin was asked by the leading Soviet literary journal to comment on new, post-Stalinist approaches to the study of literature and culture. In his brief open letter to the journal, he applauded a variety of new methods and then remarked: "There exists a very strong, but one-sided and thus untrustworthy, idea that in order better to understand a foreign culture, one must enter into it, forgetting one's own culture, and view the world through the eyes of this foreign culture" (Bakhtin 1986, 6–7). Bakhtin does concede that some sort of an "entry as a living being into a foreign culture . . . is [of course] a necessary part of the process of understanding it" (Bakhtin 1986, 7). But he is just as apprehensive about a potential *excess* of identification, a sort of overenthusiastic fusion with the other under guise of sympathy toward it, as he is about the failure to find common ground. He draws two strong conclusions. First, he insists that it is our responsibility, when studying other times, places, and values, to *remain ourselves* (or at the very least, not reject ourselves): "*Creative understanding* does not renounce itself, its own place in time or its own culture; and it forgets nothing." He then generalizes on this point: "[I]t is immensely important for the person who understands to be *located outside* the object of his or her creative understanding" (Bakhtin 1986, 7). For this to happen, one must remain consciously alien, specifically *not* a duplication or a reflection of the other, and one must never apologize for separation or difference. "Outsideness," he remarks, "is the most powerful factor in understanding" (Bakhtin 1986, 7).

This is a provocative thought. Its origins can be traced to Bakhtin's earliest writings on moral philosophy and the psychology of the self, which date from the early 1920s. Among his most striking metaphors in those early writings is the experience that all of us have with mirrors. Bakhtin distrusts mirrors intensely. They give rise to the illusion that I can see myself as others see me (which is, of course, the only way we care about "being seen"), and this error creates havoc. For however earnestly I try, Bakhtin insists, I can never see myself as others see me. Or rather, when I do try to see myself in that way, as when I peer into a mirror and grin vacuously, mimicking someone who (in my fantasy) is pleased to see me and calls forth my responsive smile, all I can register on my own face is ghostliness, lack of definition, fakery, because in this exchange there is only one consciousness at work. Such a singularity or closed loop must always be false. "What I look like," Bakhtin insists, is always conditioned by the response in me that you, a genuine other gazing at me, bring forth. Thus I can never (in any nontrivial way) see myself—although I *can* see an authentic image of myself reflected in the pupils of your eyes.

It would appear that for Bakhtin, individual selves, whole peoples, and entire cultures all work much the same way. As he concludes in his 1970 open letter: "[I]t is only through the eyes of *another* culture" that the singularity of my own culture, my own identity, can be revealed "fully and profoundly" (Bakhtin 1986, 7). This is because, given the openness and fluidity of my own inner sense of self, I do not, and cannot, cohere for myself. I cohere (rightly or wrongly, fairly or unfairly) only for you. And although you, vis-à-vis me, are always elsewhere, with your own needs calling out to be satisfied, I always stand in grateful relation to you because you bestow upon me borders and delimitations, which I cannot bestow upon myself. Until you look at me and respond to me, I literally do not know what I look like, what I need, or who I am.

This is a radical and controversial stance, given the negative press such concepts as "the gaze" have received in literary and cultural studies in the West. Conventional wisdom has long taught that "to gaze" at someone is to appropriate that person, to reduce a living image to your own appetites and prejudices, to reify it, colonize it, and erase its distinctive boundaries. Bakhtin says just the opposite. Until some other person has passed judgment on me from an alien and outside position, I do not *have* a boundary. Unseen and unjudged by others, my image is simply a smudge, a blur. It can't talk and doesn't know where it begins and ends. Thus the activity of gazing on someone else from an outside position is not a violation of that person's rights as an autonomous being; autonomy in that sense was meaningless to Bakhtin, as absent from his arsenal of true values as was the word for absolute privacy or aloneness. To gaze at another is an obligation, a service, and a benediction.

Crucial to Bakhtin's argument here is the influence of the Russian Orthodox Church, which espoused a special, non-Renaissance notion of what it means to "see." For centuries, the Eastern church has defended the worship of icons against accusations of idolatry by insisting that icon worship was not a survival of pagan fetishism, but rather an expression of reverence for the sacred processes of incarnation and transfiguration. The fact that iconographic art observes reverse perspective, presenting the outside viewer with mobile and often multiple vantage points, protects Eastern Christian visual art from the charge so often leveled against the Western practice of perspectivalism (indeed, a trace of this hostility is present in the current invective against "the gaze"): that the "seeing eye" rigidly, statically fixes the seen object in place and thus diminishes it, making it a passive object of the viewer. On just such grounds did Father Pavel Florensky, the twentieth-century art historian, research chemist, priest, and Russian Orthodox theologian, censure the perspectivalism characteristic of Western "realistic" art as a crafty illusion, a reductive and demeaning trick. Its sole selling point, Florensky conceded, was that it simplified matters for those of us on the outside by offering only one way in. He contrasted this Renaissance narrowness with the more generous, inclusive, shifting optics of the medieval icon, which, in his view, was an emblem of far richer self-other relations. Bakhtin, as an Orthodox believer, was doubtless sympathetic to these ideas, although he did not develop any theory of visual multiplicity equivalent in scope and power to his verbal heteroglossia.

KEEPING A LOW PROFILE: THE RESPONSIVE SELF

We have mentioned the reciprocal gaze, the need for boundaries, why difference is so desirable, and why mirrors are so bad. What we have not talked about is power. The omission is not accidental. Bakhtin, it appears, did not feel that power was especially important—at least not in our everyday lives, and not in the relationships that matter. Like many Russian moral thinkers, he was something of an anarchist in this regard: the institution of the state was so horrendously omnipresent and so arbitrary in its dispensations, if you took it on in an oppositional way your self would get nothing else done. Best to duck it, build your life around its edges, value only what you can see or respond to in person and on a small scale, avoid all provocative public visibility. During most of Bakhtin's adult life, the famous and ambitious creative personalities were being incarcerated or shot. Bakhtin as philosopher and classicist was also clearly attracted to the "politically irresponsible" schools of ancient thought: the eccentric Cynics, Epicureans, and Stoics who pursued two of philosophy's fundamental questions— how do we know? how should we behave?—while ignoring the third, how should we govern? The wisdom of such teachings was: *avoid* power, don't fall for it. Power—which, in the world according to Foucault, is almost all there is—is never a starting point for Bakhtin. He begins, rather, with trust.

And indeed, why not assume a posture of trust? If I'm wrong, it's too late anyway; if I'm right, chances are good I will learn something new. Perhaps because of his chronic illness, perhaps because of his life under Stalinism and his carnival worldview devised in part as a response to this life, Bakhtin appears to have believed that evil and pain, as centers of concentrated power, could not be directly confronted; they could only be evaded, tricked, laughed down, diluted, and confused by abundance. Students of Bakhtin have variously considered this position spiritually advanced, politically timid, or simply naïve, but whatever one's response to it, its underlying logic is wholly coherent. Bakhtin insists that when you look at me and tell me frankly what you see, this dynamic does *not* make me helpless or dependent upon you in a humiliating way. We neither reduce to one another, nor do we, most of the time, wipe one another out. Your gazing at me, and my gazing at you, does not result in one of us "staring the other down." It does not compromise the authority of either of our unique positions, because, Bakhtin insists, human beings do not relate to one another primarily in terms of power. To think thus would be to think that what we want most of all is to control people, whereas in fact what we want is for others to find us interesting. And if we are indeed linked to one another not vertically-politically but horizontally-*relationally* in an ongoing, shifting narrative, with author and protagonist changing places all the time, then power structures are always out of date, boring, at best the butt of satire and carnival. This is clearly not a Cartesian model of the self, which seeks integration and cohesion through unmediated self-reflection. As we have seen, Bakhtin admits of no such possibility. In his view, there is only one sort of continuity reliably available to the self: a continuity made up of my responses to you.

Now, does not my constant horizontal orientation outward, my striving to grasp the role that I play in others' utterances and their role in mine, suggest a world of multiple, unstable, incommensurate value centers? In other words, a relativistic world? Are not the values that each of us hold made "merely relative" vis-à-vis the other? Bakhtin vigorously denied being a relativist. To him, that word designated a person who believed that an individual's values were exempt from judgment, who did not care about ultimate value, did not seek it, and in principle avoided passing inner judgment on it. As we noted above, Bakhtin was a *relationalist*. Relationalism puts its faith in the local, lateral ties that bind; these horizontal obligations create absolute Good. And of course, those ties and relations can (and must) shift minute by minute.

Bakhtin was *not* a Platonist. He rejected the conventional wisdom that "true things are forever" or "good things don't change." True things change constantly, Bakhtin insisted. Plato's prejudices here have had a disastrous effect on Western ethics. (Consider how we associate the words "shifting" and "shifty.") Just because an event or situation cannot be precisely repeated (as in a laboratory experiment) does not make it any less true; experience cannot be reduced to an experiment. In terms of experience, the thing that occurs only once is the most authentic thing. But Bakhtin goes further. It is precisely because there are no single fixed points for all time but rather many valid consciousness-centers, that moral judgment—and one's responsibility for making such judgments over time—is indispensable. There are no other benchmarks. For each of us, absolute values do exist. It could even be that these values are absolutely ranked, that is, that one is more true and eternal than the others But—and here's the crucial point—there is no position available to me from which I might confirm that ranking absolutely. My convictions are irrefutably true only from my singular position. In my strivings to confirm this truth in deeds and attitudes, I must test it constantly, reaching out and intersecting with other singular positions that inevitable see things differently. Bakhtin is a pluralist. But this is not, in his view, incompatible with being an idealist. Because such a combination can be baffling to a nation such as ours, with relativism and pragmatism deep in its bones, let me expand.

THE IDEAL AS ORIENTATION, NOT DESTINATION

Bakhtin received his early training in classics and in Kantian philosophy. He belonged to an astonishing Russian generation that produced a score of eminent religious and aesthetic philosophers, some who remained at home (Pavel Florensky, Aleksei Losev), others who matured in emigration (Nicolas Berdyaev, Semyon Frank, Sergei Bulgakov). An early task of many of these thinkers was to revive idealism as a bulwark against the crude faith in materialism and positivism that had conquered the nineteenth century. In Russia, positivism was associated in the popular mind with progress, empirical science, Pavlov's salivating dogs, realism in literature, civic duty in society, and with the courage to see the world head-on, "as it really exists." In that climate, idealism was felt by many to be pie-in-the-sky, a dreamy, abstract, mystical realm, and thus reactionary. But Bakhtin and other religiously inclined thinkers (who were by no means political reactionaries; Bakhtin had many close, sincere Marxist friends) saw clearly the abusive ends to which dialectical materialism could be put, and they wished to rehabilitate idealism, to make it tough, concrete, and practical. They would do this by redeploying Kantian ideas of moral duty in a truer, less transcendental account of the daily experience of living by ideas—or, as they preferred to call it, living by the ideal.

This new idealism offered few loopholes for the lazy in spirit. Consonant with the teachings of his great countryman Leo Tolstoy, Bakhtin wished to rehabilitate the ideal and its relationship to other selves without resorting to miracle, mystery, authority. Although himself a devout Orthodox Christian, he was reluctant to invoke the authority of particular confessions or denominations. Bakhtin wished to accomplish this task wholly "on this side," from within the concrete world of mortal behaviors and attitudes, which is a world that even empiricists might accept. Prior to doing so, he had to define what an ideal could and could not do, and cleanse it of confusing attributes falsely adhering to it. So, what were these confusions?

First, an ideal—just because it is spatially or temporally distant—does not for that reason abstract experience, or homogenize it, or depersonalize it. Bakhtin was a committed personalist who took his inspiration from Kant's "subjective idealism," with its insistence that the human being is an end in itself and not a means. Although Bakhtin learned much from Hegelianism, in this area he continued to prefer Kant to those more monistic, objective idealisms (such as Hegel's) that aim to restore lost unity in some future Absolute. In Bakhtin's variant of philosophical pluralism, there are potentially as many ideals as there are persons. And thus the responsible relationship to be worked out is not among various impersonal ideals—for ideals do not need to arrange themselves in some attractive, coherently integrated "design in the sky"—but between an individual person and the ideal which that person posits as a guide. For Bakhtin that guide was most likely the same one he posited for Dostoevsky in his study of that great writer: the person of Christ. Second, an ideal need not be a fixed or permanent value. The content of an ideal can change. All that is fixed is the status of the ideal within a given personality and event-horizon. The ideal is that particular absolute *which calls out to me*—and while I should never apologize for it, I do have an obligation to respect the absolutes that call out to others. Third, living by ideals is not, in the usual sense of the word, *idealistic*. Quite the contrary. Absolute ideals—unlike the material utopias so popular with the positivists and later with the Communists—are not posited because one expects ever to arrive at them or live comfortably in them. I posit an ideal because I want to be oriented by it and move toward it in my own life, in a world that otherwise offers me little by way of security, reasonableness, or reward.

That sort of grim, aching world was exactly what Bakhtin woke up to every day. Over his long, precarious, and pain-filled life (he suffered from chronic bone disease) the practical need for this sort of transcendence must have confirmed him as an idealist. For idealism is completely alien to those utopian sorts of naïveté that counsel us to wait for, or even to engineer, a change in the larger environment, a miracle cure, which will then bring about (automatically and magically) a change in the self. Such mechanical solutions are castles in the air. In contrast to such utopian thinking, living by ideals is supremely realistic, since at no point is coherence or justice expected from the outside world, nor imposed upon that world. If there was one thing Bakhtin knew from his own experience, it was that external events, "what happens to happen to us," can never be counted on to cohere for our benefit. That is not the way the world is made. Each self has only minimal control over "events that happen." But a self always has the option of becoming answerable for its own set of *responses* to events, a competence that the ideal facilitates. It is not the pattern of our experiences as much as the pattern of our *responses* to experience that constitutes what others recognize, over time, as our distinctive personality. Those responses are monitored by an ideal. Thus positing ideals makes some sort of wholeness possible in my life, no matter how broken and unreliable its fate.

Thus, life contains absolutes. We sense this, without daring to define fully their content, and call it a sense of God. At any given moment, my position is absolute for me—and I must answer for it, with, Bakhtin writes, "no alibis." Those who do me the favor of finalizing me (for their own sake and for my own) do not become "relativists" vis-à-vis me, or vis-à-vis one another. The very notion of relativism is derived from (and tainted by) its origin in single-point perspective presumed as the norm. Bakhtin begins elsewhere. He posits multiplicity of perspective as the norm. This guarantees for each of us permanent mutual outsideness in a world where we (and our ideals) live among a mass of mutually incompatible, mutually supplementary points of view that will never add up to a single "realistic" picture. It is the world as lived in an Orthodox icon—and it should not surprise us that it delivers a valuable lesson in humility. I am not at the center of other people's worlds. I do not stand at their door, ready to stroll in at my convenience. I am only an edge, and to others, things look different. Every time my ideal comes up against your ideal, we must renegotiate.

Thus does the *I-for-myself* slowly gain a foothold in the world of *I-for-the-other* and *others-for-me*. On balance, this is good news. For just as I enjoy, by virtue of my position, the right to combine and select others' gazes, so am I also (of course) able and obliged to gaze back at you. In fact, it is your image projected on to me that prevents my identity from becoming a merely relative thing, a floater, determined solely by my inner moods, narcissistic desires, or the arrows of outrageous chance. What is created out of me by you is an objective fact, it exists on a boundary that we both share and is a real relation, not merely an "opinion" belonging to you or to me. Your gaze, along with other gazes, is what gives my identity its truth. And again, to repeat, the possibility that you might wish to kill me with your gaze, or maybe kill me period with any instrument at your disposal, or just hate me for no reason, is not for Bakhtin an interesting theoretical problem.

MODELS OF THE PERSON

With this benevolent vocabulary in place, let us now, in the final section of this essay, return in more detail to Bakhtin's three models of personhood. Each is made up of an *I-for-myself* nourished by a multitude of I-for-others, but in varying proportion. Each has tremendous advantages, as well as some serious drawbacks. Only two of these models—the dialogic self and the carnival self—became world famous. The model that preceded them both, the "architectonic self," is more complex, and for that reason its explication has been the burden of this essay. It is both singular and idealist, relational and absolute, a self-on-the-border but nevertheless a self that is continuous within our consciousness. Bakhtin's "architectonics of the self" was unknown outside the Russian-speaking world during the most active years of the Bakhtin Boom. It was buried away in faded, handwritten notebooks that the aging, ailing Bakhtin had filled with moral philosophy during the 1920s and then stored —or better, abandoned—in a woodshed throughout the Stalinist years. These notebooks were exhumed, transcribed, and selectively published in Russian after Bakhtin's death. They were translated into English in 1990.

I would like to consider these three selves, then, not in order of their chronological emergence but in order of their fame. The most celebrated (and arguably least profound) is the carnival self. Bakhtin elaborated it in the 1930s, giving it its most detailed treatment in his doctoral dissertation of 1946. That scandalous dissertation (verbal obscenity and the "lower bodily stratum" were not routine topics of discussion in the High Stalinist academy) was sanitized for public consumption in the 1950s and became Bakhtin's bestselling book of 1965, *Rabelais and his World*. Its translation into Western languages and its inspirational effect on Parisian radicals in 1968 helped launch the Bakhtin Boom.

The key to the carnival self is that it is largely a *body*—and more specifically, a robust, fertile, grotesque body "on holiday." It has all the advantages of a body under such conditions: it needs others, it can communicate with them without having to learn a complex verbal language, it is cheerful and free from shame and embarrassment, it opens up to every new experience. It is not rushing to get anything done. It is an easy self to affirm because it does not require discipline or self-control to maintain. And crucially for Bakhtin, it laughs. Carnival laughter coming out of the mouth is fearless, indifferent to death, and thus a great deal more important than *words* that come out of the mouth (carnival words are mostly obscene). Laughter is even more important than gazes that come out of the eyes. The carnival self barely has eyes; it is all lips, cheeks, breasts, and buttocks. And like these protuberances, it is completely outward- and other-oriented.

Clearly this self is social, integrationist, eager to interact with others—all positive traits. But because this type of self remembers so little and regrets so little, it is difficult to say exactly why it needs any *specific* other at all. Although it takes in an endless stream of *others-for-me*, it doesn't seem to do much with them or leave a significant mark on them; others simply pass through, or gestate and are born, because the carnival body is above all a conduit. And thus, paradoxically, we are left at the end of the day with a swollen, but somehow impoverished *I-for-myself*, a mass of interchangeable sensations and impulses that neither learns nor ages. This is (at least for me) what makes carnival selves so tedious. But in the contexts of terror and famine, this generous, open-ended, well-fed self must have been an inspiration. We know that Bakhtin was deeply enamoured of carnival selves, valuing them for their courage and egolessness.

Next, the dialogic self. Bakhtin devised this model in the late 1920s and tinkered with it throughout his life. The key to the dialogic self is that it is largely a voice—or better, an overlay of voices. Its great strength is that, although sharing constantly and attentively with others as do carnival selves, it discriminates, listens, and remembers. It can hear a dozen voices embedded in every utterance, and a personality behind each voice. Dialogic selves are above all conscious and laden with memory; indeed, their primary spiritual task might be to increase the amount of consciousness in the world. (In that special novelistic form of extreme dialogism, which Bakhtin called "polyphony," authors design characters who potentially know as much about themselves as their authors do, and this knowledge permits them to develop autonomously and to surprise even their author.) The primary obligation of the dialogic self is to fulfill, console, and supplement others by seeing, or hearing, what that other cannot see or hear for herself. (Bakhtin's earliest sketch of this scene was two people facing each other across a table, needing each other because neither knew what was threatening him behind his back, and only the other could see.)

If the skills natural to a carnival self are fertility, species survival, and fearlessness in the face of death, then to the realm of dialogue belong mutual sacrifice, supplementarity, open-endedness, and love. The specificity of this love is important. The *I-for-myself* here is selective. Much might pour in, but only certain intonations are chosen, because the dialogic self is vulnerable and, of course, mortal. So important are trust, love, and second chances to this realm that one detects a serious drawback in the model, namely, that there is almost too much *I-for-the-other* in it. The self is not willing to close down around its own word, and utterances dangle on the border, belonging partly to my mouth, partly to your ears. If reality is constituted *between* us rather than within us, then what is the status of reality should you and I begin (seriously, fatally) to disagree? In short, the dialogic realm, grounded as it is in the shared utterance, can breed irresponsibility and lies. Most of us live in this realm by default, but we can live there carelessly, or well.

Finally, we return to the parent model, the wise and patient architectonic self. When Bakhtin's early writings first came out in English in 1990, no one could believe how difficult they were to read. After the frolic of the carnival square and the soberly concrete "discourse charts" on the double-voiced word familiar from the book on Dostoevsky, it seemed as if Bakhtin had slipped back into some obfuscating Teutonic mist. But this was in fact a most natural air for Bakhtin to breathe. He had grown up speaking and reading German; by his mid-teens he was already thoroughly at home in German philosophy. In his early writings (very few of which were prepared by him for publication), his philosophical style was still deeply influenced by Kant and by the twentieth-century German existential thinkers. The contours of the architectonic self are derived from abstract categories of continental philosophy: "Being," "Becoming," "Eventness," the "Ought" [*Sollen*]. But retroactively, knowing the selves to come, we can see how the discipline that this self asks of us, if properly mastered, would alleviate many of the problems faced by the carnival and dialogic selves. For the primary task of the architectonic self is not to swallow or get swallowed (as in carnival), nor to talk and/or listen (as in dialogue); its primary task is to *act*. And to understand what constitutes an act, to learn *how* to act and how to answer for one's acts, are mental and spiritual reflexes that should be well practiced and firmly established before the cunning of language, and before the safety-valve, or holiday, of carnival as well. Bakhtin devotes an entire essay, "Toward a Philosophy of the Act" (1993), to the nature of this activity. It turns out that the architectonic self is the most morally responsible structure in all of Bakhtin, because it balances inner and outer pressures, demands of self and other, perfectly. Learn to do that, and you can visit the dialogic and carnival realms at your leisure and without risk.

We need a philosophy of the personally performed act, Bakhtin argued in 1921 on the ruins of the First World War, because in these terrible times we (the intellectuals) have succumbed to the temptation to escape from lived life into culture. Reasons are easy to find. A cultural event can exist without a responsible author; it is complete in itself. Naturally we would rather live there, because an artwork, as part of culture, acknowledges norms and inner necessity whereas our lives are simply shapeless, open, out of control, a mess. Kant was of no help here, because the general or universal case, like the transcendentally categorical "as if," could too easily begin to function as one more distanced "cultural event," as a transcription of my life and not life itself. Henri Bergson was of even less help: if our lives are all vital force and unfixable flow, then we are tempted even more powerfully to stand to one side and watch this flow, or to melt namelessly and irresponsibly into it. There must be a way, Bakhtin mused, of persuading ourselves that *obligation* in our personal acts is equivalent to *form* in a work of art in culture, and thus that assuming obligations can bring us rewards equivalent to aesthetic pleasure.

Here Bakhtin works with the simplest possible parts, again borrowed from German philosophy. The world is made up of two types of things, he writes: "that which is given" (*dan*) and "that which I posit to myself as a task" (*zadan*) (see, for instance, Bakhtin 1993, 20). Life presents me with givens (formless disasters, undeserved illnesses, mindless revolution, unexpected good luck). I respond by "signing" these situations—which is not to say that I caused them, or deserved them, or approve of them, or even that I know how to deal with them, but only that I admit that they happened; thus, I sign my name to them and agree to participate in them. This is the first and crucial step in every act. Questions such as "Who is to blame?" and "Why me?"—those worthy political and romantic questions—bother Bakhtin not at all. He functions here as a stoic and a pragmatist, creating value as he goes along. Identity and value begin for me not where I have managed to scrape together some unity of content (for there is no such unity) but only where my obligation begins. Whatever I sign, I must work with; if I make a habit of refusing to sign, for whatever reason, I forfeit identity.

It goes without saying that this is exceptionally hard work. Such hard work, in fact, that when carnival time comes along we might well feel we have earned the right to collapse temporarily into it. One is reminded here of the "active love" that the Elder Zossima teaches in *The Brothers Karamazov*: regardless of how your acts are received by others, love endlessly, work without cease, and judge not. At last we have a balanced self. In contrast to the generous, permeable, reversible, unstable give-and-take model of the dialogic self, and also in contrast to the transitory, wordless, ever-leaking and ever-consuming carnival self (really more a body than a self), the seasoned architectonic self is complexly responsible, ego-oriented, and integrated. Of all Bakhtin's models of selfhood, this earliest one is the one most concerned about becoming an individual and answering for itself among others. It is not yet fully dialogic, but it is readying itself for the challenges and pitfalls of dialogue. For entrance into dialogue, I would like to think, requires some disciplined preparatory work. Neither a mechanical fidelity to rules, nor mere instincts and intuitions of love, will suffice for long. We're too frail. There must be a core, a habitual core, that moves instinctively to assume obligations toward others. These others will always be different from myself. Where did this profoundly personalist thinker find his role model?

Bakhtin was not, of course, at liberty to publish his thoughts about the person of Christ. But at several points in his early notebooks, he comments on the Christ of the Gospels in terms of the contrary pulls of *I-for-myself* and *I-for-the-other*. The proper proportions are easy to lose. Why is the balance so difficult? This we all know from our everyday experience. Too much self, even if it is a morally pure self, and we forget what others need; that is, we forget the validity of other people's perspectives. But too much other, and our own self dangerously empties out, loses its ability to make moral judgments or take responsibility, gets swayed and swamped.

But in Christ, Bakhtin wrote, "we find a synthesis of unique depth, the synthesis of *ethical solipsism* [by which Bakhtin meant: infinite severity toward one's own self] and *ethical-aesthetic kindness* toward the other" (Bakhtin 1990, 56). Christ was the first recorded example of an "infinitely deepened *I-for-myself*," one that was not cold and mute but responsive and discriminating. This was, as Alan Jacobs has written, the inspirational model of "kenosis that is not self-annihilating" (Felch and Contino 2001, 38). The moral life requires no less, and Bakhtin strove to point the way.

II. Love, Values, and the Self

3

The Role of Love in the Development of the Self:

From Freud and Lacan to Children's Stories

Karen Coats

The philosophical conception of the self in modernity has been dominated since the Enlightenment by a Cartesian dualism that isolates the individual in a nearly solipsistic inner world of rational contemplation. Descartes' famous *cogito, ergo sum* situates the self as a disengaged isolate at the center of perception, constructing and ordering the world of ideas and representations through its thinking activity. Under such a conception, being involves detaching the self from material existence in order to understand it for what it is: a merely instrumental extension of mental life that facilitates our survival but is itself inherently meaningless. Understandably, this conception raises the hackles of many thinkers, including Christians, in that it situates the thinking, disembodied self at the center of the universe. And while Descartes himself eventually suggests that his method of radical doubt leads to a greater understanding of the nature of God, the secular uptake of his thinking has ultimately led to the privileging of an antirealist philosophy that situates not only the self, but the entire universe, as the outcome of the noetic processes of a disembodied thinking self. In other words, the Cartesian self does not so much encounter the world as it creates it, which obviously causes problems within a Christian worldview.

But this disengaged rationality has been challenged from another quarter as well. Sigmund Freud effected what he considered the third and fatal blow to such narcissistic pretensions as those of self-evident rationality with his development of psychoanalytic theory. The first blow came from Copernicus, who informed us that the earth was not the center of the universe, even though our senses told us that the sun revolved around the earth, and not vice versa. Darwin shook the conceit that we are essentially differ-ent from the animals around us by positing a common ancestry. And finally, Freud introduced the unconscious, which in effect dethroned man as the uncontested master of his own rational faculties. Instead, our lives and our decisions, our loves and our hates, are more often the result of forces working elsewhere than in our conscious mind, and we are the dupes of those forces, rather than their master. Naturally, the simple formulation of "I think, therefore I am" cannot possibly take into account the myriad and unpredictable effects of the unconscious on our perception, our memories, our use of language, and our affective engagement with the world. Indeed, thinking, as Descartes conceived it, accounts for considerably less than half the story of our being in the world.

Because Cartesianism reflects such a profound estrangement from a physical and social reality distinct from ourselves, and because it forcibly ignores the effects of the unconscious and the body as even an archaic expression of our subjective mind, it has been discredited by postmodern critics. The *cogito, ergo sum* allows no room for irrational, or even pararational, engagement with the world. I would contend that the problem with Descartes' formula is that it is not a *true* or complete expression of being, and while untruths or partial truths can hold enormous sway for long periods of time and wreak all sorts of havoc, in the end, they necessarily fail. So what, then, is a better expression of the self's ontological status? French psychoanalyst Jacques Lacan playfully quipped that in contemporary society, a better formula might be "I complain, therefore I am." We've all seen bumper sticker philosophy—"I eat," or "I drink," or even, as I saw on a baby T-shirt, "I nap, therefore I am"—which, though absurd, are nevertheless obviously the antithesis of Descartes' formulation in that they would define being entirely through the material rather than the mental. Hence, while antithetical to Descartes, they are no less Cartesian in their separation between mind and body. However, if we are to account as fully as possible for the way we live in the world in which we find ourselves, we need a formulation that takes into account the fact that we not only encounter a world, but that we act on it as well, in the modes of both passive reaction and active response, both reflective contemplation and affective engagement. In what follows, then, I'd like to suggest that the best way to think about the ontology of the self, what the self *is*, consists of the following: "I love, therefore I am."

This formulation doesn't simply critique and utterly abandon modernism's claims to individuality, agency, and rational autonomy, as postmodern critics such as Michel Foucault and Judith Butler have attempted. These critics of modern subjectivity treat the self as the mere effect of cultural power dynamics; the fact that we even think or talk about the self at all is a result of a cultural mandate for responsibility before a repressive law that, for instance, defines crimes in such a way as to require criminals (see Foucault 1970; Butler 1993, 1997). Structures require subjects to animate them, rather than the other way around. For such thinkers, the self is nothing other than the nodal point at which a number of independently functioning discourses—discourses of race, gender, ethnicity, class, and so on—come together. To a certain extent this is no doubt true; we are tremendously influenced by the experiences and valuations that our particular embodiment and material situatedness entail in the culture in which we find ourselves. Hence their critique is well taken, but it does not offer a positive response, nor does it locate a viable site of potential resistance or agency. For both Foucault and Butler, agency is only conceived in terms of one's ability to subvert the normative expressions of culture, and of course, subversion is neither creative nor productive in and of itself. Love, as we shall see, does not operate independently of the cultural power dynamics in which the subject is enmeshed, but it is also both productive of individuality and agential in its expression.

Just as the formulation "I love, therefore I am" does not abandon modernism nor collapse into postmodern critique, it does not retreat into what appears to be a new version of biological reductionism or determinism, a direction currently fueled by advances in neuroscience that indicate, for instance, that immoral and otherwise negative behavior is causally linked to malfunctioning brain chemistry, or that our understanding of the self will somehow be exhausted in the study of brain function. In *A General Theory of Love* (2000), for instance, psychiatrists Thomas Lewis, Fari Amini, and Richard Lannon present the neuroscientific evidence of the mammalian limbic system, memory, and early attachment relationships that they assert establishes the neural location of love. According to their theory, any animal with a developed limbic brain and a history of attached mother-child behavior can and does love. While this book certainly presents a fascinating picture of the biological necessity of mammalian relatedness for the development of both mental and physical maturity, it does not meet the claims of its title to provide "a general theory of love." The attachment behavior that they illuminate, while providing a precondition for loving relationships, is not itself love, ontologically speaking, nor does it account for the complex role that language and fantasy play in human relationships and the development of the self (see also Stratton, this volume, on the distinction between love and attachment).

"I love, therefore I am" can thus be characterized as an attempt at an adequate understanding of the transmodern view of the self (see Vitz, Introduction, this volume). The claims of modernism cannot be simply and utterly dismissed, nor would we want to dismiss the individual's obvious inclinations to willed rational and representational thought. However, two salient features of the self that have been systematically overlooked or discredited in Western philosophy—the self as embodied, the self as relational—need an account that is more far-reaching than the *cogito* allows. We love and are loved with our minds (both consciously and unconsciously), our bodies (both consciously and unconsciously), and our spirits, which comprise, in a psychoanalytically inflected Christian understanding, that part of us that is (or should be) in communion with God.

DEFINING LOVE

But in order for such a formulation as "I love, therefore I am" to be compelling, or to even take hold as more than a bumper-sticker slogan, we need to know what love is, and how it actively constructs the self. While love is the most potent and creative force in the world, it is probably the most undertheorized major concept in Western thought. When people do try to think or talk analytically about it (and I should note that I am excluding the poets, playwrights, novelists, and lovers who have written countless billet-doux over the centuries, and limiting my discussion to what the various analytical discourses have to say about love) they tend to produce taxonomies, antinomies, classifications, attributes, manifestations, and hierarchies rather than straightforward ontological definitions. In fact, the trepidation of philosophers, scientists, and theologians to define love makes the *Oxford English Dictionary*'s attempt seem almost an impertinence. Nevertheless, according to the *Oxford English Dictionary*, love is "that disposition or state of feeling with regard to a person which (arising from recognition of attractive qualities, from instincts of natural relationship, or from sympathy) manifests itself in solicitude for the welfare of the object, and usually also in delight in his or her presence and desire for his or her approval; warm affection, attachment." If I were to assemble in one room the theorists who have thought or written about love over the past three thousand or so years (and believe me I wouldn't need a very big room), and read this definition, I imagine there would be a moment or two of agitated silence, followed by a wild irruption of objections: Is love primarily or necessarily a state of feeling, or is affect only one of its contingent manifestations? Do we love someone for his or her attractive qualities, or is there a gestalt that transcends qualities? How, exactly, do "instincts of natural relationship" give rise to love? Is attachment or warm affection synonymous with love? Can we talk about objects when we talk about love, or are objects more properly in the domain of narcissism or demand? Don't some forms of love care little for the welfare of the object, especially if it is in fact considered at the level of object? And doesn't love often cause something other than delight in the presence of the beloved?

What, then, is love? Since we are working at the intersection of trinitarian thought and psychoanalysis, we must look for definitions from both of those quarters for a full account of our topic, and, oddly enough, we find some agreement regarding the ontological nature of love. Paul Tillich and Sigmund Freud, though they came from two very different traditions and had very different life philosophies, both agreed that love is a force permeating animate nature that is directed toward unity. We'll need to parse this definition in order to gain a full understanding of its implications: love as force, love as found throughout animate nature, and love as a striving for unity. We'll start with the last bit: love as a striving for unity.

LOVE AS A STRIVING FOR UNITY: BETWEEN PSYCHOANALYSIS AND CHRISTIANITY

Tillich (1954) maintains that, while it is important and useful to distinguish between different kinds of material expressions of love, it is equally important to remember that in its ontology, "love is one" (27). Each of its qualities, from *epithymia* (desire), to *philia* (brotherly love or friendship), to *agape* (disinterested love for our fellow man) to *caritas* (love directed to and from God), are expressions of the same force toward the unity of something that is separated. Whereas Nygrens (1957), for instance, is at great pains to tease out the fundamental differences between *agape* and *eros*, and in so doing critiques Augustine for his synthesis of the two into *caritas* (although Augustine breaks his discussion down into the distinctions between *caritas* and *cupiditas*), Tillich emphasizes that all of love, whatever its explicit aim, implies this drive toward unity. Love seeks the dissolution of the space between existences. For Tillich, this striving for unity contains within it both the notion of an originary unity and a subsequent separation: "Love is the drive toward the unity of the separated. Reunion presupposes separation of that which belongs essentially together. . . . Therefore love cannot be described as the union of the strange but as the reunion of the estranged. Estrangement presupposes original oneness" (Tillich 1954, 25).

Obviously, Tillich's original oneness must be understood as oneness of spirit; that is, it is metaphysical in nature. Our embodiment is, on the other hand, both material and our own; it is the space of the body that is marked out as distinct, incapable of union because, despite the rhetorical confusion of the pro-abortion forces, it was never originally one with anyone else's body. Even in sexual relations, we never completely lose sight of the distinctness of our own body, and we are aware that the oneness we seek can only be metaphorically expressed through sex. Tillich extends this embodied separateness to consciousness itself when he stresses that love can only be realized in the bridging of a gap between two "self-centered" beings; that is, he presumes an already self-conscious subject who reaches out in love to bridge the gap with another, equally self-conscious subject. Like most theorists of love, he focuses our attention on love between equals, that is, adult people who already have a strong sense of "self." The questions that remain include how one becomes such a self-conscious subject, and wherein lies the original unity that the two self-conscious subjects are trying to reclaim. An answer to these questions seems to lie within a psychoanalytic theory of subject development that takes seriously the idea that we are made in the image of a trinitarian God.

Psychoanalytic theory, though it varies widely in its perspectives and emphases and has usually been (quite rightly) regarded as antagonistic to the claims of Christianity, serves an important purpose in that it reminds us that the prototype for understanding loving relations is not male-female, or friendship between equals, but parent-child. Even Christian thinkers often make the mistake of taking adult I-Thou love as the foundation upon which we should build our understanding of the self-in-relation, without considering the ways in which this self or its relations develop. Indeed, the Trinity has within itself this parent-child relationship. Furthermore, if we are to understand who we are with relation to the "I am," then we have to think in terms of a love based on hierarchical assumptions that lead to development through identification with and idealization of a higher order of complexity.

In this context, it is worth considering a few of Jacques Lacan's innovations on Freudian theory as they help explain the functions of identification and idealization in the giving and receiving of love and how these facilitate the development of the self. Lacan takes issue with the way Freudian concepts have been taken up by ego psychologists; he accuses them of working out of the same Cartesian model that Freud himself claimed to have unsettled.

Lacan wants to trouble the very idea that the self can ever be adapted to the reality in which it finds itself, and that this maladaption is precisely what leads to the necessity of love in the first place. Adaptation is the central focus and goal of ego psychology, and it is only when the self has achieved a certain developmental milestone that he or she can truly love another person, again reinforcing the notion that love is only possible between adults, and that it has no real bearing on the passage from child to adult. Even Freud at times capitulates to this view, most forcefully expressed by Fairbairn

(1986), who writes, "The gradual change which thus occurs in the nature of the object-relationship is accompanied by a gradual change in libidinal aim, whereby an original oral, sucking, incorporating and 'taking' aim comes to be replaced by a mature, nonincorporating, and 'giving' aim compatible with developed genital sexuality" (77–78). In other words, given the proper environment, the child's psychological development will successfully mirror his or her physical development, and the result will be an other-directed person able to give generously and love fully.

On Lacan's account, however, such a goal of adaptation to reality, where love and pleasure can be fundamentally connected through development maturity, is not simply difficult or ideal, but *structurally impossible* for the self to attain. This is because, for Lacan, the subject—that is, the human being who accounts for himself through the use of linguistic signifiers such as I or his proper name—is an effect of the language he uses, and language and the body are of two heterogeneous orders, such that one cannot be adapted to the other. In Christian terms, the Word is responsible for the creature, and not vice versa. Our subjectivity, founded in language and yet profoundly alienated from its incarnational ability, seeks reunion with that creative Word, but we are unable to effect it on our own. Hence the self in Lacan is represented as a barred subject—a body subjected to but not completely subsumed by its own imago and its position in language. The fundamental gap between the subject and its imago is covered over by identification, but the gap between the subject and its world, or, to use Lacan's terminology, the gap between the subject and the Other, between the symbolic and real, is covered over by love.

For Lacan the symbolic is the linguistically ordered system of law and meaning through which the subject structures reality and the self. The real, on the other hand, is that which resists symbolization. When we have attempted to account for some phenomenon in language, we may be sure that we have not captured it in its materiality, because the order of the real is precisely that which exceeds and escapes symbolic reference; more than that, it is inimical to such symbolization. This dualism is often dismissed by Christian thinkers as antirealist, but I think that in leaving room for a real that escapes totalization by human knowledge and linguistic endeavor, that in fact radically resists the notion of such totalization as even a possibility, Lacan seems to be one of the few thinkers of the twentieth century who takes sin—separation from God—entirely seriously as an irreparable (from the human side at any rate) break. It is not enough simply to posit that since we are made in the image of God, we will be capable of intellectual, creative, and loving activity as if the Fall never happened, or even to suggest that conversion unfetters us to the point where our cultural and ideological heritage and influence can be eradicated. Instead, Lacan's concept of the subject structured by lack maps with uncanny precision onto the Christian notion of person separated from God by sin. Of course, Lacan's atheism leads him to say that there is no Other of the Other, that there is no Presence that authorizes, finally and completely, both the symbolic and the real, and to think otherwise is merely a paranoid fantasy. But from a Christian perspective, one might go so far as to say that Lacan's atheism rendered him unable to see the unconscious truth of his own discourse: that there is in fact an Other of the Other, and he has a name which we cannot speak, but which we signify as God. And while the subject comes into being through his or her interaction with the Other of the symbolic order, this Other of the Other is the foundation on which both the subject and the symbolic order depend for their existence. Profound in his alterity, this God nevertheless desires communion with his creatures, and our lack is most aptly understood as the self's alienation from and desire to return to unity with God.

Thus far we have established that the Lacanian self is ontologically grounded in love, and that love should be understood as a force that seeks to reunite that which has been separated. We have distinguished our approach to the understanding of love as being grounded in the hierarchical sense of parent-child, rather than love between equals, the importance of which will become evident in the following section. Further, we have shown that a psychoanalytically inflected understanding of Christianity points us in the direction of understanding the nature of the unity that has been disrupted, namely, that it is a gap between the symbolic and the real. We will now proceed within the model we have established to articulate specifically the mechanisms by which love leads to the development of the self.

FROM INFANT TO SELF-CONSCIOUS SUBJECT

For Freud, life begins in a state of "oceanic plentitude" where one's consciousness is not wholly distinct from one's surroundings but rather is intimately tied to the psyche of the mother. Lacan posits the infant as an undifferentiated bundle of needs with no clear sense of the boundaries between self and other. He punningly refers to this infant as an "hommelette," a little man and an egg running in all directions. Developments in infant observation research challenge this notion, suggesting quite strongly that infants do in fact distinguish themselves from others, and have a clear sense of the limits of their own bodies. But Freud's or Lacan's insight need not be troubled by this new information, for they suggest that this sense of unity is more a psychical than an actual state of affairs for the infant, based on a fantasized unity rather than an experiential one. The "mother" needs to be understood figuratively in this context; she is the (m)other, the first representative of the Other that the child encounters. As such, her constant (psychic) presence preserves in the child a sense of unity or continuity with the otherness that surrounds him, and her periodic (actual) disappearances facilitate his growing awareness of his separateness from that otherness. Hence the first movements for the newly self-conscious infant are regressive; they seek a return to the oneness they experienced with the mother, suggesting a first guise of love as a drive toward unity with the mother.

Freud recognizes this drive toward unity with the mother as only one direction that love understood as a force can take, and it is a dangerous one. In fact, the drive toward this type of unity is in the service of the death drive—that is, it is a regressive desire to merge with the mother, to return to an earlier state of psychic stasis and bodily satisfaction. Freud's oedipal triangle, especially as developed by Lacan, is explicitly designed to prevent such merging: the father stands in the way of the child's desire to be one with the mother. The father's prohibition inaugurates the subject into the world of cultural and social substitutes for the satisfaction he or she once felt in being in a place of undifferentiated psychic unity with mom. But this points out a bothersome weakness in Freud's account: If the mother is the site of needs met, and the father is perceived as nothing more than a threat, then why in the world would the child make the momentous choice to change allegiances, to sacrifice the warm cozy maternal relation for a profoundly cold and precarious position on the side of culture and the father? When a young child is threatened, chances are he's not going to growl back but return instead to the safety of the maternal space. In Lacan's gloss on Freud's theory, we see that the paternal prohibition covers over the impossibility of returning to that presumably safe space; moreover, we see that the space of maternal unity is not necessarily safe at all, since it would entail our own annihilation as separate subjects. Love emerges in this scenario as first of all an unconditional demand for oneness with the mother, which is met squarely by its own impossibility and undesirability.

To illustrate how this works, we can see how in the well-known children's story *Where the Wild Things Are* (1963), love is everywhere equated with incorporative cannibalistic desire. The kind of love that Max expresses in the first part of the book is melancholic, regressive, and consuming; the child seeks to reclaim the space of oneness that he feels he has lost by incorporating and cannibalizing the (m)other. "I'll eat you up!" Max says to his mother. The mother responds to his aggressive impulse by taking away the thing that has guaranteed her presence, and hence, in the child's eyes, her love, since infancy—food. She sends him to his room without supper. Here, he constructs a fantasy jungle populated by wild things who also say to him, "WE'LL EAT YOU UP—WE LOVE YOU SO!" Clearly, this guise of "love" would lead to a certain kind of "unity" of the self and other—ingestion? digestion?—but it does not lead to the development of the self, and must be rejected, both by Max and by his mother.

Instead, Max must come to identify with his mother in a particular way, rather than trying to swallow her whole. When his mother sends him to bed without supper, he is angry. He responds by fantasizing a space where he is in charge. Both his anger and his assumption of control reflect his mother's actions; hence he is not trying to be one with her, but instead he is trying to be somewhat like her by identifying with a select few of her particular characteristics. This distinction of incorporating the other versus taking on her characteristics seems overly subtle until we look closely at how Max handles his wild things. Instead of imagining a scenario where he does in fact eat his mother or her surrogates, which would indicate a melancholic incorporation, he imagines that he himself is in danger of being eaten by these wild things that love him, and like her, he does not allow it. His process of mourning the loss of his mother involves identifying with one of her traits—her sternness—rather than attempting to become one with her, and losing himself in the process.

In the example of Max, it becomes clear that attempting to become one with the (m)other entails the regressive kind of love that constitutes the loss of the self, but that identifying with a single trait preserves the alterity of the other and helps the child to develop his own characteristics and abilities through imitation. This is the second direction love as a force can take, according to Freud. Though Freud does not develop his insights as fully as he might, Jonathan Lear, in his book *Love and Its Place in Nature* (1990), interpolates from what Freud does say to describe the way in which love acts as a force for individuation, and hence, development of the self.

THE IMPORTANCE OF THE LOVABLE WORLD

Lear's account of Freud's insight begins with the notion that emotions are an archaic, embodied attempt at a rational orientation to the world. Freud found that in treatment, symptoms were relieved, not simply through the expression of emotion, but when the errant emotion found its proper object. In the case of Max, his mother doesn't deserve his aggression or his anger; once he turns his aggression toward its proper object—his own wild things—he can work it through and emerge refreshed. According to Lear, Freud later came to realize that this archaic rationality of emotion, directed at a lovable world, would necessarily lead a child to respond by loving the world back. In other words, love reflects our emotional orientation toward a world that somehow equally receives, reflects, and deserves our love. The notion of a lovable world is thus indispensable to Lear's gloss on Freud; hence the second part of our ontological definition that love permeates animate nature.

In this guise, then, we have to understand love's relation to the development of the self in its passive dimension. Before a child can invest his or her world with love, he or she must be on the receiving end of the loving attention of the Other. I use the definite pronoun and a capital letter to designate that these ministrations come from sites other than the mother or primary caregiver. If we believe that God is active in the world, then the lovableness of the world is a necessary, and not a contingent, feature of our experience, no matter what the relative adequacies of our caregivers. Julia Kristeva (1987), a French psychoanalyst and philosopher, posits what she calls an "imaginary father" who is active in all of us as we work to separate from the mother. When the child realizes, in the oedipal drama, that he cannot be one with the mother, he still only reluctantly capitulates to the demands and prohibitions of the symbolic order. Kristeva's "imaginary father," who is linked to Freud's "father of individual prehistory" has the characteristics of both mother and father, that is, he is loving, nurturing, and fully supportive of the child, but he is also powerful, even omnipotent. His presence makes it both safe and desirable for the child to separate from the mother, unlike the threatening, punitive father of Freud's original oedipal drama. In this "imaginary father," we have a way to think about the Holy Spirit's intervention in every person's life as a call to consciousness as a distinct individual and the inaugurator of a loving responsiveness to an already lovable world.

According to Lear, our emotional orientation to that world, despite being structurally archaic, nevertheless develops over time. Initially, the child can only invest his or her world with partial drive energies—forces that demand fulfillment or satisfaction at the level of bodily needs. It is precisely the movement between fulfillment and frustration that causes the world to have psychological meaning for him, that is, while the child reaches out to the world with his need, the world responds both only partially and, I would add, in excess. The world can only respond partially, because the drive contains within itself that regressive desire for the obliteration of separation, and because demands must always be expressed in language, which, as we have noted, always separates us from the real of our experience. But the world also responds in excess, because not only does the child receive care from the world, he also receives an anticipatory, as yet unrequited, profoundly complex love. There is nothing simple about the parents' love for their child—it is embodied, present, hopeful, anxious, desiring, and imperfect. And it is not always, though it can be, incorporative. In other words, it does not seek simple obliteration of the separation between us. Instead, it desires our otherness. Parents long for the day when their child seems to recognize them, when their child will be able to talk to them. From the start, they afford the child the gift of a separate identity, even though the child doesn't yet have the skills to claim it. But it is nevertheless a gift, an act of excessive generosity. We love God, our parents, the world, because they first loved us. In other words, "I am loved, therefore I come to be."

In particular, the world gives children the gift of an articulated system of differences that we have been calling the symbolic order. The real, because it resists symbolization, is a formless and inchoate space. Because the symbolic is ordered and rational, the child can come to be in it, can achieve a degree of psychic organization that enables it to become a self at all. One of the most important things the symbolic order gives to the child is its own body. Though it is difficult to posit a body that is not already inscribed and valuated by language, we have to remember that the baby learns to mark his or her body through the caregiver's attention to it. Thus the eyes, the mouth, and the genitals get marked from the beginning as distinct and privileged sites for the baby, and they remain privileged throughout life. Another way of saying this is that the subject's body is given to him through the loving attention of the Other. The loving Other reaches into an undifferentiated muddle of needs and sensations and articulates a structure that becomes the bodily imago of the child. Obviously, this is one of those sites where culture significantly mediates the relative lovableness of specific bodies through setting different values on different bodily imagoes, but the initial response of care for the body sets the fundamental course in the direction of love, even for those bodies that are culturally disprized.

A TALE OF TWO PIGS

Further concrete illustrations of the way love leads to the development of a self can be found in both *Charlotte's Web* (1952) and the popular children's movie *Babe* (1995). While the main conflict of both these stories can be considered in the light of a movement from the dangerous potentials of an incorporative type of unity to a nonincorporative love relationship, it would be ludicrous to follow Fairbairn (1986) in assuming that Babe's and Wilbur's development depends on developmental maturity proscribed by biological necessity. But just how will Wilbur and Babe move from being *objects* that persons would love to eat to being *persons* who love and are loved precisely for their status as persons? We see quite clearly in these two cases that infants start to become persons when someone loves them. Fern Arable, an eight-year-old girl with a clear sense of justice, objects to her father's decision to kill a runt pig simply because it is too small. So her father gives her the pig to raise as her baby. Fern attends to the pig's needs—feeds it, and makes sure it is warm—but she also loves it, that is, she identifies with its characteristics of smallness and vulnerability, invests it with her time and attention, and idealizes it. Likewise, Farmer Hoggett goes beyond attending to Babe's needs into actions of love toward the pig. He invests time and attention in the pig, and eventually comes to idealize the pig as well. In so doing, Fern and Farmer Hoggett take their beloved pigs out of the realm of objects and invest them with a caring attention that renders them human.

Both E. B. White and the filmmakers of King-Smith's story set up decidedly lovable worlds for their protagonists to inhabit. White lovingly describes the barn in which Wilbur comes to live, ending his two-page description by saying "It was the kind of barn that swallows like to build their nests in. It was the kind of barn that children like to play in" (14). Farmer Hoggett's farm is breathtakingly beautiful, nestled in a peaceful green valley and impeccably maintained. In addition, both worlds are peopled with loving companions. When Fern has to sell Wilbur, he is at first unbearably lonely, disdained or ignored by the other animals, until he hears a small voice from above who says, "'Do you want a friend, Wilbur? . . . I'll be a friend to you. I've watched you all day and I like you'" (31). Babe watches his mother get loaded onto a meat truck, but he is soon transported to the Hoggett farm, where he finds his place as surrogate son of the sheepdog Fly, and friend of the anorexic duck Ferdinand. Because of the loving attention that these two receive, they reach out in love to others. Wilbur is portrayed as open and childlike, loving and friendly even to the nasty rat, Templeton. Babe is a friend to all the animals who will have him and is described by the narrator as having an "unprejudiced heart." Both of these characters find their places in the world through the mediation of characters who act as "imaginary fathers" with the power to shift the terms of the little pigs' very existence. Charlotte writes words in her web that commend Wilbur to the attention of a wondering and adoring public, and Farmer Hoggett saves Babe's life by singing to him (an expression of love) and trains him as a "sheep-pig" who does the unthinkable by herding and managing sheep as if he were a dog. Because of the value conveyed on these two culturally disprized figures—what is more worthless than a runt pig?—Wilbur and Babe grow into kind and generous selves who make a real difference in the worlds that they inhabit.

FROM PASSIVE ACCEPTANCE TO ACTIVE INVESTMENT

The examples of Wilbur and Babe clearly show how love received enables a self to emerge. But how and why does the self move from a state of passively receiving the loving ministrations of the Other to actively reaching out to that Other in love? Lear points out that because the world responds only partially to the infant's needs, he or she must do something with his or her frustration, must metabolize it in some way. It is the frustration that causes us to act, and the excess of love in the response that provides the quality of the action. The world is always the world as it exists for me; Freud learned through his study of melancholia that the self is emotionally invested inwardly as well as outwardly, so that "psychic structure . . . is created by a dialectic of love and loss" (Lear 1990, 160). What is lost? As we have seen through Lacan's account, it is the sense of oneness with the real that has been figured or represented as the loss of oneness with the mother. How does the child respond? First, by consolidating his own ego as a defense against the loss of connection with the mother, and then by reaching out from that ego in loving investment toward the mother to regain the sense of lost unity. Insofar as she is a loving mother, he will, through his imitations of and identifications with her, gain the *form* of love, which we might call attachment, or more precisely, responsiveness, through that imitative behavior.

What the child learns very early in his interaction with his mother is that she has desires and commitments that have nothing to do with him. Her periodic absences, her distractions, the fact that she does not always respond immediately to his needs all indicate that she has interests elsewhere. This is in some respects catastrophic knowledge, but through a process of identifying with her desire, he can come to understand that there are things in the world that are desirable. As he follows her example by investing his libidinal energies into the world, which is another way of saying as he loves the world, he idealizes the objects that he invests. Love is metonymic in this way—we take a part or a quality and turn the whole into an idealized love object. But Lear reminds us that "because my love affair is with a distinctly existing world, I must be disappointed by it. A distinctly existing world cannot possibly satisfy all my wishes" (160). What happens then is that the child mourns the lost ideal image by incorporating some of its qualities into his own psychic structure. As Freud says, "When the I assumes the features of the object, it is forcing itself, so to speak, upon the it as a love-object and is trying to make good the it's loss by saying: *Look, you can love me too—I am so like the object*" (Freud 1961, 30). Because he is identifying with something outside of himself, the child becomes more than what he was, that is, he develops. When he then reinvests libidinal energy into the world, he does so from a more complex or developed psychic position, and hence encounters an ever-more complex world.

Imaginary and Symbolic Identifications

But as we have seen, we must be careful of the kind of unity that we desire; love proceeds by way of identification and idealization but is not to be confused with these processes. Tillich's definition of love depends as much on its failure as on its continual striving to succeed. "Fulfilled love is, at the same time, extreme happiness and the end of happiness. The separation is overcome" (27). That is, love can only be love in its failure to close the gap between the self and other; otherwise it is not love, but a regressive and self-destructive fantasy.

In our discussion of Lacan, we identified two separate orders: the symbolic and the real. But he identifies a third order that operates in connection with these two, and that is the imaginary. Perhaps the most famous notion of Lacanian psychoanalytic theory is his concept of the mirror stage. At some point very early in a child's life, he will recognize his image in a mirror. At first, there will be a moment of alienating anxiety, but that is replaced, according to Lacan, with "the jubilant assumption of his specular image" (1977, 2). What happens in that moment is that the child has made an identification with that image; he claims it as a representation of himself. But what is more interesting is that the image does not match his bodily experience. Whereas the image is whole and coherent, he experiences his body as fragmented and disconnected. Whereas the image appears in control of itself, he feels as if his body escapes his control. Whereas the image is separate and distinct from other bodies, he feels at least partially connected, still, to his mother's body. Thus the image functions as an imago, an ideal image that he will hereafter strive to achieve.

It is important to realize that we don't only encounter these imagoes in the mirror. Rather, once the mirror-stage has been achieved, imaginary identifications take place all the time; they are characteristic of our way of approaching the world. It's also important to note that this sort of identification is both a totalizing fantasy and a fantasy of totalization, that is, it covers over the gap between the symbolic and the real that we introduced earlier in two ways. First, the subject sees the imago as complete in itself, as if what you see is all there is. Second, the act of identification covers over any gap between the image and the self; the self collapses into the image and says "I am he." This, obviously, represents two forms of unity, such that we might say, under Tillich's definition, that imaginary identification is an expression of love. As we noted earlier in our discussion of Freud, love tends to operate under a metonymic and idealizing logic. We see in part, but then we cover over the lack in what we see with an idealizing fantasy; that is, we construct an ideal with which we identify as a totality. The problem is that when we identify with something in this way, it can just as easily become our rival as our ideal; in either case, we perceive it to be like us, and in so doing we erase its otherness. Hence we cannot simply say that we love that with which we identify, since we have not fulfilled the first condition of Tillich's definition, that of separation. Insofar as the gaps are actually closed, that is, insofar as unity is achieved in this illusory way, we know that we are dealing with something other than love which depends for its proper existence not only on the striving for unity, but on the recognition of separateness.

Fortunately, Lacan indicates that one may not only identify in the imaginary, but also in the symbolic. Symbolic identifications do not involve totalizing logic, because it is precisely in the symbolic that we recognize the impossibility of totalization. Not only is there an unbridgeable gap between the symbolic and the real, the gap between creature and Creator, if you will, but there are also gaps and inconsistencies within the symbolic order itself—places where language and structures undermine themselves (for instance, what Lacan might call unconscious discourse and Christians might call revealed truth) and/or get undermined by intrusions of the real (for instance, what scientists might call anomalies and Christians might call miracles). Hence we can never believe in the totality of the symbolic order as we do in the imaginary. Thus, what we identify with is a single trait, a characteristic of the thing, rather than the thing itself. Imaginary identification consists in collapsing the space between the self and the other, rendering the other the same, whereas symbolic identification involves the investment of the self into the other, locating specific points of connection but retaining the sense of the otherness of the other.

The investment of the self into the other as other is fundamentally different from the desire to incorporate the other, and it eventually leads to greater levels of individuation. When we identify at the level of the imaginary, we are mapping one illusory whole object onto another—the distance between the self and the other collapses. This is yet another way to understand the proscription of the making of images in the second commandment. The logic of the imaginary is such that we take parts for wholes and then believe in the possibility of that wholeness, that we have captured the thing in its ideal essence. When we then proceed to cover over the distance that separates us through imaginary identification, we see the other as a version of the self, or as the self's rival. What is not maintained is the otherness of the other. Hence we could presume, in imaginary logic, to be like gods. But when we identify at the level of the symbolic, we have to take the gap between the real—the realm of experience and being—and the symbolic—the realm of language and structure—into account. Hence we can't swallow a person whole, but rather we identify with particular features or traits. We identify, precisely, with the other's status as incomplete and in need of further development.

This difference helps us understand that our love for God must operate under a symbolic logic. To produce an imaginary image of God is to produce an idol; hence it is forbidden as well as impossible, much like the desire to merge with the mother in the oedipal drama. This could render my appropriation of Kristeva's term "imaginary father" to designate our Loving Mediator an unfortunate one, unless we remember that this is only one frame of reference that we have for him, and that he permeates the real, the imaginary, and the symbolic all at the same time. He may access us from any of these positions, but we may only access him in the symbolic. Knowing that we can't totally or completely signify God, we nevertheless attempt to use our flawed human language to approximate his qualities. We idealize those qualities and seek to love him by identifying with and attempting to take on the characteristics of say, humility, forgiveness, forbearance, patience. But such totalizing qualities as omnipotence and omniscience are closed to us because they are, by definition, features of imaginary and not symbolic logic.

As paradoxical as it may seem, love, in its striving for unity, produces ever greater individuation and development of the self, as that self moves from receiving the love of the Other to reinvesting itself into the world. In the process, the self suffers the loss of love-objects as ideal, and builds its own ego from the bits and pieces that remain as the ideal shatters. Hence we strive toward unity while maintaining our separateness. In the sense that we are defined in both the separateness and the striving toward unity, we can affirm the transmodern self as the *amo, ergo sum*.

4

Persons as Obligated: A Values-Realizing Psychology in Light of Bakhtin, Macmurray, and Levinas

Bert H. Hodges

[T]he self itself is a compound of facts and norms, of what *is* as well as a consciousness of what *ought* to be. The essence of being human is value. . . .

—Abraham Heschel, *Who Is Man?*

The world is not given to us "on a plate," it is given to us as a creative task. It is impossible to banish morality from this picture. . . . Our ordinary consciousness is a deep continuous working of values. . . . This is the transcendental network, the border, wherein the interests and passions which united us to the world are woven into illusion or reality. . . .

—Iris Murdoch, *Metaphysics as a Guide to Morals*

The modern self was born over three centuries ago when Descartes divided existence into two realms, the moral and mechanical. As moral beings, humans were autonomous, answering only to the clarity and logic of their own thought. Thinking not only guaranteed their existence ("*Cogito, ergo sum*"), it was the great dignity of human life, giving people the possibility of gaining "mastery and possession" over nonthinking nature. The nonthinking mechanical world was without freedom, dignity, or worth, except as it could be put to various uses by humans. Most poignantly, Cartesian believers found their own identity torn asunder, their bodies treated as meaningless mechanisms, while their disembodied thinking could create meaning and value at will.[1]

In a real sense, Descartes' modern self was lost from the beginning. Humans were jettisoned from a meaningful world in which they had enjoyed a central place and a divine purpose and were consigned to be isolated, free floating intellects, while their bodies were reduced to (placeless) space and (purposeless) time. In a real sense, the Cartesian self is schizophrenic—lost in thought and separated from reality.

To a large extent, psychology has lived in these two realms of the moral and the mechanical ever since. Comparing medieval and modern views of persons, John Shotter (1984) concluded: "If we are ever to study ourselves without disempowering ourselves in the process . . . it is Descartes' account of our being in the world (his ontology) and the accounts of how we came to know its nature (his epistemology) that we must replace" (34).[2] My own attempts to overcome the separation have proceeded primarily along two lines. One has been to explore an ecological approach to psychology (e.g., Hodges 1987), an approach pioneered by James Gibson (1979) and developed by others (e.g., Costall 1995; Michaels and Carello 1981; Reed 1997; Warren and Shaw 1985; Turvey 1990, 1996).[3] Two of its central theses relative to humans are (1) that humans and their environments are not separable, but intimately involved with each other, and (2) that humans have the "extraordinary" ability to act intentionally (Turvey 1990) and appropriately, not because they are (mechanically) caused to do so, but because they are properly informed by environmental information (i.e., perception).

The second and more important way I have tried to overcome the Cartesian heritage has been to develop a psychology of values (Hodges 1985, 2000; Hodges and Baron 1992; Martin and Hodges 1987). It is this psychology of values that will be highlighted in this chapter, with hints of the ecological approach.

In addition, a third line of inquiry has attracted my attention. Three important thinkers, none of them widely known to psychologists, were introduced to me by colleagues in psychology, who also have worked to overcome the Cartesian divide.[4] Mikhail Bakhtin, Immanuel Levinas, and John Macmurray are better known in philosophical and literary studies than in psychology, but each has influenced psychological theory and research (e.g., Davis 1995; deRivera 1989; Trevarthen 1980; Shotter 1993; Uzgiris 1996; Williams 1994). Each can be understood as postmodern in their sensitivities; for example, each attacks the view of persons provided by Descartes and those who followed him (e.g., Locke, Hume, Kant, Hegel). At the same time their deepest concerns seem not to lie in deconstructing modernity but in appropriating ancient biblical perspectives for addressing the reductionistic tendencies of modernism and the relativizing tendencies of postmodernism. In doing so, they are implicitly transmodern.

I will begin with an introduction to a values-realizing view of persons, turning then to Macmurray, Bakhtin, and Levinas to elaborate and enrich our understanding of human personhood.

WHAT MOTIVATES HUMANS?

What motivates human behavior? Where do our actions, feelings, and thoughts come from and where are they going? What do they accomplish, if anything? These questions are as hard and as crucial as any in psychology, and perhaps in all of science. The hypothesis I have explored for the past several years is that human behavior is motivated by values. Values, which will be described more formally below, are the goods to be realized in existence. With respect to humans, values are what is actually good for human persons; among them would be truth, justice, freedom, and love.[5] In short, I am claiming that humans are motivated to be moral.

I am not alone in making this claim, but psychology as a whole overwhelmingly rejects such a view. As Solomon Asch (1990), the distinguished social psychologist, put it: "[H]ere [is] a theme central to my thought: that there is an inescapable moral dimension to human existence. It follows that investigation must take account of that proposition. Yet psychologists have been among the most determined opponents of this claim" (53).

It is important to note that neither Asch nor I are arguing that people always think, do, and feel the right thing. We are only arguing that a crucial dimension of human action is evaluative; that is, action, thought, and emotion are themselves evaluative, concerned with realizing (both in the sense of discerning and of enacting) values, "the vectors that we designate with the terms right and wrong" (Asch 1952, 357). For example, anger is an emotion generated primarily by a perception of injustice, and puts the body in a state of readiness to redress the injustice (Sabini and Silver 1982; deRivera 1989). If values are an intrinsic aspect of the phenomena psychology studies, it follows that psychological research and theory should address these matters (Martin and Hodges 1987). The descriptive and explanatory activities of psychologists as scientists will themselves be evaluative; among other things, scientists intend to be accurate and fair in their portrayals. An irony here is that psychologists often understand their own behavior as motivated by values, truth for instance, but seem less inclined to see this motivation in others. Asch (1990), for example, chided his social psychological colleagues for failing to appreciate "the love of truth as a psychological reality, and the power it can command" (55).

If values such as truth are not seen as powerful motivations in human life, what does motivate us? What status, if any, does morality, right and wrong, have in psychological science? To answer these questions, we might begin by asking where value went in Descartes' scheme. Value vanished from the world to be studied by science. Machines do not differentiate good and evil; they do not evaluate and choose. However, the mechanistic world could take on one kind of value, namely, instrumental value, if a human thinker decided that it could serve as a means to his or her ends (i.e., goals). In this case, value is an imposition, determined by an act of intellect and will. Values, thus, really exist only in the mind of the Cartesian thinker.

This view of values as something imposed by a person or persons on external matters (including other persons' bodies) continues as perhaps the dominant view within psychology. Perhaps the most familiar version of this perspective at work in science currently is the social constructionist movement (e.g., Cushman 1990, 1993; Gergen 1991, 1994), but if one looks at social psychological research on values (e.g., Feather 1999; Miao and Olson 1998; Rokeach 1973; B. Schwartz 1990; S. Schwartz 1994; Seligman, Olson, and Zanna 1996), they are taken to be "attitudes," "meta-attitudes," and other psychological states that are preferential but not perceptive. That is, there is no reality being tracked by the attitude, belief,and so forth, except, perhaps, other people's social constructions. These social realities may have quite real physical and social consequences (Sabini and Silver 1982), but there is no reality posited to which all the relevant parties have access that guides or constrains their constructions. Ultimately, values are arbitrary impositions of individual or collective wills.

There have been two other common ways of dealing with values with roots in the Cartesian dualism. Many psychologists have followed a positivist path (e.g., Kendler 2000) which simply enshrines Descartes' dualism; that is, humans may be moral, but since science is about mechanics, it is morally obligated to be as "value-free" as possible. Other psychologists (e.g., Buss 1999; Skinner 1953), uncomfortable with such dualism, have followed a naturalistic path, asserting that values are invariably realized in some natural, lawful process, such as natural selection or reinforcement. In short, positivists believe morality and science (or values and facts) are completely separate; naturalists believe they are completely fused. In either case values "disappear" from scientific accounts.

This "disappearance" has hampered psychology's ability to carry out its scientific task (Brown 1996; Flach and Smith 2000; Hodges 2000; Martin and Hodges 1987). Psychological acts—feeling, remembering, imagining, speaking, perceiving—are inherently "prospective," that is, constituted in a region between "is" and "ought," between what the person is and what she will become "for good or ill" (Gibson 1979). Psychological activities cannot even be identified, much less understood, without at least implicitly invoking standards of evaluation. For example, to identify an act as "learning" implies not just a change, but an *appropriate* change in what the person knows or can do with respect to his or her environment (e.g., Martin, Kleindorfer, and Buchanan 1986). Similarly, to claim that a person has "perceived" is to claim that he has successfully picked up information about his surroundings; it, like learning, is a term of achievement (Katz 1987).

So, what do these post-Cartesian perspectives propose motivates human behavior? Answers vary, of course, but they include self-esteem, self-consistency, self-interest, reinforcement (i.e., instrumental value in maximizing preferences), inclusive genetic fitness, fear of self-annihilation, self-actualization, and self-expression (e.g., Baumeister 1995; Gergen 1991; Pyszczynski, Greenberg, and Solomon 2000; Schwartz 1986). In varying ways all of them focus on the self as the source and end of motivation. As Baumeister (1995) wryly notes: "Instead of regarding the self as the enemy of virtue and value, modern individuals focus on the self's entitlements" (58). Motivation for humans is a matter of autonomy, simply a matter of desire. Some desires may be seen as unavoidable (i.e., essential to survival) and referred to as needs. From these post-Cartesian perspectives, values are just desires or needs.

But what if the self is not the locus of values? What if human motivation supercedes needs and desires? Perhaps being a person in the world entails goods greater than being myself (i.e., desiring and needing).

To explore the nature of values I have contrasted them with laws and rules (Hodges 2000; Hodges and Baron 1992), perhaps the two most common ways scientists have of talking about psychological phenomena. Laws are universal patterns (e.g., all spoken human languages are phonemic), while rules are more localized patterns (e.g., the syntax of English in a given place and time). It is important to note that both laws and rules refer to stabilities, differing primarily in the temporal and/or spatial scale over which they hold. Laws are usually assumed to be necessary and invariant; rules, by contrast, are taken to be contingent and revisable. Furthermore, explanations framed in terms of laws have tended to be oriented to the past, that is, they take the form of causes and consequences; while explanations framed in terms of rules have tended to be oriented to the future, that is, they take the form of means and ends, where the ends are usually goals. Explanations given in terms of laws tend to stress the unintentional character of existence, while explanations given in terms of rules tend to stress the intentional character of existence.

Accounts of human activities framed only in terms of laws and rules are inadequate (e.g., Hodges 2000; Hodges and Baron 1992; Martin et al. 1987). For example, we have a need not only to talk articulately, grammatically, and meaningfully, but to say something of *worth*, to say the *right* thing.[6] Values designate the *oughtness* of what is or is to be said, done, or felt. This oughtness is neither simply found in the laws governing things and persons, nor in the rules followed by persons in their interactions with each other and the things surrounding them. How then, shall we talk of values in a way that can usefully guide scientific understanding of affect, behavior, and cognition?

Scientists have usually treated values either as universals—biological needs, for example—or as personal or socially constructed preferences—cultural rules, for example. Simply put, values are either a form of laws or a form of rules. Against this we argued (Hodges and Baron 1992) that values are "neither laws nor rules, but a set of constraints that both precedes and emerges from the existence of laws and rules. Ontologically, values are the global constraints on ecosystems," the boundary conditions that "provide not only the initial conditions for the system but . . . also underwrite the system dynamics" (270, italics omitted). Thus, values are "the intentions of the world as a self-organizing system" (270) and are not reducible to mental processes, or more colloquially, simply matters of personal choice or cultural convention. Rather, values are ontologically basic, "higher than societies and more fundamental than biology" (271).[7]

This is an audacious claim. We are stating that values are fundamental to the nature of reality. Values are the boundary conditions of an ecosystem (the universe being the largest one we know of) that provide for the dynamic directedness of the various aspects of the system. Values are the goods toward which the system as a whole is moving, as well as the ways of being within the system that sustain and enrich it.[8]

Consider a visual system. James Gibson (1979), perhaps the foremost perceptual theorist in twentieth-century psychology, describes a visual system as follows: "The visual system hunts for comprehension and clarity. . . . Exploring and optimizing seem to be the functions of the system (219). Knowledge of the environment, surely, develops as perception develops. . . . Perceiving gets wider and finer, and longer and richer and fuller as the observer explores the environment (255). A perception, in fact, does not have an end. Perceiving goes on (253). A perceiver can keep on noticing facts about the world she lives in to the end of her life without ever reaching a limit" (243). Gibson claimed his whole approach to psychology was an attempt to replace a psychology of stimulus with a psychology of values (cited in Reed 1988, 296). We do not perceive because we are caused to by prodding from visual sensations,[9] but because we are actively seeking clarity, coherence, comprehensiveness, and complexity (Hodges 1985). We might think of these values as being the boundary conditions of the system. What makes the system "visual" is that it is always exploring the structure of reflected light in order to reveal the environment more clearly, more coherently, and more extensively than before, including the complexities that will undermine previously achieved clarities, coherences, and understandings.[10] Gibson claims that what this looking reveals is opportunities for action, invitations to "good or ill." These "affordances," as they are called, are the distributed values within the visual ecosystem that provide its resources and riches, making it possible for persons to flourish.

It is important to note that values such as clarity, comprehensiveness, and complexity are not goals. Rather, as Gibson's quotation makes clear, perception is a lifelong commitment, an ongoing journey to sort out what is good and worthwhile and what is not. The values that serve as the boundary conditions of the system leave it open to further development. Thus, vision is prospective; it is always trying to see what is coming and where we should be going.

If values are the boundary conditions that define an ecosystem, what is the role of laws and rules? Reuben Baron and I (Hodges and Baron 1992) have proposed that values are the "medium within which laws and rules are coordinated"; they "provide the ontological resources that open up the causal possibilities and guide the selection of goals that focus organismic activity." Virtually all interesting human activities seem to depend on both laws and rules, but how they do so is enigmatic (Harré and Secord 1972; Kugler et al. 1991; Shanon 1993; Turvey 1990). Kugler et al. suggested that what is needed are laws that function like rules, and rules that function like laws. Baron and I (1992) hypothesized that values function in just that way; however, rather than being a form of laws or rules, values have priority over laws and rules.

For example, driving a car entails laws and rules. What we call traffic laws are rules in the scientific sense; they are cultural conventions that are intended to constrain our actions on the road. An example of a scientific law used in driving would be our ability to detect visually the time it will take a car to reach the position my car will be in if I proceed into the intersection; my perception of "time to contact" also constrains my behavior. Without these laws, driving would be impossible, and without "rules of the road" it would be considerably more difficult. But driving is not finally about laws or rules; it is about values.

Values are naturally social, developmental, and moral as well as ontological (Hodges 1997; Hodges and Baron 1992). First, values are social in the sense that they are necessarily plural. Any given psychological activity is guided by and partially realizes multiple values. Let us return to our car-driving example: What makes for good driving? One criterion that many researchers have looked at is accuracy (Caird and Hancock, 1994). Unless I perceive accurately the rate of approach of other cars, I cannot control my own actions appropriately. This sounds quite sensible, but researchers have often found that perceptual judgments in driving tasks are not nearly as accurate as they expected them to be. The reason, I have suggested (Hodges 1995) is that "driving, like all perception-action skills, involves many values." Driving is a moral activity, not just a technical one. It involves many values that must be balanced with skill and care if we are to be "good drivers." Good driving is "edgy." It moves to the edge of maximizing accuracy, and safety, and speed (i.e., efficiency), and tolerance (i.e., kindness) for other drivers, without actually maximizing any of them.

Furthermore, I have argued that the relationship among these multiple values is *heterarchical*, in other words, there is no fixed, hierarchical ordering of values. At some particular moment in driving, safety may take the lead with respect to other values, at other times speed, or accuracy, or kindness may be paramount. In the long run all of the values are honored equally, but this entails appropriate shifts over time. To summarize the social nature of values, no situation is governed by a single value and different situations may be guided by different orderings of values, but these values, when viewed across all situations, are presumed to be equal. Values are just those kinds of goods that cannot be ordered without distorting them. If love always "trumps" truth, love will not last. Similarly, if truth takes permanent precedence over love, it will be false.

Second, values are inherently dynamic, intrinsically motivating developmental change that is both telic (i.e., directed) and open-ended, revealing increasingly the nature of the values themselves. Unlike goals, which must be specifiable, values are revealed in learning and development. What it means to be a good driver cannot be revealed by a specific set of tests, but is revealed in our driving over time. As we become better drivers we may give up accuracy (e.g., cutting it as close as we can) in order to increase safety or kindness. As our eyesight fails or our reflexes slow, if we are good drivers, we make appropriate adjustments. The open-endedness and tacit nature of values may appear to be imprecise, but it is their very looseness that allows for the "play" necessary for them to work (Hodges and Baron 1992). What looks like a weakness of values is, in fact, their strength.

The heterarchical and development aspects of values leads to skilled activities having an "edgy" quality. Consider the case of music making. Playing music is constrained by laws (e.g., the physics and biomechanics of bowing a cello) and directed by the rules of the score and perhaps a conductor. But playing music is more than a goal (Winold, Thelen, and Ulrich 1994); it is a value-realizing activity that requires learning to bend and stretch the rules of the score and practicing to push the lawful limits. For example,

Palmer (1989) found that skilled pianists unknowingly increased the clarity of the melody in several ways. Melodic notes were struck twenty milliseconds sooner than the other notes in a chord, and phrases were dramatized by varying the temporal interval between them. It is in the tension of laws and rules that music comes into existence and finds its value, and it is this tension that we literally feel that embodies our perceptual appreciation of a great musical performance. Values are what guide our bending or breaking of rules and what encourages our pushing the lawful limits.

Third, values are essential to legitimate the epistemic, aesthetic, and ethical activities of humans. Understood in this way, values function as the criteria by which we evaluate our desires, choose our goals, convene our cultural practices, and revise those desires, goals, and practices from time to time (e.g., Asch 1952, 354 ff.; MacIntyre 1981; Murdoch 1970). Values "are capable of inducing valences that are not a result of the person's own needs or will . . . . [They] may even command us to perform some activity not in our personal self-interest" (deRivera 1989, 13).

It is often assumed that goals are sufficient to explain action, cognition, or emotion. This overlooks numerous difficulties with goal-oriented accounts (e.g., Valsiner 1987; Martin et al. 1987). I will mention only three. First, goals (e.g., I want to graduate from college) are virtually never self-justifying; they have to appeal to a higher-level goal, which has to be justified by an even higher-level goal, which leads to an infinite regress unless a single ultimate goal can be identified. Second, since goals, by definition, are precise, definable end-states that would serve as "stop conditions" for a computational procedure, it is unlikely that any such ultimate goal could be realistically posited. Even more proximate goals often turn out to be fuzzy or unknowable prior to carrying out the project that leads to the goal (e.g., I don't know what the finished poem will look like until I have written it). Third, goals are virtually always multiple, always difficult to coordinate, frequently conflicting, and thus not able to be ordered in a simple hierarchy (which is required by any rule-following procedure). When we consider goals, we always find ourselves having to evaluate the question: What goals are worth pursuing? The question of worth requires an appeal to values: Which goals will contribute to my being more free, more loving, more just, more truthful? Which goals will increase the clarity and coherence of my vision, the comprehensiveness and complexity of my emotions and actions?

To conclude this section, humans are motivated to realize values, that is, to be moral. This moral aspect of human activity is not restricted to a special class of actions that we might label "ethical" (e.g., deciding to steal in order to save a person's life), but applies to all kinds of ordinary, skilled performances and activities (e.g., looking, speaking, driving, music making). These activities may quite properly be described as law-governed, goal-directed, and rule-following, but these stabilizing tendencies within the activity are constrained and guided by a larger dynamical context of values. These values are plural, mutually interdependent, historically unfolding constraints that give ontological life and moral legitimacy to human activities.

PERSONS AS REALIZERS OF VALUES

Who are we as persons according to a psychology of values? Persons are participants in a web of relationships, physical, social, and cosmological—an ecosystem, if you will—that both locates them and gives them direction. Values are the fundamental ontological patterns that give rise to this web of relationships and that provide for its dynamic and directed character. Humans then exist as enmeshed, embodied beings (see Vitz, "The Embodied Self," this volume) that are dependent and responsible agents (of values for the ecosystem). The fundamental motivation of human behavior is action directed toward realizing the values that define life within all the ecosystem relations. Humans act to realize a diverse array of values—truth, justice, freedom, love, beauty, for example—that provide the criteria necessary for psychologists to give a meaningful scientific description of their various cognitive, emotional, and perceptual acts.

Values are multiple and heterarchically related; that is, the values themselves form a community and cannot be realized apart from each other. Stated more negatively, attempts to realize a value (a good) in isolation yield evil. Heterarchy is a principle much like mutual submission, in which various values, at varying times and places, may take the lead in guiding action, but at other times and places follow the lead of other values. Over all times and places there is an equality within a particular set of values rather than there being some systematic, permanent ordering (i.e., a hierarchy) of those values.[11]

The implications of these characteristics for personhood are that there are rich (diverse and constrained) possibilities for realizing values, but these possibilities harbor the risk of doing evil as well as good. As just noted, one form of evil is the failure to acknowledge the social character of values; a second is the failure to acknowledge the developmental character of values. What defines persons then is their being social, historical agents, responsible to realize values, yet always confronting the risk of doing evil, which leads to distortion, dissolution, and death within the ecosytem.

A values-realizing approach to persons refuses to understand persons as a product of natural laws alone, but it also refuses to understand persons as social constructions alone, rule-following goal seekers. While our lives may be lawful and rule-following in important ways, neither of these ways of understanding persons is sufficiently comprehensive and complex to account for our actions, feelings, and thoughts. A values-realizing approach to reality takes the world neither as something "given" to us, nor as something to be "constructed" by us; rather it is "entrusted" to us. Humans are agents, responsible to and for what grants them life. This responsibility can be carried out more or less well; thus, life for humans is problematic. Life is actually lived in between what "is" and what "ought to be."

The problematic aspect of this in-betweenness needs to be further explored.

Frustration and Suffering

Frustration is built into the very fabric of physical existence. Several years ago I found myself surprised by a sentence I read in a scientific study of the art of juggling. If you've ever tried it, you know juggling is a perception-action skill that is fun to watch and difficult to do. In discussing their results, the authors (Beek, Turvey, and Schmidt 1992) said this: Biological actions systems are "to a considerable extent *'frustrated'* . . . meaning that [they] are *subject simultaneously to very many different physical requirements that they cannot possibly satisfy fully*" (91, italics added). What their results demonstrated was that good jugglers do not do what they do by virtue of planning or by following some set of rules. Neither did their patterns of movement settle into the zones that the laws of biomechanics would predict would be most stable and comfortable. Rather they found that the better the juggler the farther away from what might be called a zone of stability and comfort their movements were. Juggling, they found, seems to be best "on the edge of the law" (Hodges 1995).[12]

The point, of course, is that juggling is values-realizing, and values, we have seen, are inherently frustrated. They are maximums that cannot be maximized, ideals that cannot be idealized, realities that cannot be completely realized.[13] We can never have too much clarity or too much justice, but we cannot achieve perfect clarity or perfect justice in any given instance, nor can we even articulate exactly what perfect clarity or justice would look like. Nonetheless, we must act.

Let me briefly allude to another example of frustration and values, one that I have been studying and experiencing recently (Hodges and Geyer, in preparation). Since it is from the social domain rather the physical, it may help the reader feel the tension and awkwardness of values-realizing

"juggling" better. Solomon Asch's (1951; 1956) famous experiments on conformity were not actually about conformity. They were about truth. Asch
thought (Campbell 1990) that if people were presented with a simple,
straightforward truth to tell (e.g., about relative lengths of lines), they would
tell it, even if others refused to acknowledge it. He was surprised to find,
though, that sometimes people gave wrong answers to easy questions when
everyone else (Asch's accomplices) had given a wrong answer.

What are the frustrations? They are many. First, Asch's experimental
participants were (by design) in a frustrating situation. They saw one thing,
but heard other reasonable people describe it quite differently. Since they
were not allowed to talk to their peers, but only to answer the experimenter's
question, they were stuck with a seemingly impossible trade-off, either deny
the validity of their own experience or deny the validity of others' experience. Neither of these is good.

A second frustration concerns Asch's understanding of his studies.
He saw the choice facing subjects as a simple moral one between good (truth)
and evil (consensus). We argue the situation is better understood not as a
choice, but as a challenge to coordinate multiple goods, all crucial to integrity. A third frustration is the way most social psychologists (Cialdini and
Trost 1998) have interpreted the results; rather than see them as a testament to the power of truth in the face of social opposition, they cite the
studies as a classic demonstration of people's turning their back "on reality
and truth" (Moscovici 1985). The simple fact is that most people, most of
the time gave correct answers (Harris 1985; Friend, Rafferty, and Bramel
1990). A fourth frustration is how we can challenge the conventional interpretation of these studies, and even Asch's more truthful analysis, in a way
that will be understandable to our colleagues in psychology. The situation
facing us is not unlike the one that faced Asch's subjects, how to state one's
own view of the situation (what one takes to be true) when it is socially
aberrant. All of this is difficult, delicate, and complex.

One of the clearest of Asch's results was that participants were dis-
tressed by their task (Campbell 1990). They realized that they were in a
frustrating situation and it clearly showed. What does one do in such circumstances?

According to a well-worn psychological theory (Dollard et al. 1939),
frustration produces aggression; however, Sabini and Silver (1982) noted
that frustration may just as likely produce resignation or learned helpless-
ness. What seems truer to say about frustration, though, is that it produces
suffering. Whether I whimper, lash out, or work quietly to improve the
situation, I suffer. Even if frustration yields skill and sensitivity, as in the
example of juggling, it is only after suffering long hours of practice and

innumerable failures. In fact, frustration and suffering may be defining marks of personhood, since the consciousness of pain, loss, and death may be peculiar to humans (Hodges 1997; Weaver, this volume).

What do we make of the surprising emergence of frustration and suffering from the promising prospects of a psychology of values? It has an awkwardness that feels strangely postmodern. An awareness of overwhelming demands, frustration, delicacy, and a fear of inflicting suffering might be argued to be characteristic signs of postmodern consciousness. Where might we turn for hope?

To explore this further I turn now to Bakhtin, Levinas, and Macmurray.

HOPEFUL, SUFFERING SELVES: A PROPER POSTMODERNISM?

Understanding values as fundamental ontological and moral constraints on our existence challenges any modern or postmodern understanding of the autonomy of the self. Much more promising is the deep insight, shared by Bakhtin, Macmurray, and Levinas, that we exist only "in relation" and "before an Other" to whom we are "obligated" and "answerable." The fundamental character of human existence is, thus, social and ethical. As Macmurray (1961) puts it:

> Being nothing in ourselves, we have no value in ourselves, and are of no importance whatever, wholly without meaning or significance. It is only in relation to others that we exist as persons: we are invested with significance by others who have need of us; and borrow our reality from those who care for us. We live and move and have our being not in ourselves but in one another; and what rights or powers or freedom we possess are ours by the grace and favour of our fellows. Here is the basic fact of our human condition; which all of us can know if we stop pretending, and do know in moments when the veil of self-deception is stripped from us and we are forced to look upon our own nakedness.
>
> . . . The fundamental condition for the resolution of the problem of freedom is our knowledge of one another. But this knowledge is one in which the dissociation of fact and value is impossible. . . . For the knowledge of one another, and so of ourselves, can be realized only through a mutual self-revelation; and this is possible only when we love one another. (211–12)

According to Macmurray, then, love is the precondition for self-awareness. Levinas sharpens the ethical primacy of our existence as selves. He goes so far as to claim that the ethical command to serve the Other is prior to any other description or claim that can be made. As Perperzak (1997) describes Levinas's views:

> Finding myself facing another awakens me to responsibility: an infinite responsibility for the Other, who is in need of everything that is necessary for a human life. By addressing myself to another I practice this responsibility, be it reluctantly or not. A total refusal of it would express itself through murder. Total acceptance would coincide with perfect love. (67)

Responsibility is "prephenomenal and preontological." It is there before I am aware of it. It is not the result of some decision, contract, or convention, an act on my part or society's.

Action is primary for both Levinas and Macmurray. Both reject Descartes' "*Cogito*" as a proper starting point for understanding our existence. Levinas rejects it because of its totalizing "egology," its presumption to be the "center and end of the world and the source of all its meaning" (Peperzak 1997, 8). Any such totalizing ego excludes the possibility of being confronted by the infinite: "the Other condemns my monopoly on the world and imposes an infinite number of demands on me" (11). Macmurray (1961) argues that the "*Cogito*" "institutes a formal dualism of theory and practice; and . . . this dualism makes it formally impossible to give any account, and indeed to conceive the possibility of persons in relation . . ." (73). In rejecting the primacy of thinking and accepting the "I do" as the primary certainty, one rejects the subjective-objective dichotomy that has forced persons engaging in science to proclaim as subjects that the Other is an object (e.g., a machine, an organism). Humans are neither subjects, substances, nor organisms, but persons, agents in relation. Macmurray asserts that "[a]ny dualistic mode of thinking is incompatible with religion. For the root of dualism is the intentional dissociation of thought and action. . . . [R]eligion . . . demands their integration" (1961, 206).

Bakhtin, who is the earliest and perhaps most prophetic of the three voices, focused his attention (as Levinas often does) on language. For Bakhtin, to speak and to listen are to act; neither speaking nor listening is an instantiation of a formal rule system (e.g., Chomsky) nor a communication (e.g., Saussure). Addressing and being addressed are embodied social acts for which the persons involved are ethically responsible; this accountability is unique and irreplaceable (see Emerson, this volume). "There can be no formula for integrity, no substitute for each person's own project of selfhood, no escape from the ethical obligations of every situation at every moment" (Morson and Emerson 1990, 31). "[T]his is the aspect of it [utterances] that pertains to honesty, truth, goodness, beauty, history" (Bakhtin 1986, 105).

Bakhtin has argued that conversations involve not only the person who addresses and the person who is addressed, but a third party which he calls the "superaddressee." Although we often may have little or no awareness of it, Bakhtin claims that in addressing another person we speak also to an Other, a powerful if invisible presence that functions as "the witness and judge" of what we say and do. This Other, which might be understood as "God, absolute truth, the court of dispassionate human conscience, the people, the court of history, science, and so forth," can be counted on to be understanding and just with us, even if our immediate conversant is not able or willing to do so. "This third party . . . is a constitutive aspect of the whole utterance, who, under deeper analysis, can be revealed in it" (Bakhtin 1986, 126–27). Thus, God, human community, history, and the natural order frame our conversation—our words and other actions must answer to them—but our conversation itself participates in and contributes to the revelation of the Other. What we say helps us to understand God, others, and the world and history within which we interact.

One might argue that the superaddressee embodies the "principle of hope" (Morson and Emerson 1990, 135). Without someone who will understand us and judge us rightly we would hardly dare speak at all. This suggests that our words are sacraments of a still larger hope, a hope that *all* conversants and their speaking and listening will be judged rightly, that all good sayings (i.e., benedictions)—those that realize love, justice, beauty, and truth—will remain; and that all corrupt, cruel, ugly, and false words will cease. In conversing with each other, we are, according to George Steiner (1989), always making "a wager on transcendence," for "any coherent account of the capacity of human speech to communicate meaning and feeling is, in the final analysis, underwritten by the assumption of God's presence" (3). Paul Grice (1991), famed for his papers on the pragmatic principles of conversation (e.g., Grice 1975), has argued that language use is based in values, which in the final analysis are grounded in absolute value. Macmurray (1961) has argued that "the fundamental unit of personal existence is two persons in relation to one another," or, more exactly, "two persons in community in relation to a common Other which includes them."

In one sense it might be argued that all three writers see persons in terms of vocation, a calling by God to love our neighbor and to take care of the world. More properly it might be understood as "sentness" (Hodges 1983); it is not as if we are "sitting still" in the world, waiting for God or our neighbor to call us. We are already sent. The obligation to act for good or for ill is already upon us, or as Bakhtin (1993) puts it, we have no "alibi in Being" (40). The world is not ready-at-hand, as Heidegger proposed, waiting to be put to our purposes and designs. Rather, it is a world, according to Levinas, in which persons are encountered by demands for

> passion and affection, vulnerability and suffering. . . . To live for Others is to suffer. . . . Transcendence is . . . the humble endurance of everyday life, touched, affected, burdened, wounded, obsessed, and exhausted. A human subject is an inspired body. It is moved by a breath that comes from an immemorial past. As respiration between this inspiration and the expiration of tiredness, old age, and death, a human life is breathing for Others, the repetition of obedience to God's command. The Good itself can neither be chosen nor contemplated, but only loved by accepting the responsibility for goodness in the world. (Peperzak 1997, 169)

Humans are called to transcendence, but this is found in suffering and endurance, in a "repetition of obedience." Such a view of persons poses a considerable challenge to psychologists, whose mantra is optimism, control, and self-esteem, and who think of obedience only in terms of Milgram's studies (1974) or in terms of authoritarian parenting.

The transcendent vocation of persons to act together in the "principle of hope" to realize the values by which we name God (e.g., Love, Justice, Truth) is an ongoing responsibility, one for which there is "no alibi." Bakhtin argues that the ethical demands of conversing with others before the Other cannot be finalized. Language creates "loopholes" as well as "answerability." Nothing we ever say is final. Even when we think we have spoken the "final word," we learn sooner or later, that it was a "penultimate word." Likewise, Macmurray (1957) argues that agency, the possibility of real action and the real change it produces in the world, means that the world cannot be fully determinate. It is because the world is incomplete that action is possible, and any "I do" actually takes the form "I am doing this," where the "this" is always open to further specification. The openness and unfinalizability of existence sometimes unnerves scientists and Christians, but it should be understood as constitutive of what it means to live life by faith. Levinas describes that faith as crucial to what it means to be human: "The human is the return to the interiority of non-intentional consciousness, . . . to its capacity to fear injustice more than death, to prefer to suffer than to commit injustice, and to prefer that which justifies being over that which assures it" (1989, 85).

Beyond and Before Modernity/Postmodernity

For Bakhtin, Levinas, and Macmurray, persons are embodied agents, eco-logically situated in an incomplete, frustrated, and suffering world. Per-haps the chief fact of our existence is that we are obligated. Values and the ethical demands of the Other are primal, not emergents of some preexist-ing ontology. Goodness is originary. Life for us is passionate, "all and al-ways on the boundary" (Bakhtin 1993). Yet the burden of the infinite and irreplaceable responsibility of the Other is ultimately one too heavy for any individual self to bear. It must be borne by an Other who suffered for us with a love so heart-rending that it makes it possible for us to hope. In obedience we can find transcendence; we can live an "answer" to the enigma of evil although we can offer no totalizing explanation and often no prac-tical solution. Yet through the frustration and the suffering, our lives, con-stituted by faith, can still remain hopeful.[14]

Notes

1. Dualism was not new of course, but the separation of bodily life from morality was, as was the claimed autonomy of our individual ideas. The illusion Descartes and later enlightenment thinkers lived under was that if individuals followed the dictates of their own thought, rational concordance would result.
2. Notice that Shotter still seems to be subscribing to the ethical project of Descartes, namely, empowerment. On the other hand, it may be that Shotter is just show-ing that Descartes' own ethical project is undermined by his ontology and epis-temology.
3. There are a number of related movements in psychology that I have followed as well, which would include authors such as Givón (1989), Lakoff and Johnson (1980; 1999), Shotter (1984; 1993) Still and Costall (1991), Varela, Thompson, and Rosch (1993).
4. John Shotter (1993) and Zazie Todd (1993) made me notice Bakhtin, Joe DeRivera (1989) introduced me to Macmurray, and Richard Williams (1994) challenged me to read Levinas.
5. Actually I will claim that values are good for any given ecosystem as a whole, not just humans.

6. This suggests that the most fundamental level of language, the one that is most directly accountable to values is pragmatics, as opposed to the more rule-governed levels of phonology, syntax, and semantics.

7. Charles Taylor (1989) and Mary Midgley (1993) use related metaphors to describe the values that make genuine moral judgment possible. Taylor refers to values as a horizon that marks out a moral space. Midgley argues that the evaluative dimension (or morality) is a necessary condition for us to imagine human life at all, but especially as it takes the form of a community of persons conversing with each other. Morality is a precondition of thought. She also suggests that values are in the world, and ultimately perhaps in God.

8. They are the ontological "boundary conditions of ecosystems," what Taylor (1989) suggested is the "horizon" we use to orient our vision and guide our movements in discovering where we are and where we should go. If we take "locating" values to be "pinning them down" so they can be objectively scrutinized, it is much like a person trying to approach the horizon to take a close-up photograph of it. The worth of the horizon is revealed dynamically in its use. Thus, values might be thought of as being located distributively, that is, incarnated throughout the ecosystem within which persons act as agents (Macmurray, 1957).

9. Prod is the original meaning of "stimulus." Gibson's theory is much more radical than most casual observers suppose; even knowledgeable commentators often confuse his ecological theory with a "stimulus theory" (e.g., Zebrowitz, 1990). Similarly, Gibson's theory is often viewed as a passive theory, but it, not cognitive theories, posits an agent who is active, seeking, and "for" something, namely, discerning "good and ill."

10. Thus, a visual system includes the parts of the body involved in locomotion (e.g., legs) and those that bring objects and events into view (e.g., hands), as well as eyes, nerve tracts, etc.

11. This heterarchical hypothesis contrasts with most social and personality theories which treat motivations as competing (e.g., Sedikides, 1993) or hierarchical (e.g., Rokeach, 1973).

12. Great juggling is neither a matter of conscious, rule-following control or unconscious, lawful automaticity. In short, all the usual ways psychologists try to talk about behavior, thought, and emotion don't really capture what seems to make an activity like juggling interesting and valuable; laws and rules cannot explain what make juggling good.

13. For just this reason, people like Laudan (1984) take them to be impractical. If something is unachievable, it is by definition unrealistic, and should be deemed useless to serious scientists. See Martin (1989) for a reply.

14. I hope that there will soon be a richer psychology of suffering and hope than now exists. Suffering could be argued to be the basis for the clinical practice of psychology, yet there is almost no scientific psychology of suffering of which I am aware. Much of the psychology of hope (e.g., Snyder, 1994) still remains far too tied to realism and/or romanticism to be genuinely hopeful. It seems particularly anemic in the face of genuine and deep suffering (Lazarus & Lazarus, 1994).

5

Finding a Self to Love:

An Evaluation of Therapeutic Self-Love

David M. Holley

Every culture has its sources of guidance about how to live. One notable form of guidance may be found in the proverbial sayings people invoke as concise reminders of important practical truths. Typically proverbs are fairly loose in their application. The truths they convey are general, and there is room for differing opinions on whether they are relevant and helpful in a particular case. In some cases alternative proverbs offer apparently conflicting advice. Nevertheless, these sayings function to shape our awareness of features of situations we encounter in ways that can influence our judgment. Imagine, for example, someone hesitating about a risky choice until he or she thinks, ""Nothing ventured, nothing gained."

An important, though often unrecognized, source of contemporary proverbs is the practice of psychotherapy and its derivatives in popular culture. While the counselor may sometimes take a pose of neutrality, psychotherapy becomes unintelligible without some normative understanding about what constitutes healthy functioning. Explicitly or implicitly, the counselor commends ideals of good living that underlie the therapeutic value system (Browning 1987; Lomas 1999). Some of these ideals have become fixtures in popular consciousness through a range of pithy sayings, such as, "Let the anger out" or "Get in touch with your feelings" or "Learn to set boundaries." Such expressions of therapeutic guidance about how to live have acquired an authority akin to older sources of wisdom. Like traditional proverbs, they convey norms of good living that exert a powerful influence on people's thought and behavior.

One example of the compelling force of such sayings may be found in a therapeutic proverb that has assumed the status of a cliché: "You need to love yourself." At opportune moments we repeat this cliché to each other or recall it for our own edification, and sometimes when we attend to it, we gain what seems like an illuminating insight, for the proverb calls our attention to the danger of neglecting something vitally important. It functions as a reminder of a truth that we surely know, but might have failed to put into practice, and such a reminder can serve as a stimulus toward reshaping our priorities.

The reminder to love yourself is sometimes portrayed as an implicit, though possibly unnoticed, element of a more ancient saying: "You shall love your neighbor as yourself" (Lev. 19:18). The ancient instruction appears to be built on the assumption that we will in fact love ourselves, but are in danger of failing to extend that love to the neighbor. The modern variant shifts our focus. Loving yourself, it suggests, is not something to be taken for granted, but a task that demands attention and effort. Furthermore, in therapeutic contexts the achievement of self-love is often portrayed as a foundation for other types of love. Unless you love yourself, we are told, you won't really succeed at loving your neighbor, and a premature effort to love others may squeeze out the kind of love that needs to be directed toward yourself. So the proper mental health strategy is apparently to get our own house in order before we dissipate our energies on a fruitless effort to love others. One popular song by Whitney Houston even extols loving yourself as "the greatest love of all."

While there is surely legitimate insight in this therapeutic way of thinking, there is also something significantly askew. It is as if our modern addendum to the ancient teaching has been allowed to overshadow its main point. The task of loving the neighbor is shifted from a primary focus to a potential obstacle. Instead of being ready to get started on this task, we are directed toward a presumably more fundamental project, and this preliminary project can easily become so absorbing that it eclipses any prospect of extending love beyond the self.

Much depends, of course, on what exactly it means to love yourself, for there are many possible versions of this idea, and some of the apparent agreement about the desirability of loving yourself masks potential differences about what kind of self-love we should aspire to have. Some ways of construing self-love presuppose pictures of good living that are in significant tension with the ideal of love for the neighbor, turning self-love into an egoistic preoccupation (Vitz 1977, 1994; Browning 1987; Wallach and Wallach 1983). But self-love can also be conceived in ways that allow us to affirm its value and importance, while giving due recognition to the place of individual selves within a larger communal context (Chazan 1998). The central problem with popular therapeutic thinking about self-love is a tendency to view the self as an isolated and independent entity, disconnected from a larger social context in which the love of self might be integrated with other important human values. The result is that while therapeutic thinking about self-love contains ideas that are sometimes practically useful, the guidance it provides is apt to misdirect us when we lose sight of its limited applicability.

The Oddness of Self-Love

Before considering specifically therapeutic versions of self-love, it is worth noticing that there is something a little peculiar about the idea of loving yourself. The oddness is similar to what arises with other concepts that gain their primary meaning in contexts involving interpersonal relationships but are by extension applied to something that goes on within a single person. For example, we speak of self-deception or self-pity, relying on interactions with other people for our primary understanding of what it means to deceive or pity. Self-deception or self-pity is something analogous to what we do in deceiving or pitying someone else. But applying these concepts to the self requires an adjustment, for part of what pity or deception means in the interpersonal case is altered when we try to think of the self as both the giver and receiver. For example, if you think of deceiving yourself as a matter of telling yourself a lie, it will be puzzling how you can know the truth in order to tell the lie and yet believe the lie anyway. Self-deception is a real phenomenon, but we can be misled about its nature, if our thinking about it is tied too closely to the interpersonal model.

Oswald Hanfling underlines the oddness of the idea of self-love with the observation that if you were asked to name the people you love most, it would be absurd to name yourself (Hanfling 1993, 153–54). Quite so, for self-love is not a paradigm application of the concept of love, but an extended one. If you were asked what languages you know, it would be strange to list a computer language alongside German or French, for ordinarily that reply would show a misunderstanding of the question asked. We can speak of computer languages easily enough, but we should not assume that since the term language is the same, the extended use can always be grouped beside the more paradigmatic uses.

Hanfling's concern, however, goes beyond the oddness of applying the concept of love to oneself. He thinks that certain uses of the term are misapplications. In particular he raises a question about whether the idea of loving yourself in the biblical injunction to love your neighbor as yourself makes sense. He argues that since interpersonal love requires feelings, if we talk about something that does not involve feelings toward oneself, we are not really talking about love. There is, of course, no problem in imagining feelings toward oneself that might be associated with love—

Hanfling mentions such feelings as pride or vanity. But this kind of self-love, he observes, cannot be what the biblical injunction is about.

On that score, Hanfling is surely correct. When we talk about love in this context, we are not focusing on the feeling element, but on a valuational feature of love that might be thought to be more fundamental than the feeling component. Self-love is a metaphorical extension of what occurs in more intimate interpersonal relationships, but the extended applications will lack the characteristic feelings associated with these paradigmatic experiences of love. In cases of romantic love, the valuation typically takes the form of admiration that is combined with a need component and a desire to benefit the other person, working together to produce what we think of as romantic feelings (Bird 1964). If there are feeling components connected with self-love, they are less prominent and less important. However, even though self-love may lack parallels to features that are central to romantic love or mother love or love for one's friends, we may still see enough relevant similarities at a fairly general and schematic level to speak of it as a member of the same family. To love yourself is primarily to value yourself in a way that is connected with a concern for your own good. In therapeutic contexts, however, self-love tends to mean something much more specific.

THERAPEUTIC SELF-LOVE

The injunction to love yourself in the ubiquitous self-help literature is sometimes addressed to the person who has become so wrapped up in responsibilities that there seems little room for enjoyment. To such a person the suggestion, "You need to love yourself," functions as a permission to become less concerned with meeting the expectations of others and more deliberate about seeking out your own gratification. In this version, a failure to love yourself is a failure to leave room for the kinds of activities that will bring you pleasure. So you display self-love by going for a manicure or having a soak in the hot tub or allowing yourself to sleep for an extra hour or eating your favorite food. The spirit of this form of self-love is exhibited in the shampoo commercial in which the actress revels in the pleasures of washing her beautiful hair, while confidently proclaiming, "I'm worth it."

Unquestionably, the advice to make sure that your pursuits have not squeezed out opportunities for pleasure is often very appropriate. It is clearly possible to deprive ourselves unnecessarily of the kinds of things that could increase our enjoyment or sense of satisfaction. C. S. Lewis (1952) suggests in the *Screwtape Letters* that a diabolic strategy is to get people to spend their time on things that are neither what they ought to do nor what they enjoy. But as an interpretation of self-love, the instruction to include more pleasure in your life seems relatively shallow. We can recognize the wisdom of accepting release from our overly ascetic tendencies, but surely there is more to self-love than attending to our own enjoyment.

Furthermore, while the advice to seek out enjoyments can be helpful, it can also be counterproductive. The appropriateness of this therapeutic form of self-love depends in part on the traits of the person to whom it is addressed. The advice to allow yourself a few indulgences works best when given to a person who already has a good degree of self-discipline. The ability to put aside immediate gratification in order to pursue long-term projects is a crucial component of living a meaningful or fulfilling life, and habits of giving in to attractions of the moment can easily disrupt activities and aspirations that are vital to achieving such a life. So allowing too much room for indulgence can be a sign of failure to love yourself in the right way. Someone whose discipline has turned rigid may lose sight of the importance of pleasure, but focusing on pleasure can result in losing sight of valuable things in life whose pursuit is made futile by a preoccupation with pleasure.

If we do identify self-love with pleasure seeking, it is pretty clear why we might regard too much attention to others' needs as an obstacle to self-love. Time that you devote to others is time that you could have spent on more direct gratifications for yourself. Given such an account, the admonition to make self-love a priority amounts to the instruction to make sure that you have your fill of gratification before you worry much about others. But that is just the kind of thinking that is likely to keep you from getting around to the neighbor at all. Evidently, this version of self-love is not the type that is implicit in the instruction to love your neighbor as yourself.

Related to the interpretation of self-love as a permission to indulge yourself is another therapeutic construal: that loving yourself is a matter of focusing on your own needs. The idea is that you can get so wrapped up in attending to others' needs or performing your obligations that you fail to give proper attention to your own needs. Clearly, there are circumstances in which such an insight is valuable. In some cases people do neglect their own needs, and such a neglect can be a sign of a failure to value themselves properly and, hence, a lack of self-love. But it would be a logical leap to move from this possibility to the conclusion that loving yourself is primarily about focusing on your needs. For you can be completely focused on your needs without loving yourself at all, and you can love yourself profoundly even though your attention is hardly ever focused on your needs.

It is possible to be either too little or too much concerned with your needs. You can neglect your needs because you think, "I'm not important" or "I'm not worth much." That would be a real lack of self-love. But becoming more concerned with your needs is not the same as acquiring self-love, and if you become too concerned about your needs, this indicates not self-love, but self-absorption.

To become self-absorbed is to narrow your world. It is to view everything else through the lens of self-directed concerns. Other people may be useful for achieving your purposes, but it is hard for a self-absorbed person to see them as valuable or interesting in their own right. As a result, self-absorption blocks the ability to genuinely love or care about others, since such cares must go through the filter of a self with a narrow and single-minded point of view. For anyone who assumes that point of view, it is also difficult to genuinely love and care about oneself, for the ability to recognize worth in oneself is connected with the ability to recognize it in others.

There is genuine insight in both of these therapeutic versions of self-love. Sometimes loving yourself does involve doing things that will bring you enjoyment, and sometimes it calls for making sure that your needs are not neglected. However, these activities are only expressions of genuine self-love when they occur in the right kind of context. When they become the central focus, the result can be a caricature of the kind of love for self that is worth developing.

Therapeutic versions of self-love are best seen as correctives to problems arising from an obsessive moralism or inordinate self-criticism. A person can acquire an oppressive sense of obligation or unrealistic standards of personal assessment, leading to a devaluation of the self. Someone whose life is dominated by feelings of inadequacy and a reflexive tendency toward self-criticism needs to learn how to break the cycle that produces such senseless misery. When a therapist encounters an individual who is caught up in inordinate negative personal assessments, encouraging the person to learn to think more positively or to pay more attention to personal wants and needs might be a step in the right direction.

It is relatively easy to fall victim to a variety of cultural ideals that lead us to feel inadequate about matters such as our physical appearance or career success or family life. Or we may continue to carry around ancient parental messages that repeatedly remind us of our shortcomings. Rejecting the standards that lead to unreasonable assessments may require considerable therapeutic work, and part of that work will involve learning alternative ways of thinking that allow for more positive assessments. So when confronted with examples of people who exhibit something akin to self-hatred in the way they treat themselves, it is understandable why a therapist might seek to produce a higher level of charity toward the self.

Nevertheless, while such guidance can be warranted in particular cases, when it is treated as general advice, we run the risk of going from one extreme to another. It may be necessary to declare one's independence from certain standards that are becoming self-destructive for us, but this kind of liberation is ill-conceived when we are liberated from any standard that might bind the self. Therapeutic admonitions to self-love can easily become permissions to disregard what is inconvenient or difficult in the name of caring for the self. Hence, these instructions need to be understood within a normative context where the value of the self is integrated into a wider scheme of values.

When we try to conceive of self-love independently of any awareness of what is valuable apart from the self, we are apt to think of the self in terms of a collection of desires to be satisfied. But one of the problems of thinking of this acquisitive self as the object of love is that such a self fails to inspire the kinds of reactions we usually associate with love. I may try to fulfill my desires, but attitudes of respect or admiration that are needed to regard myself as an object of love call for a conception of myself as something worthy (Schmidtz 1995, 103ff.). The kind of self I can conceive in this way will be one that is formed by ideals or aspirations that help to constitute my sense of who I am. Loving myself is, therefore, bound up with cherishing ideals that are central to my identity.

Although some thinkers have celebrated the emergence of a postmodern self, characterized by a multicentered plasticity, we need selves with the kind of moral structure that is stable enough to support an identity. It is our ideals and convictions that enable us to become selves who are recognizably human, and thinking of ourselves in a way that abstracts from any kind of stable evaluative structure that defines the self leaves us with an entity that is hardly recognizable as a self (Taylor 1989). In much of therapeutic discourse this evaluative gap is filled with an implicit assumption of a self that is egoistically defined and given permission to break free of any other kind of oppressive normative structure (Rieff 1966, 61). But loving this kind of self is a very different sort of project from loving the kind of self that is genuinely capable of loving the neighbor. The problem with therapeutic versions of self-love is a tendency to direct love toward the wrong self.

Aristotle on Self-Love

The idea that self-love might be misdirected is not new. In fact it is precisely what Aristotle suggests in his discussion of self-love in the *Nicomachean Ethics*. Aristotle focuses his analysis on the question of whether self-love is a good thing or a bad thing. More particularly, he asks whether it is a good thing to love yourself more than you love others. He states the argument of those who find self-love objectionable as follows:

> People criticize those who love themselves most, and call them
> self-lovers, using this as an epithet of disgrace, and a bad man
> seems to do everything for his own sake, and the more so the more
> wicked he is—and so men reproach him . . . while the good man
> acts for honour's sake, and sacrifices his own interest. (Aristotle
> 1941, 1086)

Aristotle's answer as to whether self-love is good or bad is that it depends on what we mean by the term. The sense of "self-love" that is objectionable, he says, is one in which it applies to people who "assign to themselves the greater share of wealth, honours, and bodily pleasures" (1086).
The people Aristotle has in mind seek to gratify their appetites by acting as
if their claims had a kind of priority over those of others. In what sense do
these behaviors show a love of self? Aristotle's answer depends on a distinction between different parts of the self or soul. Within an individual
are what Aristotle thinks of as irrational appetites, lower parts of the self,
which are to be contrasted with the higher elements that include capacities
for reasoning and forming ideals of virtuous behavior. The kind of self-
love that is worthy of reproach, suggests Aristotle, is exhibited by the person who loves the gratification of the appetites, exercised in isolation from
these higher human capacities. The self that such a person loves is identified with his or her appetites.

There is, however, another kind of self-love, and it is exhibited by the
person whose appetites are under the control of what Aristotle calls the
rational elements of the soul. He says the following of this kind of person:

> [B]ut such a man would seem more than the other a lover of self; at
> all events he assigns to himself the things that are noblest and best,
> and gratifies the most authoritative element in himself and in all
> things obeys this. . . . He is most truly a lover of self, of another
> type than that which is a matter of reproach, and as different from
> that as living according to rational principle is from living as pas-
> sion dictates, and desiring what is noble from desiring what seems
> advantageous. (1087)

Hence, Aristotle answers the question of whether self-love is good or
bad by saying in effect that it depends on what kind of self you are loving.
If the self is a bundle of unstructured appetites, then loving such a self is
undesirable, both socially and individually. On the other hand, if the self is
in good working order, with desires under the control of the human capacity for judging and caring about what is good or valuable, then loving that
self plays an important role in living a worthy life within the community.

Thus, for Aristotle, loving yourself is a good thing if you are a virtuous person and a bad thing if you lack the right kinds of concerns for what is good or the kind of self-control needed to pursue the good. In other words worthy self-love is inseparable from proper moral development. It is not a matter of valuing whatever you happen to be, but of valuing the kind of self that is worthy of admiration. The person who is capable of the sort of self-love that is worth having is one whose psychological constitution is formed by an admiration of and a desire for what is just and noble and good. Hence, this kind of self-love becomes a kind of affirmation of the ideals with which the person has identified and is expressed by activities that are in accordance with those ideals.

As a corrective to therapeutic versions of self-love, Aristotle's account reminds us that the self is a normative structure that might or might not be in good working order. In a properly functioning self, the desires will be ordered by the human capacities for reason and valuation. In such a hierarchical self, self-love involves a kind of reflective endorsement of the ordered structure by which one is constituted as a self. If we pick out some element of the hierarchy to love apart from the organizing structure that makes us into selves, our efforts produce a distorted form of self-love. The kind of ordered self to which Aristotle calls our attention is formed by identifying with ideals of good living that we recognize as worthy and use to shape our desires. If these ideals are genuinely worthy, love for the self is inseparable from love for a way of life that transcends egoistic wants and needs. From Aristotle's perspective, therapeutic ways of thinking, by omitting the normative structure that makes us into fully human selves, run the risk of turning self-love into an affirmation of the kind of self that is lacking in the capacities and concerns needed for good living.

SELF-LOVE AND SELF-PREFERENCE

We might wonder whether there is a halfway house between Aristotle's virtuous self and the anarchic self that is a prisoner of irrational appetites. What about a self whose desires are under the control of some conception of a desirable life that is defined in nonmoral terms? We can imagine an individual who has some view of his long-term interests and has developed the discipline needed to efficiently pursue those interests. While this is not the kind of self-love Aristotle commends, it may be the model that underlies some therapeutic versions of self-love.

If we think of self-love as a concern for one's own good, where that good can be described independently of any moral norms, is it a good or bad idea to tell people to develop greater love for themselves? One cause for concern is whether the practical effect of promoting this kind of self-love would be to produce greater selfishness. One might have thought that most of us are already too much concerned with our own benefit and too little concerned with the good of others. Won't telling us to love ourselves more be likely to increase a bias toward our own interests that is far too strong as it is? When we offer people instructions that help them feel good about giving greater attention to essentially self-directed desires, don't we enable them to rationalize behavior that downplays the needs and desires of others? In short isn't the problem that we are already too selfish and don't need encouragement to become more so?

Answering these questions calls for some clear thinking about what selfishness is. It is much too simple to assume that selfishness is simply to be identified with self-love or with inordinate self-love. Much of the behavior that we call selfish is not really conducive to the interests of the individual who displays it. Typically, when I insist on having my own way and minimize the desires or concerns of other people, I poison my relationships in a way that hurts me more in the long run than any benefit I might gain. When I mindlessly pursue some addictive pleasure that causes suffering for both myself and my family, I may be acting selfishly, but I am also acting against my own long-term happiness or well-being. Much of the behavior we call selfish is characterized by an inadequate concern with what is genuinely good for us. Reflecting on the extent to which we disregard our own interest, the eighteenth-century thinker Joseph Butler concludes in a famous series of sermons that we need to develop more self-love. All too frequently, people become caught up in particular desires or impulses that overshadow their concern to seek their own good (Butler 1950, 15–16).

In Butler's account self-love is a reflective concern that motivates us to act for our overall good or happiness. This kind of concern relies on the human capacity to weigh negative and positive consequences and judge what is in our long-term interest. Butler contrasts the reflective capacity for self-love with what he calls the particular passions. People are moved to act by a variety of immediate impulses. They act to satisfy curiosity or to protect themselves from danger or to appease hunger. They are moved by jealousy or the desire for revenge or the urge to show off. They are motivated by friendship or sympathy, as well as by hatred or lust. Deciding whether it is beneficial in a given case to be motivated by a particular impulse calls for judgment. It may thwart your larger purposes to express anger toward the boss or to yield to a sexual enticement. So a person with genuine self-love will need to develop the capacity to overrule strong desires and powerful emotions. Butler was struck by the extent to which people fail to coordinate and control their impulses in a way that is conducive to their own good. In commenting on this failure he remarks, "The thing to be lamented is not that men have so great regard to their own good or interest in the present world, for they have not enough" (16).

So if it is inadequate to think of selfishness as self-love or too much self-love, how should we think of it? Butler's remarks suggest one possible answer. Immediately after his comment on the need for greater self-love, he says that there is also a need for greater benevolence or concern for the good of others. He thinks that the weakness of benevolent motivation is connected with people becoming "so engaged in the gratification of particular passions unfriendly to benevolence, and which happen to be more prevalent in them, much more than to self-love" (16). Following this suggestion, we might think of the selfish person as one whose concern for the good of others is squeezed out by more powerful self-directed concerns. Such a person becomes caught up in the quest for things such as money or sex or prestige, with the result that concerns for the good of others play too small a role in her motivational economy. The problem is not so much with self-love, whose job it is to coordinate a person's impulses to achieve overall happiness, but in the fact that self-love must operate with the raw materials provided by the particular impulses that actually move the person. In other words self-love is being applied to a defective self.

Self-love reflectively promotes the person's conception of her own happiness, but what constitutes happiness for a given individual depends on the concerns and dispositions that person actually has. One who has developed little concern for the good of others is unlikely to have a conception of happiness in which benevolent impulses play much of a role. Acting for the good of others can be an important source of personal satisfaction for the person who has learned to care about and appreciate others, but in someone who has not developed the appropriate capacities, benefiting others faces a greater competition with other opportunities to benefit oneself. Butler is at great pains to show that there is no necessary conflict between benevolence and self-love. But the harmony proposed depends both on one's individual development as well as the right kind of social circumstances (Adams 1998, 501).

Of course, it is sometimes the case that one can judge a change of dispositions to be conducive to a more satisfying way of life. I might come to see some of my efforts at happiness as being sabotaged by my inordinate concern for career success or by my limited interest in personal relationships. Hence, I might undertake an effort to modify my motivations in a direction more conducive to a satisfying way of life. But there is no guarantee that the kind of life I would judge to be more satisfying will have a central role for genuine concern for others, as opposed to a general policy of treating others decently so as to get decent treatment in return. If self-love goes to work on the dispositions of an essentially egoistic self, what we might expect is better efficiency at pursuing long-term egoistic interests. Someone who has developed altruistic virtues and learned what it is to care about others may be convinced that the satisfactions of a benevolent way of life exceed any drawbacks, but someone with different traits will probably rate those satisfactions less highly.

So is advising greater self-love a good idea? It depends on what we want to achieve. The person who acquires greater self-love in Butler's sense of the term is likely to behave with greater prudence, and, as Butler makes clear, a great many examples of immoral behavior are also examples of a failure to attend adequately to one's own good. So greater reflectiveness about how to achieve one's long-term benefit may lead to behaviors that are more socially desirable than we might expect from the person who is controlled predominantly by immediate impulse. On the other hand, telling someone whose pattern of concerns is essentially egoistic to love herself more seems like an implicit endorsement of her egoistic self. Given that most people are already biased in their thinking towards their own perceived benefit, the advice to love yourself more seems likely to increase vices of self-preference unless it is accompanied by clear instruction about the kind of self that needs to be loved.

Butler's claim that our self-love is often too weak has merit, but he is far too sanguine about the expectation that the exercise of self-love by itself tends toward moral living. He says, "Self-love . . . does in general coincide with virtue and leads us to one and the same course of life" (48). Admittedly, Butler does not claim a complete harmony between seeking your own happiness and doing what is right. It is only "in general" that the two tend in the same direction. At points Butler suggests that if we take God and the eternal perspective into account, the harmony is complete, but he thought that even in terms of earthly life, the motivations of self-love and conscience lead to similar modes of life.

A central problem with this claim is that the kind of happiness that would be valued by an agent with a moral identity is different from the kind of happiness that might be valued by someone who lacks such an identity. For the first kind of agent, moral concerns are presupposed in the kind of life one can call happy. For the second kind of agent, moral behavior may be a means to an end, but one who construes her end in nonmoral terms will find that moral living is sometimes at odds with achieving that end (Sidgwick 1962). Prudent selves may be better than the anarchic selves that Aristotle contrasts with those capable of a superior love of self, but there is still a significant gap between loving a self that is ultimately motivated by personal advantage and loving a self that has incorporated fundamental concerns for things beyond the self.

SELF-LOVE AND NEIGHBOR LOVE

How is loving your neighbor connected with loving yourself? In the context of the Old Testament commandment, self-love seems to be something that is taken for granted. The instruction in Leviticus occurs in the middle of a list of harmful actions one might do to others in the community (Lev. 19:18). Don't spread slander. Don't pervert justice. Don't endanger your neighbor's life. Don't seek revenge. In such a context we could understand the kind of love we have for ourselves in terms of a concern that we not suffer harm, a concern that we can ordinarily assume to be established through biology and socialization. As physical organisms, human beings are "hard-wired" to resist certain intrusions, and we typically learn in the socialization process to extend the self-protective dispositions to a wider range of harms. The commandment instructs us to refrain from doing to others in the community the things we want to protect ourselves against.

By the time we get to the New Testament, Jesus has extended the meaning of the ancient command. When he instructs his followers to love their neighbor as themselves, it is no longer just a matter of refraining from acts of harm. Neighbor-love, or the lack of it, is revealed in the kinds of attitudes one has toward others and the positive actions undertaken to do them good. Jesus taught that we need to treat other people as if they mattered, since they do matter in God's sight. When he used the parable of the Good Samaritan as an illustration of neighbor-love, he offered a picture of the kind of regard for another's benefit we might want from others, even if we do not expect it. The Samaritan is able to see and respond to the neighbor, not just as an obstacle, but as a person who is worthy of compassionate treatment.

Even here, the injunction sounds like a call to extend to the neighbor the kind of positive concern we are assumed to have for our own good. There is not really a command to love oneself. Nevertheless, as we reflect on self-love, it is relevant to consider the therapeutic insight that our self-love may be defective. In therapeutic contexts, the kind of defect that gains most attention is the danger of becoming so focused on fulfilling obligations or balancing relational demands that one fails to make room for a proper degree of self-regarding behavior. It is consistent with a biblical perspective to remind a person that he or she is of value and that submitting to degrading conditions or expectations is not necessarily a sign of virtue. Although one may sometimes relinquish certain rights or perform acts of self-sacrifice, it takes some discernment to decide when such acts of self-renunciation are productive and when they are destructive. Not every kind of losing of the self is an ideal to be emulated (Hampton 1993; Charry 2001).

It should not escape our notice that such claims about defective self-love contain implicit moral judgments about the value of the individual and proper self-respect. When we urge people not to be doormats and to learn to stand up for themselves, we are implicitly or explicitly appealing to moral ideals that can be neglected in a moral education that focuses too exclusively on the need for giving to others. The best kind of moral education teaches us both to regard our own good as important and to care about the good of others as well (Adams 1998, 509–12).

It is easy to assume that there is a sharp conflict between seeking your own good and seeking the good of others, between loving yourself and loving your neighbor. But whether there is a basic conflict depends on how we conceive our good. Some interests are narrow in the sense that they belong to an individual as an individual. I may be concerned with *my* finances or *my* reputation or *my* health. But most of us have wider interests as well, those that involve identifying ourselves with some larger unit than the individual. A woman may find herself concerned about benefiting her family or friend or church. Many of the things we care about most involve an identification of the self with something bigger than the individual. We acquire what Bernard Harrison calls "extended personal interests" (Harrison 1989, 307).

In telling us to love our neighbors as ourselves, Jesus stretches extended personal interests to the bursting point. We are to view the stranger much in the way we might a family member whose good is inextricably part of our own. We are to develop the kind of self that cares even about the distant neighbor who is a fellow child of God. We might think that such a teaching is an impossible ideal; nevertheless, it reminds us of the possibility of acquiring varying degrees of extended interests that enlarge our conception of what constitutes our good. Some people come to think about their work for the good of others in ways that make that work an integral part of their identity (Colby and Damon 1992). In other words some people become the kinds of selves whose good is bound up with care and concern for others. For such a person loving the self means loving the kind of self who has incorporated a concern for the neighbor in a fundamental way.

Developing such extended interests does not mean that there is never a conflict between doing what you think best for yourself and doing what is best for another. Human beings have limited time and resources, and even if another person's good is bound up with your own, you may not be able to do all you want for another while taking proper care of your more self-regarding needs. But the sort of conflict between benefiting yourself and benefiting those you care about is not markedly different from the conflict we all face in reconciling conflicting self-regarding desires. An individual with both self-regarding and other-regarding desires must make judgments about which have higher priority in a given situation.

Although we may worry about potential conflicts between self-love and neighbor-love, we can think of the two as mutually interdependent. There is a close connection between being able to see the neighbor as some-one who matters and being able to see yourself as someone who matters. To see yourself as an object of value presupposes an awareness of what is valuable from a point of view that transcends your individual concerns. The relevant kind of value will not be merely what serves your needs and wants, but something you can recognize as worthy independently of whether you find it convenient. When you try to think about whether you are valu-able from this wider perspective, you will be hard-pressed to think of your-self as valuable, if you cannot think of human beings generally as having value. Whatever reasons you have for regarding your own life as important are likely to be reasons for regarding other people to be important as well (Annas 1992).

So if you are reflective enough, a recognition of your own worth can implicitly be a recognition of other people's worth. Because of the connec-tion, blunting your awareness of the value of the neighbor can blunt your vision of your own value. So the therapeutic idea of learning to love your-self first before you start trying to love your neighbor is misleading. When self-love is reflectively integrated with other value judgments, the task of loving yourself is intertwined with the task of loving your neighbor. Learn-ing to see yourself as one who matters and learning to see the neighbor as one who matters are thus complementary elements of the same project.

The sort of self-love that can harmonize with neighbor-love is love for a self who has incorporated concerns for the good of the neighbor as an aspect of her own good. In practice, one's actual concerns are likely to fall short of one's ideal self-conception. However, loving oneself is not merely an affirmation of just what we are now, since our identity is constituted in part by the ideals that we claim as our own. We cannot fully say what we are while leaving out the ideals, yet to affirm our ideals is to affirm possi-bilities that may or may not become real, depending on how we live. In one sense, loving the self whose identity is defined by certain ideal possibilities is displayed by behavior that makes the possibilities into realities. When our ideals include concerns for the good of the neighbor, the project of loving the self involves efforts to become the kind of self who is able to love the neighbor (Holley 1999).

THERAPEUTIC THINKING

Therapeutic thinking often centers on achieving health through various kinds of liberation. Sometimes we run into problems when trying to fit into a social structure that is overly confining or oppressive. So therapeutic guidance tells us to declare our independence of alien forces that threaten to consume the self (Rieff 1966). Such guidance can be of great help when the forces we are rejecting are genuinely alien. However, if we simply assume that any limits that restrict freedom or any concerns for things transcending the self are to be treated as external, we have a recipe for emptying the self of the kind of structure that makes it genuinely human. There comes a point at which the project of liberating the self leaves us with little self left to liberate.

When liberation is conceived in terms of removing anything that might interfere with autonomous choice, the idea that there might be values worthy of recognition, which are not merely functions of individual wants and needs, can seem like a restriction. But when we try to liberate ourselves from such values, we discover that we cannot form selves substantial enough to respect and love. Learning to love ourselves involves shaping our concerns in the light of values that we recognize as having a kind of authority over us. Doing this need not be any more oppressive than the restriction involved in subordinating our beliefs about the world to a recognition of truths that are not just a function of what we would like to believe. The kind of liberty we should aspire to is not liberty from our own best judgments about what is valuable, for it is our recognition of value that enables us to form the kind of selves that we can find worthy of our own admiration.

With regard to moral values, the trick is to be able to distinguish between what can be treated as external to the self and what must be regarded as a vital element of the self. If we imagine a self that is morally constituted, the question of how to love it is very different from the question of how to love a self that is unstructured by moral concerns or constraints. To love a morally constituted self must surely involve efforts to maintain the ideals and convictions that are essential to the identity of that self. In other words such a love is inseparable from what we call integrity, using that term in the etymological sense of the virtue that protects the wholeness or unity of the individual (Chazon 1998; Holley 2002).

However, therapeutic thinking generally attempts to remain neutral about substantive moral commitments, and in order to do so, it must treat moral structures that might form the self as matters of individual choice. But who is it that is supposed to be making such a choice? If we imagine a self that is morally unformed, it is hard to see how moral concerns could be construed as anything other than means to egoistic ends. So trying to think about healthy selves in a way that treats those selves as existing independently of moral formation tends to alienate the individual from his or her own fundamental moral convictions.

The instruction to love yourself seems like an obvious truism. But the kind of guidance given depends greatly on how we construe the nature of the self that is the object of love. If the self to be loved is unified by an identification with ideals affirming the value of other selves, then the project of loving the self is not at odds with the project of loving others. Indeed, it is inseparable from efforts to become the kind of self that can live in a way that expresses those ideals. For such a self the love of others is not a secondary project to be approached, only after self-love has been achieved. It is rather an element of valuing a self that is partially constituted by other-directed concerns.

So with regard to the therapeutic proverb, "You need to love yourself," the relevant question is, *What kind of self do you need to love?* This therapeutic instruction misdirects us if it suggests that loving the self involves an endorsement of desires that have not been shaped by an awareness of what kind of self is worthy of aspiration. The aspirations that define such a self will express moral valuations, and the attempt to live by those aspirations is a moral project. Loving the self is in part a project of integrating aspirations and actions to genuinely become what we respect or admire. In an important sense the self that we most need to love is the one that has not yet been brought into being.

III. The Body and the Self

6

The Meaning of Embodiment: Neuroscience,

Cognitive Psychology, and Spiritual Anthropology

William B. Hurlbut

In August 1938 an expedition from the American Museum of Natural History, searching for undiscovered birds and mammals in the interior of New Guinea, made the first outside contact with an isolated population living with Stone Age technology (Brown 1991, 155). It is difficult to say how long this community had lived in the island interior, cut off from the rest of the world by the dense jungle that separated the valley from the coast a mere 115 miles to the north or south. They had no concept of the ocean and had never seen a white man. They were terrified that they were seeing the ghosts of their ancestors and were comforted only after realizing that these men, too, defecated as do all natural creatures. The two encountering cultures were about as different in color, custom, and cosmology as could be imagined. There, in that moment of human drama, stood two groups of men whose eyes looked outward from minds as dissimilar as any that have ever existed on the earth. Nonetheless, as dramatic as the differences were, what was equally evident were the similarities of facial expressions, gestures, general sensibilities, and their capacity to communicate across the vast gulf of thousands of years of physical and cultural separation.

How long these two groups of human beings had been separated genetically and culturally is difficult to know. Studies of mitochondrial and Y chromosome DNA, as noted by L. Cavalli-Sforza (2004), seem to confirm the evidence in the fossil record that suggests a common ancestor for all of humanity about 100,000 years ago. From a small East African ancestral population of about 2,000 they burst forth to occupy the far reaches of the globe, displacing other hominid species in the process. Genetic evidence suggests they first migrated eastward populating the coast of Southeast Asia, then spread northward and further east, reaching New Guinea by about 40,000 years ago. By 10,000 years ago human beings had occupied virtually every inhabitable coast and canyon, valley, and island in the world.

During the many millennia of this great human diaspora, our evident external differences in color and form evolved, probably mainly in response to environmental conditions.[1] In geographical separation, cultural differences between groups developed as well. Now, however, as we experience the beginnings of a great global reconvergence we are confronted with the challenge of communicating across our differences to establish global cooperation.

On the one hand, these differences constitute a valuable human resource, reflecting the freedom inherent in our capacity for symbolic representation and creative imagination. They encode the repository of human experience, wisdom, and spiritual understanding. Over the sweeping panorama of our evolutionary origin they can be seen as the culmination of a generalized freedom that is inherent in the entire evolutionary process, as ever more novel and complex forms arise with greater and greater flexibility to respond to their environment. During the past century, however, anthropological studies have over-emphasized the variability between peoples, resulting in a pessimism as to the possibility of achieving any global consensus.

However, closer consideration of cultural differences and evidence from cognitive neuroscience is now giving us an awareness of the great extent to which all humans share a common neurophysiology that leads to basic similarities in our modes of consciousness and sociality. In perceptual interpretation, conceptual categorization, and cognitive strategies there are remarkable similarities in individuals across cultures. Our capacity for freedom (and the cultural diversity that results) arose in the larger context of our shared biological origins. Our scientific understandings, therefore, provide a basis for reimagining humanity in a way that preserves the strengths both of our diversity and our unity, and on that basis offers hope for the possibility of genuine intercultural communication, understanding, and moral consensus.

If we reconsider from the perspective of modern scientific knowledge our place in the cosmos and the evolutionary process that formed us, we can better understand the natural groundings of both our freedom and our common humanity out of which our freedom arises. From the study of biology it is clear that we have been formed and fashioned by the forces of the earth and intricately interwoven with the whole physical and biological world. And this is the meaning of the word "human"—in its Latin root it comes from the word "humus," meaning earth or soil: we are creatures of the earth.

Throughout evolution we see the development of increasingly complex external morphology with the concomitant refinement of internal mental capacities. Differentiation of the head region, with its organs of sensory perception and communication, was paralleled internally by cerebral structures capable of processing more complex impressions of the surrounding environment and of regulating the feelings and functions of the organism. With upright posture came coordinated revisions of body form, increased range of motion, and radical cerebral reorganization that made possible new relations with the world.

Our transformation to upright form is reflected in nearly every detail of our deep structure, both somatic and psychic. The freeing of the upper limbs and the refinement of the "tool of tools," as Aristotle called the hands, allowed the emergence of greater fine-motor control and the cerebral capabilities that could coordinate and sustain more complex actions on the world. During the transition to bipedalism, earlier primates underwent the retraction of the snout and the development of bilateral stereoscopic vision. Whereas smell required direct chemical contact, and sound gave formless information, as sight became the prominent sense it gave a knowing and accurate encounter with the form and unity of wholes and allowed rapid perception of objects and actions at great distances.

Our reliance on visual stimuli, and the interpersonal relationships that reliance helps make possible, allows the openness in awareness, appreciation, and receptivity that is best exemplified in our direct, face-to-face encounter with other human beings. Along with visual sensory predominance, thinning of primate facial fur allowed the face to emerge as a canvas of self-presentation. Upwards through mammalian evolution, there was a progressive refinement of the structures of the face and improved neurological control of the facial muscles that facilitated active and increasingly subtle communication. Studies on monkeys have shown that special ensembles of cells in the brain respond only to faces. With more than thirty finely tuned muscles of facial expression and vocal control, human beings are capable of a wide array of communicative expressions of emotions and intentions.

The detached beholding of sight also allowed a deeper and more accurate apprehension of the reality of things; sight allowed insight. The cerebral processing and storage of visual images led to the detachability of object from image, symbolic representation, and the emergence of imagination and its creative powers. We have the capacity to imagine possibilities and try them out (in a kind of dress rehearsal) without the expense of time and risk of resources in the process.

If we look at the fossil record, around 1.5 million years ago the simple chipped tools found in layers representing a million years of hominid history are suddenly transcended by an artifact that bespeaks a significant cognitive leap, the production of the hand axe. "These symmetrical implements, shaped from large stone cores, were the first to conform to a 'mental template' that existed in the toolmakers mind" (Tattersall 2000, 61). The significance of such an innovation of mind is extraordinary and far-reaching. The capacity to form a mental image, to hold it in the mind, and work to achieve its realization bespeaks intention, planning, and implementation of ideals. What began as the visualization of an axe within a stone would become, in another million and a half years, the capacity to generate the images and ideals of a complex technological and moral culture.

The capacity to imagine and bring to completion an ideal gives an extraordinary freedom to human beings. Whereas most creatures live in an unbroken immediacy of life, humans have the freedom to pull the past into the present from learning stored as memory and the freedom to pull the future into the present through the creative imagination. Together with the ceaseless drive to organize the unexplained, what has been called the "cognitive imperative," the capacities to calculate, extrapolate, and recombine are used to reconfigure that which is into that which could be. Whereas most creatures are pushed by circumstances, we are pulled into the future by our dreams and images of fuller flourishing. For human beings it is not the determinism of physics that is the cause, but something previously unseen in the story of nature, the freedom of coherent aspiration, of a moral ideal. Leon Kass writes, "Desire, not DNA is the deepest principle of life" (Kass 1994, 48). In our early environment of evolutionary adaptation, our ability to actualize our desires was constrained by the limitations of nature on our awareness and capacities for action. Now the future will be controlled increasingly by the character of our desires.

Across the scope of evolution one can see an ascent toward full human freedom in the emerging complexity of the vital powers of awareness, actions, and drives in response to the challenges and opportunities of the environment. We have evolved not for pure instinctive response or narrow adaptation but for adaptability itself; not for a particular niche but for unpredicted possibility; and for comprehension and control, for flexibility and freedom in thought and action. Without some form of guidance channeling and controlling our desires and will, however, freedom could itself become a danger to our survival, as we carry out actions that prove harmful or destructive of our individual and communal life. Through evolution human beings have developed complex constraints of morality to provide a balance between innovation and stability, change and continuity, to preserve and promote both the freedom and flourishing of life.

Research into the neuroscience of the human brain is giving us an increasingly complex understanding of the universal biosocial context of human life in which our freedom is grounded. The philosophers George Lakoff and Mark Johnson summarize a large body of research findings and conclude that the "mind is not merely embodied, but embodied in such a way that our conceptual systems draw largely upon the commonalties of our bodies and the environment we live in" (Lakoff and Johnson 1999, 6). Time, for example, is understood by its representation through the experience of movement in space. Antonio Damasio, also a neuroscientist, drawing on cases of neural injury, shows how the body, as represented in the brain, provides the indispensable frame of reference for a sense of self, consciousness, personal identity, and awareness of the world. As he states, "our very organism rather than some absolute external reality is used as the ground reference for the constructions we make of the world around us" and goes on to say that "our minds would not be the way they are if it were not for the interplay of body and brain during evolution" (Damasio 1994, xvi).

The evolved embodiment that provides a common ground for self-consciousness and conceptual categories also provides a basis for the desires and intentions that shape our shared system of values. With increasing organismic complexity, the central values of evolutionary success, survival, and reproduction are served by pleasurable intermediate activities that become valued ends in themselves. The most obvious of these are the pleasures associated with eating and with sexuality. Notwithstanding the great variety of cultures and diversity of personalities, there is a solid central core of basic biological need that forms the shared desires and dreams of human community.

Our particular evolved human form of embodiment, with the physical and mental capacities we share, provides a common "language" of mental categories, emotional responses, and shared needs. These common characteristics are the basis for intelligible communication, mediated by the crucial process of empathy, which enables genuine social community. In such community, an individual develops a sense of self, as well as an awareness of the inner personal nature of others.

Simply defined, empathy is the ability to identify with and understand the situations, motives, and feelings of another. In this sense it has a meaning that is much more general than the notion of mere "sympathy." It is a form of intersubjectivity in which the observer actually participates in the feelings of the other. Neurologically, the process of empathy seems to work as follows. Because the human organism is a psychophysiological unity, an emotional state of anger, for example, generates in an individual visible expressive manifestations such as facial expression. Observing such facial expression subtly activates in the observer the same muscular movements and nervous system responses that together constitute the physical grounding of an inwardly felt subjective state that would be represented by such a facial expression. We experience this, for example, when we see someone yawn or grimace in pain. Such physical response in the observer translates into the corresponding emotional state in the observer, thus establishing an empathically shared psychophysiological state between the observer and the one being observed. Such a shared state becomes empathic communication as the observer reflectively distinguishes the other as distinct from self.

This empathetic intersubjectivity seems to provide the patterning for personal identity and the platform for cultural awareness. From earliest infancy there is an interactive engagement between mother and child that sustains a shared conversation of reciprocating rhythm and unifying emotional resonance. The long period of childhood dependency assures that social stimulation plays a formative role in the maturation of the mind. By age three and a half months the baby can control his gaze and initiate face to face encounters, gaining a sense of himself as an agent or actor that can alter the dynamics of interpretation. In a process that the psychiatrist Daniel Sterns (1985) has called "attunement," there is a reciprocity of small repeated exchanges, a kind of facial "duet" in which the mother responds, not with an imitation but with a reply that lets the baby know that she has understood his feelings. Mutual gaze provides the crucial lessons of pure social interaction, the ties of attachment, and the nonverbal foundations upon which language will later be built. Indeed there is evidence that our very concept of person, of a distinct subjective locus of life, replete with intentions, hopes, and fears, is formed in a uniquely human extension of the neurological substrate that processes facial and vocal expression.

This primary grounding of communication and trust, based on shared biology, bridged by empathy, and built by personal interaction, provides the foundations for language, moral awareness, and community of culture. The basic congruency of feeling established between mother and infant is slowly extended into a broader conversation that reaches out in exploration and evaluation of new and unfamiliar experiences. In a process of "social referencing" that builds a common set of values, the infant will point or gaze at an object to establish joint attention and then observe the mother's reaction. The mother's spoken responses begin to carry specific semantic content. A web of meaning is formed within this linguistic system, empathetically grounded in symbolic gestures, the coded concepts on which all human cultures are constructed.[2]

With language we move beyond the imperatives of the present to the creative constructions of cultural meanings and values. We weave an interpretive story, rich with ideals and aspirations, a narrative by which we navigate the world. In a kind of "reenvoicement," the child begins to structure his understanding of the world, the very pattern of his thoughts, by the echo of the words of others. In this frame, the social significance of the self is placed within a pattern of moral meanings and transcendent truths. Slowly the child is entrained to the society in which he is born, raised to a realm of beliefs and hopes inaccessible to an isolated individual.

In an orderly developmental progression, a child begins to crystallize a sense of self and other, to recognize the differentiation of animate and inanimate beings, and to discover the inner mental world of private beliefs and intentions. With conscious personal identity comes awareness of the distinct identity of others. Indiscriminate emotional contagion, with its blurred boundaries of self, gives way to cognitive empathy, a willed and knowing stepping into the role of the other. In one study, a twenty-one month child responded to his mother's simulated sadness by: (1) attending to his mother; (2) peering into her face to determine what is wrong (accompanied by verbal inquiries); (3) trying to distract her with a puppet; (4) looking concerned; and (5) giving his mother a hug while making consoling sounds and sympathetic statements (Zahn-Waxler and Radke-Yarrow 1990, 107–30). This series of actions demonstrates the complex understanding of emotion and empathetic interaction already developed at a relatively young age.

Within this profound resonance of mutual understanding, between the second and third year of life children develop an appreciation of the symbolic categories of good and bad and learn to apply these to their own actions, thoughts, and feelings. With a growing understanding of the relationship between present actions and future outcomes, a child begins to develop a conflict between acting on present desires and recognizing when to do so would have negative consequences on self and others. Before the age of five, children have difficulty governing their actions, but by around six the sense of self-control, and therefore accountability, allows shame and guilt but also the happy sense of virtue, of consonant goodness of self. Free moral choice becomes increasingly the central moral axis and, guided by the emotional pull of empathetic communion, leads to the poignant and powerful drama of the individual self in the quest for a sense of ethical worthiness. Jerome Kagan writes, "I am tempted to suggest that the continuous seeking of evidence to prove one's virtue is, like Darwin's notion of natural selection, the most potent condition sculpting each person's traits over their lifetime" (Kagan 1998, 157). As a child matures, with the greater cognitive empathy acquired comes greater sensitivity to the needs of others, as well as the associated moral imperatives.

Moral thinking is inherent in the development of human consciousness, for as the self becomes aware of other selves, the ethical issue inescapably arises as to how one person should treat another. The mind is irreducibly transactional, defined in a "conversation" that is grounded in empathy and experienced in community. The categories of thought based on our shared biology are placed in a web of meaning as our consciousness is constructed through the inter-communion of our minds. Our ideas of self, society, and the significance of life, are all formed within the language of a shared cultural narrative. As the philosopher Charles Taylor writes, "[T]he genesis of the human mind is . . . not 'monological,' not something each accomplishes on his or her own, but dialogical" (Taylor 1991, 33).

Albert Einstein, (as quoted in the *New York Times*, April 19, 1955) said, "[T]he most incomprehensible thing about the world is that it is comprehensible." The reciprocal significance of this statement is the astonishing fact that the cosmos has produced a creature capable of comprehending its order. That the human mind can penetrate to the foundational principles of the material world is evidenced in our mathematical physics. But dare we extend this confidence to the realm of the moral, to attempt to discern a moral order in the world? Does not the moral, as Hans Jonas poses the dilemma, "originate in ourselves and merely come back to us from the putative scheme of things as our reflected voice?" (Jonas 1966, 282). As Pope John Paul II (1987) said, when we look into the eyes of another person we know we have encountered a limit to our self-will. Such awareness, together with our inwardly felt sense of significance, becomes the sense of a moral meaning within the cosmos that transcends the particularities of local culture.

When morality is recognized as serving both the flourishing of life and the freedom that is our crucial strength, as twin essentials of our individual and communal human nature that is part of nature, it is possible to step beyond relativism and locate moral grounds on which individuals and even cultures may be judged. Communities themselves exist to serve the individuals within their groups and for that reason morals must seek to keep social order and individual autonomy in a dynamic balance. Humbly acknowledging such perspectives may help foster genuine intercultural communication and understanding.

It is an irony of history that the word *humility* also shares with the word *human* the Latin root *humus*, meaning earth or soil. If we draw back from our self-created urban civilization and try to see with clear eyes from where we have come, we are stirred by the majesty of its meaning. These "creatures of the earth"—Homo Sapiens Sapiens (doubly wise)—formed and fashioned from the material and by the very powers and processes of the natural world, have emerged from it like bright colored wings from a chrysalis—unexpected, unexplained, and radiant with possibility. We have not yet, however, learned the humility to appreciate the portent and promise, the singular significance of the human form and its open and unexplored extensions. We seem unable to recognize our extraordinary place within the order of nature as cosmic matter come to consciousness, freedom, and moral awareness—nor the awesome dignity and responsibility these imply.

Preservation of true freedom, and the open possibilities for human flourishing, may depend on our finding a new and more profound understanding of our human nature. We have argued here for a conception of our nature that encompasses the fullness of human possibilities. Perhaps we will preserve our freedom only if we dare to acknowledge that our moral sense is not relative, but relational, and based on the fundamental character of nature itself, which human nature reflects and reveals.

Pascal noted that human existence is located between infinities, between the infinitely large and the infinitely small, the vast realms of cosmic space and the tiniest particles of matter (Pascal 1965, Meditation 72). Brought into life by the fundamental forces of the cosmos, we are just the right size in form and function for genuine empathy, for sensitive awareness of other persons. We are cosmic matter come to community and moral consciousness. Indeed, the whole of the material world may be seen as an intelligible "language" of being and the foundation for the extraordinary extensions of personal and social existence that allow the expression of genuine altruistic love. Just as our body and mind have been formed and fashioned by the cosmos from which we have emerged, could it be that the manifestation of love further complements and completes that which is, revealing and reflecting both the fundamental nature of the universe and the full significance of human life.

NOTES

1. The variations within humanity may be analogous to the different breeds of dogs; no actual mutation are involved in creating Chihuahuas, Great Danes and Wirehaired Fox Terriers, just different concentrations of genes. Intermating of the various dog breeds results in the original dog, the mutt, in just a few generations. Likewise, with the reconvergence of humanity, we may see the return of a more basic human stock, the human "mutt."

2. The neural basis for understanding language appears to be grounded in the structures used in primates for interpretation of facial and simple vocal expression. The central role of emotional expression in language is becoming more fully appreciated as we try to create computers that are capable of deciphering spoken language. Without the accompanying pauses, prosody, and postural cues, language is deprived of an important part of its communicative value. This difficulty is partly overcome in written texts by conventions in structure that carry intended meanings. Spoken language, however, is very different from written language, as anyone who has ever tried to read a transcription of a meeting or a court hearing can attest.

7

The Embodied Self: Evidence from

Cognitive Psychology and Neuropsychology

Paul C. Vitz

Many **postmodern theorists today** claim that there is no human nature; that is, there is nothing important that is intrinsic to the human being. Consistent with this general assumption, postmodern theorists have also claimed that there is no self or at least no natural or true self. What postmodernists mean by this statement is that the self is a socially constructed concept and therefore essentially plastic and capable of being constructed in whatever way one might wish. There is, therefore, no natural self with basic universal characteristics. Likewise, the more general idea of a human nature is also seen as a socially constructed idea.

In this essay, I challenge this postmodern viewpoint. Specifically, evidence will be assembled here that identifies *universal characteristics* of the human nervous system, including higher cognition, and of our experiences that contribute to the concept of the self. The existence of these characteristics, I believe, puts severe limits on the notion of an arbitrary social or self-constructed identity.

Among the sources of the self for each individual are universal forms of infant sensory and perceptual experience, invariant early interpersonal interactions, common early language learning, childhood interpersonal relationships, and other universal cultural factors. All of these types of experience are solidified and particularized for each self through the action of memory. In addition, this self is consciously understood as a consequence of our various universal cognitive processes. Of course, there remain aspects of the self that are culturally constructed and are especially problematic today. But the common core to the self should not be overlooked. In many respects, the self that develops through the operation of universal factors described here is the same self that de-develops or deconstructs under the impact of Alzheimer's dementia, as treated so intelligently and movingly in Glenn Weaver's essay in this volume.

THE ECOLOGICAL SELF

In *The Paradox of Self-Consciousness* (1998), José Bermúdez summarizes powerful evidence that the self emerges through early visual, auditory, and other sensory and perceptual experience. Specifically, there is a very strong prelinguistic self common to all infants and young children, and of course this same foundational self continues throughout a person's lifetime. Bermúdez begins by paraphrasing an important point made by the prominent psychologist of perception J. J. Gibson in *The Ecological Approach to Visual Perception* (1979). Gibson makes clear that the visual field specifies the existence of the self. For example, the visual field is bounded by the edges of what we can see in front of us at any particular moment. That is, the visual field comes with an edge all around it—and that edge continually identifies the boundary of the visual self. We also know that the visual field, in the direction of our gaze, is in front of us. And that behind us, the visual world exists but cannot be seen unless we turn around. As Bermúdez puts it: "The boundedness of the field of vision is part of what is seen" (105).

What Gibson means by the powerful but indirect visual creation of the self is that the visual field is not only bounded but also that much of the visual world is hidden at any particular moment and that as you move around in the visual environment you keep changing the boundaries of the visual field. And the "changer"—the source of all those changes—is your self, an invariant consciousness present during each of those glimpses of the world.

In addition, Bermúdez notes that we know visual fields contain within them the visual experience of parts of our body. For example, our nose in many respects, however dimly aware we are of it, constantly defines, as a minor mountain, the direction of our gaze and the presence of our face in the visual field. Other parts of our body are often visually present. Our hands and feet give us a distinctive bodily self-awareness of our presence in the visual world. We know that our hands and feet are not part of the outside visual environment but part of the self—that is, part of what is attached to us. Furthermore, as we move in the visual environment we are especially aware, though often unconsciously, of our body parts moving in the field; our hand passes in front of our face, our feet precede us, and so forth. Gibson goes on to argue for still other perceptual information of a more complex kind that also specifies our self in the visual field, and hence helps to define a perceptually based self.

Certainly one other major aspect of the self, besides consciousness as it operates in the visual field, is the experience of agency. In other words, we are aware that where we look in the visual field is subject to our intention. I look at what I want to look at. My will, my motives, my desires determine what I see. Let us use the word *agency* to describe this primarily conscious experience. As Bermúdez (1998, 150) puts it: "It seems fair to say that the limits of the will mark the distinction between the self and the nonself just as much as does the skin, although in a different way."

Still another major sensory experience that gives rise to the notion of a self is proprioceptive feedback from the body, that is, internal experiences tell us the state and location of our bodies. These experiences give rise to what Bermúdez calls "the bodily self" (Bermúdez 1998, 131–62). These cues include: (1) information about pressure, temperature, and friction from receptors on the skin and beneath its surface; (2) information about the relation of body segments from receptors in the joints; (3) information about balance and posture from the inner ear; (4) information about muscular fatigue from receptors in the muscles; and so on. In short, there is a vast array of internal proprioceptive information telling us about our bodily self. In addition, this kind of information is intimately coordinated with the visual information previously described.

Finally, another important source of information is what comes from hearing. We know much about the spatial world in which we move from the constantly changing auditory experience that identifies us at the center of an acoustic field. These bodily based acoustic and visual fields are all in a sense spatial, and they are closely coordinated so as to give rise to the idea and experience of a single multisensory space at the center of which is the perceptual self.

It is not just adults who know these things, or children who have been around for a while, but even tiny infants have a rudimentary notion of this sensory space and of themselves as located in it. For example, a three-minute old infant when a click is sounded on one side or another of its head will reliably shift its eyes in the direction of the click (Wertheimer 1961; see also Butterworth 1981; Muir and Field 1979; Clarkson, Swain, Clifton, and Cohen, 1991). This capacity begins long before an infant can even move its own body. Infants of a month or two in age pay much less attention to an object that is outside of their reach than an object which is reachable. Work by T. G. R. Bower (1972) suggests that this discrimination begins as early as two weeks. (Also see Von Hosten 1982.) Likewise, babies, when observing a looming object that gets bigger as it comes nearer, will move their heads away if the object is on a collision course but will just observe it if the object's course will miss them (see, e.g., Dunkeld and Bower 1980; Nanez 1988).

As a summary of the very early infant sensor-perceptual-motoric capacities with respect to the self, consider the following quote from the well-known cognitive psychologist Ulric Neisser (1988):

> The information that specifies the ecological self is omnipresent, and babies are not slow to pick it up. They respond to looming and optical flow from a very early age, discriminate among objects, and easily distinguish the immediate consequences of their own actions from events of other kinds. The old hypothesis that a young infant cannot tell the difference between itself and its environment, or between itself and its mother, can be decisively rejected. The ecological self is present from the first. (40)

THE EARLY INTERPERSONAL SELF

Human infants, long before they are capable of speaking, have normally developed a large number of interpersonal skills that demonstrate their awareness of a self in the context of interpersonal relations, most of which are with the mother or mother-figure. To begin, infants as young as three days prefer their own mother's voice over that of another infant's mother (DeCasper and Fifer 1980). There is evidence that by two weeks infants are more likely to stop crying on hearing their mother's voice than when hearing that of a female stranger (Bremner 1988, 157). Some of this voice preference might have been the result of pre-natal experience, but there is similar evidence with respect to infants' preference for faces. By an average age of forty-five hours, infants reveal a clear preference for the face of their mother over that of a stranger (Field, Woodson, Greenberg, and Cohen, 1982).

It has long been known that infants respond to the crying of other infants by crying themselves. An early study by Simner (1971) was replicated by Martin and Clark (1982) using infants averaging just 18.3 hours. Further, they observed that infants stopped crying or cried less when they heard a recording of themselves crying. That is, the researchers found reliable evidence that newborns recognize their own crying as distinct from that of others—a clear case of self-perception (see Bermúdez 1998, 124–25).

Even more striking results have been reported with respect to facial imitation in very young infants. Meltzoff and Moore (1977) found that infants twelve to twenty-one days in age could imitate successfully three distinct facial acts—lip protrusion, mouth opening, and tongue protrusion, as well as finger movement. Later Meltzoff and Moore (1983) looked at the same capacities in newborns ranging from forty-two minutes to thirty-two hours old. These infants imitated mouth opening and tongue protrusion. And T. M. Field (1982) found that two-day-old infants could imitate adult smiles, frowns, and expressions of surprise. In short, socially coordinated behavior develops very quickly between the infant and others.

By the time they are two months old, infants engage in extended coordinated "dialogues" or protoconversations with their mother or mother-figure. According to psychologist Trevarthen (1993):

> Babies six weeks or older focus on the mother's face and express concentrated interest by stilling of movement and a momentary pause in breathing. The infant's interest as a whole conscious being is indicated by the coordination and directedness of this behavior, which aims all modalities to gain information about the mother's presence and expressions. Hands and feet move and clasp the mother's body or her supporting hand, the head turns to face her, eyes fix on her eyes or mouth, and ears hold and track her voice.

The next, and crucial, phase is signalled by the infant's making a "statement of feeling" in the form of a movement of the body, a change in hand gesture away from clasping the mother, a smile or a pout, a pleasure sound or a fretful cry. The mother, if she is alert and attentive, reacts in a complimentary way. A positive, happy expression of smiling and cooing causes her to make a happy imitation, often complimenting or praising the baby in a laughing way, and then the two of them join in a synchronized display that leads the infant to perform a more serious utterance that has a remarkably precocious form.

> This infant utterance is the behavior, in that context of interpersonal coordination and sharing of feelings, which justifies the term *protoconversation*. It looks and sounds as though the infant, in replying to the mother, is offering a message or statement about something it knows and wants to tell. Mothers respond and speak to these bursts of expression as if the infant were really saying something intelligible and propositional that merits a spoken acknowledgement. (130–32)

There is even an experimental paradigm supporting this persuasive case for describing this early interpersonal behavior as a form of conversation. Murray and Trevarthen (1985) used closed-circuit television to create remote interactions between six- to eight-week old infants and their mothers. Each infant and each mother saw a life-sized face-image of the other. Although this environment was somewhat artificial, the mother and child established a fairly normal protoconversation of the kind just described. The experimenters then broke the closed-circuit link and began replaying to the infants the video tapes of their mothers filmed earlier in a real-time interaction. The infants showed significant distress at this change even though the videotapes showed the same images of the mother that had recently given them pleasure. Of course the missing element was the contingency between their mother's utterances and the expression of their own response. In short, the babies saw half a dialogue directed at them from their mother, but they had no sense of participation in the dialogue and they didn't like it!

This kind of interactive conversation already present at two months continues to steadily evolve in complexity as the months go by. By approximately nine months, a new element enters into the infant's repertoire. Previous interactions had been diadic, that is, the infant related to a person or sometimes to an object. At nine months triadic interaction becomes possible, that is, the infant can look at an object that the mother is looking at and then relate to the mother with respect to the object. The mother and infant can jointly attend to an object. What has been mastered, as Jerome Bruner (1977) puts it

> is a procedure for homing in on the attentional locus of another. It is a disclosure and discovery routine and not a naming procedure. . . . It has, moreover, equipped the child with a technique for transcending egocentrism, for insofar as he can appreciate another's line of regard and decipher their marking intentions, he has plainly achieved a basis for what Piaget has called decentration, using a coordinate system for the world other than the one of which he is the center. (276)

In other words, the nine-month-old is capable of joint visual attention with its mother. Again we see, before the development of language per se, the beginning of social interaction involving the coordinated communication between two selves.

Early Language

It is very clear from the experimental literature that all humans are strongly preprogramed to learn language. Here I present a summary primarily taken from Coren, Ward, and Enns (1999, 370). Infants are born with a remarkable ability to respond to human speech (for technical discussions see Jusczyk

1986; Kuhl 1987). Recordings of the electrical activity of the brain have revealed that even premature infants of thirty to thirty-five weeks gestational age can discriminate among vowel sounds (Cheour-Luhtanen et al. 1996). At birth, infants move their limbs in synchrony with connected adult speech but not with other sounds, such as tapping sounds or disconnected vowel sounds (Condon and Sander 1974). In addition, infants show much the same patterns of responses to spoken phonemes that adults do. For example, infants as young as one month of age discriminate speech stimuli better across phonemic boundaries than within phonemic categories, showing categorical perception in the way that adults do (Eimas, Siqueland, Jusczyk, and Vigorito 1971). Because, at one month of age, infants have had only minimal exposure to speech sounds and their utterances consist only of cries, screams, and babbles, they clearly have not yet learned language. Their ability to make speech discriminations similar to those of adults has thus been taken as evidence of an innate mechanism for speech processing.

Other developmental evidence for an innate speech system comes from studies of children's babbling (Lennebert 1967; Locke 1983). By seven to ten months of age infants normally engage in vocalizations that are characterized as repetitive (e.g., saying "dadada") and syllabic in structure (i.e., consonant-vowel clusters), without apparent reference or meaning, and that progress through a well-defined series of stages. Some critics have dismissed babbling as nothing more than evidence that motoric aspects of the vocal speech apparatus are developing. However, severely hearing-impaired infants reared by parents whose only linguistic communication was American sign language (ASL) produce "manual babbling" that, although made with hands and fingers, is indistinguishable in its time course, structure, and function from the vocal babbling of hearing infants (Petitto and Marentette 1991). Thus, babbling seems to be related to the development of an *amodal* language system. Interestingly, hand and finger movements of the hearing infants bear no resemblance to those of the young ASL "signers" in the study of manual babbling.

Another very impressive demonstration of infants' speech perception ability is that infants can integrate auditory information and visual information about speech. For example, Aronson and Rosenbloom (1971) showed that one to two-month-old infants exhibited distress when hearing their mother's voice displaced in space from the mother's visual location. In one study, four-month-old infants were presented with two video displays of the same person's face speaking two different vowel sounds (Kuhl and Meltzoff 1982). At the same time, each infant was presented (from a loudspeaker midway between the faces) with the sound of the person's voice producing one or the other of the vowel sounds. The voice and the two faces were all in synchrony with each other, but the voice corresponded to only one of the face's articulatory movements. The infant spent about 73 percent of the time looking at the face that was articulating the vowel sound it was hearing. Thus, very young infants also demonstrate cross-modal integration of speech cues, just as adults do, even though they have had only limited experience with such cues and do not yet speak. Moveover, this ability is apparently a function of the left hemisphere of the brain in infants, just as speech production is a function of that hemisphere in adults (MacKain, Studdert-Kennedy, Spieker, and Stern, 1983).

In short, we find a linguistic structure rooted in our nervous system that gets elicited and specified through a universal form of experience, namely the learning of one's mother tongue. This foundational language for each individual creates a linguistically understood aspect of the self that will be completely resistant to any later attempts to remove or change it. And of course one of the first things—roughly around age one and a half—that every child learns is the notion of "me" and "mine." This, again, represents the child's linguistic description of the previous even earlier perceptual awareness of self and other. Very quickly with early language a child learns his or her name, the names "Mama" and "Papa," and the names of other family members. The child's name, although coming from the culture, becomes part of him or her on a permanent basis.

EARLY INTERPERSONAL RELATIONS: OBJECT RELATIONS THEORY

The only serious understanding of early relationships of an interpersonal kind—at least with regard to later mental and interpersonal problems—is that found in the psychoanalytic tradition known as object relations theory. This theoretical approach is primarily concerned with the internal psychological representations, called "objects," of early interpersonal relationships, such as the baby's representation of its relationship to its mother. There are different theorists with different emphases: for example, Melanie Klein proposes that early internal representations of the mother or mother-figure, and of the self, are innate. Others, such as D. W. Winnicott, propose that these representations of the other and the self are primarily the result of early experience. (For discussions and summaries of object relations theorists, see Greenberg and Mitchell 1983; Summers 1994.) It is an important theoretical issue whether we have quite specific innate interpersonal templates or whether early interpersonal patterns are primarily laid down by experience. Still, this issue with respect to the self is not especially relevant to our concerns. Even if these early internal representations are largely the result of experience, the basic experience between a child and a mother-figure is universal to all children. The worst that can happen is that there is no such relationship because there is no functional mother; in such a grim case, the child either dies or is so psychologically crippled that the issue of social construction of the self is moot. Such individuals simply don't function.

In addition to the internalized representation of the mother and of the self, rather quickly after the first year or so, similar representations of other members of the family are established, for example, the father, siblings, nannies, grandparents, and the like. Again, the basic family structure is pretty universal, although the particular cast of family characters will be unique to each individual. In short, object relations theory establishes a common structure for the foundation of the interpersonal self in childhood.

DRAWING AND DEVELOPMENT OF ART

There is also a very remarkable similarity in the development in children's drawings, all over the world. Kellogg (1970) and others have shown that children begin drawing between two and three, and that their drawings follow the same developmental sequence up until roughly puberty. By approximately age six, some particular cultural elements will be present in children's art, but the structure and general character of these drawings are remarkably similar around the world. Presumably this universal artistic development underlies the fact that human beings appear to be able to appreciate the art and imagery of other cultures with relatively little difficulty. Again, there is a cultural specificity to the art of each people, but the capacity for art is not merely an arbitrary, socially constructed thing.

PEER RELATIONSHIPS

Another almost universal aspect of the developing self is the common peer experience especially important between the ages of about six through twelve. Throughout the world's cultures, this is a time of early friends, early social and sports activities, and almost always it is a time of schooling and learning how to relate to a variety of peers. (For a theoretical understanding of this period see Erik H. Erikson's school age or latency stage, e.g., Frager and Fadiman 1998, or Monte and Sollod 2003.) Again, each individual has a particular set of these experiences, but the general nature or structure of the self as it emerges through these experiences is roughly the same. In addition the specific experiences for better and for worse mark a person for his or her entire life. One cannot decide to create oneself in such a way as to erase the impact of these years any more than one can erase the still earlier impact of one's family life and first language.

ADULT CHARACTERISTICS OF THE SELF

Here it will be useful to identify certain properties of the adult self that are not open to arbitrary change or reconstruction. Some of these are perhaps obvious, but they nevertheless need to be noted. Memory is certainly a universal human characteristic and much of our memory starts with the understanding of our own life as a sequence of narratives or episodes, but our memory also includes factual information both about such things as our birthdate, where we have lived, and so forth, and also factual information related to our education, specialized knowledge of certain kinds, skills, and the like. These two kinds of information, one episodic or narrative, the other propositional or semantic, have been well identified in cognitive psychology (Tulving 1983; Bruner 1986; Davidson and Hugdahl 1995; for a discussion of this distinction, see Vitz 1990). The point here is that both kinds of information provide an understanding of the self that remains highly resistant to arbitrary change. Episodic memories of interactions with parents, siblings, childhood and high school friends, early romances, successes and failures in school or in sports—all this kind of information is part of who we are, and the idea that as adults we can dismiss it—forget it—is simply false.

Moreover, there are all the other kinds of things we can know in the semantic sense, such as our mother's birthday, the state capitals, and friends' telephone numbers. Or perhaps we know a lot about electrical engineering or Spanish literature. Such information is also an important part of who we are. The basic problem caused by the pathology of amnesia is the problem of losing this previous information. And in recovering this information, we recover much of what is meant by "our self." It is meaningless to claim that we can choose who we are in such a way as to reject or even neglect this kind of memory.

EMOTIONAL "WEATHER" AND INTERIORITY

A different kind of memory—a third type, if you will—is the memory we have of our emotional states. We remember feelings of sadness, loss, anxiety, joy, relief, boredom, embarrassment, and so on. For each of us, these emotions have a different frequency of occurrence—a different prevalence or relative dominance. Some people are often anxious, others are commonly sad, others seem to be always optimistic and happy, and so on. Each of these internal emotions can be thought of as a kind of internal weather, and over the years each of us becomes familiar with, and has a memory of, our recurring pattern of emotions. This memory is also part of our self that cannot be changed. You might be able to change some of your emotions in the future, but not, of course, those in the past. For many people an important aspect of their self is their knowledge and memory of these characteristic internal affective states.

INTIMACY

One of the uncommon but very important ways in which we know the self is through the experience of intimacy with another. Intimacy is a kind of awareness of the basic nature or essence of another. We become aware of the other self and of its unique qualities. In many respects, intimacy most reliably occurs between a mother and her child. Such intimacy is perhaps best described in a passage by the philosopher Kenneth Schmitz (1986):

> Metaphysically speaking, intimacy is not grounded in the recognition of this or that characteristic a person *has*, but rather in the simple unqualified presence the person *is*. . . . Indeed, it seems to me that the presence in which intimacy is rooted is nothing short of the unique act of existing of each person. Presence is but another name for the being of something insofar as it is actual, and in intimacy we come upon and are received into the very act of existing of another. We are, then, at the heart, not only of another person, but at the heart of the texture of being itself. No doubt it is true that the person is incommunicable in objective terms insofar as he or she is existentially unique. But in intimacy, as we approach the very act of self-disclosure, we approach the center of all communicability. It is this "secret" that we share with the other person. It is the sense of being with another at the foundation not only of our personal existence, but of being with each other in the most fundamental texture of being itself. Put in the most general terms—though we must not forget that each intimacy is through and through singular—the "secret" that we discover through intimacy is this: *"that reality is not indifferent to the presence of persons."* (45; emphasis in original)

Though Schmitz is describing the metaphysical nature of intimacy, the same understanding is at the core of psychological intimacy. Intimacy thus becomes a major characteristic of a person. This intimacy—set up by closeness and openness—is not cognitive knowledge based on abstraction, but intuitive knowledge based on experience, on union with the other. The memory of these experiences is part of how we know our true or real self and of how we know the selves of others.

LOSS OF SELF-COHERENCE IN THE POSTMODERN WORLD

Many of the postmodern deconstructors of the self, namely those who argue that the coherent self is ceasing to exist and that this is a good thing, have failed to address the issue raised by the psychological condition once called "multiple personality disorder" (MPD) and now called "disassociative identity disorder" (DID). For example, in this condition, there is the presence of a number, sometimes as many as fifteen or twenty selves in the same person, each one capable of taking over behavior under some circumstances. This condition defines a person without a coherent self, without psychological integration. The result, however, is not joyful liberation, but psychological suffering and serious mental malfunctioning. Such people seek help to bring integration and unity into their personality. This is not to say that a healthy person's self is a completely coherent, noncontradictory, harmonious phenomenon. But it is important to make clear that the seriously unintegrated condition, as in DID, is a pathology. (See the DSM-IV-TR, 529. For a specific analysis of DID with respect to postmodern personal identity, see Davis 2000.)

The prevalence of the postmodern self—which is increasingly pastiche like, saturated, polyvocalic, and incoherent—reflects an increase in personal pathology in response to the social pathologies of our society. Thus, family breakdown, social isolation, virtual relationships, and sexual abuse are moving our population toward an environment that increasingly fosters DID and multiple personalities. As a consequence of this interpretation, the growing pervasiveness of the postmodern self is something to fear, not something to cheer.

SOME REFLECTIONS ON THE COHERENT, DEVELOPING SELF

It is time now to summarize and integrate the implications of the preceding material for our understanding of the self. We saw at the very beginning of life that the infant begins quickly to develop a perceptual self that integrates the different senses within a general space, a space in which the body moves about and which can be thought of as the first conscious experience of the self. Keep in mind that this perceptual self continues to exist throughout our lives. It remains with us at all times and indeed slowly changes as our perceptual and bodily characteristics change. The point is that this early perceptual self is not buried and forgotten but continues to exist as a living and developing aspect of our self throughout life. Likewise, the early interpersonal self—prelanguage—once set in motion continues to develop and be present throughout our lives. Anyone who has learned a new dance step as an adult is perfectly aware of how this nonverbal interpersonal aspect of the self is still alive and functioning, and of course in countless other ways we keep in interpersonal touch with people in nonverbal ways, that is, we keep in *touch*.

Meanwhile, the verbal understanding of our self constantly remains and develops and is an obvious and familiar part of self-identity. Likewise, our early family relationships remain part of us. Indeed psychology has often shown that many adult relations are deeply rooted in our first family-based relationships. Why is it that so many children of alcoholics marry alcoholics? (On this topic of early attachment relations as affecting adult lives, see Ainsworth 1989; Collins and Read 1990; Simpson, 1990; Feeney and Noller 1991; Hazan and Shaver 1994; Kilpatrick and Davis 1994; Solomon and George 1999.)

Many specifics of how the different aspects of the self are brought into existence are not especially clear. And no doubt there are parts of each of us that are in conflict with other parts. Nevertheless, this general understanding of the self is one of continual growth and integration.

Some theorists have suggested that the true self of a person can't really exist because each of our different selves is rather like the layer in an onion. And who is to say which layer of an onion is the real onion, the real self? Of course, this whole analogy is seriously flawed, since each layer is very much like the others and the true onion is the whole integrated onion with the spirit of growth within it. But for the moment let's take the onion metaphor seriously. Implied in this metaphor is that there is no true self and that when you've taken away all the layers there is nothing left to find. Let me suggest a more appropriate vegetable for our metaphoric purposes, namely an artichoke. For example, the leaves are all rooted in the basic stem but perhaps one could say that the leaves are not the best or truest expression of the artichoke. That honor goes to the heart of the artichoke. The fuzzy things on top of the heart are still different from the leaves and even leaves are part of the self of the artichoke, but the core, or the heart, of the artichoke is still there and is perhaps the best symbol of our core self.

THE CRISIS OF HUMAN IDENTITY AND FREEDOM

The previous material from psychology and biology has strongly, though implicitly, argued that there are major restraints on the human self. We are brought into existence and remain structured by many forces that we do not choose. These include such varied elements as bodily limitations, preexisting perceptual capacities and brain structures, our parents and siblings, our first language, our emotional temperament, and the social world of our childhood and youth. The evidence marshaled makes clear that any idea that we can construct and reconstruct ourselves in any thorough-going fashion is simply not possible.

But of course it is *very* true that we can change our lives, we do have some important measure of freedom, and we can certainly move ourselves toward various goals both good and bad.

In fact, in the modern and postmodern period one of the most distinctive changes has been the great increase in personal freedom, and this brings us to the heart of the postmodern self as conceptualized by certain theorists. Although these theorists have seriously overgeneralized, they are far from completely wrong. There is, indeed, in the contemporary world a crisis of the self or a crisis of identity, as experienced by many young adults. We might call this the problem of the adult social self. There is evidence that this self has become increasingly ambiguous, multicentered, saturated, or in other words, increasingly less coherent and less and less determined by the past. This crisis has been brought about by increases in personal freedom, by the new technology, and by an increase in the number of different social choices for how to live that now face people. And all these possibilities have been combined with significant weakening of the older more traditional social supports for the self, as shown by the effects of family breakdown, and so forth. In important respects, this crisis of identity is a serious and, I suspect, historically new phenomenon.

Here, let me propose that there are essentially three responses to this crisis, each of which assumes a person's free capacity to choose. One of these choices is not to do anything and just float with the chaotic and often disintegrating tides of life. A second possibility is to choose to make changes in the social self, based upon whatever personal criteria the individual wishes to use. In this case, the postmodern theorists have identified a genuine new kind of adult social self—however much it remains conditioned by the earlier constraints of biology, language, and early interpersonal relations. Please note, however, that these theorists assume that we have the freedom to so choose. This freedom is another intrinsic part of human nature.

The third choice is to respond to an important and, I believe, universal aspect of human nature that has been much ignored. As human beings grow and change and become interpersonally and intellectually more mature, they recognize a process and a *trajectory of transcendence* in their own life. That is, they come to understand that they have over time transcended—moved beyond and above—their previous self-understanding. In time we all become aware of this movement. This experience creates and at the same time expresses a deep longing of the human heart. Whether one sees this trajectory of transcendence as something aimed at God or a higher spiritual existence, or as some kind of self-constructed identity is not the point here. Instead, I would like to propose that this trajectory of transcendence is universal and part of the highest level of human nature. Indeed, in proposing that human beings can construct themselves, the postmodernists are assuming this trajectory of transcendence as part of our nature. Whether we will choose to find the self's identity within the higher spiritual levels of transcendence or not is one of our choices. As already noted, some may choose to transcend their former self on hedonistic or narcissistic or ideological grounds so as to construct their "new" adult social self from the choices provided by the commercial world and our increasingly neopagan society. They are free to do so—even if the choices provided by this world are controlled by economic and political forces. I believe that if such postmodernists continue over the years to make such choices, in time they will find their supposedly "new" self increasingly disorganized and out of personal control. As a result, ironically, they will become imprisoned within the laws of their biology and of their social environment.

However, the choice to seek identity through one's relationship to God or the higher spiritual levels of transcendence provides a new way to construct a coherent self or identity, connected to one's past but not controlled by it. This new self is controlled more by what we have freely chosen to move toward than by our personal past or our social present. That is, this choice allows the person to escape both the restrictions and the lack of freedom in the traditional self and the arbitrariness and incoherence of the postmodern self.

8

Losing Our Memories and Gaining Our Souls:

The Scandal of Alzheimer's Dementia for

the Modern or Postmodern Self

Glenn Weaver

We arrived early. The waiting room was crowded, and we took seats in an area where we could see doctors hurrying back and forth along a carpeted corridor in their white jackets. I saw my doctor a couple of times and pointed him out to Joyce. Finally he came into the waiting room and took us to his little office with his kid's paintings on the wall.

He asked us to sit down in two straight-back chairs arranged in front of his desk. He sat opposite us and held a sheaf of documents with both hands. He looked uncomfortable, almost hiding behind his papers, creating a clear separation from us. It appeared almost as if he were trying to mask his face while handing down an unpleasant verdict, a routine he may have developed as a way to protect his own humanity over a number of stressful years of handing out bad news.

He looked at us both uncomfortably; then he looked at me. He was quiet and controlled.

"Have you received the final report?" I asked.

"You have Alzheimer's," he said matter-of-factly.

For me now, any question of identity becomes profound and difficult. Without memory you lose the idea of who you are. I am struggling more than ever to find answers to questions of identity. I am flooded with early memories in protected places of my brain

where Alzheimer's does not reign supreme. These memories become the last remnants of my search for who I am.

> —Thomas DeBaggio,
> *Losing My Mind: An Intimate Look*
> *at Life with Alzheimer's*

In these passages from his clinical autobiography, Thomas
DeBaggio conveys the apprehension with which he and his wife, Joyce, received his diagnosis of Alzheimer's Type dementia and the subsequent effects this disease came to have on his experience of identity (DeBaggio 2002).
My argument in this essay is that the human condition rendered by
Alzheimer's dementia challenges much of what characterizes both modern
and postmodern understandings of the self. The experiences of suffering
that Alzheimer's dementia entails can be interpreted through distinctively
Christian understandings of the human self and enrich, as well, these Christian understandings in an empirical theology of our common human condition.

In its early stages, the Alzheimer's disease process most aggressively
destroys nerve cells in the hippocampus, a structure located in the temporal lobes of the cortex in the brain. The hippocampus is very likely the
single most important part of the brain that sustains our ability to encode
and store in memory experiences which have just happened to us, so that
we can recall these experiences and relate them to our consciousness of the
present at future points in time. When this ability is impaired, one suffers a
form of anterograde amnesia. That is, there is a void in memory of events
that have just happened, memory that would ordinarily connect awareness
of the immediate present with impressions of what happened long ago. For
many Alzheimer's patients there is a resulting sense of being cut adrift from
one's immediate past.

These memory deficiencies have identifiable effects on the experience
of self. There is evidence that even well into the middle to late stages of
Alzheimer's dementia persons potentially retain an identifiable experience
of self-identity similar to what one can infer from DeBaggio's reflections.
This marker of self-identity has been referred to by Steven Sabat as a sense
of the "personal present" (Sabat 2001). A century ago William Stern described it as "a natural center from which and toward which everything
pertaining to it extends" (Sabat 2001, 232). It refers to the sense of one's
present experience as an individual in the world, the location, in relation to
the place of embodiment, of one's psychosocial space of beliefs, attitudes,
feelings, and reactions. We may presume that this experience of self is the

reference of the pronoun "I" that DeBaggio expressed when he wrote : "*I am flooded with memories preserved in protected parts of my brain*" (DeBaggio 2002, 42).

The relatively enduring core of self-identity that I've just described provides the base from which persons can measure changes in the other meaningful dimensions of the self. Persons who suffer Alzheimer's dementia frequently describe the most troubling of these changes to be what we might call a breakdown in the narrative unity of their lives. Now lacking their previous abilities to store and recall from memory experiences that have just taken place, gaps open up between the present, the past, and the anticipated future. In the experience of a patient with similar damage to the hippocampus, it was as though "he was awakening each moment for the first time" (Wilson and Wearing 1995). The experience of self tends to be contracted to a "blinkered moment in time." This contradiction may actually drive persons to search for a coherently narrated self in more accessible memories of the distant past. But lacking continuity between these memories and the persons that they are now, it is difficult to know how to relate these episodes to the "personal present" self, other than to translocate the self wholly into these memories so that in recalling them persons may actually become that little girl or little boy once again.

The breakdown in narrative unity of self, along with frequently progressive disorders of spatial perspective that accompany Alzheimer's dementia, make it increasingly difficult to connect intentions with any sustained action. These deficits take a toll on another meaningful dimension of the experience of self, a person's sense of agency. Brain disorders of the kind we are describing erode the sense that one has the power to intend goal-directed action simply through the exercise of the will. DeBaggio (2002) describes the difficulty that these changes caused him when writing his book: "With failing memory it is difficult to write long passages without getting lost in the words. Where does the story go? Why does the pencil tremble? I am often able to write only a sentence or two, enough to sketch what was to be brawny and complex. Do you understand I am not dying, just disappearing before your eyes" (157).

Biographies of persons in the middle stages of dementia contain many examples of failures to initiate action because the persons forgot that a given activity was one that they could perform based on memories of having done so in the past. Even though she had been an accomplished swimmer all of her life, the British philosopher Iris Murdoch's dementia caused her to fear the water and hold back from stepping into it until someone she trusted led her in and her well-preserved procedural memory for swimming took over and allowed her to enjoy it (Bayley 1999). The Dutch-American painter Willem De Kooning became notably lethargic and no longer able to recognize and discuss his artistic identity as his dementia progressed, yet his manner shifted abruptly into an energetic, passionate professionalism when he walked from his kitchen to his adjacent studio. It was largely through his reunion with his estranged wife, Elaine, and her motivating him to get up and walk to his studio that he was able to complete some 341 critically esteemed paintings throughout his illness before his death (Shenk 2001). In persons with advanced dementia, failures of agency are even more comprehensive and profound in their effects and often become the threshold measure for institutionalization when loved ones conclude that these persons simply can't care for themselves any more.

A third dimension of loss, in addition to the breakdown in narrative unity of the self and an eroding sense of agency, lies in damage to one's cognitive representations of self ordinarily related to a number of higher mental processes. Alzheimer's dementia progressively impairs abilities of abstract, operational thinking. These problems are in part related to the inability to compare quickly present events with memories of events in the past in order to determine similarities and differences between them. The loss of cognitive operations also results from the direct effects of eventual damage to the frontal lobes of the cortex that mediate mental functions such as planning, organizing, sequencing, and categorizing. For some patients, these failures of higher order operational processes encourage an increasing paranoia that other persons must be manipulating their possessions because these patients can't remember handling the possessions themselves and can't operationally think their way into the perspective of a neutral observer to conclude that they themselves objectively could have been the only persons to handle these possessions at a specific point in time.[1]

CHALLENGES TO MODERN AND POSTMODERN CONCEPTIONS OF THE SELF

These glimpses of the changes to self that accompany the brain damage associated with Alzheimer's dementia seem most clearly to deliver a blow to the hubris of modern understandings of the self. The person who lives with Alzheimer's dementia can no longer locate her conviction about her self-identity in the functions of her autonomous rationality. "*Cogito ergo sum*," Descartes' rationalist argument for grounding self-identity in abstract, self-reflective thinking, can carry little or no force for this human condition.[2] Nor can one's exercise of agentic will any longer open the way to the discovery of true self, the path that was recommended by romantic transcendentalists such as Emerson and Thoreau.[3]

If Willem De Kooning's considerable exercise of individual creativity in his painting had once provided a center for his identity in his predementia condition, that self-aware creative center steadily dissolved, and in his later years shadows of it only occasionally returned to tease him as a cruel joke. In addition, for most persons who are experiencing early Alzheimer's dementia, the burden of failing work skills and the financial drain of medical bills strip away the possibility of grounding self-identity in one's productivity or financial wealth. In fact, the cruelest irony in contemporary culture may be that many who thought that they had found their identities in the individualism, rationalism, romanticism, and materialism of Western modernity over the past century now find these foundations crumbling beneath them as they enter the journey through dementia at the end of their lives. Dickens's character Ebeneezer Scrooge built his early identity around a singular sense of self-reliance and material gain but was later forced to recognize these commitments as shackles preventing discovery of his true self when he encountered the spirits of Christmas. Similarly, postmodern persons may sense that our culture's prior commitments to self-actualization, financial success, or individualization have separated them from the very resources through which their human identities can be sustained.

If the human condition of dementia forces an existential encounter with the breakdown of all of these grand narratives in the pursuit of self but also reveals that it is impossible to realize certain inescapable moral claims within a wholly postmodern understanding of existence, perhaps we can think of dementia as a distinctively *postmodern disease*. In this respect we can interpret the postmodern condition to bear the inevitable fruit of earlier modern enterprises, even as it marks their dissolution.

Modern empirical science led to developments in medicine that rescued the post–World War II generation from common, sudden, premature death, at ages when we would have been caught up fervently in the modernist visions of that age. Extended life-spans eventually made this generation vulnerable to the slower, self-deconstructing death of Alzheimer's dementia that catches up with us when our lives often have fewer ideologically based supports and many persons have become spiritually weary beyond their years. Today, the burgeoning caseloads of dementia threaten the viability of Western health care systems still strongly biased toward modernist, technological medicine when instead there is now great need for long-term human supportive care. DeBaggio's account of the day he received his Alzheimer's diagnosis conveys his critical reaction to modern medical professionals ill-equipped to offer him the help he needs.

Alzheimer's dementia manifests this postmodern character in contrast with the AIDS epidemic, perhaps the other most visible public health problem today. AIDS is caused by a virus largely transmitted through high-risk human behaviors (promiscuous unprotected sexual intercourse, sharing unsterilized syringes when using certain drugs), which we like to think may be epidemiologically controlled. Such high-risk behaviors correlate with social conditions (poverty, low levels of education) that modernist cultural projects frequently seek to overcome. At least in technologically developed western cultures, AIDS has seemed to present the kind of circumscribed public health problem that fits the parameters of modern bureaucratic, medically informed solutions, although that scenario is now undergoing some change.

But Alzheimer's dementia appears to involve multiple causal processes (genetic, previous brain traumas, certain environmental conditions, the aging process itself) much more perplexing for science to unravel. The causes don't easily map onto the life conditions that modernist cultural projects have sought to redress. Quite the opposite, the causes are related to at least one of the supposed major benefits of modern western technology, our extended life expectancies, and the effects of aging on our human brains.[4] The projected increase in future incidence of Alzheimer's dementia is staggering, expanding from approximately 4 million cases in the United States in 2002 to 15 million by 2050 (Shenk 2001, 31). Even if some effective drug intervention were to be discovered, the implication that the disease carries for human self-identity remains clear: our material human brains that carry the self-identities we know have a time limited warranty under any of the policies that have been received from modernist understandings of life.

The projects of modern medicine have created the possibility of extending human life beyond what the human body would ordinarily bear if all external threats to its functioning (including infectious diseases) were removed. Epidemiologists refer to this extension of life as "manufactured time" (Shenk 2001, 176). We colloquially call it "borrowed time." More than ever, this possibility raises issues about when a community of caregivers should stop manufacturing more time through medical intervention and simply allow a person to die. These situations starkly pose the question of just what defines when a viable human self-identity ceases to exist. Debates about quality of life ensue. When is it morally justifiable to pull the plug of life support? But if it is the case in postmodern culture that the meaning of a viable self-identity can only be decided by the person who experiences it in his or her own unique, local context, and this person can't form or communicate a decision because of progressive dementia, then there simply is no coherent argument through which these moral dilemmas can be resolved.

Much of modern nineteenth and twentieth century psychology celebrated the cult of the individual autonomous self, for example, in the form of positivist epistemologies in psychological science and humanistic, psychoanalytic, and cognitive-behavioral understandings of psychopathology and psychotherapy. In combination with much of the rest of high intellectual and popular culture of this age, psychology affirmed values and meanings regarding human identity that challenged the importance and viability of interpersonal family, community, and ecclesiastical relationships. (E.g., with the influence of televangelism in the Christian tradition even one's eternal salvation has been promoted as a largely personal, individual affair.)

As the ideologies that supported this cult of the autonomous individual self now lose much of their previous power, the institutions that might support a different apprehension of human self-identity are those that have been most weakened by these ideologies and so have become inaccessible to many persons. This is a modern legacy to our postmodern condition. A pervasive loneliness runs deep through much of contemporary Western culture. Research documents that this sense of loneliness is far more prevalent in those cultures that emphasize developing self-identities separate from, or even over against, traditional reference groups such as extended families, for example North American culture, than in those cultures that have continued to emphasize these ties, for example Hispanic culture (Rokeach et al. 2001). Research also indicates that this deep sense of loneliness progressively becomes a greater risk among the elderly in these cultures than in it is among younger age groups (Lehmann 1982). The threat is no more evident than among persons whose Alzheimer's dementia results in removal from their home, family, and familiar life routines. Too few can rely on a strong, enduring network of interpersonal relationships to help bear them up.

Finally, postmodern hermeneutics employ sociohistorical critical methods in order to interpret texts in different contexts of meaning. These approaches argue the possibility of assuming a variety of different voices when constructing and interpreting stories about any sequence of events. For example, in stories about politics and government one may assume the voice of persons who hold established power over institutional processes and decisions, or the voice of persons who passively experience themselves controlled by this exercise of power, or the voice of those who have distanced themselves from these relationships of control.[5] Different contextual orientations support very different stories and construct very different realities for those who assume them.

Applied to one's experience of self-identity, these kinds of polyvocal transpositions lead some theorists to disconnect, or deconstruct, the story about "self" from what might have previously been taken to be the facts of interconnected events in one's past (Anderson 1998; Lifton 1993; Gergen

1991). These transpositions facilitate moving personal present experiences of self-identity fluidly into many possible different stories constructed from fragmentary impressions of specific contexts surrounding one's life.

By separating consciousness of the personal present from memories of an interconnected, receding past, Alzheimer's dementia also makes possible a variety of identity transpositions to different contexts in one's present or one's past. One's experience of self may be reconstructed around television images (e.g., a religious service or political rally) that draw out a well-rehearsed repertoire of responses (singing hymns or shouting slogans) so that one lives at that moment as though one is really there. Or, one may assume the voice one remembers having as a twelve-year old child by reconstructing this identity from a complex of strong impressions in the present (memory fragments relating to childhood, emotional feelings of sadness needing comfort).

The most one can confidently accomplish in these psychological conditions is to enact temporary, micronarrative episodes of assumed identity that may seem like endless awakenings to self-identity for the first time. Just as our individual processes of aging more and more frequently overtake our brain functions and render grand, unifying self-narratives inaccessible in dementia, so postmodernity more and more frequently overtakes our cultural consciousness and renders the possibility of coherent, unifying self-narratives inaccessible and apparently obsolete.

The idea that we can develop a concept of a *postmodern disease* from the symptoms of Alzheimer's dementia may be an interesting one to pursue even further. But in this essay I also want to argue that there are threads of hope running throughout the many experiences of dementia that challenge important aspects of both modern and postmodern interpretations of the self. These experiences increasingly have been recorded in autobiographical/biographical accounts such as Thomas DeBaggio's account of his illness and John Bayley's reflections on his life with Iris Murdoch through the stages of her dementia (Bayley 1999) and have been studied in programs of in-depth interview research such as those done by Tom Kitwood and Steven Sabat (Kitwood 1993; Sabat 2001).

Describing postmodern literary deconstruction of whole narrative texts, Joseph Davis writes that "fragmentation and malleable identities are sometimes championed as a form of personal liberation. Some postmodernists celebrate a self characterized by variation, by change, by flux, by an irony toward life and a free-floating approach to work, ideas, attitudes and feelings. The self is not stable and centered but 'nomadic,' experimenting with and resymbolizing itself, linking disparate identity elements in a constant stream of new combinations." (Davis 2000, 156).

Davis notes that in certain postmodern clinical theory (e.g., Brown 1997) one can even find praise for some persons diagnosed with dissociative identity disorder, also called multiple personality disorder, who have learned to take on different identities in a "creative" fashion (Davis 2000, 156). Such recommendations to continually renarrate one's life assume a richness of narrative material (represented in our memories) and considerable agentic storytelling abilities. The metaphor that comes to mind is that of a wealthy consumer in an upscale Western megastore, a shopper at Nieman Marcus, overwhelmed by an embarrassment of items for purchase, trying each one on for size with no clear sense of what will satisfy. The attitude frequently described in this sort of repeated self-deconstruction and self-reconstruction is that of playfulness, perhaps punctuated by moments of ennui.

These are not the typical experiences that one finds in first-hand accounts of dementia. The assumed riches of narrative agency and creative inventions of multiple meanings (polysemic possibilities of texts) are precisely the resources that dementia has taken away. The story of Alzheimer's disease is more akin to that of a beggar on the street in a third world country who is struggling to find food of any sort to nourish her child. Persons with Alzheimer's dementia more commonly voice their experiences as struggles to regain their hold on something specific about the meaning of their life narratives that is fading away. But just as the image of the beggar seeking bread for her child offers a greater sense of value and real hope about human self-identity than the image of the Nieman Marcus shopper, the sad experiences of Alzheimer's patients and their loved ones carry greater hope than the free play of postmodern storytellers, because they witness to something specific and precious, the loss of which brings genuine suffering. The nature of this suffering lays out some directions for discovering anchors of the human self.

DIRECTIONS FOR REDISCOVERING THE HUMAN SELF

Where do these anchors of the self lie? In dementia each anchor might be identified as a substantial *limit* on the experience of self that, like the limits of gravity or our need for oxygen or food, conveys a reliable sense of who we really are. These limits are closely related to Charles Taylor's idea of the moral claims of "goodness" that we come up against in our lives, claims which define a "space" within which we discover our significant voices and participate in the unfolding of our life stories (Taylor 1989).

The first of these anchors can be found in our physical embodiment. I think that all of us have moments of epiphany when we realize the profound degree to which our physical being defines who we are. I've noticed small such epiphanies during classroom exercises in perception when my students come to realize that they all have a blind spot in their visual fields of which they are unaware and that no amount of exercise of the mind or will can overcome it. Thomas DeBaggio had an epiphany regarding self when he was shown a PET-scan of his brain for the first time revealing the progressive damage to the hippocampus that was causing his memory loss (De Baggio 2002, 175).[6]

He describes how his sense of biological limits grounded his identity in a specific historical life story:

> Here is what life taught me. You can do all the healthy stuff touted as a way to extend your life, and you can believe in the 200-year-old human, but do not forget that you had parents, men and women who were the result of centuries of genetic swapping. Some of those important codes on some of those genes can become damaged. Although it feels light, every morning you wake up with the weight of your genetic history. It is not your fault you have a battered gene that will kill you, but it is your burden now. Smugness in the pursuit of health is a risky attitude. (DeBaggio 2002, 69)

Alzheimer's dementia reveals that the amazing powers of self extension I know in rational thinking, creative storytelling, or technological cyberspace transportations are finally rooted in and vulnerable to injuries to the particular configuration of matter which is my body.

In his book *The Feeling of the Body,* Antonio Damasio argues persuasively that the core of the human self, the self of the "present moment" as we referred to it before, lies not so much in reflective thinking but in our immediate feelings of body limits and physical changes, feelings that are mediated through higher levels of the brain stem (1999). These brain stem structures, including parts of the thalamus, the insula, and the tegmentum, mediate our feelings of changes in such dimensions as body position, body chemistry, and temperature. They also function in mediating experiences of basic emotions, such as fear and joy. Typically, these parts of the brain continue to function throughout most of the course of Alzheimer's dementia up until near the point of the person's death. Cartesian dualism may be redirected here toward an experiential embodied self-monism of "I feel, therefore I am."

The second anchor of self lies in our relationships with other persons. Damasio suggests that the brain stem mechanisms just described actually support a core sense of self-identity by connecting our representations of our own feelings with something beyond our bodies, including the physically limiting contacts that our bodies have with the bodies of other persons. Progressive dementia leaves persons inescapably aware of their dependency on others who care about them and who take care of them. And from this awareness one can recognize that all of the higher cognitive processes through which self has frequently been experienced as "autonomous" are really by nature interpersonal, social processes. So, for example, rational thinking acquires meaning in communities of interpretation; human agency involves acting with, or in response to, or over against other persons; memories are socially influenced representations of the past subject to negotiation with others who experienced those events as well.

Tom Kitwood (1990) proposes that the pathology of Alzheimer's dementia can be better understood as an interpersonal-biological dialectic rather than through the distinctively modern Western medical model of individual disease. Too often the interplay of early changes in memory, agency, and rational processes with social, interpersonal experiences that express modern and postmodern assumptions about the self leads to a downward spiral that diminishes one's experience of personhood.

For example, a person's early loss of some efficacy in performing complex tasks may bring them up against modern cultural expectations that tasks need to be completed efficiently, leading coworkers prematurely to take over the tasks that the person had been performing and create a sense

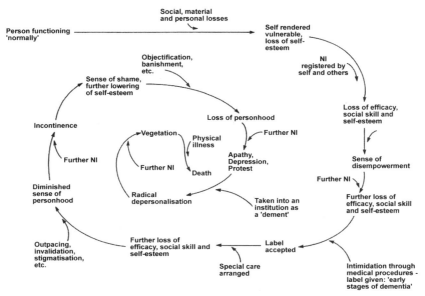

Figure 1. The dementing process. (NI = neurological impairment)

of disempowerment. Changes in a person's social demeanor interact with modern, individualist assumptions that one must be continually evaluated on the basis of individual characteristics (e.g., beauty, intelligence, friendliness), causing the person to become deeply self-conscious and withdraw further from social contacts because of shame. One's early loss of control over certain aspects of daily routine brings great apprehension because of the postmodern fluidity and inconsistency in group relationships, resulting in inevitable reliance on institutional care. Kitwood's representation of this dialectic process is illustrated in figure 1.

On the other hand, Kitwood documents numerous cases in which the consequences of advancing neurological impairments are offset or mitigated by positive person-work carried out by caregivers. To quote Kitwood (1996):

> The holding provided by caregivers is sufficient to enable the person with dementia to tolerate powerful feelings of anxiety or grief; the facilitation of self by others is such that many competencies are at least partially retained; there is enough celebration for life to have joy and meaning. In this kind of way a person is able to "relax into" his or her dementia; although there is anguish and devastating loss, there is an underlying security and well-being. So a different kind of interaction is set up; in a sense the process is more truly dialectical than the first, because it is derived from contradictory rather than mutually reinforcing tendencies. There is no radical loss of personhood. (278)

Kitwood's conclusions are born out by David Snowden's pioneering longitudinal studies of the development of dementia in members of a Roman Catholic religious community, the School Sisters of Notre Dame, a group among whom possible environmental, life-style factors influencing the disease could be readily identified and well controlled (Snowden 2002). The women in this religious community in Wisconsin, many of whom live to advanced ages putting them at increased risk of Alzheimer's dementia, have agreed to a long-term cooperation with Snowden's research by regularly participating in tests of their cognitive functions and willing their brains for medical analysis following their deaths. Thus far, the research confirms the causal role that the neural pathology of Alzheimer's disease (physical changes in the brain) plays in the onset and progression of dementia. However, the studies also indicate the influence of social factors that may enhance a person's ability to sustain a healthy sense of self-identity despite these changes. Snowden describes one exceptional participant in the study, Sister Mary, who remained actively related to others in this closely knit community and continued to function cognitively at a relatively high level until she died at the age of 101 years, despite clear signs of Alzheimer's disease pathology in autopsy samples taken from her brain (Snowden 1997). In this regard it is interesting to note that in the accounts of Thomas DeBaggio's, Iris Murdoch's, and Willem De Kooning's journeys through Alzheimer's dementia it was regular interaction with a devoted, sensitive, continually present spouse that focused and upheld their experiences of valued self-identity throughout the disease.

Those examples of marital support provide a good lead into the discussion of the third anchor of self. This is the experience of love. Sabat's research documents that the ability to express love and to respond with appropriate emotions when love is given to one or when it is withheld is retained long into the course of Alzheimer's dementia (Sabat 2001). The love that persons with dementia realize seems to be a progressively simple form of love. They no longer enjoy realities so much in terms of the complex meanings these realities held for them in the past, but rather as they impinge on one's self in the present moment. De Baggio (2002) analyzes how increasingly living in the personal present intensified his appreciation of the nature of small things in his life and deepened his love for them.

> I am more aware of the world now, the tiny insignificant things. I am beginning to be more childlike. (150)

> I have grown to enjoy the surprises of everyday life and self-discovery it brings. I cling to dirt and watch marvels rise from it. I watch the robin high up in the unused greenhouse, patiently warming her five blue eggs in the fuzz of her feathers. I wait as anxiously as she to see new life. (201)

One of the earliest signs I noticed of my mother's long journey through Alzheimer's dementia was her increased fascination with the particularities of nature, a childlike fascination that allowed her to watch silently a small bird or moving clouds for hours and remark, "Aren't they beautiful?" Later these expressions of simple love took on an even more obviously physical form as Mom would tenderly run her hands across my small boys' faces whenever they visited her. It is this kind of love that sustains one's experience of self-identity despite real suffering, as persons with Alzheimer's dementia develop the sense of increasing separation from realities that are precious and valuable in themselves.

CHRISTIAN INTERPRETATION AND
ENRICHMENT OF CHRISTIAN FAITH

I'd like to conclude by reflecting on three aspects of a Christian understanding of persons that may help us interpret the larger significance of these three anchors of the human self. This interpretation of the significance of anchors of self-identity is echoed in the biblical idea that God has graced all humans with a particular "glory" (II Corinthians 4:17).

Elaborating on C. S. Lewis's exposition of this theme in his book, *The Weight of Glory* (1949), Cornelius Plantinga writes: "Personhood is not an achievement but a given. The same is true of our dignity—the natural weightiness and worthiness of creatures designed to look like God. A person with dignity has a low center of gravity and is hard to topple" (Plantinga 2002, 40). The Christian understanding of the person that I'll summarize can itself be enriched and brought more fully into our own life stories by listening carefully to the voices of persons who have had dementia experiences.

To begin, Alzheimer's dementia reminds us that the Bible pictures humans as thoroughly materially embodied creatures. From the earth we were created and in our natural condition at death to the earth we return (Eccles. 3:20). The present body with all of its potentials is the blessing of our finite existence. When we come up against the brokenness of the body, its decay which can produce not only physical pain but real spiritual suffering as well, we realize that our bodily existence in a fallen creation is also our bane. Human persons (centers of self-identity) properly recognize their creaturely dependence, and in their preserved longings to realize what is genuinely precious and valuable in life, hunger for an eternity which they cannot by themselves achieve.

Such creaturely humility is an important part of knowing our right relationship with God. Our *longing* for eternity rests in the way in which God has made us, an aspect of our glory. Our *hope* of eternity can't be based on anything that we ourselves provide. My understanding of the Genesis account is not that we have souls as something eternal implanted within us, but rather that as the dust of the earth we were made "soulish" in a particular set of relationships with God; and it is God who holds our fragile beings in this existence.[7] Because of his victory over sin and death, Jesus Christ has promised by grace to provide us an eternal existence as particular embodied selves, new creations, in the resurrection. The high regard that God holds for this embodied aspect of our human glory is made clear in the Incarnation—God the Son eternally embodied in identification with our human condition.

The divine relationship through which we are upheld as particular selves in our fragile material existences is the amazingly rich relationship of love by which the persons of the Trinity are bound. Increasingly today, theologians in the confessing traditions of Western Christianity are developing understandings of the three-in-oneness of God that have long been emphasized in Christian traditions of the East. Cornelius Plantinga and Colin Gunton, for instance, interpret the Trinity through a social or community metaphor of God's personhood (Plantinga 1989; Gunton 1997). That is, Father, Son, and Holy Spirit are taken to be "three distinct centers of knowledge, will and action"—three persons (Plantinga 1989, 22).

The oneness of God expresses the inseparable relationship, the communion, among these persons, which the Bible describes as the outcome of their divine, self-giving love (Gunton 1997, 10). In the Bible, the Gospel of John uses the similar Greek words *en* (in) and *hen* (one) to describe the divine internal communion. "According to this concept, each Trinitarian person (Father, Son, Holy Spirit) graciously makes room for the other in his inner life and envelops, or enfolds, that person there. Each is in the other two." (Plantinga 1989, 25) At the highest level, the inner life of the Trinity, this social, interpersonal communion defines what it means to be a person, what it is to experience self-identity.

So, a trinitarian confession that humans have been created in the image of God proposes that we have been created to experience our self-identities in this manner. The anchor of self lies on our inescapable relatedness to other persons through God's provision of enduring, intimate structures of deeply valued relationships, for example, family, friendships, neighborhood communities, the church, even encounters with strangers who provide opportunities for us to express hospitality, relationships in which we can realize self-giving love. Through the work of the Holy Spirit these kinds of relationship witness to and draw us into the reality of God's continuing presence in our lives.

Here is the transcendent dimension of the anchor of love often experienced through dementia. Loving wives, husbands, children, friends, and communities, such as the Sisters of Notre Dame, enfold their diseased loved ones through continuing identity projects: motivating them to engage in familiar actions they can still perform; providing critical cues to fill in the gaps of significant memories from their past; holding and feeding them through sensitive, familiar contact that sustains the core feelings of their own bodies; retelling stories of the enduring spiritual significance of their lives, so that their identities are not forgotten even when they can no longer remember those identities on their own.

Finally, I want to return to the theme of suffering. Here I will borrow insights from the French author Simone Weil and a Christian philosopher who has interpreted her work, Diogenes Allen. Simone Weil describes a form of inexorable suffering that she experienced during her own life. She calls it "affliction." Diogenes Allen (1990) interprets it this way:

> Affliction is not primarily physical suffering; it can be caused by physical suffering, if it is very prolonged or frequent, and affliction has physical effects, such as when one has difficulty breathing at the news of the death of a beloved person. For there to be affliction, there must be some event or events that uproot a life and affect it physically, socially and psychologically. Physical distress keeps the mind fastened on one's affliction, but the source of affliction is primarily social. A person is uprooted from the fabric of social relations, so that he or she no longer accounts for anything. There is social degradation, or at least the fear of it. Even more horrible, psychologically the afflicted person inwardly feels the contempt and disgust which others express toward one who is socially of no account. (198–99)

Affliction describes the suffering of Job; it is also the story of many persons with Alzheimer's dementia. How can one experience the love of God through this seeming loss of value in one's life? Weil believes that God's love is deeply revealed by our drawing very near to the creation in our affliction, by our realizing that we are part of the creation in our intricately organized, fragile, material brains and in our bodies, which establish our inescapable connection to all of creation's other structures. In affliction we draw intimately close to the creation in the way that God is intimately close to it in his moment by moment sustaining power, and with God we feel both the precious value of the creation as God intended it and its estrangement from God.

In these experiences, our suffering can become more than a brute fact of existence for us, it can be at least partially an act in which we submit ourselves, not just to the suffering itself, but to the call God has given us to accept his forgiveness, adopt the mind and heart of Christ, and share in his redemptive love on the cross. Through even small manifestations of that quality of divine love in us we become powerful vehicles of God's presence and our lives open to the hope of the Resurrection and to eternal life. Here lies the weight of glory in which human self-identity is secured.

NOTES

1. Theorists call the ability to assume cognitively an objective other's perspective on one's own behavior a working Theory of Mind. Damage to this ability is associated with other forms of psychopathology in addition to Alzheimer's dementia, e.g. autism.

2. The Cartesian dictum "*cogito ergo sum*," I think therefore I am, is commonly considered a bedrock historic argument supporting a rationalist intellectual tradition that locates self-identity in individual human minds.

3. John Steadman Rice points out that in American romantic transcendentalist literature one realizes her or his self most clearly by willing actions against conventional social expectations which thwart the unfolding of the divine spirit within (Rice, 1999).

4. Although the Alzheimer's disease process is not an inevitable consequence of aging, for every five year increase in age up to age 64 the incidence of dementia triples, then the rates double between ages 65 and 75. By age 85 nearly 50% of all adults are thought to be at risk.

5. See Lyotard, J-F., *The Postmodern Explained*, for elaboration of themes running through postmodern critical interpretation.

6. PET-scans refer to a technique called positron emission tomography which uses radioactive tracers to measure metabolic activity, or lack of activity, across various regions of the brain.

7. This Christian monistic understanding of human personhood recently has been elaborated by theologians such as Jurgen Moltmann in *God in Creation*; by philosophers such as Nancey Murphy in W. Brown, N. Murphy and N. Maloney, *Whatever Happened to the Soul?* and by psychologists such as Malcolm Jeeves in *Human Nature at the Millennium*.

IV. Contemporary Society and the Self

9

Self-Construction through Consumption Activities:

An Analysis and Review of Alternatives

David J. Burns

There is general agreement on the increasingly postmodern nature of much of Western society (Ferguson 1996; Gay 1998). Similar to the
changes experienced in the transition from premodernism to modernism
(see Cummins 1996; Gay 1998; Lyon 1999; Wachtel 1989), the transition
from modernism to postmodernism has involved redefining many of the
fundamental aspects of society (Martin and Sugarman 2000; Gay 1998).
One of the primary consequences of this transition is a change in the nature of the self. The self is "a set of ideas we have about ourselves" (Ornstein
and Carstengen 1991, 491). Changes in the self, therefore, have the potential for far-reaching effects. The aim of this essay is to examine the nature
of the self in today's postmodern society. First, the role of consumption
activities in self-construction is identified. Second, problems with basing
the self on consumption activities are reviewed. Finally, ways that the self
can be "reclaimed" are explored.

THE POSTMODERN SELF AND CONSUMERISM

One of the primary qualities of the postmodern self is a weakening of each
of its historical bases—the family, community, and religion (Fowles 1996;
Langman 1992; Magnet 1987). With the weakening of these historical bases,
a new foundation for the self needs to be developed. Specifically, instead of
being conferred through relatively stable external forces, the self is formed
increasingly through the choices and actions of individuals. In other words,
to a great extent, the self has become something to be achieved or constructed by an individual (Cushman 1995; Dittmar 1992; Wachtel 1989).
One's self, therefore, is no longer dependent on a relatively uncontrollable
external environment encountered by an individual; instead, it is increas-

ingly dependent on the conscious choices of an individual (Cova 1997; Holley 1999).

In a postmodern society, the new foundation of the self is arguably presentation activity (Landy 1993). Presentation is a personal choice through which one's chosen self can be established through displaying it to oneself and to others. The most commonly used channel through which presentation is used to construct one's self is through consumption activities (Brownlie, Saren, Wensley, and Whittington 1999; Dittmar 1992). As Slater (1997) states, "Individuals must, by force of circumstances, choose, construct, maintain, interpret, negotiate, display who they are to be or be seen as, using a bewildering variety of material and symbolic resources" (84). The link between consumption activities, specifically the acquisition of possessions, and the self has been recognized for some time (e.g., Cooley 1902, 1908; James, 1890). (Indeed, even Shakespeare recognized this relationship as did Job—arguably the oldest book in the Bible.) The difference with regard to the postmodern self is one of degree. For many today, consumption activities have become a primary, if not the only, channel for self-construction (Dittmar and Drury 2000; Solomon 1983).

In other words, the consumer culture, characterized by a substantive degree of attention to consumer activities, products, and the idea of materialism, is indicative of postmodern society and is also particularly conducive to self-construction (Fullerton 1998; Hammerslough 2001). In such a consumer culture, material possessions do not merely provide comfort or satisfy physical needs. Instead, they act primarily as tools in the process of self-construction, and only secondarily as a means to satisfy physical needs. Today, this belief is widely accepted: "[K]nowingly or unknowingly, intentionally or unintentionally, we regard possessions as ourselves. . . . That we are what we have is perhaps the most basic and powerful fact of consumer behavior" (Belk 1988, 139). Similarly, Fromm (1976) has said "I am = what I have and what I consume" (27). Indeed, Dittmar (1992) states "we magically acquire a different persona" (2) with the purchase or consumption of different possessions. For many, the self has become a "self-image resulting from the endless displacements and condensations of product images" (Gabriel and Lang, 1995, 87). The importance of consumption activities has increased to such an extent that some suggest that the self today is formed totally through presentation made possible through consumption activities (Brownlie, Saren, Wensley, and Whittington, 1999). As Ferguson (1992) notes,

> The "self" which exists potentially within us, it was held, becomes actual through the process of consumption . . . [and] all consump-

tion becomes conceivable as the desire for, as well as the desire of, the self. . . . We then seek, in consuming such objects (products), to incorporate an idealized self, to make the self more real, and to end the inner despair of not having a self (27, 28).

A key to the role of consumption activity in self-construction involves establishing a point of difference from others: to establish one's self as a distinct, independent entity (Baumeister 1986; Snyder and Fromkin 1980). It is not sufficient merely to "keep up with the Joneses"; instead, it is necessary to be different from the Joneses, or in other words, to possess a self unique from others (Rutherford 1990). Self-construction via consumption then not only concerns the quantity of goods consumed but also the extent to which the goods make "physical visible statements about the hierarchy of values to which their chooser subscribes" (Douglas and Isherwood 1978, 5). As a result, desires are often not for any particular product or quantities of products but for products that are "different" (Baudrillard 1988). Indeed, Reekie (1992) suggests that "[s]hopping appears to have undergone re-skilling, from a management task defined by the shopper's ability to select 'bargains' (or quantity at low cost), to a creative task defined by the shopper's ability to locate unusual, unstandardized, or personalized goods"(190).

If material possessions are integral components of the self, the loss of these possessions should produce an effect similar in kind to the loss of a beloved friend or family member. Such effects have been reported. Goffman (1961), for instance, observed that the loss of possessions encountered when one is institutionalized results in a lessening of the self. Similarly, Rosenblatt, Walsh, and Jackson (1976) observed that theft victims often enter a period of grief not dissimilar to that in response to the loss of a loved one. Donner (1985) noted that a college student stated in response to the theft of her bicycle, "You stole a piece of my life" (31). McLeod (1984) and Erikson (1976) observed similar grieving in response to loss from natural disasters.

This link between consumer behavior and self exists between not only personal belongings and one's view of oneself but also one's views of others: one's perceptions of others is commonly linked to the possessions that others own (Kasser 2002). Csikszentmihalyi (1982), for instance, states that "a person who owns a nice home, a new car, good furniture, the latest appliances, is recognized by others as having passed the test of personhood in our society" (5; see also Kottler 1999). Burroughs, Drews, and Hallman (1991) observed that when given a choice of possessions, behaviors, and social activities of actual students, 84 percent of observers chose possessions as their initial cue when evaluating students' personalities. Furthermore, the observers who based their assessments on possessions produced more accurate assessments than those who used alternative cues. Within a consumer culture, through the avenue of symbolism, consumptive activity has seemingly become the primary avenue through which individuals evaluate their selves and others (Rassuli and Hollander 1986).

Presentation through consumption activities, therefore, appears to be a viable and commonly used means by which individuals construct their selves in an environment where the traditional bases for the self (family, community, and religion) have lost much of their influence.

As implied earlier, the ability of individuals to use consumer behavior to establish or aid in establishing a self lies in the meaning associated with or ascribed to products via symbolism or semiotic communication (Bocock 1993; Elliott 1997). As Shields (1992) notes,

> To the extent that consumption takes on a symbolic role, and the degree to which commodities become valued for the "aura" of symbolic meanings and values than their use or exchange value, we may speak of a qualitative change in the nature of commodity consumption. . . . Mass-produced commodities have reacquired an aura of symbolic values. (99)

Through the symbolic meanings ascribed to them, products have the ability to contribute to the construction of one's self and of the communication of it to others (Dittmar and Drury 2000). In other words, the symbolic meanings ascribed to products operate in both directions—inward toward one's self (self-symbolism) and outward towards others (social-symbolism) (Elliott 1997). Products, therefore, are not only economic commodities, but, through symbolism, products can convey qualities useful for self construction (e.g., Csikszentmihalyi and Rochberg-Halton 1981; Goffman 1951; Levi-Strauss 1965). Dittmar (1992) has stated that consumer goods can be described as "symbols for sale" (2).

Although self-change is facilitated in this reality, the self is also held captive to the changing meanings given to specific products in a given society, to the polysemic quality of commodities of signs (du Gay, Hall, Janes, Mackay, and Negus 1997). Gabriel and Lang (1995) suggest that "free floating signifiers wreak havoc with our individual identities, which are ransacked by wave after wave of semiotic invaders" (88). The meaning bestowed on a product by a consumer is often the result of a relatively complex process by which consumers assign meaning (Holt 1997). A change in the meaning ascribed to products (which can be as simple as a change in fashion) has the ability to change an individual's perception of personal belongings and, as a result, to change that individual's self. When faced with such a change, individuals need to acquire self-appropriate or dispose of self-in-appropriate products to regain their original self. Dellinger (1977) calls the need to replace products at an increasingly fast speed to adapt to the changes in meaning "status pandemonium."

Constructing one's identity through consumption activities affords individuals considerable freedom of self—freedom not typically available when the self is conferred by family, community, and religion (Baumeister 1997). As opposed to a self based on external bases, a self based on consumption activities can be relatively easily adapted or changed at will. Indeed, an individual can often choose between a number of different possible selves (Holley 1999). In order to change one's self, an individual merely needs to change consumption patterns—individuals need only add to or subtract from their accumulation of material goods and/or change their shopping activities.

Individuals today, therefore, are faced with a heretofore unimaginable amount of freedom to select and construct what they would like their selves to be. Such freedom, however, is not without cost.

SELF CONSTRUCTION THROUGH CONSUMPTION ACTIVITIES: THE SHORTCOMINGS

Although constructing one's self via consumption activities can be a very successful undertaking, it is not without pitfalls. Individuals, for instance, find that self-construction becomes an ever-present concern as selfhood becomes linked to a "mall-based allocation of goods and dreams" (Langman 1992, 67). The primary problems with self-construction via consumption activities can be grouped into four categories: the ideal images presented by advertising; the need for adequate resources to engage in self construction; time poverty; and the risk of losing the self while trying to construct the self.

To build or preserve a cohesive self, an individual must place continuing attention on the symbolism conveyed by products. Since such symbolism is transitory, an individual must continually look to outside sources, such as reference groups, to monitor these changes. Although according to traditional reference group theory, reference groups are comprised of actual people (e.g., Festinger 1954), this is not a necessary requirement. In the absence of close, lasting relationships, there is often only one constant in many people's lives—television characters. For some, the relationship with television characters is so strong that they have become surrogate friends or family (Kubey and Csikszentmihalyi 1990). As Langman (1992) notes, "Consumption-based selfhood sees itself as the key figure of a TV program, movie or commercial. Thus the use of a product, driving a _____ car, drinking a _____ beer or wearing _____ clothes brings recognition not only by those in clear view, but by millions of viewers out there in television land" (56).

Of the images and characters presented on television, those depicted in advertising appear to be one of the most powerful and reliable sources of information on the symbolism conveyed by products: "The images used lure us with the promise that we will be a different person—successful, exciting, stunningly attractive, socially well-placed—if only we start to use product X" (Dittmar 1992, 98).

These images, however, tend not to reflect reality, but instead present idealized versions of reality that often bear little resemblance to real life (Pollay 1986b; Richins 1996). They typically present the best in life with all its excitement and zest. The individuals portrayed are usually extraordinarily rich (Belk and Pollay 1985) and beautiful (Richins 1995) and rarely have any shortcomings. Richins (1995) also suggests that advertising images represent edited versions of life—thirty seconds is an insufficient time to permit a complete picture of characters' lives or of their circumstances, so anything boring, mundane, or unpleasant, which are significant components of everyday life, is excluded, often creating the illusion that such experiences are absent from others' lives. Moreover, the sheer prevalence of advertising and the astonishing number of encounters that individuals have with advertising on a daily basis greatly magnifies the power that these ideal images exercise over consumers (Hammerslough 2001; Richins 1996, 1995; Twitchell 1996).

How do consumers process these idealized media images? Richins (1996) suggests that images viewed as negative or below the expectation levels of consumers are dismissed as irrelevant. On the other hand, positively viewed images are more likely to be integrated into one's expectations of what "ought to be." In other words, even though advertising presents consumers idealized attractive images, consumers further interpret the images by accepting only those deemed to be sufficiently positive. The images processed by consumers, then, become even more idealized.

The problems which can result from consistent exposure to the ideals depicted in advertising, therefore, include 1) self-comparisons with the ideal, comparisons which by definition must fall short (Richins 1996), and 2) an upward shifting of consumers' expectations and desires (Hammerslough 2001; Hoch and Loewenstein 1991). Consequently, individuals are likely to find themselves at a significant disadvantage with respect to the ideal portrayals in advertising, which, in turn, leads to negative self assessments (Smith, Diener, and Garonzik 1990). "Fortunately," most advertisements provide the solution to the poor evaluation results—buy their product or buy more of their product. The ideal images provided in advertising, therefore, have the ability to reinforce and exacerbate the perceived need for more products (Duval, Duval, and Mulilis 1992). In the end, individuals are left with images of unreachable ideals that "can lead the receiver to be dissatisfied with the realities of his everyday world—his wife, his friends, his job, even his life itself. Fantasies are a loaded gun. They may sweeten life and advance culture; they may also destroy life in a reckless pursuit of impossible accomplishments" (Toronto School of Theology, 1972, 22).

Need for Resources. The basis of the marketplace and consumer culture is exchange. For a successful exchange to occur, each party must possess something that the other values (Kotler 2000). If the self is based to a large extent on the nature and extent of one's possessions, the establishment or maintenance of the self will require the financial resources necessary to participate in the marketplace. An adequate financial base, therefore, is seemingly essential to the development and maintenance of one's self. Individuals with limited resources, however, often find that they have little to exchange in the marketplace (Alwitt 1995) and thus feel capriciously prevented from constructing a self or having a life because they lack financial resources. Indeed, advertisements become a vivid and constant reminder of their relative poverty (Pollay 1986b). Since the poor and economically disadvantaged actually have more exposure to the media than the rest of society (Xiaoming 1994), the negative effects of the ideal images presented in advertising may be greater for these individuals than for the general population.

Yet since material possessions can come to be viewed as the only tool through which a self can be constructed, many, in addition to the poor, can find themselves suffering from the effects of possessing inadequate resources to achieve the selves desired. Evidence to this effect, including excessive personal debt and increasing bankruptcy rates, increases in property crimes, and intolerance of immigrants and other out-group members, are commonly observed among middle-income individuals (Pollay 1986b; Richins 1995). The resulting jealousy, envy, and strife emanating from this search for a self seems only to make acquiring the desired self more elusive.

Time Poverty. A lack of time is a key quality of the postmodern consumer (Needleman 1991). The desire for a specific self serves as a primary motivator of activities that can enhance income generation, which in turn permits the acquisition of products essential to develop the desired self. As a result, individuals are placing more and more attention on generating income. Consequently, individuals are finding that they possess less and less free time, while they increase the time spent at work and work-related activities. Over the last thirty years, for instance, the amount of time spent by Americans working has risen steadily (Schor 1991). When the time spent at work by all of the members of a family or household is examined, the increase is even greater—the increased percentage of women and children in the job market has led to an explosion of total time invested in work activities by the members of a typical family (Schor 1998; Yount 1997). Earning money to engage in the consumer culture, then, becomes the primary focus of. life with the result that we "have become a 'harried' leisure and working class, frustrated by the demands of consumption on our time and obliged to labour more than we would like to earn the means to consume" (Cross 1993, 1).

It is not only money-producing activities that are devouring the limited time available to consumers—consumption is also a significant depleter of free time (Sarup 1996). First, the act of consumption takes time. Although consumers have altered their shopping habits over the past decade to reduce the amount of time used in this activity (e.g., Laing 1992; Miller 1997; Shoulberg 1998), the activity still takes an average of six hours a week (Hammerslough 2001). Furthermore, many products, once purchased, require significant amounts of time for maintenance and upkeep—so much so that possessions can be regarded at times as "owning" their owner. To recall Weber's (1958) comment, "The care for external goods should lie only on the shoulder of the saint like a light cloak, which can be thrown aside at any moment. But fate decreed that the cloak should become an iron cage"(181).

Losing the Self while Attempting to Find the Self. In the past, when identity was primarily conferred through external channels, most individuals found themselves greatly constrained in the extent to which they were in control over their identities. This scenario forms the basis of several movies based in small, rural towns where young adults are lured by the prospects of the big city where they can "find themselves," "prove themselves," or "be their own persons": in other words, where they can possess increased control over their identities. Yet, is the ability to construct one's self through one's own choices a freeing experience as it is commonly depicted? Some argue no. Cushman (1990) and Vitz (1994), for instance, suggest that the contemporary self, based on choice and consumption, remains empty. Indeed, basing the self on consumption appears to be more enslaving than basing it on traditional means. For instance, Slater (1997) suggests that "Society comes to dominate the individual, not least through the material world of objects and interests, which are essential not merely for meeting needs but for being or finding a self" (83). When one is attempting to construct one's self via consumption activities, the desired self can be sought successfully only through prescribed paths—through those activities that are thought to symbolize or be associated with the identity which is being sought. Many consumption activities, as a result, are controlled to a great extent by the symbolism associated by society with specific products, instead of individuals' own wishes and desires. Indeed, all consumer decisions become "decisions not only about how to act but who we are" (Warde 1994, 881).

Since consumption decisions also bear the weight of identity formation, the risk associated with making an incorrect choice becomes much greater—the risk is finding not only whether one's physical needs are satisfied by the product, but whether the product truly reflects the identity desired by the individual (Beck 1992). The ability to construct one's self, therefore, involves a significant amount of personal responsibility—one must be adept at self-construction. A suboptimal consumer choice can have potentially devastating effects on one's self, particularly "as consumer culture also speeds up and dislocates, through the fashion system, planned obsolescence and so on, any sense of what a 'right choice' might be today as opposed to last week or next week" (Slater 1997, 85–86).

In the end, the self itself becomes a salable commodity (Cushman 1995). It is produced in the marketplace, and it is sold in the marketplace as a means to intimate relationships, social standing, jobs, or a career (Slater 1997; Giddens 1991). Consequently, "In the rush of modern industrial society, and in the attempt to maintain our image as successful persons, we feel that we have lost touch with a deeper, more profound part of our beings. Yet, we feel that we have little time, energy, or cultural support to pursue those areas of life that we know are important" (Dass 1981, 14).

The State of the Self in Postmodern Culture

Although the freedom experienced by individuals in the process of self-construction has undoubtedly provided some benefits while providing for a virtually limitless array of opportunities for marketers, at what costs does this freedom come? While the search for identity has become pervasive in society (Baumeister 1986), the result has been a significant degree of insecurity and uncertainty about who we are (Sarup 1996)—what Elliott and Wattanasuwan (1998) call a "looming state of personal meaningless" (131). Some have even questioned whether a singular self exists for most individuals anymore (Gergen 1991; Holstein and Gubrium 2000). Grodlin and Lindlof (1996), for instance, suggest that as the self becomes multivocal (where individuals possess a number of different selves to be expressed in various settings), individuals find that they no longer have a central core, or a center self—they become decentered. Life no longer is a coherent entity, but a splintered array of different, disconnected spheres. "The historical unity of the image of human self is liquefied and lost in an ethereal play of possibilities and momentary selves" (Young 1992, 141). Ewen (1989) calls this self the "consumable self, the buyable fantasy" (85). The self becomes a "symbolic project" (Thompson 1995), an ongoing activity of using available products to weave a congruent self. As Kottler (1999) notes:

> The final consequence of materialism is the loss of the essential self. Because of the emphasis on external symbols of status and identity, on projecting an image that is defined by what is owned, there is less opportunity for people to face who they are, stripped of trappings. Problems are addressed not by examining underlying issues but by choosing materialistic self-medication (62).

The freedom afforded individuals in self-construction, therefore, comes at a price. Instead of living a life confined within a conferred self, life becomes a process of self-construction and self-maintenance. In other words, *instead of a life imprisoned within a difficult-to-change conferred self with the freedom to operate within that self, life has become trapped in the self-construction process in which the only freedom is the pursuance of the self.* Since the self-construction process is carried out primarily through consumption, the self becomes enslaved to this activity. It becomes enslaved to the offerings, and more importantly, to the images that are associated with the products by marketers (Burns 2001). Freedom is only the freedom to choose the type of images and symbols to be acquired, and individuals are forced to acquire those products consistent with the construction of the selected self-associations determined beforehand by marketers. Indeed, the purchase of products with self-consistent images becomes a primary, or more correctly, *the* primary orientation of one's life—a materialistic lifestyle must be pursued. It would appear, therefore, that instead of providing individuals with increased freedom and autonomy, self construction through consumption acts to enslave individuals to a much greater extent than other bases of the self, namely the historical foundations of family, community, and religion.

RECLAIMING THE SELF

For most, the consumer culture and its accompanying shortcomings are givens, with little thought given to alternatives. In theory, the solutions should be simple—individuals have led lives not dominated by materialism and the market place for millennia. Moreover, individuals have for millennia possessed successful selves not based on consumption activities. To replace consumption activities as the basis for the self, however, can prove to be a very difficult undertaking, "as difficult to carry out as would curing a heroin addict by telling him to stop using the drug and, instead, to do something constructive" (Csikszentmihalyi and Rothberg-Halton 1981, 229). Changes in four areas need to occur.

Work. Benton (1987) believes that the preeminence of consumption in many societies is often the result of the unfulfilling nature of many individuals' work. He proposes that by making work more fulfilling, it can become a successful basis for the self. Although some maintain that the value placed on income and consumption by members of society would correspondingly decline, the facts, however, do not seem to indicate that making work more fulfilling would materially affect the dominance of the consumer culture. Indeed, in Western society, there seems to be little evidence suggesting that a relationship exists between the nature of one's work (whether it is viewed as meaningful and fulfilling or not) and one's reliance on consumption for self-construction.

Marketing. Dholakia, Firat, and Bagozzi (1987) suggest that the process of marketing needs to be rethought and reconceptualized with the objective of changing society. The outcome of redefining marketing would be to change the way business is conducted. The ways suggested to accomplish this reconceptualization include infusing humanistic values into marketing; fostering enlightened, responsible practice, developing holistic and integrative frameworks, and deepening our historical understanding of the discipline and practice of marketing.

Kotler (1987) defines humanistic marketing as

> a management philosophy that takes as its central objective the earning of profit through the enhancement of the customers' long-run well-being. It assumes that: the customer is active and intelligent; seeks satisfaction of both immediate and larger interests; and favors companies that develop products, services, and communications that enrich the customer's life possibilities. (272)

Humanistic marketing in this context must be differentiated from current marketing practice. In current marketing practice, the concept of customer satisfaction is defined as providing customers with products they desire, regardless of the source or nature of these desires (e.g., Kotler 2000; Massnick 1997; Wirtz and Bateson 1999). In contrast, the concept of humanistic marketing embodies a more broad-reaching recognition of the long-term good of customers and of society. It is, therefore, not sufficient merely to produce products that best meet a customers' expressed needs. Instead, it is necessary to demonstrate that the products provide for the long-term good of customers and of society.

Dholakia, Firat, and Bagozzi (1987) suggest, however, that although humanistic marketing may be a profitable endeavor for some businesses, current marketing practice will generally be more profitable. Although there are examples of businesses that have adopted a humanistic approach, there is no evidence that this approach is widely accepted today. Furthermore, since adherence to this philosophy likely involves diminished profits, there seems to be little motivation for many businesses to adopt such an approach. Indeed, pressure from investors for short-term profits may preclude many businesses from pursuing a humanist approach regardless of what management's intentions may be. It would seem that a necessary precondition for the widespread adoption of a humanist marketing orientation is the existence of strong and continuing societal pressure, but such pressure does not presently exist nor is there evidence that it will materially exist in the near future (Miller 1987).

Similarly, although Dholakia, Firat, and Bagozzi (1987) believe that by fostering enlightened, responsible practices amongst marketers "many of the problems attributed to marketing would disappear" (375), it is more likely that this claim is wishful thinking. First, simply encouraging marketers to be more responsible ignores their commitment to the bottom line, the measure by which most are evaluated. Most marketers are not evaluated on the responsiveness displayed toward the true needs of society, especially since there is no societal agreement on what these true needs are.

Possibly even more of a problem, however, is establishing what is responsive or ethical. There exists a wide heterogeneity of opinion when it comes to answering the question "what is ethical?" or "what is responsive?" Indeed, Lewis (1985) suggests that "defining business ethics is like nailing Jell-o to a wall" (377). Each of the primary ethical systems often lead to different, often contradictory, declarations of what is right and what is not (DeGeorge 1990). The lack of a single widely accepted ethical basis or foundation for making business decisions prevents, or at least severely limits, the successful implementation of this recommendation. It is not merely that there is no agreement on minor nuances, but also that different ethical perspectives often generate vastly different, often diametrically opposed, prescriptions.

Developing holistic and integrative frameworks of the effects of marketing activities on individuals and society would unquestionably be a requirement for reconceptualizing marketing. Such frameworks would permit a clear understanding of the effects on individuals and society of marketing activities. All outcomes resulting from individual marketing choices, then, could be seen and evaluated, permitting improved decision-making by marketers. Although attempts have been made to develop holistic and integrative frameworks (e.g., Warren and Burns 2002), their applicability has generally been limited. Since the effects of marketing activities upon individuals and society are far reaching, the complexity of such frameworks often make them unwieldy and difficult to use. The development and use of holistic and integrative frameworks, however, would only provide a foundation for analysis. The frameworks, in and of themselves, would be insufficient to prescribe appropriate actions.

Finally, Dholakia, Firat, and Bagozzi (1987) suggest that a deep understanding of the historical basis of marketing would provide a better understanding of today's environment. Many marketers, for instance, have little understanding of the history associated with the development of marketing. It is commonly assumed that marketing has always existed as a dominant societal force, with the possible exception of communist and other centrally planned societies. The consumer culture is assumed to be the norm and often no alternatives to this philosophy are generally known (Lessnoff 1994). Although there is an increasing awareness of the history of marketing in academic circles, this interest has not affected practitioners.

Knowledge of history, however, merely provides the basis for understanding the present (and possibly predicting the future). This knowledge in itself does not necessarily result in a realization of the optimal or the "right" choices for society today. Such an optimal or "right" choice would necessarily be contingent on a societal agreement on basic personal and societal goals and objectives. There appears to be little evidence that such a consensus can be reached at the present time.

Advertising. Pollay (1986b) suggests that the importance placed on material belongings in a consumer culture can be affected by changing the nature of advertising. Because of its pervasiveness and its singular attention to consumption, advertising, probably more than any other single institution, promotes the philosophy of the consumer culture. As Pollay (1986a) notes, advertising induces us "to keep working in order to keep spending, keeping us on a treadmill, chasing new and improved carrots with no less vigor, even though our basic needs may be well met" (25).

In response, Pollay (1986b) identified seven policy options available to governments to control advertisements:

1. ban or prohibit all or specific forms of advertising;
2. control advertising by state-run organizations that produce, monitor and/or provide clearance for some or all advertising material;

3. impose quotas to limit the total quantity of advertising;
4. impose requirements to determine what advertising is deemed worthy;
5. establish guidelines, policy statements, and councils to provide moral suasion;
6. encourage self-regulatory processes; and
7. do nothing.

Kasser (2002) makes several similar suggestions. Pollay, however, recognizes that it is unlikely that the broad-based public support necessary for governmental action can be developed. Furthermore, the media are not likely to impose changes in the nature or frequency of advertising without outside pressure, since they profit by providing an audience of potential consumers to advertisers (Elgin 1993). Indeed, it is to their advantage to aggressively promote a high-consumption culture.

Thus, it appears that it would be difficult for changes in marketing and advertising alone to structurally lessen the dominance of the consumer culture in the lives of most individuals. Although marketing and advertising have played key roles in the evolution and development of the consumer culture, they do so with tacit or even overt support from society—"consumerism is not forced on us" (Twitchell 1999, 11). Instead, it appears that if changes are to be made, if the emphasis on consumption as the basis for the self is to be lessened, the impetus must come from society itself. History shows that the imposition of alternatives, such as that attempted through the ideology of communism, is doomed to failure. Instead, society itself and the values it supports must change first (Kasser 2002).

Society. Several writers (e.g., Anwal 1994; Frow 1997; Vitz 1998) suggest that such a societal change may have already begun. Specifically, they suggest that postmodernism, and its reliance upon consumption activities as the primary basis of the self, may be drawing to a close. In its place, it has been suggested that a new philosophy, transmodernism, may slowly be gaining adherents (Rushing and Frentz 1995; Vitz 1995, 1998). Transmodernism is important since it may prove to be a way that the self can be reclaimed and restabilized. Specifically, transmodernism marks the birth of

> a spirit of hopefulness; a desire for wisdom; a concern with religions and transcendent spiritual themes; a rediscovery of the importance of truth, beauty, goodness and harmony; a concern with simplicity and the quest for a mature and balanced understanding of experience. It is not so much a spirit of new theories or ideolo-

gies, but an integration of existing valid intellectual approaches, including those from a premodern tradition (Vitz 1998, 113–14).

It can be said that transmodernism involves a reemergence of quasi-archaic values (Cova 1996). Transmodernism, therefore, does not reject all things premodern, modern, or postmodern. Transmodernism holds that the wholesale rejection of everything associated with premodernism in response to the rise of modernism, and the wholesale rejection of everything associated with modernism in response to the rise of postmodernism was not only unnecessary but destructive. The rejection of premodernism, for instance, involved the conscious suppression of much of what it means to be human, such as the relatively permanent basis of the self in family, community, and religion. Transmodernism includes the reestablishment of these historical bases of the self as an alternative to the present consumption-based self.

In essence then, transmodernism marks the return of a measure of stability to the self. Instead of being something solely to be constructed, individuals possess selves because of their very existence—selves are conferred at birth. This is not to say that the self is not open to change or cannot be supplemented if an individual so desires. It does say, however, that the empty self described in much of postmodernism (e.g., Cummins 1996; Jameson 1991) has been addressed. Under transmodernism, individuals are still free to affect their selves to some extent, but they are *affecting* their selves, not constructing them.

Rushing and Frentz (1995) suggest that transmodernism must meet several requirements:

1. place attention on the individual—the sovereign rational subject;
2. recognize that spirituality is an integral part of the self and cannot be denied; and
3. posit a cohesive whole, relatively permanent self.

The idea of the existence of a sovereign rational subject is of modern origin. Within modernism, the individual, specifically the ego, is in control and individualism reigns (as opposed to collectivism, which is dominant in premodernism). Individuals are able to exercise their wills and make choices that can affect their environment. Transmodernism continues with this conception, but not to the same degree. The sovereign rational self exists, but it exists within a relational framework. The relational framework provides the field within which the sovereign rational self can be exercised. Sovereignty of the self, therefore, is not total under transmodernism as it is under modernism. Instead, it is constrained, operating within a framework established externally through relationships, many of which are established by forces under which an individual has little control, such as family.

Throughout the history of humanity, spirituality has played a significant role in individuals' lives. It has only been since the advent of modernism that religion has been regarded as an expendable part of life by a sizable percentage of the population (Berger 1990). Transmodernism posits that spirituality represents an integral part of individuals as it did in premodernism and consistent with the views of depth and transpersonal psychologists (Hartley 1999; Luyckx 1999). Research seems to agree on the importance of spirituality and its resurgence in recent days (Gergen 1991). A recent Gallup poll on spirituality in the United States, for instance, found that 53 percent of respondents say "religious beliefs or spiritual practices will become an increasing force in people's lives in the next 100 years" (Hargrove 2000, B9). Furthermore, nearly two-thirds say that religion and spirituality will "change the way we think," and 81 percent say that it is either likely or very likely that "individuals will experience advancement in religious beliefs or spiritual growth" (Hargrove 2000, B9). Such opinions are clearly in contrast to beliefs held under modernism or postmodernism that regard spirituality as superfluous (Ingram 1997).

In addition to the reintegration of spirituality, transmodernism posits the reinstitution of the ties between the self and society. As under premodernism, where the self is defined primarily through relationships (both spiritual and personal), external familial and societal ties and the resulting relationships play a large role in self-formation under transmodernism. Indeed, Shweder and Bourne (1988) suggest that the self cannot be found or understood apart from its relationships with others. (See also essays in this volume by Bailie, Emerson, Coats, and Vitz.)

In summary, transmodernism gets its name from its ability to transform and transcend other orientations. Transmodernism includes and integrates the key points from each of the other orientations, but within a larger context that acknowledges and includes the necessary interaction between all parts of the self and reality (Ingram 1997). It involves a philosophy of life that is in many ways in direct opposition to that espoused by postmodernism. The cohesive, relatively permanent self is an important, necessary component of a successful and meaningful life—something that is not possible when one's self is merely an amalgamation of symbolism acquired from products purchased.

A transition from a postmodern society to a transmodern society has not yet occurred. The shift from one societal orientation to another takes place over an extended period of time since it necessarily involves major changes in a society's institutions and systems. One such change would involve lessening the importance of the institution of marketing. This change would look similar to the voluntary simplicity movement, which, as expected, is also gaining more adherents (Castro 1991; Crocker 1998). A key to voluntary simplicity is the rejection of the consumer culture and signs and product symbolism through which it operates. Instead, attention is placed on the alternative, traditional bases of the self, namely family, community, and religion. Increased importance is placed on relationships with others and religion as substitutes for consumption. Voluntary simplicity involves avoiding external clutter that is not essential or does not enhance one's relationships with others and/or with God. A key component of voluntary simplicity, therefore, includes investing more time in family and friends and less time generating income and engaging in product acquisition and consumption (Yount 1997).

Interestingly, research indicates that a lifestyle consistent with transmodernism and voluntary simplicity is able to increase one's happiness. This finding is opposite to the popular view that additional income and/or wealth or life in the consumer culture leads to increased happiness (Roper Starch Worldwide 1994). Although most would agree that a larger house, a new car, a better entertainment center, new clothing, air conditioning on a hot summer's day, and the like, would increase their happiness level, research results are not consistent with this contention (Kottler 1999; Myers 2000). Several researchers (e.g., Diener, Sandvik, Seidlitz, and Diener 1993; Myers 1992; Sirgy et al. 1995; Veenhoven 1991) have not observed any evidence that participating in the consumer culture increases one's happiness. Allen observed, "We have no proof that more material goods such as more cars or gadgets has made anyone happier—in fact, the evidence seems to point in the opposite direction" (Packard 1980, 246). Instead, Argyle (1987) and Myers (1992) both observed that friendship, family, and close relationships comprise the only matters that were clearly able to positively affect an individual's happiness. Paradoxically then, within postmodern consumer culture, individuals seemingly sacrifice the only thing that has been shown to lead to happiness (interpersonal relationships) for the sake of obtaining what is believed to lead to happiness (money and belongings), but which cannot deliver (Lane 1994; Pollay 1986b). Transmodernism and voluntary simplicity, therefore, seemingly can deliver the happiness that a postmodern consumer culture cannot. Indeed, voluntary simplicity is "a matter of living which is outwardly more simple and inwardly more rich" (Elgin 1993, 25).

Schwartz (1994) suggests that the acceptance of voluntary simplicity, and ultimately transmodernism, will be based on the force that originally constrained the development of a consumer culture in the first place—religion:

> If as individuals we are too vulnerable and as a nation we are too unresponsive to restrain the influence of the market and change our collective social direction, where else can we turn? A possible candidate, suggested by Tocqueville, is our religious institutions. As he pointed out almost two hundred years ago, it is religious commandments—largely mediated by the family and, within the family, by its women—that rein in the pursuit and abuse of political and economic power. By strengthening our religious institutions, and by strengthening our commitment to participation in those institutions, we might thus be able to reintroduce the language of responsibility and morality into our public life. Membership in religious communities might protect us from the very harsh consequences we would otherwise face if we chose as individuals to reject the pursuit of material wealth as our primary objective in life. (318)

The self is an important individual construct. It is the means by which an individual takes a place in society, and provides a basis for communication with others (Baumeister 1997). Flanagan (1996) states that "If something—if anything, that is—is necessary for a life worth living, it is this: that I develop an identity and that I express it" (5).

It does not appear, however, that consumption activities must completely determine self-construction. Unquestionably, in a postmodern society, consumption represents the primary, if not the only, means for self-construction. Any changes from the supremacy of consumption activities as the primary source of one's self, however, does not seem to be possible if it is to be implemented by the business community. Regardless of any role that marketing may have played in the rise of the use of consumption activities in self construction, it is unable in and of itself to materially change this orientation—any changes must originate in individuals themselves. Given that self-construction via consumption activities appears to have been unable to appreciably improve the qualities of individuals' lives, the possibilities for the introduction of alternative philosophies, such as transmodernism, seems likely. Transmodernism suggests the return to several of the externally oriented, relatively permanent bases (family, community, and religion) for the self as experienced under premodernism. Although any shift to a transmodern orientation will likely take decades to totally manifest itself, evidence exists which suggests that such a shift may have already begun. It appears that the driving force behind a transition to transmodernism is spirituality.

Through transmodernism, the self has the potential to be "reclaimed," where the self is no longer totally dependent on one's own choices and behaviors but becomes a self that can exist in a more stable fashion, permitting individuals to once again focus attention on living their lives instead of constructing them.

10

The Self at the Human/Computer Interface:

A Postmodern Artifact in a Different World

Kent L. Norman

We **come to know things** at points of interaction and change (see the discussion of Bakhtin by Emerson, this volume). This claim seems particularly true with the concept of the self. Indeed the self is so entwined with culture and with the material world that it cannot be understood in its present context without considering transitions in worldviews from modernism to postmodernism and beyond and its immersion in the technology of the day. In turn, our understanding of most things starts from a perspective, a central vantage point, from which we organize the rest of the world. In psychology, this point is the self. From the perspective of the self, we view our world, we relate to other people, and ultimately as Christians, we consider our God. It is this dual and recursive nature of the self as both perspective and object that makes it a most interesting and challenging study.

There are many ways of approaching the self as suggested by the essays of this volume. This essay will focus on the self as it leaves its imprint in the machinery of the human/computer interface as digital artifacts. We will turn to the implications of this interface for the self in light of changes in worldview and perspective, with special reference to technology in the transition from modernism to postmodernism. Finally, I will argue for a reevaluation of the person as a mind/body/spirit unit that is inherently incongruent with the machine.

SETS OF SELVES

First, the enigmatic question: "What is the self?" The concept of the self has long been the topic of philosophy and since the twentieth century the subject of work in clinical and counseling psychology (e.g., Alder, Jung,

Maslow, Rogers), social psychology (e.g., Baumeister 1987), and cognitive psychology (e.g., Snodgrass and Thompson 1997; Bermúdez 1998).

While we use the term "self" to an increasing degree in the world today and we seem to know what it is subjectively, there is little agreement on the formal definition of the term. Instead, it is a multiplicity of conceptualizations. We seem to be at the heart of a very postmodern phenomenon. The self is a set of many perspectives. It is a narrative, a frame, a voice, a situated model. In order to capture the concept, we cannot operationalize it in any one way, but rather must take into account a set of selves, or a polyconceptualized self. Table 1, gives a partial list of such approaches. It is not a question of which conceptualization is correct; all are needed in concert to gain as full an understanding of the self as possible.

The self works as an executive to plan, carry out, and evaluate the activities of the person. It operates from a set of goals to achieve its desired outcomes. Within this conceptualization of the self, research studies it as an agent solving problems and making decisions. The self may also be conceptualized as a repository of attitudes, beliefs, memories, and all that is somehow encoded and internalized in our neural systems. We are very much the product or sum of everything collected and retained. The self is also a

Table 1: Recent Conceptualizations of the Self

CONCEPT OF SELF	REFERENCES	QUESTIONS
Self as an executive (homunculus)	Metacognition (Shiffrin and Atkinson 1969; Flavell 1979)	How does it make plans, evaluate plans, and carry them out?
Self as a repository	Collection of memories, experiences, feelings (Cushman 1990)	What does it hold in its personal storage?
Self as a referent	Point-at-able, relational (Snoddgrass and Thompson 1997)	Where is it? To what is it referring?
Self as an entity	With properties and characteristics (Bermúdez 1998)	What are its specifications?

referent. In thought and conversation, the self is a point-at-able entity. Conceptually, we locate ourselves in time and space. Our language and thought gives reference to our selves and other selves as subjects and objects of activities and relationships. Finally, in this discussion, the self is an entity. It has properties and characteristics like any entity. Some of these are common to all people, some are common to sets of people, and others are totally unique to the individual. These properties and characteristics make the self a fertile subject of cognitive psychology, social psychology, personality theory, and psychometrics.

THE HUMAN/COMPUTER INTERFACE

In order to set the context and focus on the self of the twenty-first century, I shall use the lens of the machine, namely the human/computer interface. The interface allows us to observe something about the self because we leave as it were, the residue of our selves in the artifacts of creative works, our doodles, our preferences, and the chronicles of our actions. In the analog world, we leave our writings and paintings, our arrangements of furniture and flowers and decorations, and so forth, as artifacts of our selves. In the digital world, these are stored documents, our desktops, our preferences files, access codes, and every record of a click and a keystroke. In a sense, we are what we leave in the wake of the flow of life.

Moreover, to an increasing extent, our lives are being lived at and through the human/computer interface. We work, we play, we shop, we socialize at and through the interface. Statistics indicate that 176 million Americans have access to the Internet. The average amount of time people spend on-line per week is 21 hours at work and 9.5 hours at home. We are increasing both the amount and variety of things we do on-line. Our interactions include e-mail and chat sessions, viewing and transmitting still and video images, and sending files back and forth. The Internet and our interactions through it cover nearly the full gamut of human activities, private and public, personal and impersonal. One is hard pressed to think of some area of human endeavor or desire, good or bad, that is not represented and pursued on-line. Although such interactions are not yet uniform across either the whole of society or the whole of a person's life, they are moving rapidly in that direction.

In order to understand the implications of these trends, we need to consider more than exponential increases in computer power and capacity or increases in frequencies and proportions of time spent on-line. First, developments in theories of self and self-consciousness (Lakoff and Johnson 1999; Snodgrass and Thompson 1997; Bermúdez 1998) need to be taken into account as we understand the role of the "user" as an agent immersed in the digital/electronic environment. Second, the prevailing shift from a modern worldview to postmodernism cutting across views of science, technology, culture, and the arts (Natoli and Hutcheon 1998; Powell 1998; Taylor 1989) needs to be taken into consideration to understand a shift in viewpoints and a reframing of roles and values by the self at the human/computer interface.

As technologies mature and permeate the market, they change society. This is particularly true when it comes to computers and the Internet. Older views of the definition and design of the human/computer interface for efficiency, functionality, and usability are giving way to less utilitarian and pragmatic approaches that allow for personal preferences, individuation, and aesthetic design. Rigid, hierarchical, systems approaches to computer design are being deconstructed to yield personal interface spaces.

Moreover, as we interact at and through the human/computer interface, we find a greater need to redefine the "user" and ultimately to remove the term from our lexicon altogether in favor of a multiplicity of roles. Instead, we find ourselves as "selves" at the interface in dialogue with the machine and with others through the machine.

To understand the development of this new self at the human/computer interface, we must turn to the changing worldviews of science, technology, the arts, and culture. The science and technology that gave rise to the modern human/computer interface is rapidly shifting from a modern to a postmodern worldview.

There are many definitions of the interface between the human and machine. Primitive definitions place the interface at the point at which electronic circuits become displays that present information to the human sensory and the point at which motor movements are converted to electronic signals (Card, Moran, and Newell 1983; Norman and Draper 1986). From the physical/mechanical/neural interface, theorists have quickly moved to cognitive conceptions to account for how intentions are mapped to actions and computer output is imbued with meaning (Norman 1991b). Indeed the interface is much more than meets the eye. It includes all of the cognitive processes that lead up to a mouse click on the side of the human and the computations that result in a pattern on the screen which are intended to display information in an active window in front of another window. For the most part, they show the human and the machine at the same level, working side by side interacting through models of each other. On the one side, these models account for how the human understands the operations of the computer by using mental models of the system. On the other side, they account for how the computer anticipates and interprets the actions of the human through models of the user. Both sides engage models that address the self in terms of the conceptualizations listed in Table 1. Each side asks of the other the questions listed in the last column of the table.

Shifting Perspectives

To this point we have begged the question: "Why do we use computers?" The stock answer is to do what we want to do faster, more effectively, more reliably, and better. Computers help us to meet our potential, expand our abilities, and achieve our goals whatever they may be. It has been proposed that human/computer interaction is a synergistic relationship (Licklider 1960) and a multiplicative function (Norman 1991a). The computer multiplies by some factor our human abilities to produce a new enhanced, synergistic performance.

Humans have high-level goals, whether voiced or unvoiced: the need for knowledge, the need for power, the need to travel, and the need to communicate. At the ultimate extreme we would like to be omniscient, omnipotent, and omnipresent. While computers cannot make us gods, they seem to move us in that direction. We can obtain the qualities of quasi niscience, quasi nipotence, and quasi presence that mimic the attributes of God (Norman 1991a). The unfortunate consequence is that when we move God out of the relationship and move the computer side-by-side with ourselves, we lose a sense of vertical orientation and are left with only the horizontal. In the classic worldview, God was at the top, the material world at the bottom, and the human creature somewhere in between.

In the modern view, the human, the machine, and the interface are all physical. All is material. As such, we rely on science, technology, and rational thought. We seek a unified, grand scheme of things, a cognitive science that will hold all things together in one grand framework. Whether framed in evolutionary or reductionistic terms, all is matter interacting with matter. This view leads us to the dissolving of the self into the machine. Figure 1 attempts to diagram this shift in orientation. The classic worldview is shown in phase 1. We view God above ourselves and machines below. Phase 2 removes God from consideration in either an atheistic or a secular worldview. With the orientation of an absolute God missing, the positions of self and machine are unstable and quickly move to the same plane in phase 3. With advances in technology and artificial intelligence, it becomes conceivable in phase 4 that the computer could become superior to the human mind and body. The final phase could go in either of two directions. In phase 5 the human self is eliminated. It may become extinct in some evolutionary transference of life from the carbon-based biological organism to silicone-based digital machines, or the self could be united through the interface with the machine. In this scenario, there is no true distinction between the human mind and the machine. In Ray Kurzweil's book *The Age of Spiritual Machines* (1999), the future is only a question of whether we meld our bodies with the hardware of the machine or whether our selves are transported into the machine as portrayed is such movies as *Lawnmower Man* and *The Thirteenth Floor*.

The driving force behind this progression of phases is not entirely clear. There are however some lines of force. First, technology seems to have an inherent motivation to go one better in terms of speed, efficiency, and quality. Second, while psychology would be well served by a unifying theory, it has become more elusive than ever. We find ourselves on ever shifting sands of empiricism and relativism rather than on the bedrock of theory. In every area, we find a proliferation of microtheory rather than general theory. Finally, cognitive science actually has as its ultimate goal the creation of an artificial intelligence. The purpose of the study of the human self is really to pirate its architecture so as to build a machine in its image. While bolstered by the interests of commercial development, the human/computer interface falls at the dangerous cross roads of conflict

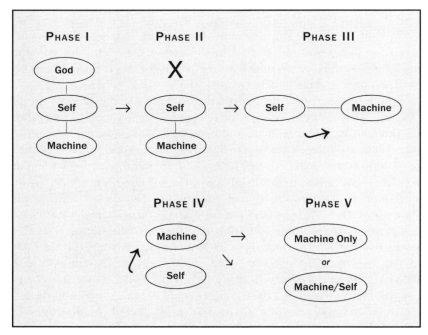

Figure 1: The five phases of the shifting orientation at the interface.

between science and technology, objectivity and subjectivity, and between absolute precepts and relativity.

Modern/Postmodern Views

In order to understand the predicament of our understanding of the self at the human/computer interface, we will turn to the remarkable shift in Western culture from the modern to the postmodern worldview. This change has permeated nearly every area of human life.

While any characterization of modernism will no doubt be a gross oversimplification, its central marks have been a reliance on empirical science, the belief in materialism and rationalism, and the pursuit of individuality. Modernism began with the Renaissance and the Reformation, reached its height at the Enlightenment, and has since then set the standard and paradigm for scientific thinking.

While many people have written about postmodernism in literature, philosophy, and the sciences, it is hard to give it a good definition. In a sense, by its nature it defies definition. It is a critique and a reaction not only to modernism but to itself as well; it involves the deconstruction of ideas; it recognizes the framing of values and perspectives and attempts to step beyond them; and it allows a multiplicity of voices, narratives, and performances (Hassan 1987; Natoli and Hutcheon 1998; Powell 1998).

With persuasive authors and a broad audience, postmodernism has moved into many spheres of human activity and thought. Its influence is seen in contemporary art, literature, and the media as well as in science and technology. As the effects of postmodernism permeate the thought and activities of individuals and society and as the human/computer interface is extended across those activities, we experience a collision of two waves. The current human/computer interface is in a state of flux. It was the creation of modern systems engineers and interface designers; and today it is the mutant product of postmodern user modification.

The shift from modernism to postmodernism can be seen in a number of changes in computer science and particularly at the interface where the machine overlaps with human thought and activity. A number of the distinctions between modernism and postmodernism map to analogous shifts in human/computer interaction. As a guide, I will use parts of a table provided by Hassan (1987). Table 2 shows the terms identified by Hassan for modernism and postmodernism in the middle two columns. The left-most column lists instantiations of modernism and the rightmost column instantiations of postmodernism in the human/computer interface. These two columns are the result of my own work (Norman 2001).

Table 2: Contrasting terms in modernism and postmodernism with side instantiations in the human/computer interface

Modern Instantiation (Norman 2001)	Modernism 1945–80 (Hassan 1987)	Postmodernism 1975– (Hassan 1987)	Postmodern Instantiation (Norman 2001)
Top/down stepwise refinement in programming and in system architecture	Vertical	Horizontal	Object-oriented programming, communities of software agents[1]
Hierarchical menu selection systems, Hierarchical structured databases	Hierarchy	Anarchy	Hypertext, World Wide Web
Text, Icons	Symbolism	Dadaism	Backgrounds,[2] Negative spaces[3]
Productivity Utility/ functionality	Purpose	Play	Games/Entertainment Edutainment
Systems approach	Design	Chance	Opportunistic/ Serendipity
Text, audio, graphics, video	Form (Conjunctive, Closed)	Antiform (Disjunctive, Open)	Digital code Quicktime[4]
Expert-novice user distinction	Mastery/Logos	Exhaustion/Silence	Consumers, audience
Product release Versions	Art Object/Finished Work	Process/Performance/ Happening	Beta testing[5] Continuous versioning[6]
Non-invasive: Clear separation of user and computer, separated by interface code, mouse, keybd.	Distance	Participation	Invasive: Blurred distinction of where the human ends and the machine begins Neural implant
Packages, bundles, Software suites	Creation/Totalization	Decreation/ Deconstruction	Viruses, Pirating

Table 2 (cont'd)			
User-Centered Design Mainframe, Client/server	Centering	Dispersal	Community, stand alones,[7] personal pages, My whatever[8]
HyperText/ Embedded Menus	Hypotaxis	Parataxis	Jumpstations[9] Webliographies
"Works like" explanations	Metaphor	Metonymy	Graphical user interface objects[10]
Single task/ Single windows	Selection	Combination	Multitask/ Multiple windows
Server/Download	Root/Depth	Rhizome/Surface	Node/Network Napster, Limewire[11]
Consistency/ Single mode	Narrative/ Grande Histoire	Anti-narrative/ Petite Histoire	Insistency/Situational/Contextualized
One language/One OS/One platform	Master Code	Idiolect	Portability/Platform independence[12]
Predictable, expectedoutcomes/ results	Determinancy	Indeterminancy	Unpredictable, Unexpected outcomes/results
(Human)/(Computer)	Transcendence	Immanence	(Human-Computer)

The modern view of the interface, and for that matter all computer hardware and software, was hierarchical. Programmers were taught to generate code in a process of top-down, stepwise refinement (e.g., Fortran, Cobal, C). The function of the main program was broken into subroutines and subroutines within the subroutines. It was vertical. In contrast, the postmodern orientation is horizontal. Today programmers are taught object-oriented languages (e.g., C++, Java). Programs are composed of communities of programs, routines, and objects that talk to each other. There is little or no hierarchy in their network. They are often at the same level and even their order of occurrence in the code is irrelevant.

In the modern world, there was an ethic that what we do should have purpose, utility, function, and count for something. Consequently, interfaces should support work and personal productivity. The proliferation of personal productivity software on PDAs (personal digital assistants) was a product of this trend. In the postmodern world, play, entertainment, and just doing something for the fun of it are valid activities. In the postmodern software bundle, solitaire is installed with every Windows system and a tile puzzle with every Mac.

In the modern era, usability testing sought to craft a user interface that would be efficient, require minimal time, and be easy to learn, meaningful, and free of errors. Nearly every software corporation opened up a usability-testing lab to record task performance time and user errors, while focus groups helped to reveal user frustrations and the need for additional program functionality.

During modernism, standardization was the key and efficiency was the lock. Computers were impersonal, colorless (putty or beige), and all alike. While screen savers started as utilities to prolong the life of monitors and reduce energy consumption, they evolved in the postmodern world to make a statement with a splash of color and beauty. While the modern world established an individuality based on purpose, the postmodern world embraces a different kind of individuality based on arbitrary preference. Consequently, the postmodern Mac came in six colors to choose from with endless options to set the personal appearance of the interface and the preferences of the user.

Computer scientists such as Shneiderman in his book *Leonardo's Laptop* (2002) are well aware of the change from "old computing" focused on the machine to "new computing" in pursuit of human goals and values. Central to the new computing of postmodernism is the self. The self is the center of the model of the computer user. All of the conceptualizations of the self in Table 1 are in some way instantiated in the "new computing" and its digital code. The self is an agent in network gaming and a buddy in chat rooms. The self is a set of internalized values, encoded in preference files, user profiles, and transmitted via "cookies" on the World Wide Web. The self is a referent. It is an e-mail address; it is the URL of a personal Web page; it is an avatar in a chat room (Suler 1996).

Who we are is determined in a number of ways. The first and foremost is our genetic identity coded in our DNA (hardcode). The second is the encoded information from the environment stored as memory. Finally, we have our own positioning of individuality and identity. Our selves are embodied, but we also create external identity by selecting user names, screen names, and avatars, publicly and privately through passwords. Passwords are our inner, secret identities.

In many ways, the postmodern interface is used to enhance the self. The self is augmented at the human/computer interface with a new shot of digital, synergistic, global relationship. The digitally connected self is everything and everywhere.

Moreover, there is a strong movement to install intelligent agents at the human/computer interface as wizards, personal agents, and assistants. Some take a very modern view that agents should not usurp control from the user (Shneiderman 1998). Agents should inform the user of their actions. They should not be anthropomorphic. There is no utility behind portraying agents as human. But the postmodern view embraces intelligent agents as both playful simulations and serious voices at the human/computer interface. In this view, the machine is more than an extension of the self; the self indwells the interface.

A DIFFERENT WORLD

As postmodernism runs its course and the events of history have their turn, we find ourselves in a different world. The question is how it will affect the self and our conceptual notion of the self. My fear is that as the line of the human/computer interface elevates the machine to the level of an idol, the self will become more like the machine than the converse. Then the words of the Psalmist take on a new meaning, "The idols of the nations are silver and gold, made by the hands of men. They have mouths, but cannot speak, eyes, but they cannot see; they have ears, but cannot hear, nor is there breath in their mouths. Those who make them will be like them and so will all who trust in them" (Ps. 139:15–18).

To avoid such a fatality, two things are required. First, we must resist the tendency to deify or to even humanize the computer. Simply put, machines are machines. There is no need to stifle research and development in artificial intelligence. We need only remember that no matter how intelligent a machine is, it is still only a machine and nothing more. It has no soul; it has no rights; it is only a machine. Pinnochio and the movie *A.I. Artificial Intelligence* are engaging fantasy stories, not reality. Kurzweil's (1999) vision of a melding of the human and the machine is not just science fiction; it is philosophically illogical (Stalder 2000).

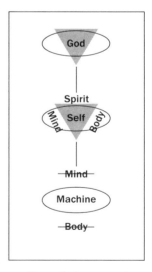

Figure 2: A geometric congruence with the Triune Godhead and the human personal and incongruence with the machine.

Second, we must view the self as more than a mere, symbol-processing agent. If nothing else, the self is embodied in a very analog body and its complexity exceeds by many orders of magnitude any conceivable digital model of it. Still as Christians, we must assert there is more to the self than listed in Table 1. The self is not only more than the sum of its parts; it is more than itself. It includes its relationships with others and with God himself. Yes, there is an embodied self, instantiated in the world, navigating the analog and digital worlds; but more importantly, this is a self that is an agent of pure freewill and the object of God's love. Thus, if technology is the defining point of the self, we are lost. If God is the defining point of the self, then he also provides the model. From the Trinity and its analog, we see the trifold concept of mind, body, and a spirit. Figure 2 attempts to illustrate graphically the geometric congruence between God and the human person and the incongruence with the machine. In our study of the self and technology, we must maintain these distinctions. While a computer is a material object and according to some, may even have a mind, it does not have spirit. "Flesh gives birth to flesh but the Spirit gives birth to spirit" (John 3:6). Thus, there is congruence and a true connection between God and the self, but not between the machine and the self for the human spirit is unable to birth spirit into the machine.

As a postnote, in the modern world, psychology has been quite fearful about the spiritual and, consequently, excluded theology from its conceptual world. The most radical form has been behaviorism. Over time in pursuit of a more complete description of cognition, ideas of self and consciousness have reemerged. Still, without God, the puzzle of science will never be complete. We study the tessera but not the mosaic. Analogous to the letter tile puzzle, we shift the letters in one limited space to make sense, but it doesn't work with the rest. Even in the postmodern world, to allow God back into the mix of science at secular universities is inconceivable, thus limiting us to a minutia of knowledge, the most empirical, focused areas of science and depriving us of grand, unifying theories. Consequently, in the area of self and technology, while the questions and issues will be addressed by the secular world, the answers will come from Christian scholarship.

NOTES

1. Sets of artificial intelligence programs with different functions that "talk" to each other by exchanging information.
2. Patterns or wall paper used on computer screens and Web pages.
3. Empty space on the computer screen.
4. An application that displays videos on the computer screen.
5. Field testing of computer programs prior to their commercial release.
6. Software updated continuously via the World Wide Web rather than released in discrete versions.
7. Computers not connected to a network running programs that do not rely on shared data.
8. Programs marketed to personal lifestyles
9. Web sites that provide links to jump to other Web sites.
10. Images on screen that look and act like buttons, sliders, containers, etc. and make the computer easier to use.
11. A program with an associated Web server that was used for sharing mp3 music files between users.
12. The idea that a program can run on any computer independent of the hardware and the operating system.

11

Technology and the Self: Approaching the Transmodern

John Bechtold

But their idols are silver and gold,
made by the hands of men.
They have mouths, but cannot speak,
eyes, but cannot see;
they have ears, but cannot hear,
noses, but they cannot smell;
they have hands, but cannot feel,
feet, but cannot walk;
nor can they utter a sound with their throats.
Those who make them will be like them,
and so will all who trust in them.

Ps. 115:4-8

David Noble, in *The Religion of Technology* (1999), states that "modern technology and modern faith are neither complements nor opposites, nor do they represent succeeding stages of human development. They are merged, and always have been, the technological enterprise being, at the same time, an essentially religious endeavor" (4–5). Noble echoes the sentiment of the Psalmist, reflecting the faith humankind places in its own accomplishments. Likewise, Marshall McLuhan (1964) a generation earlier, commented on these same verses: "The Psalmist insists that the beholding of *idols*, or the use of technology, conforms men to them" (55). As these authors suggest, technology has long been recognized as both a powerful extension of the self and as something worthy of human emulation. But such imitation is not on a material level. We can't transmit ourselves over telephone wires, nor can we project ourselves onto television screens, but we do aspire to the godlike qualities that technology approximates. These classical godlike attributes of omnipresence, omnipotence, and omniscience

are qualities that are reflected in much of our present-day technologies under the guise of technology's pervasiveness, its efficiency and autonomy,
and its vast amount of data touted as knowledge. As we consider technology in light of the Psalm, we will explore technology's godlike qualities
and consider what those qualities mean in terms of the self that experiences them, for the self emulates technology by exaggerating human qualities of presence, efficiency and autonomy, and knowledge. As we will see,
humankind is at an important crossroads between the postmodern, or in
technological terms the hypermodern, and the transmodern, a proposed or
predicted historic and social period that takes the basic positive contributions of the modern and transforms them, often by putting them in a new
context. Transmodernity also involves a significant transcendent element,
whether that be religious, spiritual, or idealistic (see Vitz, "From the Modern and Postmodern Selves to the Transmodern Self," in this volume).

TECHNOLOGY'S PERVASIVENESS

While technology (i.e., human invention) has been around for thousands
of years, most of that technology has been simple and specific to a certain
task. Historically, technology was initially implemented to aid humanity in
its relationship to the natural world. Technology, as reflected in human tools,
amplified human abilities and made their work easier to accomplish
(Schuurman 1995). This was largely true up to the industrial revolution
and the twentieth century advances in science. Coping and adapting to nature, then, gave way to controlling and recreating nature. From that point
on, technology not only began to dominate nature but also to replace it
and to control and fabricate what were seen as natural processes and materials. What marks modern day technologies as significantly different from
the past are their complexity and lack of specialization, which has resulted
in modern technology's pervasiveness.

For example, mobile phones were first introduced in the 1960s. By
today's standards, they were fairly simple and were largely reserved for
emergency personnel. Now, current cell phone technology enables an ever
expanding population of users to call, check weather and stock reports,
find locations via maps and Global Positioning Satellites (GPS), and send
and receive digital photographs. In remote and rural locales, especially in
developing countries, cell phones conveniently appear where no telephone
lines can economically go. As cell phones become ubiquitous, they contribute to what Neil Postman (1993) calls a technopoly, a culture in which
all aspects of life submit to the domination of technology and technique.
Technology becomes the "ground" for most if not all human and cultural

activities, so much so that the technologically "unnatural" seems "natural."

Consider for instance, the environment conducive for "natural" conversations. Historically, the town well was a site where persons conversed about the events of the day and caught up with family and friends. In the more recent past, the "watering hole" might have been the office water fountain or coffee machine. Now such "conversations" occur via instant messenger, which enables the worker to carry on "conversations" while multitasking other activities. The mere presence of technology seems to have a socially sanctioned expectation that we use it more and more. Cell towers and satellite dishes are constant reminders that one can be "connected" anywhere. "Smart" houses, "smart" cars, "smart" businesses, and "smart" bombs ensure that the technological invasion will continue to the saturation point of our daily lives.

TECHNOLOGY'S EFFICIENCY AND AUTONOMY

Clearly an essential quality of technology is efficiency. This quality represents the cultural values of precision as well as the economy of time, effort, and money (Winner 1986), but the efficiency of many modern technologies seems to have no boundaries. Computers are an obvious example. Computers over the past fifty years have gotten about 70 million times cheaper and computing costs have halved essentially every eighteen months (Rawlins 1998). All the while, the ability of computers to do more and more things increases. "Every year, size, energy needs, waste heat, and costs drop, while speed, power, reliability, yields, sales, expertise, and complexity rise. It's hard to grasp what such a rate of change can do because we're not used to it in everyday life. We're used to things that increase slowly" (Rawlins 1998, 121). And yet things that increase slowly are disappearing from the two environments in which we spend much of our lives—education and business.

Technology in the classroom was once considered a threat and an intrusion on the teaching abilities of the teacher (Benjamin 1988), but now it is embraced as a necessary part of nearly every aspect of the curriculum, making for a more efficient and autonomous classroom. Individualized instruction via the computer can occur simultaneously while the teacher gives group instructions, students in junior high no longer take "typing" but "keyboard" monitored by automatic programs, and senior high students surf the net, send instant messages, and access databases as naturally as students of the past tuned their transistor radios. Combine the pervasiveness of technology with its efficient and autonomous use in the classroom and you get youth well prepared to ride the crest of technology's wave into the future.

Coupled with technology's efficiency and display of power through efficiency is technology's autonomy, or display of power through its own apparent self-sufficiency. Egbert Schuurman (1995), summarizing observations made by Jacques Ellul, states that one of the most important characteristics of modern technology is its autonomy: "For Ellul this means that technology becomes a world of its own, subordinating everything to itself and putting its mark on it. This all-pervasive technology will become so influential that people will subject themselves to it with the reverence of a religion" (34). Autonomous technology is complex technology. It gives the appearance of running on its own, without any sense of a "programmer" or "technician" behind it.

Furthermore, the business environment is constantly changing as a result of increasing technological efficiency and autonomy. In the past, businesses and labor were constrained by the capability of individual workers to keep account, deliver goods and services, create and sell products, and transact in person; such activities would be called human labor intensive. The extent of such human labor, however, has been progressively reduced as a result of technology, for "what once took 100,000 hours of work to accomplish in the mid twentieth century, can now be completed in just 10,000 hours thanks to technology. And in the next generation, that work will be completed in a mere 1,000 hours" (Harrison and Klein 1995). The more technology in business, the more efficient and autonomous that business becomes. And the more efficient and autonomous, the more power is exercised over both human and material capital.

TECHNOLOGY'S KNOWLEDGE

It is no wonder that one of the descriptors of our modern and postmodern world is "the age of information." It is also no wonder that behind many of our solutions to problems is the phrase muttered under our breaths and spoken in the back of our minds, "We have the technology!" (Or if we don't have it, we soon *will have* the technology.) Technology seems to be the answer to all of our problems, and those who understand and control technology have the answers. Mere literacy, the ability to read and write, is no longer the measure of an educated person. Rather to be computer literate, media literate, and technologically literate are the standards of value for most individuals today. With information increasing at a phenomenal rate, there is essentially only one way to manage it, and that is through technology. And only those who are technologically literate will be able to find—and control—that.

Sven Birkerts (1994), writing on the demise of the printed text, suggests that libraries will soon be no more than museums, since most of the information people need will be directly accessible from computer terminals. Books, newspapers, and academic journals are now available in a digital form and the advantage of electronic books from an economic standpoint is remarkable. From the reduction of printing, storage, and distribution costs, to the increase in accessibility, permanence, and revisions, electronic media will transform text as much as the Gutenberg press transformed text in the fifteenth century (Rawlins 1996).

However, knowledge acquired through digital text is only one way in which information is shared via technology. When the visual component is taken into consideration, even more possibilities are accessible. Virtual reality, telepresence, and remote presence are all ways of knowing available through technology (Heim 1993). These sources are more than just informative in the way a National Geographic Special informs about polar bears. These sources provide experiences of knowing that approximate real experiences in significant ways. And these are the ways that truly highlight the godlike qualities of omnipresence, omnipotence, and omniscience. For example, virtual reality can create a sensory immersion into a virtual world (Heim 1993). A person who suffers from acrophobia can be submerged into a virtual reality display that mimics a high and lofty place. Through repeated exposures to gradually increasing virtual heights, a person can learn to overcome the fear through various relaxation techniques associated with the virtual environments. No real environment associated with the fear need ever be experienced, yet the fear can be extinguished. The person can experience multiple virtual "places," experience control and power over the situation appropriate to his or her abilities to cope, and experience the "knowledge" that comes with overcoming that fear—all brought about through the powers of technology. Hence, the omniscient quality of technology lies not in some assumed consciousness on the part of the technological "hardware," but in its power to hold the raw data of knowledge and experience for anyone's use and manipulation.

And herein lies the danger that technology's pervasiveness, efficiency and autonomy, and knowledge, all of which imitate the classical attributes of God, will tempt us to substitute technology for God, turning it into an idol.

The Reflexive Nature of the Self

The verses from the Psalms cited at the beginning of this chapter suggest that those who create the idols that can neither see nor hear become like them. This idea resonates with the essays of Gil Bailie and David Burns in this volume. For Bailie it is in mimetic desire, the imitating of the other, that one knows oneself as a person. For Burns, it is the identification with consumer products that aids in defining the self. I refer to these aspects of human perceptions as a person's *reflexive nature*; that is, people tend to perceive themselves as like those things that they worship or see as having power in their lives. These perceptions are not always conscious, nor are they always responses to attributes others may see as most prominent, yet they have influence over the individual. In contrast to Bailie's emphasis on mimetic desire, a human's reflexive nature can reflect inanimate objects as well as other persons, and in contrast to Burns, the reflexive quality of humans operates on a deeper level than that of mere identification with the status of certain consumer goods.

Langdon Winner (1986) suggests that the tool-like qualities of many technologies, as they become woven into the fabric of everyday life, are incorporated more or less into our very humanity. Or as Rawlins (1996) puts it, "Once we start using a tool extensively, it also starts using us . . . . Ultimately it may change how we view reality itself" (24). Our reflexive nature suggests that what we see in technology we eventually begin to see in ourselves and we then identify with it in more subtle ways. For example, McLuhan (1964) observed the transformation that occurred in the workplace with the introduction of the typewriter. It provided a certain status, especially for women, as the typist became "a style-maker who was also eager to follow styles" (228). But more importantly, for poets and authors it became a way to transform language and literature and "indeed, the very mental habits, themselves, of writers" (228). For poets, McLuhan notes, the typewriter became the "mimetic instrument" that allowed them to imitate the "colloquial freedom of the world of jazz and ragtime" (230).

The typewriter also changed our view of the office worker. There was a time that office conduct transited from handwriting to manual and then to electric typewriters (as if they were no longer manual) and the efficiency of office work increased. Such efficiency, being highly valued, transformed the perception of the office with electric typewriters as a more efficient office than those without them. However, Winner's point is not that technology merely becomes more efficient, but that such expectations of efficiency become incorporated into our own existence and we begin to expect the efficiency of technology to be present in ourselves, or at least in others. Not only was the electric typewriter more efficient than the manual one, but it became a centerpiece for a more efficient office and the extension of an efficient person. We looked in the "modern" office of the day and said, "My, aren't your workers efficient?" instead of, "My, aren't your typewriters efficient?" In fact, identifying the worker as efficient became a valued label. The value placed on technology quickly became the value placed on ourselves. This is the reflexive nature of humans, to see reflected in technology an image of ourselves.

If we see technology reflected in ourselves, its marvels are also seen as a way to transcend much of our human existence, hence providing a certain kind of power to be sought after and worshiped. Technology promises much, and to a culture that defines progress largely in terms of the material and the cognitive (Swenson 1992), technology becomes a worthy object of faith. Although most would be hard pressed to consider the worship of technology as a bonafide religion, it still appeals to many as providing a means to improve the self. I propose that of the many ways technology effects the self, due to the human's reflexive nature and in accordance with technology's characteristics, three are most important: I call them "hyperpresence," "hyperefficiency and hyperautonomy," and "hyperknowledge," where the prefix signals an exaggerated quality.

Hyperpresence. Although hyperpresence cannot make us omnipresent, it offers us the next best thing. Hyperpresence is an exaggerated sense that we have been in at least two places at once. Sherry Turkle in *Life on the Screen: Identity in the Age of the Internet* (1995), writes that "today people are embracing the notion that computers may extend an individual's physical presence. Some people use computers to extend their physical presence via real-time video links and shared virtual conference rooms. Some use computer mediated screen communication for sexual encounters" (20). Any one individual can by way of a Web page present information about himself or herself to thousands simultaneously, twenty-four hours a day. This Web page can contain textual information, pictures, animation, sound, connections to other areas of personal interest, and even real time pictures of a person's activities by way of a Web cam. Of course, it is not really "you" in the fullest sense, that is presented, but the simulacrum is convincing. In addition, real time conversations can be conducted with the people next door or on the other side of the world. Video and teleconferencing extend such capabilities even further.

Furthermore, information technologies, with powerful search capacities, allow endless discoveries at the click of a mouse. Such "engines" search through vast databases in a matter of seconds, bypassing a tedious and time-consuming linear search from source to source in a library to look in parallel fashion through many databases simultaneously.

But even more astounding than the "connected" and networked hyperpresence, is the potential one has with going "wireless." At my daughter's fifth grade music performance at the state capitol in its rotunda, she and her classmates, surrounded by many proud parents and our state representative, sang and played to the delight of all. However, standing near me, a proud father of one of Hannah's classmates could not be "joined" by his wife—at least not physically—but there he was, with cell phone out-stretched, giving the unavailable mom the sense of being there as well. Cel-lular and satellite communications can put stock information, baseball scores, and your present location via a Global Positioning Satellite (GPS) all in the palm of your hand. That same hand can hold technology allow-ing anyone with the right means to reach you anywhere as well, creating a tremendous sense of hyperpresence.

Indeed, we need not be bound by reality at all. Again, Turkle describes how computer users can create and "inhabit" alternate cyberworlds called Multi-User Domains (MUDs) and by so doing create and recreate them-selves. They can "exist" in several MUDs at once and through the course of a day find themselves "cycling through" the real world and several virtual worlds. Gender surfing and other forms of identity experimentation allow a person not only to "be" at another place at the same time, but also to be someone else in the process. Gender surfing allows a person to play a dif-ferent role and have others respond to that role via chat rooms and e-mails and Instant Messenger.

Even the television remote provides a sense of hyperpresence. Whereas once we had to get up out of our seat to change a channel, we now do it "remotely." Furthermore, remote abilities have been extended from the tele-vision, to movements and interactions in virtual worlds by way of elec-tronic headsets that monitor our head movements, gloves which allow us to "pick up" things in a virtual or remote room, and whole body suits that allow us to move around in remote and virtual rooms. The possibilities of being in more than one place at the same time as broad as the imagination, and it is an all-pervasive technology that gives us such hyperpresence.

Hyperefficiency and Hyperautonomy. One of the characteristics that seems to distinguish many Americans is their rugged individualist mental-ity and their valuing of autonomy and freedom. It is no wonder that the reflexive nature of humans should likewise perceive technology as granting them omnipotence in the guise of efficiency and autonomy.

Hyperefficiency is the exaggerated sense that we are operating at our highest capacity, and its consequences can be far reaching. The postmodern primary classroom buzzes. Students no longer sit in rows. Multiple activi-ties occur throughout the classroom at different times, with students work-ing at computers at their own pace and receiving immediate feedback and encouragement. Students and teachers seem to have become hyperefficient. But that is not all; the cyberclassroom has taken a quantum leap in educa-tional efficiency. Students can now learn at home, connected to other students and teachers in remote sites from all over the world. Such distance learning is no longer reserved for colleges and universities. Although, in looking at such educational uses of technology, typically the efficiency of the process is not foregrounded, nonetheless the bottom line is that the technology wouldn't succeed unless it was efficient in terms of time, space, and resources. The consequences of this efficiency are a reversal of the decline in academic standards that was occurring in the classrooms of the 1970s and '80s where "open" classroom models were popular (Brooks 2001). Efficiency is now expected of both teachers and students. No longer are students learning only the three "R's," now they are getting sex education, AIDS awareness, diversity training, anger management, emergency drills, and character lessons. Students must be more efficient today in order to process the demands and information of our postmodern world, and with the aid of technology, the hyperefficient person is that much closer to omnipotence.

The endpoint for many of hyperefficient students is a college education, where their tendency toward efficiency is honed even more. An article in the *Atlantic Monthly* describes what the most privileged college students look like. Brooks (2001) observes students at Princeton, organized to the hilt in terms of their activities and relationships. He also notes that they don't seem to mind. They have accepted the rules of "the system" and they don't try to resist them—they strive to accommodate them. With their eyes fixed on the goals of worldly success, they seem unwavering in their pursuit. One student, asked if students at his institution ever felt like workaholics, replied, "Sometimes we feel like we're just tools for processing information. That's what we call ourselves—power tools. And we call these (holding up his satchel) tool bags" (40). The offspring of the efficient technologies is the hyperefficient, human, "power tool."

In a parallel vein, hyperautonomy is also at work in the individual. The efficiency and skills created in working with technology in the classroom prepare the person for greater success in the business world, which expects not only efficient but autonomous workers. Hyperautonomy is an exaggerated sense of our self-sufficiency in a widely technology-mediated world. Our hyperautonomy allows us to manage the consistent and often mundane aspects of our lives automatically, freeing us up for more important matters. We have direct deposit for our paychecks, autowithdrawal for our bills, and automatic transfers with a simple phone or internet transaction. Once set in motion, many of these procedures continue with unforgiving regularity with the result that the moment we "take charge" of our financial situation is the moment we relinquish it to technology.

Our hyperefficient and hyperautonomous lives in America are no more apparent than when we turn our attention to travel. We become our own travel agents and tour guides through the powers of the Internet. One exceptional example was recounted in a *Newsweek* essay written by a woman who has been living with her husband for eight years aboard their sailing ship, traveling about the world (Ginsberg-Klemmt 2001). This self-described "technomad" is the epitome of the hyperautonomously "connected" person. Able to reach friends and family any time day or night, regardless of their geographical position (hyperpresence) her autonomy is maintained by a vast array of technological gadgets. Through her high-tech modem connection, she claims that her communication with others helps them to be "virtually" on board with her. Hence, they can respond to her adventurous accounts as if they were actually there. Upon recounting the distressing ordeal of losing their pet cat overboard and sending the news hyperefficiently to "hundreds of people who were following our Pacific crossing," she writes, "During the next days we downloaded many touching messages of condolence, love and letting go. Nothing could have been more comforting for us as we sailed with the southeasterly trade winds toward the Marquesas." Welcome to the hyperautonomous reality of technology. The essay ends as she gives birth to their daughter on a Hawaiian shore, hoping to share more of this marvelous planet with her child and anyone else who would like to sail with them "virtually." Her life at sea actually becomes a metaphor for the autonomous self and technology. The rugged individualist no longer roams the wild west with a six-shooter, but sails the high seas with a laptop.

From financial management to the South Seas, technology contributes to an "I did it myself" mentality. There are many things we choose to do through modern technology because we can do them at our own convenience and on our own time. Technology offers us hyperefficiency and hyperautonomy as we identify with the presumed omnipotence of technology.

Hyperknowledge. The old adage that "knowledge is power" is more true today than it has ever been. Considering technology's capability to store and convey information, hyperknowledge is the exaggerated perception that having the information technology is analogous to having the knowledge. And having the knowledge is akin to having the omniscient nature of technology. Since information is so powerful in today's world, this quality of technology can be the most seductive of its attributes. Three aspects of technology's "omniscience" have an especially mesmerizing effect on humans—its accessibility, its quantity, and its speed of delivery. Having information so readily available "24/7," allows the person essentially to have information on demand. No longer is someone constrained by the hours of operation of the bookstore or library. No longer is place even an issue in terms of traditional sites of information. With wireless technology, a PDA or laptop computer can access electronic data from literally anywhere in the world making the sense of hyperpresence all the more powerful. And the degree of status that goes with the conspicuous consumption of digital devices creates an immediate advantage and power for the user.

Along with unlimited access, the quantity of information available is overwhelming. It is not uncommon for various databases to have over one million entries. Search engines can find information on any topic imaginable from the "spork" to "how to make a letter bomb." Interest groups, therapy groups, self-diagnosis of illnesses sites, encyclopedias, language sites, history, current events, shopping, games, weather, maps, music and more are readily available for downloading. And that is just on the Internet. There is also cable and satellite television offering hundreds of channels, and our airwaves are filled with cellular phones, walkie-talkies, subscription radio services, and various types of audio/visual broadcasts. And that is just the electronic sources. Junk mail continues to stream through our mail boxes, and print media, newspapers, popular and academic journals keep the flow constant. With every new or improved outlet of information, there is the cadre of advertisers telling you of more sources of information and products. Information is one of the few resources that is not being depleted. With the right technology, there is a world of information available.

Databases and search engines are a large component of the easy access to information. Once information is digitized, it is worthless unless it is accessible through either databases or through various search engines. The other crucial component is time. Much of the information accessible today has been accessible in the past, given the resources and the time to acquire it. However, now, access is almost instantaneous and involves little labor, giving rise to a sense of hyperknowledge.

We thus have come full circle in understanding the reflexivity of the human as he or she interacts with technology. Although the godlike qualities of technology are themselves illusions, they are powerful enough to shape its creators and in turn, produce a "hyperindividual," one that seemingly knows no boundaries, is able to accomplish any task efficiently and without another's help, and can quickly access information anytime and anywhere.

THE END OF THE HYPERMODERN SELF

So what results from our emersion in the hypermodern? Aren't hyper-presense, hyperautonomy and hyperefficiency, and hyperknowledge to be desired? Doesn't our evolutionary hard wiring require that our "selves" adapt to the world of technology? Bruce Mazlish (1993) suggests that it does. In fact, he claims the last stage in our evolution is the realization of the continuity between humans and machines. Mazlish (1993), in his book on the "co-evolution of humans and machines," suggests that the human will become the "prosthetic god":

> Humans will, indeed, also become more mechanical, both in body and in mind. In body, they are increasingly hooked up to mechanical parts—the macabre end point manifesting itself in life support systems from which they need a "right to die" in order to free themselves from such unwanted, purely mechanical "life." In mind, Carlylean mechanization is now supplemented by metaphors of programming and artificial intelligence; and since humans think and feel in terms of metaphors, they approximate more closely in this regard to the mechanical-cum-computer. All in all, something like a new species will eventually emerge—Homo comboticus— that will compete with and very likely replace (or convert) most of the human types that have existed before about 1970; that is, precomputer Man. (228–29)

Mazlish argues that we are becoming more machinelike as we interact with technology. And technology is getting harder and harder to avoid. It sucks us in to its world. When technology is present, it seems to compel us to use it. If we reflect the "human power tool" metaphor, the future of humanity lies in our technological visions not merely of computer/human interaction, but computer/human integration. Humans may even become merely the "sex organs" of technology, for it is by humans that technology is created or "produced." Yet, we need technology to cope with technology.

The End of Hyperpresence? As a result of such technology, the self finds itself in a unique position. Never before has it experienced such god-like qualities transcending time and space. The author of Psalm 115 could not have anticipated the extent of human creativity in technology. Yet the consequences of this technological progress have not all been positive for the self. With hyperpresence has come fragmentation as the self is deconstructed into a variety of contexts that are constantly changing. The self is disembodied as it moves from face-to-face communication to the computer screen, from the world of reality to the cyberworld. It also becomes more vulnerable because virtual presence is just a click away from nonexistence. Full technological immersion cheapens the person, who becomes just another interchangeable part of the machine.

Yet eventually we have to come back from the cyberworlds we create or that are created for us, even when we recognize that our cyberselves are more appealing than our actual selves. Spend enough time in such alternate worlds and the value of direct experience of the real world is diminished (Turkle 1995). The more we experience hyperpresence the more we experience things "remotely" and while there is a greater sense of power there is a diminishing direct experience with the material world (Heim 1993) that should provide the context for human activity. Consequently, experiencing hyperpresence removes the self from the context of the material world and into the context of multiple cyberworlds. Such multiplicity can be valued in a postmodern world where all things are subject to multiple interpretations, but "by offering us a reality divorced from the world, from the limits and responsibilities of presence, [it may] offer us as well a glimpse into an utterly amoral universe" (Slouka 1995, 13).

Furthermore, hyperpresence allows what Kenneth Gergen (1991) calls multiphrenia—the splitting of the self into a "multiplicity of self-investments" (74). He notes that

> As one's potentials are expanded by the technologies, so one increasingly employs the technologies for self-expression; yet, as the technologies are further utilized, so do they add to the repertoire of potentials. It would be a mistake to view this multiphrenic condition as a form of illness, for it is often suffused with a sense of expansiveness and adventure. (74)

There is no question that the experience of hyperpresence offers a sense of expansiveness and adventure, and life is enriched by such experiences. However, whereas the technology is seemingly ever increasing and boundless, humans are not. Gergen lauds the multiphrenic self for its openness to adventures and potentials. The multiphrenic, or "saturated" self lacks a sustained coherence because of its emersion into so many diverse social settings that accentuate the loss of boundaries. Nevertheless, the saturated self, unlike a technological hyyperpresence, is still sustained by an embodied self that ultimately has boundaries and is finite. If Gergen is attentive at all to the world, he must know that "self matters." In spite of Gergen's numerous examples to the contrary, and in spite of the technology that would suggest otherwise, there is still enough of an embodied self, a core unified sense of being, bounded by reality, to defeat the dream of hyperpresence.

The End of Hyperautonomy and Hyperefficiency? As for hyper-autonomy and hyperefficiency, far from true freedom and autonomy, the self becomes tethered to technology for support. The woman who sails the high seas with her husband is surrounded and even comforted by technology. She received notes of condolence at the loss of her cat, but what would have happened had her laptop "drowned?" Which death would have been more tragic? We only seem autonomous as long as our technology is running smoothly. Far from being hyperautonomous, or even autonomous, the reality is that we are highly dependent people, and our dependence on technology is truly more of a reflection of our lack of autonomy than we give technology credit for. We are blinded by our reflexive nature that says, "you did do it yourself!" Reality hits when we have to do without . . . or the power goes off, or the disk goes bad . . . or the battery dies . . . or one moves out of range.

Our hyperefficiency is also a sham. Humans as finite beings cannot hope to compete with technology in terms of its tireless, indefatigable pace. Hyperefficiency challenges the boundaries of any known limits to performance—I can go faster, acquire more, expend less energy, and produce more accurately and effortlessly than ever before. The fact of the matter is, we were never designed to perform at the pace of our modern technologies. As with most technologies, the increase in technological efficiency comes with higher expectations on human behavior. We buy in to hyperautonomy and hyperefficiency, technology's omnipotence, to our own peril.

The End of Hyperknowledge? Although around-the-clock instant access to vast amounts of data may initially seem quite appealing, there are costs involved. Information anxiety, decontextualized information, and relational numbing, are among such costs. Richard Wurman (1989) notes that "Information anxiety is the black hole between data and knowledge" (34). When we have access to a sea of data, getting what we need to know becomes a more difficult rather than a less difficult task. We may gather data, but can we acquire knowledge? This dilemma becomes acute when we realize that "the total of all printed knowledge doubles every eight years" (Wurman 1989, 35). Information anxiety arises as the production of information outpaces our ability to understand that information.

> The explosion of data—along with general societal secularization and the collapse of what the theorists call the "master narratives" (Christian, Marxist, Freudian, humanist . . .)—has all but destroyed the premise of understandability. Inundated by perspectives, by lateral vistas of information that stretch endlessly in every direction, we no longer accept the possibility of assembling a complete picture. (Birkerts 1994, 75)

Along with information anxiety due to too much information, there is also a sense of anxiety when not enough information is available. Vast amounts of electronic information are useless if the information we seek is not digital or is inaccessible through technology. To have so much information and yet not be able to find what we are looking for amplifies our anxiety. Not only does such lack destroy our experience of hyperknowledge, but it also subtly alters how we view knowledge all together. Digital information becomes valued over other forms, dramatically narrowing what is considered knowledge. The net becomes authoritative as the printed text became authoritative over oral traditions.

Hyperknowledge is also deficient because as the print medium gives way to the electronic, a sense of permanence is lost. Information can seem evanescent and detached from any history or narrative (Birkerts 1994). The lack of any metanarrative is at the heart of postmodernism and is amplified by technology. Information is captured in the moment, the perpetual "now," where no structure or hierarchy is observable, just isolated data accessed from a sea of information: "The more we grow rooted in the consciousness of the now, the more it will seem utterly extraordinary that things were ever any different" (Birkerts 1994, 130). Hence, any historical perspective will easily be lost from the information we access. With information decontextualized, we as humans can also lose our sense of place in the historical reality of our lives. Much of television news, for instance, where events are juxtaposed with other events in a constant stream of information, lacks historical perspective. Likewise, dramas, sitcoms, and "reality" based shows flash across our screens only to be replaced by other similar shows, each self-contained and largely independent of any continuous narrative. Our own sense of self can seem equally detached and impermanent, a mere blip on the screen, as easily deleted as it might be saved.

A third consequence of the experience of hyperknowledge occurs as a result of our ability to connect with people all over the world for the purpose of "staying in touch." So-called relational numbing occurs when you reach your limit of people wanting to "connect" with you. Returning from a long weekend, you may encounter a hundred e-mails or the friendly message from your phone server: "Your mailbox is full." Relational numbing occurs when you are engaged in some enjoyable activity only to be beckoned by your cell phone or pager to meet someone else's demands. Technology, in this instance, alienates you from the face-to-face contacts that make up traditional human relations. Electronic sources, especially when they accumulate, can push you further away from others. In an ironic reversal, you become the source of information that some technology is trying to access. Whereas face-to-face conversations strengthen *relationships*, most mediated communications are reduced to the verbal sharing of *information*. This distinction has led Birkerts (1994) to comment, "Never so much utterance, so much flow, and never before so little sense of connection or mattering" (172).

Technology promises more than it delivers in terms of hyperpresence, hyperefficiency and hyperautonomy, and hyperknowledge. As much as Mazlish and others would entertain the thought of greater adaptation of humans to technology, the costs in terms of the self seem too great. Fragmentation, dependence, stress and anxiety, loss of meaning are all costs incurred by the hyperindividual. For Birkerts (1994), such a crisis of the self will lead to three possible outcomes: (1) an increase in interest in religion and the grand narratives and the sacred space that they provide; (2) a rush to therapy where the "fragmented self will be brought to trained professionals for reconstitution" (197); and (3) a resurgence of the arts where coherence and meaning are found. If nothing else, postmodernism provides a critical time to reevaluate the nature of the self.

AT THE CROSSROADS: THE TRANSMODERN

Postmodernism has propelled us into a hyperindividualism where people have a disembodied voice, with no centralized controls either internally or externally, a high value on change, and a low value on any unifying system of reality. They have no past to weigh them down nor a singular future to which to conform. They exist in communities of their own making, and through language call into being their own realities. These changes could only happen in a technologically driven society that enables and empowers people to see these qualities realized at least in cyberspace, if not in physical space. This hypermodern world is at a crossroads. As Paul Vitz (personal communication, May 23, 2002) has noted, toward the end of certain historical periods there has been a rather exaggerated expression of that period. For example, at the end of the Middle Ages there was what was called "flamboyant Gothic," where architecture took on extreme or exaggerated Gothic styles. We may possibly be at the end of another era where the hypermodern use of technology has produced an exaggerated view of the self to even godlike proportions.

Yet hyperpresence, hyperautonomy and hyperefficiency, and hyperknowledge are not as satisfying as they pretend to be. Hyperpresence challenges the notion that we are bounded by our own physical presence by giving us a sense of omnipresence. But the fact remains that we are embodied selves. Hyperautonomy and hyperefficiency challenge the notion that we are limited and need each other by giving us a sense of omnipotence.

But the fact remains that we are relational selves. Hyperknowledge challenges the notion that we do not have all the answers to our problems by giving us a sense of omniscience. But the fact remains that we are humble selves.

The transmodern allows us to reconnect with our self in new ways. An embodied self realizes the limitations of the self and technology to transcend reality and is acutely aware of our own physical presence in the context of time and space. Such an understanding should allow us to be in the right relationship to others. A relational self understands that we cannot truly have a reflexive nature beyond our limitations. Hence, such mimetic desires need to be grounded in human relationships, not high tech wizardry. Such an understanding should allow us to be humble before others. And a humble self recognizes that there will always be mystery in our own limited understanding of things. Such an understanding should compel us to seek the only relationship that will completely satisfy the desire to know and be known as a person. That relationship is with the One not made by human hands, Who has eyes and truly sees, Who has ears and truly hears, Who has a mouth and truly speaks, Who has feet and truly walked among us in the person of Jesus Christ.

V. College Students and the Self

12

Personal Identity: Postmodern or Transmodern?

A Study of College and University Undergraduates

at the Turn of the Millenium

Jim Norwine, Allen Ketcham, Michael Preda, Michael S. Bruner

Just as our grandparents' experience was essentially one of modernity, ours is an essentially postmodern condition. As our grandparents expected to *discover* rather than inherit their calling and identity even as they read their Bible and their Darwin, we may choose to be devout or logical or kind but we *choose* to do so and next week we may *choose* not to. The "sacred" or nonnegotiable value in all this is not devotion, reason, or self-giving, which are but options, but choice itself. Little wonder that our fluxing mindscapes feel almost unbearably "light" (Kundera 1984).

Concede for the moment the possibility that we *are* all postmoderns (Oden 1991). Where does that leave us? What does it mean? Specifically, what does this say about personal identity at the start of the third millennium? This study is about our attempt to explore answers to that question. Our hunch concerning the answer was, to greatly oversimplify, that the condition of postmodernity tends to favor two related yet competing worldviews, which we characterize as "radical postmodern" (RP) and "transmodern" (TR). In this inquiry we endeavored to test, or at least to wrestle with, this intuition.

This project is the third phase of an ongoing inquiry into worldview shifts among university-level students. Our long-term objective has been to identify and explore the postmodern "turn," if any, reflected in the weltanschauungen of these future leaders. Our original survey instrument, developed and tested in 1990–91, consisted of value statements representing four worldviews: traditional, nontraditional, modern, and postmodern. It was administered to about 1,600 undergraduates at three public universities in Texas in 1991. Among the findings we reported (Bruner et al. 1994; Norwine and Smith 2000) were strong identification with "traditional" values such as honor and family as well as "modern" values like self-expression and technology. However, we also found that 50 percent to 70 percent of the respondents agreed with expressions of two postmodern themes: (a) the radical equality of all ideas and values, and (b) the celebration/elevation of personal choice and autonomy (e.g., "all ideas have equal worth" and "happiness is whatever makes me feel good").

In 1992 a shortened version of our Texas Survey was administered to about 1,000 undergraduates at six diverse institutions in the United States and at eight in Australia, Canada, Chile, Gaza (Palestine), South Korea, and Wales. We reported (Bruner et al. 1994) a number of intriguing findings, including (perhaps somewhat presciently) that *only* the students at the College of Science and Technology, Gaza, had a coherently traditional worldview. Otherwise, however, the results of this International Survey were largely in line with those of the Texas survey. Traditional and modern values remained even stronger at most non-U.S. universities than we had found at the Texas universities, but at the same time, everywhere (except Gaza) we found some quite evident affirmation of statements indicative of a postmodern paradigm.

Because in both traditionality (T) and modernity (M) absolutes or universals are assumed, one's personhood is found more or less "vertically." Although different, T and M are similar in that each offers a bridge or connection to a higher realm and thus to meaning and purpose. In postmodernity, however, we have crossed a border into a realm of horizontal valuescapes. Presence is absent "in an age in which a publicly accessible cosmic order of meaning is an impossibility" (Taylor, 1989). "Objective knowledge" becomes untrustworthy without personal resonance/interpretation. Lacking any clear "heart's desire," the world one inherits and inhabits becomes one of reflexively self-defined (Davis 2000) "freeplay" wherein "I create my self(es)."

Given such mindscapes, is there any choice about choice, any desire beyond desire? After all, what is most distinctive about the postmodern experience is the privileging of personal freeplay, its elevation to or even above older virtues like compassion or logic. There is but one choice about choice in a postmodern worldview: whether freeplay is its own end or whether it is an essential means to an end.

Both the radical postmodern (RP) and transmodern (TR) stances presume the necessity of all persons self-discovering their authentic selves. Both intuit that there is no going back to the straightforward verticality of meaning of traditionality and modernity. After that they part ways. Unlike TR, which is equal parts freeplay subjectivity *and* subject-to—e.g., "my self is not about me," RP by definition must always be subjective and *never* subject-to (Bailie 1995). Thus RP liberates and even empowers but appears dubious as a way to "authentic" personhood (Davis 2000; Taylor 1989).

Perhaps because RP lacks a "religiously significant prospect for ordering . . . lives" (Bailie 1995), RP is simply the "Have a nice day!" happy face self. RP must wear this face as anything-goes nihilism. We see this nihilism, for example, when scholars at major universities publicly propose that parents should be able to *choose* to kill inferior children up to age one, and that adults and children should be able to *choose* to have sex with one another (Stoeltje 2002).

A transmodern (Anwal 1994; Edge 1994; Ingram 1997; Luyckz 1999; Rushing 1995; Vitz 1995b, 1998) or "para-modern" (Larner 1998) worldview, on the other hand, *requires* real "anchor points" (McLaren 2001) to which one is subject. According to Vitz (2001b):

> Transmodern means that a person or idea has gone through modernism, including postmodernism, which is really late- or hyper-modern, and come out on the other side. More specifically, transmodern means that many of the valid modern ideas are kept but they are transformed by being placed in a new understanding or context and also transcended by the addition of an explicit transcendent framework. This transcended framework may be clearly religious, or possibly spiritual in a general sense, or possibly idealistic.

God, other people, or perhaps even the embodied natural world fulfill the function of anchor points—with which one is in relation, and so against which one's self-referential authority can and in fact *must* be tested. As in jazz music, selves in TR are free to create the unique "riffs" of themselves because they are subject to an overarching melody. Where do contemporary undergraduates place themselves among these competing valuescapes?

Having established the theoretical framework and research questions of the Transmodern Survey, we turn now to the details of the study.

METHOD

The present investigation began with the development during the summer and autumn of 2001 of a Survey of Student Values No. 2 instrument. The questionnaire was designed to explore the worldviews and values of the students, with particular emphasis on the self. It consisted of sixteen demographic questions about personal background followed by sixty statements to which students responded using a Likert-like scale of "strongly agree" to "strongly disagree" (see Appendix). Each of the sixty statements was classified as, and intended to reflect, an aspect of a "traditional" (T), "modern" (M), "radical postmodern" (RP), or "transmodern" (TR) outlook. Our goal was to use the students' responses to examine the extent to which their "selves" or identities might be characterized as the following:

- *Traditional* (T): premodern/archaic, inherited, anchored, nonautonomous; situated freedom. Possible exemplars: Chief Seattle; Marcus Tullius Cicero; Edmund Burke; George Santayana; Mother Teresa of Calcutta; Saint Francis of Assisi.

- *Modern/Autonomous* (M): self-sustaining, coherent, unitary, masterful. Possible exemplars: René Descartes; Blaise Pascal; Sigmund Freud; Karl Marx.

- *Radical Postmodern* (RP)/Self-Referential: disembodied, associative, drifting, triumphant, fluid, transient; "joyous self-creation in freeplay" (Felch 2001); "a self that is an agent of pure freewill navigating the real and electronic worlds" (Norman 2001). Possible exemplars: Friedrich Wilhelm Nietzsche; Martin Heidegger; Roland Barthes; John Lennon; Richard Rorty.

- *Transmodern* (TR)/Self- and Other-Referential: my (your, everyone's) "pure freewill"—no external authority may legitimately be imposed—is assumed to be authoritative but only if married with an equal presumption of the reality and authority of the Other. It is only through the relationship of these "authorities"—the testing, the comparing, the (in)validating of my/your personal experience—that tentative, ephemeral, contingent identity becomes my/our personhood(s). Possible exemplars: Vaclav Havel; Charles Taylor; René Girard; John Zizioulas; Garrison Keillor.

Participants. During the period November 2001 to February 2002, we administered the Survey of Student Values No. 2 to a total of 804 undergraduates at eight institutions of higher learning in the United States. Four were secular (public/state) universities, and four were church-affiliated, Christian colleges and universities, as summarized in Table 1.

The bulk of the participants were between the ages of eighteen and twenty-three. Among the participants were 486 females and 318 males. The overwhelming majority of participants were white/Caucasian except at Texas A&M University-Kingsville, where the majority were Hispanic (Latino) American.

There were 643 participants who identified themselves as Christian. The undergraduates were scattered among four primary areas of study:

Table 1: Participating Colleges and Universities

LOCATION	INSTITUTION TYPE	SAMPLE SIZE
Michigan	Church-related	115
Iowa	Church-related	71
Texas	Church-related Protestant	63
Texas	Church-related Roman Catholic	37
	Subtotal	**286**
Texas	Public/State-related	168
Texas	Public/State-related	137
California	Public/State-related	122
Illinois	Public/State-related	91
	Subtotal	**518**
	Grand Total	**N = 804**

Liberal Arts (170), Business (160), Science/Mathematics/Computer Science (115), and Education/Physical Education (110).

The Survey Instrument. The questionnaire booklet consisted of a cover letter, sixteen demographic questions about personal background, followed by sixty statements to which students responded using a Likert-like scale of strongly agree to strongly disagree. The questionnaires were completed and collected in a variety of undergraduate courses.

During the first few months of 2002, data from the student surveys were processed (a total in excess of 64,000 entries) and subjected to Pearson chi-square analysis. The results were grouped and analyzed in a variety of ways. In this essay, however, we shall restrict our discussion to statistical averages of responses to statements around which there was a "broad con-

Table 2: "Broad Consensus" Statements and Response Rates*
(N=804)

"BROAD CONSENSUS" STATEMENTS .... AT LEAST 70% OF RESPONDENTS
AGREED OR DISAGREED

34. Family is important as myself. .... 90% agree

68. Much from past . . . new and positive .... 87% agree

74. It is essential to stick to my beliefs .... 86% agree

69. . . . Come a long way since the Dark Ages .... 84% agree

70. Hard work surest way to success .... 84% agree

29. I am more hopeful than despairing... 83% agree

21. Change is good .... 82% agree

57. Some values are better than others .... 80% agree

75. (In making decisions) I trust my feelings .... 80% agree

79. I am proud to be an American .... 79% agree

66. Where my loved ones are is home .... 78% agree

18. I have a duty to serve God .... 77% agree

54. Suffering builds character .... 77% agree

58. We all are sinners .... 77% agree

46. Personal freedom has its limits .... 76% agree

76. Love is bigger than all of us .... 76% agree

19. A relationship must enhance both parties .... 75% agree

20. I must be me, but in community... 75% agree

30. Family traditions are important .... 75% agree

33. Will move from family to pursue dreams............................... 75% agree

31. Everyone's viewpoint equally valid .... 71% agree

52. Life has meaning even if I don't know it .... 71% agree

47. . . . Life is essentially meaningless .... 91% disagree

23. All religions are nonsense .... 84% disagree

59. Marriage is a non-binding commitment .... 83% disagree

35. God and Truth are not real . . . but . . . invented .... 80% disagree

*Where "broad consensus" = 70% or more of the respondents agree or disagree. "Agree" is defined as the sum of "strongly agree" (SA) and "mildly agree" (MA). "Disagree" is defined as the sum of "strongly disagree" (SD) and "mildly disagree" (MD).

sensus" and statements that elicited "mixed responses." Based on our experience with the Texas Survey and the International Survey, these two areas in the Survey of Student Values No. 2 seemed robust, significant, and intriguing.

RESULTS

Let us first turn to the areas of "broad consensus," where at least 70 percent of the respondents agreed (or disagreed) with a statement. The 70 percent cut-off point was chosen because it represents approximately twice the percentage of participants at church-related institutions. Therefore, the strong reactions to the statements cannot be attributed to church-related institutions alone. The findings on "broad consensus" items are reported in Table 2.

Next, let us report on those statements that received "mixed responses." These findings are reported in Table 3.

DISCUSSION

Inglehart (2000) posits "cultural shifts away from traditional value systems" toward "increasingly modern (and postmodern) values" but concedes that Huntington (1996) and others are right that "cultural traditions are remarkably enduring (and continue to shape) societies today." The areas of "broad consensus" in our Transmodern Survey suggest that Inglehart is correct. Far from being "slain," traditional and modern values often remain quite robust, yet the condition of postmodernity inclines us toward a major cultural paradigm shift, one which favors two related yet competing selves, which we characterize as "radical postmodern" and "transmodern."

The Traditional Self and the Modern Self can be seen quite clearly in three areas: Family, Hard Work and Progress, and God. The statement in our Survey of Student Values No. 2 that received the highest rate of agreement (90%) was no. 34: "My family is as important to me as myself." Family also was affirmed in responses to these statements: no. 66: "Where my loved ones are is my home" (78% agree); and no. 30: "It is important to me to perpetuate my family traditions" (75% agree). Marriage, a central part of family in the Traditional and Modern frameworks, also received strong support. Statement no. 59, "Marriage is a nonbinding commitment," was overwhelmingly rejected (83% disagree).

At the same time, the participants revealed commitments that run counter to traditional views of family, such as no. 33: "I plan to pursue my own life and dreams, even if that means moving far away from my family"

(75% agree). This emphasis on "me" reveals another type of self.

In an area that we might label Hard Work and Progress, the undergraduates revealed a surprising number of Traditional and Modern values. On the past and progress, the participants strongly affirmed: no. 68: "There

Table 3: Statements with "Mixed Responses"*
(N=804)

"MIXED RESPONSES" STATEMENTS	RESPONSE PERCENTAGES**
22. This life is unimportant compared to heaven.	43-16-41
26. If there is no God ... no meaning ...	47-12-40
27. None of my principles is non-negotiable.	31-20-49
28. God and I are equal copartners ...	38-15-47
38. On my own, I am nothing.	46-10-43
43. I oppose any limits on choice/autonomy.	45-28-27
44. Rather have children raised by any devout ...	23-28-48
51. I worry about my self-esteem.	46-10-43
60. My experience (tells me but needs testing).	53-32-14
64. Nobody should tell me ... but sometimes ...	48-13-38
71. Teaching any ... value as better ... wrong.	36-30-33
72. Choose lives of children over principles.	39-28-31
78. After 9/11 more optimistic about future.	39-27-33

*Statements with "mixed responses" are defined as those with which at least 31% of the respondents agree and at least 31% disagree, or which have an "undecided" rate of at least 28%. "Agree" is defined as the sum of "strongly agree" (SA) and "mildly agree" (MA). "Disagree" is defined as the sum of "strongly disagree" (SD) and "mildly disagree" (MD).

**Percentages are arrayed in this order: agree, undecided, disagree. The totals do not equal 100% in all cases due to rounding.

is much from the past that can be used again, in a new and positive way" (87% agree); no. 69: "We have come a long way since the Dark Ages" (84% agree); and no. 21: "Change is good" (82% agree).

With regard to character and hard work, the undergraduates expressed agreement with these statements: no. 74: "It is essential to stick to my beliefs, even when it is hard to do so" (86% agree); no. 70: "Hard work is the surest way to success" (84% agree); and no. 54: "Suffering builds character" (77% agree). These views of self could also be found centuries or even millennia ago.

Looking to the future, the participants responded in a mildly nationalistic tone: no. 79: "I am proud to be an American" (79% agree). In what might be encouraging news, 83 percent of the participants agreed that they were "more hopeful than despairing about the future" (no. 29).

Two items seemed to confound these affirmations. First, the participants were highly polarized about whether this life is important at all. Participants were quite divided on statement no. 22: "This life is unimportant to me compared to my eternal life in heaven."

Forty-three percent agreed while 41 percent disagreed. Second, in a pattern that reflected strong ambivalence, 36 percent agreed, 30 percent were undecided, and 33 percent disagreed with the statement no. 71: "Teaching any particular value as better than another is wrong."

In the area of God, a remarkable 77 percent of respondents affirmed no. 18: "I have a duty to serve God," and 77 percent agreed with no. 58: "We are all sinners." Continuing in this vein, 84 percent disagreed with no. 23: "All religions are nonsense" and 80 percent disagreed with no. 35: "*God and Truth are not real because they are ideas invented by people.*" In perhaps the strongest expression of all, 91 percent of the students disagreed with no. 47: "I think life is essentially meaningless."

Once again, however, these expressions were undercut by other responses. As noted above, 41 percent disagreed with no. 22: "This life is unimportant compared to eternal life in heaven." Thirty-eight per cent agreed and 47 percent disagreed with no. 28: "God (as I see God) and I are coequal partners in charting my life." Either response could be seen as undermining the omnipotence of God. And, in a significant pattern of responses, 47 percent agreed but 40 percent disagreed with no. 26: "If there is no God, there is no meaning in life."

As can be seen from this review of responses to statements about Family, Hard Work and Progress, and God, the condition of postmodernity inclines us toward a major cultural paradigm shift, one that favors two related yet competing selves, as earlier noted, which we characterize as "radical postmodern" and "transmodern" (Inglehart 2000). The Radical

Postmodern self and the Transmodern self are even more apparent when we analyze the "mixed responses" in table 3.

Let us focus on several significant items. The response rate for no. 27: "None of my personal beliefs/principles is absolutely sacred or nonnegotiable in determining the way I live my life" was 31 percent agree, 20 percent undecided, and 49 percent disagree. These statistics indicate that personal identities or the self could be negotiable for almost one-half of the students. Now examine no. 43: "I oppose any limits on my personal choice and autonomy." The pattern of responses here was 45 percent agree, 28 percent undecided, and 27 percent disagree. These data indicate that almost one-half of the students oppose limits on the autonomy of self.

Statement no. 51: "I worry about my level of self-esteem" drew a markedly mixed set of responses. Forty-six percent agreed, raising some concern about the condition of the undergraduate self. An almost equal number disagreed (43 percent). Equality or horizontality of ideas is affirmed (45 percent agree) in the students' responses to statement no. 31: "Everyone's point of view is equally valid."

Responses to statement no. 72 are among the most interesting in the survey. The students were presented with this scenario, "*If I were in a situation in which I was convinced that my most sacred principles somehow required the sacrifice of five children, I would choose the lives of the children over my principles.*" Thirty-nine percent opted for the children, 28 percent were undecided, and 31 percent chose their principles over the five children.

In sum, while many Radical Postmodern and Transmodern values were rejected, a number were either affirmed by pluralities/majorities (e.g., "every point of view is equally valid") or were the source of considerable ambivalence (e.g., "I would choose the lives of five children over my most sacred principles"). These data suggest an ongoing although perhaps early-stage shift in the self among undergraduates.

TR values reflect at least in general terms Vitz's idea that primarily giving and receiving, loving and being loved, "brings the self into existence" (2001a) or, as Zizioulus puts it, personal identity can emerge only from love as freedom and from freedom as love (1995). Thus, while RP seems to represent at best both the latest grand story—the paradigm is dead, long live the paradigm!—and hubris, that most ancient of conceits, TR is better thought of as the newest, potentially even the best, form of an old epiphany. After all, as love is possible only where freedom rules, the single form of personal autonomy which is non-negotiable is freely choosing to love (Kinlaw 2001). Thus, TR's unself-self (Balthasar 1986) reflects an internalization of God's values (Kinlaw 2001) via the "demand of the person for absolute freedom" (Zizioulas 1995).

Table 4: "Transmodern" (TR) Statements and Responses
(N=804)

"TRANSMODERN" STATEMENTS	% AGREE-UNDECIDED-DISAGREE
AGREE	
20. I must be me but (must) serve my community.	75 – 15 – 9
24. Each (must) craft (unique) life but (must serve) . . .	74 – 16 – 10
36. Human (and environmental) well-being are equal.	69 – 12 – 18
40. My life-path is different but (must) consider more . . .	68 – 24 – 6
52. (I'm sure) life has meaning (but not what) it is.	71 – 12 – 16
56. Love is bigger than all of us.	76 – 16 – 7
68. (Much from the past can be used in) new and positive . . .	87 – 10 – 2
76. True freedom is . . . choosing to be a loving servant.	60 – 22 – 16
DISAGREE	
32. God is a human invention, but love is not.	12 – 20 – 67
UNDECIDED / SPLIT VOTE	
28. God and I are equal copartners . . .	38 – 15 – 47
44. (Prefer my) children be raised by any devoutly . . .	23 – 28 – 48
48. (Important) to be spiritual but not . . . religious.	51 – 17 – 31
60. My experience (is authoritative but needs testing) . . .	53 – 32 – 14
64. Nobody should tell me what to do but sometimes . . .	48 – 13 – 38
72. (I would choose the lives of children over) principles.	39 – 28 – 31

In the early part of the twentieth century, William James claimed that the great discovery of his time was that lives could be changed by changed attitudes (Norwine et al. 2000). At almost precisely the same moment, however, Max Weber trumped James' claim with his hugely influential argument that new attitudes led to new *ways* of life: specifically, that Calvinist Protestantism had "defined and sanctioned an ethic of everyday behavior" and attitudes which helped create not just modern capitalism (Landes 2000) but a cultural paradigm-shift to a new value-system, the materialist worldview (Inglehart 2000 1990) of modernity. The present study began with the presumption that postmodernity represents a similar change of dominant worldviews, one which could turn out to be just as singular as modernity by being a stunning amalgam of James *and* Weber: changed attitudes changing lives and ways of life that in turn change not only attitudes once again but the loci of these fluxing attitudes, our individual personal identities or "selves."

Like Weber, we are interested not in ivory-tower discussions of cultural paradigm shift but in how the postmodern experience is playing "out on the ground" in the lived lives of (in this instance) the personal identities of a sample of contemporary college students. Our interest was primarily in addressing a single overarching issue—Who are these persons now and who are they becoming? Our data indicate that, in some important ways, the students' selves are becoming transmodern.

Table 5: Selected Statements and Responses at Religious vs. Secular Colleges/Universities

(N=804)

STATEMENT	WORLDVIEW	RELIGIOUS	SECULAR
"SAME/IDENTICAL" RESPONSES			
34. (My family is as important as myself).	T	86–7–6	91–5–4
41. I feel alone much of the time.	M	23–11–66	26–9–66
44. (Prefer children raised by . . . devout).	TR	32–33–44	17–28–57
67. Science has created more problems . . .	RP	19–32–47	28–30–43
69. (Come a long way since Dark Ages.)	M	81–15–4	85–6–8
70. Hard work (surest way to success.)	T	82–8–10	85–6–8
72. (Choose children over my) principles.	TR	31–36–31	43–28–31

Table 5 (cont'd) (N=804)			
Statement	Worldview	Religious	Secular
Responses Similar in Direction by Large Degree-Difference			
18. I have a duty to serve God.	T	97–2–1	66–12–21
20. I must be me but (must serve).	TR	88–10–2	68–19–13
24. Each (life must be unique and serve).	TR	85–9–5	69–19–12
27. None of my beliefs is absolutely sacred.	RP	21–15–64	37–20–40
31. (Every point of view is equally valid).	RP	59–14–26	77–10–15
32. God is (invention) but love is not.	TR	3–10–87	17–25–57
35. God, Truth not real . . . but . . . invented.	RP	4–2–95	13–14–72
36. Humans (and environment) are equal.	TR	52–14–33	79–12–9
39. Having children (is not important).	RP	13–8–79	24–10–64
45. Only education can save us.	M	10–7–82	34–11–52
46. Personal freedom has its limits.	T	91–3–6	68–8–21
49. Societal problems can be solved by science.	M	9–12–79	18–16–63
50. Shame can be good for me.	T	73–16–10	50–19–29
52. (Life has meaning even if unknown.)	TR	62–11–26	77–12–10
53. Nature operates according to . . . laws.	M	65–19–16	45–24–26
54. Suffering builds character.	T	86–10–3	71–11–14
55. If it feels good, I should do it.	RP	11–11–78	36–15–45
57. Some values are better than others.	M	86–9–5	75–11–11
58. We are all sinners.	T	96–2–2	68–8–20
59. Marriage is (non-binding).	RP	5–5–84	8–11–63
60. My experience (tells me but) . . .	TR	6–27–7	46–32–17
61. (Problems can be solved by science.)	M	11–9–80	13–18–61

Table 4 summarizes the students' responses to the fifteen transmodern statements found in the questionnaire. The most obvious result is that, quite unlike the reactions to the radical postmodern statements, a majority agreed with two-thirds of these statements (ten of fifteen). Consider, for example, the 60 percent agreement–16 percent disagreement produced by no. 76, a TR statement that is arguably as penetrating as any included: "True freedom consists of freely choosing to be a loving servant." Of the remaining five TR statements, four received "split votes," only one was rejected by a majority of the student sample, and in three of these five cases the Undecided response was at least 20 percent. In sum, the TR statements produced more agreement, and less outright rejection, than did the RP statements.

When the sample is divided into two groups, religious and secular institutions, the results are sometimes unsurprising, sometimes intriguing, and sometimes arresting. Examination of Table 5 reveals that the worldviews of the two groups were in a number of instances quite different, as might have been expected, but in other cases they were surprisingly, perhaps even disturbingly, similar.

To begin, the responses to seven statements were virtually identical. Both groups agreed with traditional statements concerning the importance of family and hard work, both agreed about modern progress, both rejected the idea that their personal experience includes a lot of modern existential angst, and both disagreed with the RP statement that science has created more problems than it has solved, although the students at public schools in particular clearly had reservations about this. The groups roughly agreed in their ambivalent responses to two TR statements, although the secular students disagreed more strongly that they would prefer to have their children raised by devoutly religious people and tended to mildly agree that they would sacrifice their most sacred principles to save the lives of five children. The profoundly divided responses to the latter statement on the part of the Christian-college students was surely one of the most provocative findings of this project.

Delving further into Table 5, we find four basic patterns. First, the value systems of the students at the church-affiliated institutions were consistently more vertical, and those of the students at state colleges and universities more horizontal. Second, notwithstanding the centrality of absolutes at the Christian schools, their responses to a large number of RP and TR statements at least imply a tilting away from the vertical toward the horizontal. Third, while traditional and modern outlooks are certainly not dead at the public institutions, they don't always appear terribly healthy, either. The responses among this group revealed an acceptance of, or openness to, RP statements that implies a shift to personal identities affected or influenced in significant degree by this worldview. The two groups were about equally open to TR statements.

Finally, in very general terms the two groups responded similarly—and broadly approvingly—to the transmodern statements. When all of the fifteen TR statements are combined, the average response at the secular schools was 56–19–22 and at the religious colleges it was 56–17–27. In fact, however, these averages are somewhat misleading. Majorities or pluralities of the students at the public institutions endorsed twelve of these statements, only rejected two, and were roughly evenly divided in but one instance. The undergraduates at the church-affiliated colleges, on the other hand, agreed with nine, disagreed with three, and were split in three cases. Some of the more noteworthy TR contrasts were the following:

- no. 28. God and I are coequal partners . . . : 27–10–63 (religious) vs. 44–16–38 (state)

- no. 36. (Humans and environment equally important): 52–14–33 vs. 79–12–9

- no. 44. (Rather have children raised by devout . . .): 32–33–34 vs. 16-28-56

- no. 48. Important to be spiritual but not . . . religious: 30–15–54 vs. 62–17–18

- no. 72. (Sacrifice my principles for lives of children): 31–36–31 vs. 42–28–31.

CONCLUSION

Are we at the end of Western civilization's story or at the dawn of its second chapter? All we know with certainty is that we seem to have reached a frontier, beyond which we peer into a thickening—or is it lifting?—fog.

The findings of this project indicate that the worldviews of approximately 800 American college and university undergraduates continue to reflect many traditional and modern values, but they have some radical postmodern and even more transmodern values. It was also shown that students attending secular institutions were much more likely to approve of radical postmodern values than students attending colleges and universities with a religious affiliation. Finally, there was some admittedly mixed evidence of a transmodern turn. It appears clear that the vertical "ladders" to meaning and identity of traditionality and modernity are being tilted toward the horizontal by the new vortex of personal freeplay. Freeplay is surely enabling each of us to explore/create/develop/invent our distinctive differentness, but what is not yet clear is whether that is leading us in the direction of authentic, or inauthentic, selfhood.

A few years ago, Pope John Paul II wrote that "*the Church proposes; she imposes nothing*" (1990, emphasis in original). Perhaps His Holiness was acknowledging, with Aleksandr Solzhenitsyn, that there is no turning back but "there could only be (a transmodern) ascent from modernity (and postmodernity), one that accepted (their) principal achievements while rooting them in a more truthful account of God and man" (Mahoney 2002).

Appendix: Survey of Student Values No. 2 (2001)

Thank you for participating in this survey of student opinion. The research team will safeguard your confidentiality by using only statistical analyses of your responses. Please work carefully and give accurate responses. Do not complete more than one of these questionnaires. Thank you, again, for your help.

<u>Directions</u>: The first part of the questionnaire asks for demographic information. Please circle selection in response to each item, and/or fill the information in the blank space.

1. What is the name of your college/university? _____

2. College Affiliation   Public or Private

3. Gender   Female   Male

4. Age category   17 or younger   18–19   20–21   22–23   24–25
                    26–49   50+

5. Race   White/Caucasian   African-American
               Hispanic American   Asian American
               Native American Indian   Pacific Islander
               Mixed Race

6. Are both your parents of this same racial or ethnic background? Yes   No

7. What is your religious creed or outlook?   Atheist   Buddhist
                                                 Christian   Confucian
                                                 Hindu   Jewish
                                                 Muslim   Shintoism
                                                 Other

8. What is your father's educational level?   less than high school
                                                 high school graduate
                                                 some university
                                                 university graduate
                                                 technical school graduate
                                                 some graduate school
                                                 graduate degree

9. What is your father's occupation?   farmer
                                          nonfarm manual laborer
                                          clerical worker
                                          technician or professional
                                          independent businessman
                                          military
                                          other _____(specify)
                                          unemployed for longer than 3 months
                                          not applicable

10. What is your mother's educational level?

less than high school
high school graduate
some university
university graduate
technical school graduate
some graduate school
graduate degree

11. What is your mother's occupation?

farmer
nonfarm manual laborer
clerical worker
technician or professional
independent businessman
military
other _____(specify)
unemployed for longer than 3 months
not applicable

12. Your current year in college/university

1st – Freshman
2nd – Sophomore
3rd – Junior
4th – Senior
5th – continuing Senior
Graduate Student

13. Area of study (major fits into one of these groups)

Liberal Arts
Science/Math/Computer Sci.
Health CareEducation/Physical Education
Engineering
Business Administration
Fine Arts
Undecided
Other

14. Do you consider yourself to be   Conservative   Liberal
                                       Moderate   None of the above

15. Your family's annual household income (optional)

<$10,000	$10,000–24,999
$25,000–49,999	$50,000–74,999
$75,000–99,999	$100,000+

16. Have you traveled outside of the U.S.A. more than twice in the last two years?

Yes   No

Please read the statements below. For each statement, please circle the appropriate choice: strongly agree (SA), mildly agree (MA), undecided (U), mildly disagree (MD), or strongly disagree (SD).

17. A person's genes largely determine his or her personality.
    SA   MA   U   MD   SD

18. I have a duty to serve God.
    SA   MA   U   MD   SD

19. A relationship is worthwhile only when it is an enhancing, growing experience for both.
    SA   MA   U   MD   SD

20. I must be authentically "me," but part of who I am is to serve my community.
    SA   MA   U   MD   SD

21. Change is good.
    SA   MA   U   MD   SD

22. This life is unimportant compared to my eternal life in heaven.
    SA   MA   U   MD   SD

23. All religions are nonsense.
    SA   MA   U   MD   SD

24. Each of us needs to craft a life that is distinctly personal or unique, but which finds its greatest meaning by serving things, such as other people, God, or the environment.
    SA   MA   U   MD   SD

25. Fact is better than opinion.
    SA   MA   U   MD   SD

26. If there is no God, there is no meaning in life.
    SA   MA   U   MD   SD

27. None of my personal beliefs/principles is absolutely sacred or non-negotiable in determining the way I live my life.
    SA   MA   U   MD   SD

28. God (as I see God) and I are coequal partners in charting my life.
    SA   MA   U   MD   SD

29. I am more hopeful than despairing about the future.
    SA   MA   U   MD   SD

30. It is important to me to perpetuate my family traditions.
    SA   MA   U   MD   SD

31. Everyone's point of view is equally valid.
    SA   MA   U   MD   SD

32. God is a human invention, but love is not.
    SA   MA   U   MD   SD

33. I plan to pursue my own life and dreams, even if that means moving far away from my family.
    SA   MA   U   MD   SD

34. My family is as important to me as myself.
    SA   MA   U   MD   SD

35. God and Truth are not real because they are ideas invented by people.
    SA   MA   U   MD   SD

36. Human well-being and the well-being of the environment are equally important.
    SA   MA   U   MD   SD

37. I deserve what I have.
    SA   MA   U   MD   SD

38. On my own, I am nothing.
    SA   MA   U   MD   SD

39. Having children is not all that important for me.
    SA   MA   U   MD   SD

40. My personal life-path is different from everyone else's, but when I sometimes lose my way in life, I get back on the right path when I consider more than just me.
    SA   MA   U   MD   SD

41. I feel alone much of the time.
    SA   MA   U   MD   SD

42. Our knowledge has limits.
    SA   MA   U   MD   SD

43. I oppose any limits on mypersonal choice and autonomy.
    SA   MA   U   MD   SD

44. If both my spouse and I died, I would rather have our children raised by a devoutly religious person of any faith than by a good, but nonreligious, person.
    SA   MA   U   MD   SD

45. Education is the only thing that can save us.
    SA   MA   U   MD   SD

46. Personal freedom has its limits.
    SA   MA   U   MD   SD

47. I think life is essentially meaningless.
    SA   MA   U   MD   SD

48. It is important to be spiritual, but not necessarily in the sense of institutionalized religion.
    SA   MA   U   MD   SD

49. The problems of society can be solved through science and technology.
    SA   MA   U   MD   SD

50. Shame can be good for me.
    SA   MA   U   MD   SD

51. I worry about my level of self-esteem.
    SA   MA   U   MD   SD

52. I am sure that life has meaning even though I am not entirely sure what it is.
    SA   MA   U   MD   SD

53. Nature operates according to orderly laws.
    SA   MA   U   MD   SD

54. Suffering builds character.
    SA   MA   U   MD   SD

55. If it feels good, I should do it.
    SA   MA   U   MD   SD

56. Love is bigger than all of us.
    SA   MA   U   MD   SD

57. Some values are better than others.
    SA   MA   U   MD   SD

58. We are all sinners.
    SA   MA   U   MD   SD

59. Marriage is a nonbinding commitment.
    SA   MA   U   MD   SD

60. My experiences tell me what I feel about something, but those feelings are more reliable when I test them against religion, nature, tradition, or other people.
    SA   MA   U   MD   SD

61. The problems of society can be solved through science.
    SA   MA   U   MD   SD

62. I keep my word at all costs.
    SA   MA   U   MD   SD

63. Nobody has the right to tell me what to do.
    SA   MA   U   MD   SD

64. Nobody should tell me what to do, but sometimes I am too stupid or foolish to make the best choice.
    SA   MA   U   MD   SD

65. Things are getting better and better.
    SA   MA   U   MD   SD

66. Where my loved ones are is my home.
    SA   MA   U   MD   SD

67. Science has created more problems than it has solved.
    SA   MA   U   MD   SD

68. There is much from the past that can be used again, in a new and positive way.
    SA   MA   U   MD   SD

69. We have come a long way since the Dark Ages.
  SA MA U   MD SD

70. Hard work is the surest way to success.
  SA MA U   MD SD

71. Teaching any particular value as better than another is wrong.
  SA MA U   MD SD

72. If I were in a situation in which I was convinced that my *most sacred principles* somehow required the sacrifice of five children, I would choose the lives of the children over my principles.
  SA MA U   MD SD

73. When making important decisions, I prefer to rely on objective evidence.
  SA MA U   MD SD

74. It is essential to stick to my beliefs, even when it is hard to do so.
  SA MA U   MD SD

75. When making important decisions, I trust my feelings.
  SA MA U   MD SD

76. True freedom is freely choosing to be a loving servant.
  SA MA U   MD SD

77. The events of September 11 have changed my outlook on life so that I am more pessimistic about the future.
  SA MA U   MD SD

78. The events of September 11 have changed my outlook on life so that I am more optimistic about the future.
  SA MA U   MD SD

79. I am proud to be an American.
  SA MA U   MD SD

13

Social Psychology and the Self: Teaching and Research

Sherri B. Lantinga

Not many of you should presume to be teachers because you know that we who teach will be judged more strictly. (James 3:1)

Teaching is a difficult calling. Excellent teachers must learn continually about their field and about their students in order to effectively make connections between the two. Christian teachers have an additional responsibility to consider how their own faith perspective shapes both what they teach and how they do so. Further, they must consider how students' faith perspectives (Christian or not) influence how they will understand the course material. These tasks are made even more difficult when undertaken outside a community of believers who support the life of the Christian mind. In a particular attempt to help Christian teachers both within and outside of Christian academic communities, I present my own approach to teaching social psychology from a Christian perspective.

Teaching social psychology from a Christian perspective would seem to be relatively straightforward. Most people have never heard of social psychology, and the field's focus on how other people powerfully influence our everyday behavior does not evoke controversial historical figures or theories. Further, the social psychological understanding of strong social influences appears to map onto a Christian understanding of the fundamentally relational nature of human beings. I have been dismayed, however, by the difficulty of teaching social psychology as a coherent subdiscipline, let alone teaching it from a Christian perspective. Within social psychology itself, one finds an internally conflicting mixture of premodern, modern, and postmodern strands among the descriptions of research methods, the field's theories and research findings, and in the implied definitions of the self. Social psychological research is conducted (and described) in a modern frame. Important research outcomes are then synthesized into textbooks by authors with often unexamined postmodern perspectives (for more on this tension, see Martin and Sugarman 2000). Further, whether people are basically relational beings or basically autonomous individuals buffeted about by situational influences is unclear in most textbooks. To make matters even worse, students who read these texts—including Christian students—may themselves hold a muddled bundle of unexamined assumptions about the nature of persons. Finally, some of the assumptions of students and of social psychology coincide with a Biblical view of persons and others violently conflict. In such a milieu, how can Christian teachers effectively convey a convincing or a coherent notion of the self?

As a social enterprise, teaching shapes selves. Helping students to examine and refine their typically implicit beliefs about the nature of people will shape their social behaviors, which in turn influences other people. In the long run, the examined life should lead to better service in the Kingdom. The challenge for the Christian social psychologist is thus to teach about the fundamentally relational and responsible self to students convinced about radical individuality in a discipline where the researchers themselves are confused about whether radical individualism or social embeddedness better describes the nature of people. In what follows, I briefly outline a biblical view of persons and historical views of the self (premodern, modern, and postmodern). I next examine social psychological and student perspectives on the nature of the self and relate those to biblical and historical understandings. In the final section, I offer some conclusions and suggestions for helping students gain a more appropriate biblical and empirical understanding of the self.

A BIBLICAL VIEW OF THE SELF

One's beliefs about the nature of reality and the nature of people within that reality are at the core of any faith perspective. This set of fundamental beliefs shapes how one understands and acts within the world, even if those beliefs are not consciously accessible (Wolters 1985). For example, a belief that people are highly evolved animals whose problems are caused by irrationality results in a different explanation for aggression than a belief that people are stewards of creation whose problems are caused by disobedience to God's will. Being able to articulate one's own perspective helps provide a coherent framework for further thought and action. It also helps in understanding others' positions in interpersonal disagreements, which may be based on a different set of fundamental beliefs. Christian teachers must articulate their own fundamental beliefs before helping their students do so. In this section, I present my own understanding of a biblical view of the self as a starting place for other Christians to begin their own task of articulation.

Christians believe that God exists. Building on that irreducible belief, we believe that God is triune, one God in three persons in a communing relationship. We believe that God created all that is, including people, through his Spirit and the Word. People are created with physical bodies on a physical earth, and men and women together reflect the image of this Creator God. People were commanded to care for the creation and to reproduce. That is, as embodied beings we are called to be responsible and to be relational as we work in the world (see Gunton 2001; Murr 2001; Wolters 1985). We live in relationship with our Creator, with other people, and with the nonhuman creation. A biblical description of the self must include all three of these elements (materially embodied, morally responsible, relationally embedded) and may not reduce the nature of persons to only one aspect. We must also recognize that sin has resulted in a distorted creation, so that our relationships, thought patterns, choices, and knowledge of the creation are twisted (Plantinga 1995). We understand from Scripture that God's grace (e.g., through salvation in Christ, through common wisdom) and not our own independent devices is the only lasting means of solving the problems all around us. Because of God's sustaining grace, we can still serve him in a sinful world and attempt to discern what is good and whole from what needs redeeming. Through grace, people can become agents of wholeness while the Spirit is still sanctifying them.

People raised in an individualistic Western culture are persuaded that individuality is primary and human relationships are secondary. However, a biblical view of the nature of persons suggests that relationships are perhaps more fundamental to persons than individuality. Indeed, the Bible does not describe any faithful Lone Rangers (indeed, even the Lone Ranger was never far from his faithful sidekick). Biblical figures who tried to make their own rules, who tried to live outside of obedient relationships with a community or with God, were punished. We readily think of Achan, who stole from Jericho things devoted to God (Josh. 7); King David's treacherous strategy to take Bathsheba as his wife (2 Sam. 11); Ananias and Sapphira's lie to the new church (Acts 5). In many non-Western cultures, as was probably the case in biblical times as well, family members are essential parts of the self: "To be without family is to be dead" (Pipher 1997, 25). The historic punishment of exile was the equivalent of a death sentence in the finality of the separation from a community of meaning. Even ignoring for a moment our inescapable relationship with God, that we are conceived at all requires some sort of human relationship (even scientific ways around the traditional means of conception still involve relationships among people). Before our birth, we are already completely embedded in an inseparable physical-social context. We are inside another human being for the first months of development; farmers, truckers, grocers, medical care professionals, neighbors, and especially our fathers provided food, social and material support, and love for our mothers that sustained them as they cared for us. From the moment of our conception, we are surrounded by people, their language, and their various cultural beliefs (for a fascinating cross-cultural comparison of social birth rituals, see DeLoach and Gottlieb 2000). Others shape our understanding of the world and of ourselves by their continual feedback and their availability as points of comparison. This social formation of the self does not end at high school or college graduation. We are profoundly and continually influenced by and influence others throughout our lives. We are meaningfully embedded in social contexts and to be abstracted from them does damage to our humanity.

SOCIAL PSYCHOLOGICAL VIEWS OF THE SELF

The focus of social psychology is to describe and explain individual human behavior as it is influenced by social contexts. Three major principles form the basis for the field (Ross and Nisbett 1991). The *power of the situation* describes the idea that situational factors profoundly influence an individual's behavior, often well beyond any personality factors. For example, as the number of other observers increases, the likelihood of any particular individual offering help to an injured individual significantly decreases (Latane and Darley 1968). The *power of interpretation* reflects the notion that how a person understands a situation, based on one's prior experiences with similar situations, significantly impacts one's behavior. For example, a man running close behind a fleeing woman would be interpreted quite differently in urban Chicago (as an assault in progress) than it would be in a small town (as a friendly chase). These different interpretations would result in different behaviors on the part of the observer (a call to the police vs. an indulgent smile). Finally, the *power of tension* recognizes that any given behavior is the result of a compromise among compelling and constraining forces on the actor, which are not necessarily at a conscious level (Ross and Nisbett 1991). For example, writing this essay is a result of a compromise or balance among social forces (e.g., the desire to spend time with my family), career goals (e.g., tenure), physical factors (e.g., the need to take a nap), and so on. Social psychology is therefore rooted in the idea that an individual's behavior is embedded in a social context that directly and indirectly influences behavior.

As its source of knowledge, social psychology relies entirely on empirical research, preferably of the strict experimental kind. The goal of such research is to determine the causes of a given behavior, either singly or, more commonly, in combination with a few other hypothesized causal factors. As a legacy of the modernist project, social psychologists conduct their research under the belief that they are objectively describing the (usually hidden) forces that shape individual behavior. Although it is not often acknowledged, this methodological commitment restricts both the kind and size of questions that can be answered in social psychology. As a result of its chosen methodology, social psychology has usually adopted a mechanistic focus on causality rather than a teleological focus on an individual's goals as explanations of social behavior. This mechanistic approach is then reflected in textbooks that introduce students to the discipline (for a refreshing goal-oriented approach, see the text by Kenrick, Neuberg, and Cialdini 2002). Situational causes and observable behaviors are more easily studied by the objective experimenter than are research subjects' personal goals; goals require consideration of the subject as a person with his or her own values, desires, and purposes.

With a primary unit of analysis as the individual person (contrasted with sociology's focus on larger groups or biology's focus on cellular systems) and a mechanistic, objective methodology, direct social psychological examination of the nature of self is strictly limited. A deeper understanding of human beings requires philosophical investigation, which is not within the purview of the discipline. Social psychologists rarely consider how historical and philosophical trends have shaped their assumptions about the nature of people; only since the 1980s have cultural influences on the content or conclusions of the discipline been considered (for an example, see Baumeister 1987). Nor do social psychologists consider how the religious beliefs of either the researcher or the study participants shape observations or behavior. As a result, a full understanding of the self is not possible within the confines of the social psychological paradigm.

Within a psychology curriculum, social psychology is the best-suited subdiscipline for addressing the relational aspect of the self. Skimming any social psychology textbook quickly reveals that people are very much influenced by others. The text title and the typical topics (e.g., aggression, prejudice) seem to require a view of the self as fundamentally relational and embedded in meaningful social contexts. Oddly enough, definitions of the self (when they are given at all) are much more modern in orientation. For example, "The self is first and foremost the collection of beliefs that we hold about ourselves" (Taylor, Peplau, and Sears 2003, 99). Another text defines the social individual (it does not use the word *self*) as "a dynamic combination of motivations, knowledge, and feelings, all of which work with one another to produce the fascinating range of social thought and behavior" (Kenrick et al. 2002, 37). Such definitions neglect the body, neglect a historical or geographic or spiritual framework, and neglect relationships with other people or with God. The self seems to be entirely subjective, interior, conscious, and individual.

Despite the subjective understanding of the self, social psychological research is more interested in objectively observed behavior than on subjective reports of feelings or beliefs (for a critique of psychological research methods, see Van Leeuwen 1982). Despite the supposedly relational emphasis of social psychology, tight experimental control requires the removal of individuals from their own social contexts of meaning; research almost exclusively addresses only the "stranger" end of the relationship continuum. Researchers recruit unacquainted participants who report to an unfamiliar setting. The unacquainted experimenter then instructs them to interact with each other for a short period of time on a specific task or with hypothetical persons described on paper. As a result, we have built a social psychology of the self-as-stranger rather than studying the behavior of people within their communities of meaning. This is especially striking in a discipline where the main focus is on how social situations influence behavior. To look at it another way, the restricted methods of empirical research have shaped our understanding of the self. These choices are analogous to measuring the height, length, and width of a balloon, and, relying only on those measurements, concluding that balloons are solid cubes. We know the approximate size, but little of the actual shape, color, texture, or content of the balloon. Worse, by looking only at the self-as-stranger view of human behavior, we have come to believe that our measurements result in an accurate picture of the object under study.

Students with unexamined beliefs about the nature of people or with naïveté about the limitations of scientific methods may all too easily accept the confused assumptions of social psychology. How can undergraduates begin to untangle the implicit and contradictory assumptions that the self can meaningfully be studied in isolation from its social context and that selves are importantly influenced each minute by their social surroundings? Within an individualistic culture, students will likely downplay the entire message of social psychology that our physical and social situations powerfully affect our daily behavior and beliefs. The internal contradictions just noted within social psychology undermine the enterprise and prevents students from fully understanding the richness of our social contexts.

STUDENTS' PERCEPTIONS OF THE SELF

Students' fundamental beliefs about the nature of people shape how they process information in a social psychology course: what they focus on, what they ignore, and even what gets distorted to fit their preexisting framework. Students raised in a Western culture likely adopt modern or postmodern beliefs; Christian students may also hold to some traditional beliefs in a creator God. How do these sources of belief influence how students understand the self?

Participants, Survey, and Procedure. I surveyed a convenience sample of 221 undergraduates from four Christian liberal arts schools, most of whom received a small amount of extra course credit for their participation.[1] Most of the participants were women (58%). Upperclassmen (juniors and seniors) represented 69% of the sample, and the average age was twenty-one years ($SD = 2.77$). Almost all of the students (98%) identified themselves as Christians; the most commonly-reported denominational affiliations were Nazarene (21%), Reformed (19%), and Baptist (14%). Most participants (97%) reported attending at least one religious service (including school chapels) in the last month, and the average attendance was nearly twice weekly ($M = 7.34$, $SD = 5.52$).

Surveys were sent to colleagues at each of the four schools, and they were administered either during class or as an outside assignment. After being informed of the purpose of the study and that their responses would be anonymous, students privately responded to the written prompt "Write an essay on what you mean by the word 'self.'" Students were given about half of a standard page to write their response (only a few needed more room than this) and then answered several demographic items.

Results and Discussion. It was clear that most students had a difficult time articulating what they meant by "self." Many students appealed to synonyms ("My self is my identity") or resorted to vague statements like "self is who I am," followed by a list of characteristics. One of the most convoluted essays was made up entirely of statements that could be individually found in many other essays: "When I think of the word self, I think of me as a person. Myself is the person that I am, including what makes me up. Self is what I see inside of me and what I try to have others see good [sic] of me. Self is who I am as a person." Despite this elusiveness, there were some common themes in the essays. I read a sample of the essays to develop a list of themes relevant to historical understandings of the self and then scored the essays for the commonality and importance of the themes on 3-point scales (where 0 = "characteristic not mentioned," 1 = "mentioned or peripheral," and 2 = "central, important, meaningful"). The thirteen scored themes included qualities of the self (exclusivity, uniqueness, hiddenness, possibility for change), content of the self (thoughts and emotions, personality, physical body, soul/spirit, behavior), and sources of the self (culture or environment, other people, God/Christ, and one's own will).

Table 1 shows the percentage of respondents who at least mentioned each theme and the percentage of respondents whose essays indicated that the theme or concept was important for understanding the self. Taken together, the data on qualities of the self suggest a subjective individuality. About a fourth of the essays note that the self is not-others (either separate or different). A fifth of the essays note that the self is dynamic; the tone of some of the essays that did acknowledge change suggested that the self *had* developed, so that the students may have felt that college graduation was the expected terminus for development. Finally, the self appears to be subjective (a fifth noted that it was hidden from others, that it was "at the core of one's inner being"), so that the self was known through internal means rather than through observable behaviors. An analysis of content themes shows a heavy emphasis on internal aspects of the self (cognitions, emotions, personality). This pattern reinforces hiddenness and subjectivity. The connection of the self to one's physical body or to one's soul was frequently mentioned, though often as part of a forumulaic list (mind, body, soul/spirit). Some students went into more detail about the relevance of genetics or appearance to the self. Many students mentioned action as part of a list of the contents of the self, but fewer seemed to believe that this was an important element worth elaborating on (e.g., "The word self includes my thoughts, feelings, actions, perceptions, and how I express myself"). The analysis of sources of the self showed that a few different types were mentioned. Some students were careful to include cultural and familial sources of the self so that their essays sounded rather premodern in tone. However, only two students mentioned specific social roles as part of the self (e.g., wife, student, friend, daughter). Other essays were rather rationalistic, so that the will and personal decisions were most important for forming the self; of course, these essays were rather individualistic in tone. Most of the essays including these sources saw them as factors that may influence the self but that are not themselves constituent elements of the self.

What is striking about the students' essays is not only what was included (implied or explicit), but also what is absent. For example, given that nearly every respondent claimed a Christian religious affiliation and attended several worship services in the last month, 72 percent of them did not even mention God (or Jesus or the Holy Spirit) in their essays. Only one mentioned any form of religious ritual or process in connection to the self (e.g., profession of faith, baptism, sanctification). None mentioned the Holy Spirit, fruits of the Spirit, or the Bible. For professing Christians, it seemed very odd that none of these were included in an attempt to explain one's understanding of the self. As another example, no students explicitly included the concepts of reason, virtue, responsibility, or morality

Table 1
*Percentage of essays containing themes and percentage of essays
where theme was important for understanding the self.*

Themes	Mentioned	Important
Qualities of the Self		
Exclusivity (self as a separate individual)	30	12
Uniqueness (self as different from others)	22	16
Change possible (development of the self)	20	12
Hidden from others	19	8
Content of the Self		
Thoughts/emotions (beliefs, values, self-perceptions, goals)	72	45
Personality	25	4
Physical body (appearance, genetics, body)	40	17
Soul/spirit	22	5
Behavior (actions)	23	5
Sources of the Self		
Creation/environment/context (society, culture)	26	11
Other people (family, friends)	29	14
God/Christ/Holy Spirit	28	16
Will, self-as-creator	25	8
	Note: $N = 221$	

in their essays. These ideas would be important for both modernist and biblical understandings of the self, but they did not appear here. It is possible that more students did not mention some themes (e.g., uniqueness) either because they did not believe they were relevant or that these qualities were so assumed that they did not come to mind. For example, 80 percent of the students did not mention the possibility of change; this result begs the question about whether these students assume changeability but did not write about it or whether they assume a static self.

These analyses allow us a way to manage a lot of information, but they do not reflect the global tone of the essays. For example, mentioning God in an essay does not necessarily convey whether the student believes that God is somewhat relevant or a critical, fundamental source of the self. As a result of this difficulty, I attempted to assess the degree to which each essay reflected the three historical periods described earlier (premodern, modern, or postmodern) along a 3-point scale where 0 = "not at all," 1 = "somewhat," and 2 = "very much so." Again, these ratings were not independent, so that a given essay could score high both on modern and postmodern, for example. The task of giving global ratings was surprisingly difficult to do, and the results (shown in table 2) should be read very tentatively. I gave higher premodern scores to essays that emphasized the importance of external persons or structures for understanding the self: "Self is an internal understanding of how the people around us view us. Self is a result of society. God has a major role in our concept of self as well." Essays with an emphasis on individualism, subjective internality, or the will were given higher modern scores: "Self is naturally the focus of our logic and reasoning because it is who we are and it is very difficult to see others as they are" or "Self is your own and who you want it to be. It is the person's choice of what they want to do with their own choice; I just hope my decision with my self was the right one to make."

Ratings of postmodernism were the most difficult. Higher scores were

---

Table 2
Percentage of essays reflecting each historical period's understanding of the self.

	NOT AT ALL	SOMEWHAT	VERY MUCH
Premodern tone	69	21	10
Modern tone	27	52	21
Postmodern tone	3	28	69

NOTE: N = 221

given to essays that reflected a jumbled confusion of paradigms, to those reflecting hypermodernism (e.g., a radical subjectivity), or to those reflecting what has recently been labeled as transmodernism (see also the Survey of Student Values and analysis by Norwine et al. in this volume). Here is an example of the paradigm confusion: "My self is something that I struggle constantly to discover, to reshape and ultimately to model after Christ. Self is the individual that I am, unique and different from anything else. It is a word of ownership, stating that I am ultimately in control of what I do, think, and say." Examples of hypermodernism include "Self is whatever you want it to be" or "The self, for me, is the stream of thought, perception, emotion, and memory that runs thru [sic] my conciousness [sic]. My body is included only in the sense that what affects my body directly impinges and affects my consciousness." The essays that reflected a transmodern perspective were fewer in number and may be what some of the "confused" essays were trying to reflect. Examples from these include "An individual person who lives within a community of other social active self's [sic]. Personal feelings/beliefs/actions [sic] that all play off of those other self's [sic] in which the self finds itself surrounded by culturally, ethically [sic], sexually, etc." or "[The self] is distinct from all others, and so has a unique perspective on the world. Yet the self lives only in relationship with others and finds its identity in those relationships." Among the essays rated high on postmodernism, the confused and transmodern versions were more common than the hypermodern versions. It is possible that the confusion evident in many essays results from Baumeister's (1987) observation of increasing historic difficulty with defining the self. Another possibility is one of sampling considerations: these students are young Christians still in the process of trying to reconcile their Christian beliefs (created in the image of God) with their cultural and historical context (we are our own gods).

An analysis of the resulting global ratings shows that most students' essays reflected postmodern themes. Premodern understandings of the firmly embedded self were uncommon, as were pure modern expressions. The postmodern paradigm reveals traces of previous paradigms but has taken them to a new level (e.g., hypersubjectivity) or has transformed them into a new idea (transmodernism).

Several related assumptions seem to lie beneath the themes identified in the essays. First, students assume that the self is consciously accessible and knowable. It may be hidden from others, but usually not from oneself. This development in describing the nature of the self can probably be traced back at least to Descartes' famous *Cogito, ergo sum.* Related to this, students seem to believe that others do not know about one's self unless it is intentionally shared. Behavior is not typically seen as an important part of the subjective, internal self. The physical body is part of the self, but it seems to serve as the wall between the "real" self and the outer world; it is usually not integrally important beyond its service as a barrier or porter. Third, many students seem to assume that the self is stable and universal. The tone of many essays was surprisingly similar to God's Old Testament declarations of "I AM." Related to this, I sensed that students saw the self as the center of the individual's universe. To pursue this further, I asked thirty-nine students from Dordt College to "draw any sort of diagram that shows what you mean by the word 'self.'" The typical response was a depiction of the self at the center (often with a list of inner characteristics) with lines connecting it to external factors (God, family, teachers, etc.). Although this approach revealed a much more embedded (and embodied) understanding of the self than did the essays, it also confirmed the self-centeredness implied in the essays. Perhaps the most striking example of this ego-centeredness was one student's essay statement, "As a Christian, God is included in my 'self.'"

In summary, even Christian students believe in an individualistic, subjective, conscious self that may have originated from God or familial sources but which they presently control independently of their social or physical context. The challenge of social psychology is to convince students that much of their behavior is not under their conscious control, but that behavior and self-understanding are very much products of current and past contexts. The challenge of Christianity is to convince students that people are inherently (not tangentially) relational creatures rather than atomistic agents. How can a Christian social psychologist even begin to help students revise their unexamined beliefs about the nature of people?

RECOMMENDATIONS FOR MEETING THE CHALLENGES

What are the implications of a biblically and empirically grounded understanding of the self for teaching and learning in social psychology? How can a Christian psychologist make sense of and shape the many sets of fundamental beliefs that come together in a social psychology classroom? In this section, I offer several concrete recommendations for in-class demonstrations or assignments that help clarify the nature of the self.

The first step is to articulate one's own perspective on the nature of the self, which requires a teaching philosophy that is grounded in a faith perspective. How does one begin this daunting task? I have found it useful to begin with my "givens" in a classroom setting and ask myself a series of "why" questions to get back to my implicit, fundamental beliefs. For example, I firmly believe it is important for me to memorize and use all of my students' names within the first two weeks of each semester. Why is this important? I do this to show respect for my students and to begin a relationship with them. Why are respect and relationships important? I believe that students learn best in a relationship of respect, where the professor is accountable to the learners and even open to learning from them. Why are these people worthy of respect? In this particular domain, I have more knowledge and experience than students do, but as fellow servants in God's Kingdom, they also have gifts and skills and experiences from which I can benefit. As believers, we work together to discern goodness and evil as we attempt to bring redemption to sin-tainted relationships. Why do we believe that we have any authority to do this work? I believe that our work in this world is part of the "cultural mandate" in Gen. 1, where men and women are *together* called to care for the creation and to reproduce. We are therefore all communally responsible for that creation (and are therefore placed above animals). This creation has been distorted by sin, and in caring for it we need understand it and bring about healing. This brief example shows how to use one's everyday actions to access the beliefs that guide behavior. Such questioning is not a static process, however. One may find that one's fundamental beliefs (e.g., that people are inherently responsible) do not seem to relate to current behaviors (e.g., imposing no penalties for students' late work), and thinking about the disconnection between the two is needed.

Once the instructor has articulated his or her own beliefs, the next step is to identify and develop one's course goals. Adopting a content goal about the nature of the self keeps this topic at the forefront and counteracts the metaphorical isolation of the self in textbooks. Pedagogical strategies and course policies are also influenced by the instructor's understanding of the self. For example, lectures minimize the physical and relational aspects of the self, whereas demonstrations or small group discussions highlight those aspects; attendance policies can reflect beliefs about relationships in terms of accountability to classmates or the instructor for contributing to communal learning. Making explicit one's implicit goals for a course helps to demonstrate one's beliefs to students.

Once the course itself has begun, I use several assignments and demonstrations to help students identify and reflect on their own and others' implicit beliefs. One useful assignment that fosters a good deal of class discussion involves having students read a chapter from their introductory text and then write a two-page paper about what "bugs" them or what is missing from a Christian perspective. Many students are able to identity the assumption of evolutionary theory as fact, the lack of any mention of God or spirituality or religion, and the assumption that nearly all social behaviors are ultimately for one's own gain. Some students remark that they have never questioned a textbook before in this way and that they would be more careful about how they read the book.

To illustrate our fundamentally relational nature, I use a ball of string to make visible the invisible connections and influences among people. Tossing the ball from student to student (with each holding onto his/her part of the string) shows the social interconnections; having different students pull on their part of the string or drop it altogether affects the rest of the "body" to a greater or lesser degree. Students understand that they are still individuals (they themselves do not turn into string), but that they are very much connected with those around them. Having the teacher (a common, external authority figure) direct the movement of the ball of string helps show the premodern understanding of the self where students are defined by how they behave and by their social connections. The modern self can be demonstrated by allowing for more dynamic social relationships, where the ball is tossed randomly (the teacher is relegated to mere observer). A few persons may choose to tug on the string, drop it altogether, or even move to different locations. The postmodern, saturated self (Gergen 1991) is more difficult, but can be demonstrated by giving students their own pieces of string (Velcro pieces may be even better here). They may then choose to wander about to connect (or disconnect) with whomever they please. The string activity involves more active learning and opens a discussion of the embedded self and its relationship to social context.

Chapters on social cognition, which focus on how people think about themselves and others, often assume an individualistic, subjective frame. In teaching about self-concept, a common suggestion is to have students complete the "Who am I" or Twenty Statements Test in which they quickly write down twenty phrases that describe themselves. As a way to encourage students to think about themselves from a fresh perspective, three versions of this classic measure could be used instead: a traditional "who am I," one with "where am I," and one with "what am I." The latter two versions help prompt recognition and discussion of the historical, cultural, physical, and social aspects of the self. Self-perception theory can be introduced with another thought-experiment, where students list their many public behaviors from the last week. Based *only* on these behaviors (no internal self-reflection allowed), have students describe themselves. What kind of a person do these public behaviors indicate? How does that correspond to the students' interior understanding of his or her self? Which version of the self is the "real" one?

Other thought experiments help students prepare for a discussion of the relational self or of individualistic and communalistic cultures. First, students consider living an entire hour without relying on *anyone*, past or present, physically present or not. They should quickly discover that the clothes they wear, the computers they use, and the chairs on which they sit all connect them to other people. In another version, students must describe a decision of theirs that did not rely on other people—one that was entirely their own. The more insightful students should see that the very language they use to think about or answer the question itself depends on a prior social context. Third, students write a single sentence that describes who they are *fundamentally*. Students exchange papers and read them aloud to begin a discussion of the extent to which relationships (to family, God, or others) or individuality feature in the descriptions. The joke about God and the scientist who agreed to a contest about who could make the better person is appropriate here: The scientist, who God has agreed may go first in the contest, bends down to scoop up some dirt in order to begin. God stops him with the words, "Make your own dirt." Even the stuff from which we try to create our modern "self-made man" has been given to us by others.

Teaching about the embedded dimension of the self can implicate two other aspects of the self. An increasingly prevalent example of the link between embeddedness and embodiment is that of eating disorders and the mass media. What people think of their bodies is based on cultural messages. Internalization of these social messages via social comparison and self-perception processes affects behavior (e.g., self-presentation concerns influence both eating and product consumption). Beliefs and behavior in turn affect relationships with others; questions are raised about the sincerity of others' love, especially that of a God who seems capriciously to assign lousy bodies to some. In this example, the relational nature of the self can be discussed within the context of persuasion. What message are television and movie viewers persuaded to believe about the kind of body that women and men "ought" to have? How do advertisers make people feel substandard and therefore in need of "salvation" via products?

The embedded self also comes through in discussions of persuasion and conformity. Research on informational influence has long demonstrated that when we are uncertain, we seek others' reactions for information about the proper way to think or act (Deutsch and Gerard 1955). We consult with those in our community (family, friends, coworkers, and neighbors) in order to understand our world and refine ourselves. Indeed, even the "teachers" in the classic obedience experiments of Milgram tried to ascertain what was actually happening to the "learner" behind the wall by looking at the experimenter's reactions; seeing that the experimenter was not alarmed, many "teachers" continued delivering electrical shocks to the "learner"

(Milgram 1974). It is a strange paradox that the postmodern self is the sole source of meaning, but this same self often does not have the ability to decide in isolation what is reality and what is not.

Postmodern understandings of the self can be rather easily undercut by attribution research. Postmodernism, when taken to its reasonable conclusion (itself not possible in a postmodern framework), is a desperately lonely enterprise. In the absence of grand narratives, in the loss of a common moral horizon, I am supposed to find my own meaning and you yours. We stand quite alone, left with only the little worlds that we have made for ourselves. Signs that this loneliness is not normative are becoming obvious throughout our culture. The increasing number of Internet chat rooms testify to the felt need to relate to other people (although through a disembodied means). Increasing numbers of "victim groups" are emerging, which might cohere around themes of dysfunctional families of origin, addictive habits, or other maladies (Cushman 1990; Vitz 1995). The paradox, and perhaps the death knell of postmodernism, seems to be that individualism is not working: if this world in which I live is mine alone, why do I feel such a need to consort with others? In a post-Christian society, victims receive sympathy (Bailie 1995). As Weiner's (1996) attribution research shows, if victims can convince others that they are not responsible for their problems, then others will sympathize and will draw near to bring what help they can. If, on the other hand, we are perceived to be responsible for our problems, then others will move away from us in anger or disgust, and will not offer help (Weiner 1996). Thus, the increasingly common strategy of self-labeled victimhood is a covert means to draw others closer, to establish some sort of social bond, however distorted it may be. This relational self persistently makes itself known even in a radically individualistic world. Indeed, even the label of "victim" implies some greater social order that has in some way not served us as we believe it ought, revealing again that we are inextricably bound up in a social system.

Discussing the fundamental attribution error (Ross 1977) in conjunction with Weiner's attribution work fits well when teaching about helping behavior. If Westerners do indeed underestimate situational factors in judging the cause of others' behavior, then Weiner's theory would predict more judgments of responsibility, more anger, and less helping behavior than otherwise. Ample research has supported this prediction (e.g, Weiner, Perry, and Magnusson 1988). The experiences and beliefs on which we base our attributions of responsibility for problems are critically important in understanding why we help some people and not others. Students, perhaps especially Christians, can then be challenged at a more personal level: Should we only help people who seem to deserve it (recognizing that we are often too harsh in our judgments) or should we help everyone (which escapes the judgment problem by offering grace to all but ignores justice)? Should we lean toward justice or toward grace?

Finally, another way to link relationality and responsibility is by using Shirley Jackson's short story "The Lottery" when discussing group processes or conformity pressures. In this highly engaging story, the citizens of a small town gather in the town square, where they chat about everyday activities and about the Lottery, which is mysterious to the viewer but apparently commonplace to the townspeople. From the slips of paper that each citizen draws, a winning citizen is eventually determined. She is then stoned to death by the other townspeople (including her own husband and children). Seeing a filmed version of the story in a classroom context always shocks students, both because of the awful outcome and because they have neither foreseen the violence at the end nor condemned any of the actions leading up to it. Students are challenged to consider to what extent each townsperson was responsible for the stoning and how the power of the situation may mitigate responsibility. They can then consider what aspects of their own lives reflect communal-level decisions and what part they each play in reinforcing those norms or traditions.

CONCLUSION

Social psychology is a joy to teach because of its immediate relevance to students' everyday lives. Students learn to think about the causes of people's behavior from a bigger perspective, understanding that situational factors and prior experiences play a much larger role in shaping behavior than an individualistic culture would have us believe. At the same time, teaching social psychology is made quite challenging by the array of unarticulated and confused beliefs present in the classroom. As a subdiscipline, social psychology shows internal contradictions: its methods are modern, its definitions of self are late modern or postmodern, and the title and topics of study assume a meaningful (and almost premodern understanding) of the importance of social context for understanding the self. Insofar as social psychology perpetuates the notion of the self as autonomous, then it fails to live up to its name. Another source of confusion is in the students' unarticulated beliefs. Christian students may simultaneously believe they were created in the image of God but that they are in control of who they are. God is believed to be very important, but so is the subjective individual. These conflicting assumptions will influence how students understand the course material and how they selectively apply it to their lives. Taken together, students may leave a social psychology course with their beliefs about the autonomous self either reinforced or perhaps merely confused by the message of the power of the situation. Neither of these is an ideal outcome. Students who leave a social psychology course without understanding how the power of the situation, of interpretation, and tension influence the fundamentally relational self (and not just the individual self) have been done a great disservice.

Christian teachers must help students examine their beliefs from a biblical perspective, both to improve students' understanding of the implications of social psychology for everyday life and to enhance their service in God's kingdom. To ignore the relational and responsible nature of the self is possible for some short time, but to do so neglects a critical part of the self and in the end it makes us less than human. As adopted by even well-meaning Christians, individualism has the capacity to destroy the church. Our errors in thinking (enumerated at length by cognitive and social psychologists) go unchecked, although we are convinced that we are quite accurate in our perceptions and thoughts. If we succumb to the notion that my choices are beyond question because I have my own sense of what is right and wrong, then members of Christ's body are no longer given the authority to hold each other in account. Cain's answer to God that he was not his brother's keeper is an eerie foretelling of our times, when the social norm "mind your own business" pervades even our churches. If the church body cannot call into question the actions or beliefs of its members, then the church fails to function as an extension of Christ. By working with students to help them understand that our relational and responsible selves require us to be accountable to others for correction, we will therefore challenge the nonbiblical influence of postmodernism in our classrooms, in our churches, and in the larger kingdom.

NOTES

1. Participants were forty-six students from Dordt College, a school in the Reformed tradition that enrolls 1300 students and is located in northwest Iowa (north of Sioux City); nineteen students at Asbury College, which enrolls approximately 1,300 students and is located south of Lexington, Kentucky; seventy-one students at Southern Nazarene University, which is located just west of Oklahoma City, Oklahoma, and enrolls 2,100 students; eighty-five students from Judson College, an evangelical college of American Baptist affiliation located west of Chicago which enrolls 830 students.

VI. The Trinity and the Self

14

Self, Attachment, and Agency:

Love and the Trinitarian Concept of Personhood

Stephen P. Stratton

The term *person* **originated** in Christian theology's developmental struggle to comprehend the nature and experience of a triune God. The derivative concept of human personhood is a gift of the Christian faith to culture. By definition, personhood is the event/being of relationship between a subject and an other (Ratzinger 1990; see also Vitz 1995). A person is a relational being who emerges when a self, as a unique particularity, communes with an other self. The result of this action is more than the sum of its constituent parts. Mark Lowery (this volume), using a more classic terminology, refers to the result as a *relational substance*. In more contemporary terminology a human person is a *communing self*—an inseparable merger of particularity and process. Personhood is life-structure and life-movement, combined.

In the beginning, however, a disclaimer is necessary: it is important to distinguish selfhood from individualism. Individualism as complete autonomy and total social isolation is a myth, a postulate at best. It has long been recognized that self cannot be reliably considered separate from its social milieu (Cooley 1968; Mead 1962). There is always a social exchange with others, either actually present, recalled, or imagined. To use the words of philosopher Charles Taylor (1989), no self exists outside of its "web of interlocution." "A self can never be described without reference to those who surround it" (35). As a subject attempts to deny the inescapability of communion, usually for protective reasons, and moves increasingly to live in the illusion of individuation, personhood is progressively diminished. This essay suggests that to whatever degree a subject denies communion for a more autonomous stance, a loss of personal balance is evident.

But an error in the opposite direction is also possible and may be seen most noticeably in non-Western cultures, such as India and Japan. These societies emphasize a highly relational "we-self," in contrast to the more Western "I-ness" (Roland 1988). Consequently, self may be submerged or hypothetically lost in relations to family or community. The self as an independent psychological agent is deemphasized in favor of the collective. A person then is defined exclusively in terms of social roles, presentations, and communication. To the degree that self vanishes amid the relational process, personhood is progressively diminished. This error tries to isolate or elevate communal movement as the primary quality of personhood, as the previous and opposite error tries to make self-structure the defining feature. Both errors of overemphasis on self or communion are distortions, the former more in keeping with modernistic leanings and the latter more predisposed to pre- or postmodern thinking.

Jürgen Moltmann (2001) seems to depict the extreme polar distortions of self and communion as *self-separated* and *self-dispersed,* respectively. The more underdeveloped the person, the more likely it is that human relations will be oriented toward some degree of defensive self-separation (the illusion of total individuation) or its mirror image, defensive self-dispersion (the illusion of complete merger). In either direction, personhood is diminished. In well-developed personhood, however, there is an inseparable complementarity of selfhood (in-itself) and communion (towards-others) that must be maintained (Clark 1993, 16, 17).

THE COMMUNING SELF AS PERSON

Selfhood and communion are two sides of the coin called personhood, different yet inseparable. Not opposites in trinitarian thinking, they coincide (Gunton 1991; Zizioulas 1985). Both contribute distinctly to life in balance and yet are indivisible for purposes of healthy, authentic living. Gunton (1997) explains:

> The person is neither an individual, defined in terms of separateness from others, nor one who is swallowed up into the collective. Just as Father, Son, and Holy Spirit are what they are by virtue of their otherness-in-relation, so that each particular is unique and absolutely necessary to the being of the whole, so it is, in our own way, for our being in society. (13)

If selfhood is overemphasized and detached conceptually from communion, it often assumes a modern flavor and drifts toward a bounded, reified abstraction of individualism that evidences little to no awareness of the importance of context or community. If communion is overemphasized and detached conceptually from selfhood, it often assumes a postmodern flavor and becomes a random, amoral process that denies the self-determining capacities of individual psychological agents. Realistically, well-developed personhood requires an authentic self-structure and a healthy communal process.

Selfhood contributes to personhood as an emergent experience of subjectivity (see Emerson this volume, and the discussion of Bakhtin's *I-for-myself*) that is multifaceted and dynamic (Markus and Wurf 1987), not monolithic or static. Self is a malleable embodied representation of whom one presently is from relational situation to situation. It is the moment by moment intrapersonal location in the dynamic flow of interpersonal relating. This temporal locational process begins developmentally with an embodied proto-self (Bermúdez 1998; Vitz, this volume) who is socially embedded from birth and exhibits a responsive core consciousness (LeDoux 1996, Damasio 1999). With continued development, one exhibits a more stable interpersonal and representational self (Neisser 1997; Nelson 1997), who has a past and a future founded in extended consciousness (Damasio 1999). The bridge between the early self and this latter self is best defined by concepts found in attachment theory, which contributes a universal foundation for understanding self-in-communion.

As selfhood is related to subjectivity, communion contributes the emergent experience of intersubjectivity to personhood (see Emerson, this volume, for discussion of Bakhtin's *I-for-the-other*). Lowery (this volume) uses the term *solidarity*. Communion or solidarity *is not* the interpersonal location of the self as it relates to others; it *is* the actual interpersonal flow between persons. It is life movement intimately connected to life-structure in healthy development and living. Action and authenticity are united and reciprocally determining. Consequently, personhood as self-in-communion is not an entity or a potential act but a *presence* experienced in the relationship between human beings (Tiryakian 1968). Healthy communion requires a self to move in coordination with an other. Indeed, medical research suggests that neurophysiological stability in all human beings depends on such a system of mutual interaction and reciprocation, synchronized with those to whom they are attached (Lewis, Amini, and Lannon 2000; Schore 2003a, 2003b).

Trinitarian Personhood: A Transmodern Approach

This approach pleases few devotees to a strictly modern or postmodern worldview. In actuality, a worldview based on a trinitarian perspective does not fit into either worldview. It probably comes closest to a perspective that is called *constructive postmodernism* (Kegan 1994) or maybe in a more hopeful way, *transmodernism* (Vitz 2001). These titles convey an attempt at a creative retrieval of elements of modernism appropriately critiqued by postmodernism and integrated into a progressive worldview. The resulting worldview provides a conducive environment for trinitarian theology.

Many modernists find fault with an approach based on the inner life of the Trinity as a prototype for personhood and selfhood. A trinitarian perspective has no place for radical autonomy or disengagement and prioritizes engagement as the essential foundation for human development, freedom, and knowledge. Indeed, relationship becomes the guiding transcendent principle for practical living with a relevant, personal God, who is not knowable rationally or empirically, but is knowable experientially. Reason no longer reigns supreme but is considered only as a way of knowing that must be accountable to messy emotions. All this is troublesome to those with sensitive modern tendencies based on essentialism and verifiable certainty.

Postmodernism, particularly those varieties that are intensely deconstructive in their method, has its own criticisms of a trinitarian approach. There is little room for arbitrariness in the concepts of person, relationship, love, and freedom when they are actualized in a triune God. It is difficult to build a worldview based in self-referential authority and extreme relativism when an external but engagable prototype is posited. A trinitarian and biblical approach balances the significant influence of the social with an awareness of embodiment, which is the foundation for human personhood.

This article develops these trinitarian thoughts about personhood as a way of considering how we actually live in relationship with others. It suggests that Attachment Theory provides a complementary research foundation for considering the development of self with others. In addition, human agency or self-movement in a relational context is a way of conceptualizing the development of communion. Finally, the first steps in a proposed model offer some explanations about what facilitates and obstructs selves-in-communion. Ultimately, such a model may offer some direction for how persons can participate in relationships with one another and with a triune Creator.

BEFORE CREATION: A TRIUNE GOD

The trinitarian narrative of God is a relational story; it is a love story. Even before creation and the garden narrative, there is one God in three Persons as a communing relationship characterized by self-giving and self-limiting love (Moltmann 2001). "Terms like king, judge, and sovereign speak of what God does, of His relationship to the creation" (Kinlaw 2001, 9), but that is not who He is. "God is love," as the apostle John affirms in his first epistle, and love is actualized first in the relational life of the Trinity. Kasper (1997) describes the inner life of this triune God:

> The Father as pure self-giving cannot exist without the Son who receives. But since the Son does not receive something but everything, he exists only in and through the giving and receiving. On the other hand, he would not have truly received the self-giving of the Father were he to keep it for himself and not give it back. He exists therefore insofar as he receives himself wholly from the Father and gives himself wholly back to the Father, or, as it is put in the farewell prayer of Jesus, glorifies the Father in return. As existence that is wholly owed to another, the Son is therefore pure gratitude, eternal Eucharist, pure obedient response to the word and the will of the Father. But this reciprocal love also presses beyond itself; it is pure giving only if it empties itself of, and gives away, even this two-in-oneness and in pure gratuitousness, incorporates a third in whom love exists as pure receiving, a third who therefore exists only insofar as he receives his being from the mutual love between the Father and Son. The three persons of the Trinity are thus pure relationality; they are relationships in which the one nature of God exists in three distinct and non-interchangeable ways. (309)

A trinitarian perspective asserts therefore that the inner life of God is triune, familial, loving, free, and dialogical (Kinlaw 2001). These characteristics describe God as he engages creation, but they also describe God prior to the creational accounts. In this eternal community

> each divine person totally surrenders Himself to the others. This total self-gift of each person within the Trinity, while preserving the distinct features of each Person establishes a complete union of wills. The love of each divine Person is a personal choice, a will-act, made by each based on a knowledge of truth. The self-donation of each Person to the others unites all three in a communion of persons. In effect, there is an attitude, a choice, to act as one. This is what love is: an act of the will to do what another wills. (Hogan and LeVoir 1985, 37)

This description is more than simply a past or current description of God. It suggests something profound and unbelievably applicable for God's created others, an act of this eternal, loving Community formed all creation. The stamp of love permeates the created order. Accordingly, this relational unity called God becomes the prototype for all relationships in the created order: humans were made by Love for love. It lies at the heart of understanding how persons image God. Indeed, human beings are confused about whom they are unless they understand the nature and experience of the God they image.

CREATION AND THE GARDEN COMMUNITY

A canonical reading of Genesis 1 sees in its peculiar language a reference to the Trinity. "God said, 'Let us make man in our Image, according to our likeness. . . . So God created man in His own image; in the image of God He created him; male and female He created them'" (Gen. 1: 26–27). Communing selves are established as the prerequisite from the beginning, modeled after the prototype.

> [Creation in the image of God] is to be understood relationally rather than in terms of the possession of fixed characteristics such as reason or will.
>
> . . . The reality of the human creature must be understood in terms of the human relation to God, in the first instance, and the rest of creation in the second. The relation to the remainder of Creation itself falls into two. In the first place, to be in the image of God is to subsist in relations of mutual constituitiveness with other human beings [relationships]. In the second place, it is to be in a set of relations [tasks] with the non-personal creation. The human imaging of God is a dynamic way of being before God and with fellow creatures. (Gunton 1993, 3)

Before the Fall: Self and Communion in Harmony. Created persons lived out their primary purpose in the Garden by choosing to accept the invitation into communion with the Trinity. They participated in communion by choosing to live out the complementary purposes of (1) loving personal relationships of mutual constituitiveness, and (2) loving stewardship for the nonpersonal creation. Purposeful participation created the conditions for God's loving actions to be realized with other human beings and with the created world. God, who is love, was realized in the relationships with others and the tasks of stewardship. In other words, participating with the triune God in these ontological relationships and tasks created the conditions for the one who is love-in-action to move without barrier. Modeled after the prototype, love is affirmed as the innate vocation of every human person (Hogan and LeVoir 1985).

Gen. 2:25 reports that as the original human beings participated in their created purpose, they were naked and unashamed with God, each other, and the rest of creation. The union of self and communion was unhindered by barriers within or between persons. Woman, man, and God shared freely and together cared for the rest of creation in complete intimacy of communion. The merger of particularity and process was dynamic and practical.

The Fall: Self Fearing Communion. The decision to step out of this type of relationship had disastrous consequences at every level—with God, with each other, and with the rest of creation. Martin Luther implies that human beings chose a self separated from communion ("a heart curved in on itself," [Kinlaw 2001, 62]) as protection from the picture painted by the Tempter. Brunner (1939) explains that this choice was motivated by anxiety. He suggests that Adam and Eve's decision should be seen as "a fear of venturing all on God alone; it is not simply impudence, but anxiety about oneself; it is not merely rebellion, it is a kind of dizziness which attacks those who ought to step over the abyss leaning only on God" (131–32). The next step is an extension of distrust in God—disengaging the self from communion to the degree that seemed secure to untrusting humans. Human agency for the first time contradicted human being.

Human hearts, initially with a passion for their created purposes, became hearts of shame and fear. In response, task and relationship were distorted into self-protective strategies, not opportunities for love. "The fall consists in the refusal to make being dependent on communion. This rupture between being and communion results automatically in the truth of being acquiring priority over the truth of communion" (Zizioulas 1997, 101–2). In other words, new conditions make it essential that particularity be protected above all else. Process becomes the tool for purposes of self-security, no longer viewed as inseparable from its complement. Personhood is distorted, and love is hindered.

After the Fall: Self-Protective Coverings. After human beings opted for self-protection, "the eyes of both of them were opened, and they knew that they were naked; and they sewed fig leaves together and made themselves coverings" (Gen. 3:7). Before the Fall, self-in-communion felt secure. Nakedness was not risky; vulnerability was life-giving and life-sustaining. After the Fall, communion became suspect, nakedness brought shame, and vulnerability was something to fear. Self-generated protective coverings became essential to creatures who had chosen a life other than that for which they were made.

Coverings are the futile attempts of human beings to reproduce the pre-Fall conditions for which they were made, without God's communion that made such a life possible. Humans seem to desire the security and intimacy of Eden—on their own terms. The problem with self-generated coverings is that they provide an illusion of security, a pseudo-intimacy. They allow short-term management of shame and fear because they promise security with terms acceptable to communion-suspicious selves. Relations with God, others, and the rest of creation are subordinated to protection. Self-separation or self-dispersion, distortions of self and communion and ultimately a deformation of human purpose, become the strategies to live with actual and imagined risks of a fallen world. Both poles of self-separation (extreme, defensive independence) and self-dispersion (extreme, defensive dependence) work by establishing relationships that objectify and control others for self-protective reasons.

As defensive self-separation becomes the central focus, communal movement is relegated to subsidiary status. The subjective takes priority over the intersubjective. Alternatively, defensive self-dispersion, if it becomes the central focus, loses the particularity of the self-structure. In both, personhood is out of balance and diminished. Fallen persons created by love and for love opt for life that gives the illusion of being protectively managed. Selfhood becomes inauthentic, and communion becomes distorted. Accordingly, unadulterated love modeled in the Trinity ceases to be the pure soil from which human personhood is cultivated. Personhood now grows in tainted soil, polluted with elements of shame and fear. Reclamation and healing of persons is now necessary in this new human condition. The next sections consider a conceptual model that explores true self-in-communion as compared with the choice of false selfhood and false communion.

PERSONHOOD VIEWED THROUGH ATTACHMENT THEORY

In the 1950s John Bowlby began to publish his research observations of children coping with separation from caregivers. These findings developed into Attachment Theory, an area of burgeoning psychological, sociological, and biological study across all age levels. Lopez and Brennan (2000) suggest that this growing body of research literature is providing an increasingly comprehensive understanding of healthy and effective selfhood. Indeed, Attachment Theory illuminates the development of self in a less-than-perfect relational world from moments after birth to the grave. It affirms our inherent relationality and suggests that our relational experiences are not simply contextual influences but actually are self-in-development. Some make the mistake of assuming that attachment is the same as love or sexual bonding. It is not. The attachment process instead creates the conditions for love to grow in a more, or less, trustworthy environment. It also provides the framework for understanding personal fears that hinder love and promote self-protection.

Attachment Theory proposes that human beings share with other species an innate safety regulation system to deal with feared conditions. Perceived threats can disrupt a sense of felt security and result in relational movement to regain protection and felt-security. The movement is relational because Attachment Theory asserts that safety is a relational construct. Bowlby (1988) believed that patterns for seeking, maintaining, or avoiding protective proximity are evident early in life and based in actual experiences with primary caregivers. Persistent or intense relational experiences, either positive or negative, become the foundation for security-enhancing working models that are neurophysiological as much as they are cognitive and symbolic (Johnson 1997; Lewis, Amini, and Lannon 2000).

> The internal working model is presumed to incorporate two discrete yet interrelated components: a *self model* regarding one's own sense of worth and lovability and an *other model* embodying core expectations of the availability and trustworthiness of others in one's social world. By definition, working models are inherently relational schema that embody not only self-perceptions but also implicit action strategies for responding to security-related threats and violations. Said differently, the internal working model comprises a set of overlearned, abstracted, generalized, and not necessarily fully conscious appraisals and expectations, as well as relational scripts for choreographing one's social behavior during circumstances perceived as threatening to the self. (Lopez and Brennan 2000, 285)

Kirkpatrick (1999) suggests that there is no theoretical reason to disbelieve that a relationship with God is managed any differently from other more temporal relationships. God, self, and others, are all perceived from the lens of working models. Moreover, the heart of all models is suspected to be an innate, adaptive, and lifelong need to love and be loved by a unique, irreplaceable other (Johnson 1997). Much like the creational account, persons who are made for love still function most effectively in loving conditions. Working models predict how much risk is involved in loving or being loved and then form an action plan that manages fear and promotes security.

Research (Ainsworth, Blehar, Waters, and Wall 1978) affirms reliable patterns or styles of attachment based on human working models. Individual differences certainly exist, but the patterns, described below, tend to be robust. Studies on cross-situational and cross-age continuity of attachment also demonstrate strong support for the resiliency of these patterns or styles from infancy through adulthood (Rothbard and Shaver 1994). Of course, the research does not suggest that patterns are unchangeable. Major life events and transitions such as marriage may afford the best opportunities for a working model to move toward greater or lesser security (Stratton 1991).

Attachment Styles and Selfhood. Attachment patterns are often classified as either secure attachment or insecure/anxious attachment. The insecure/anxious attachment pattern is divided into two different patterns: anxious-avoidant (dismissing of attachment) and anxious-ambivalent (preoccupied with attachment). The secure attachment pattern seems to suggest a communing self in which neither protective separation or protective connection dominates. The dismissing of attachment pattern seems to explain sociologically, psychologically, and behaviorally the defensive relational movement of self-separation. This pole, associated with extreme independence, destabilizes and diminishes personhood. The other insecure/anxious pattern, preoccupied with attachment, seems also to operationalize defensive self-dispersion or merger with others. This opposite pole is associated with extreme dependence and also destabilizes and diminishes personhood. Both the protective separation of the dismissing extreme and the protective connection of the preoccupied extreme seem analogous to the self-generated coverings discussed in relation to the creation narrative. Each gives the illusion of safety and intimacy but actually sows the seeds for relational dysfunction.

Mikulincer (1995) concluded that these patterns could be differentiated as follows:

> · *Securely attached persons* have confidence in the availability of attachment figures, comfort with closeness, interdependence, and trust. They seek support in times of need and rely on constructive coping strategies to regulate affect. They are conscious of both positive and negative self-attributes, exhibit highly complex self-schema, and reveal relatively low discrepancies between actual, ideal, and ought selves.
>
> · *Dismissing persons* show insecurity in assessing the intentions of others and prefer emotional distance. They rely on affect and memory suppressive strategies and devaluation of events to cope with challenges. They have highly positive and differentiated self-structures that are not influenced by emotional experiences. Yet, they show low accessibility to negative self-aspects and reveal high discrepancies between actual, ideal, and ought selves. In general,

their positive self-view appears to lack balance, integration, and inner coherence.

· *Preoccupied persons* display strong desire for intimacy joined with insecurity about others' responses to this desire and intense fear of rejection. They depend on emotion-focused coping that increases rather than decreases distress. They exhibit a negative, simplistic, and less integrated self-structure, characterized by low differentiation and low integration of self-representations, as well as significant discrepancies between actual, ideal, and ought selves.

The First Dimension of a Model: Dynamic, Centered Selfhood. Attachment patterns may be placed on a continuum (Fig. 1) that depicts secure attachment as the dynamic center for attachment processes. A securely attached person exhibits a flexibility of emotional differentiation ("I can stand alone") and mutuality ("I can stand with") from situation to situation (Stratton 1991). The position of centeredness may look more separate in one situation and in another more connected; yet, the goal in both continues to be attachment to an other. This dynamic flexibility seems to offer the optimal conditions for unimpaired communion that is depicted in the section to follow. Dynamically centered attachment experiences are relatively free from the influences of shame and fear. Communion is therefore perceived as less risky because self-definition is functional and adaptive.

Dismissing-of-attachment and preoccupied-with-attachment patterns are located toward the continuum's extremes and depict underdeveloped personhood tied to more rigid and less centered working models of self and other. Dismissing strategies defensively over-emphasize differentiation and self-separation, while preoccupied strategies over-emphasize union and self-dispersion. The goals of these patterns are primarily self-protective; they *cover* for fears associated with self-in-communion. Consequently, movement toward either pole suggests impairment of communion for self's sake.

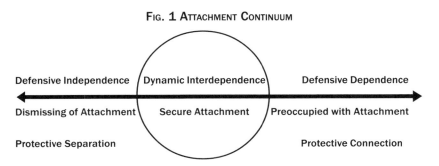

FIG. 1 ATTACHMENT CONTINUUM

One final quality of this continuum cannot be overlooked. Reminiscent of the God-designed purposes for human creatures in relation with him, attachment patterns give new significance to the created purposes of relationship and task. At the extremes of the attachment continuum, either relationship or tasks become the priority, not both. One ontological purpose is overused protectively at the expense of the other. The result is distortion of personhood, experienced as a lack of flexibility in *position*. Stability is based upon rigidity, not freedom. With the dismissing pattern, relationship is deemphasized for the safety of tasks in the nonpersonal world. With the preoccupied pattern, tasks are deemphasized for the safety of close relationships. With secure attachment, neither tasks nor relationships suffer at the expense of the other. Persons, divine as well as human, evidencing the secure attachment pattern seem to balance these purposeful goals.

Attachment Theory contributes a view that parallels and supports many trinitarian concepts related to personhood. Most significant, it describes a view of self and its development intricately tied to relationships. The next section augments this description of self and its development by focusing on relational movement as central to agency. In a sense, human agency activates the attachment process and completes the relational parameters for conceptualizing love between persons.

PERSONHOOD IN RELATION TO AGENCY

> When I act I modify the world. Action is causally effective, even if it fails of the particular effect that is intended. This implies that the Self is part of the world in which it acts, and in dynamic relation with the rest of the world. On the other hand, as subject the Self stands "over against" the world, which is its object. The Self as subject then is not part of the world it knows, but withdrawn from it, and so, in conception, outside it, or other than its object. But to be part of the world is to exist, while to be excluded from the world is to be non-existent. It follows that the Self exists as agent but not as subject. (Macmurray 1957/1991, 91–92)

Macmurray's contention that the self moves toward nonexistence as it withdraws toward theoretical individuality is consistent with the premise of this essay. So is the idea that the self-in-relation is by definition an agent. The communing self of personhood connotes freely chosen social movement. This line of thinking, certainly consistent with trinitarian thought, is vastly different from the classical definition of person given by Boethius in the sixth century. A person cannot merely be an individual substance rational in nature. This definition is incomplete since it fails to understand the essential nature of communal movement in personhood. It theoretically emphasizes self only as subject, to use Macmurray's terminology. In reality, the particularity of selfhood must embrace the relational action of communion if it is to remain healthy. It is not enough to know who we are. We must know where we are going (Taylor 1989).

The Second Dimension of a Model: Dynamic, Centered Communion. Human relational agency may be depicted as a second continuum running from aggressive action to passive action (fig. 2). Aggressiveness reflects an exaggerated, externalized defensive expression of power in a relational action. It protects self with direct, expressive behaviors in relation to others. Passivity reflects an internalized defensive expression of power in relation to others. It protects self with indirect, restrictive behaviors. Both are self-generated coverings used for protective purposes.

Both aggressiveness and passivity first reflect agency. Passivity may be indirect and even covert in many ways, yet it remains a relational action, not inaction as some assume. Second, both are self-protecting strategies. The motivation for these movements is to create the conditions for self to be safe from communion. Aggressive and passive relations with others are only important as they function to reinforce a sense of security. Protection dominates, and freedom is hindered. Humans cease to be *acting* persons in the truest sense of the word; they are *re-acting* persons when living in these extremes (Palmer 1990).

Reflecting the rich and evocative flavor of Aristotle in his *Nicomachean Ethics*, the virtuous mean of these extremes is assertiveness. Assertiveness, as the dynamic center on the continuum, is defined as personal power, disciplined and channeled for mutually beneficial relational purposes. It reflects a flexibility of positive self-affirmation and positive others-affirmation. (Alberti and Emmons 1990). It might be said that assertiveness an-

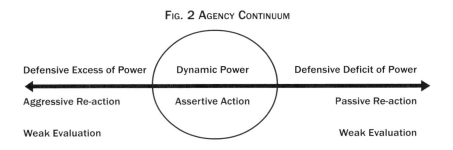

FIG. 2 AGENCY CONTINUUM

Defensive Excess of Power	Dynamic Power	Defensive Deficit of Power
Aggressive Re-action	Assertive Action	Passive Re-action
Weak Evaluation		Weak Evaluation

chors a personal power continuum that depicts how human beings act in and on their relational world.

Hagberg (1994) remarks, "[Well-developed] personal power is the extent to which one is able to link outer capacity for action (external power) with the inner capacity for reflection (internal power)" (xxi). She finds that the capacity for internal power correlates well with a more mature level of self-development. The reflected-upon action that characterizes internal power is set apart from earlier, less mature stages by "a meaningful, other-oriented life purpose" (99).

Action without this type of reflection characterizes earlier stages of personal power development, and the form it takes is defensive. It is more about acquiring, controlling, and sustaining external power through association with power holders or attainment of symbols of power. Reliance on external power validates and fortifies what feels internally insecure. Action is fundamentally self-dominated in early development of personal power, and therefore communal movement is utilized as it brings a sense of secure covering. This does not imply that actions are intentionally chosen to promote self at the expense of others. Persons in early stages of personal power are not necessarily relational mercenaries. They simply are unable to reflect on others as separate from their own protective agenda. They are underdeveloped and immature as agents of personal power and tend to be out of balance in terms of personhood.

Mature development as agents of personal power seems to coincide with stable and undiminished personhood, just as secure selfhood discussed in the previous section on attachment did. Assertiveness, or acting for the good of self and other, is the resulting movement. In fact, Hagberg (1994) reports that the later stages of development might be described as "power *for* the other" (106, italics hers), or it might be termed self acting for the other. It is only under these conditions that actions can be called spontaneous and free. This is not the case with aggressiveness and passivity where reactions are primarily self-protective. Freedom of choice is impaired. Reminiscent of Brunner's explanation of the Fall, Hagberg connects less mature agents of personal power with insecurity in the face of anxiety.

The Necessity of Strong Evaluation for Centeredness. Hagberg's research parallels Charles Taylor's (1985) writings about strong and weak evaluations and agency. The assertive reflective actions of mature personal power involve a strong evaluation process. The aggressive and passive poles of action depict less mature, nonreflective personal power, supported by a weak evaluation process. Taylor (1985) explains that in weak evaluation "good" is characterized by the fulfillment of a felt-desire. Little to no reflective process is involved other than the fact that the "good" is wanted or needed. Weak evaluation is a reaction to interpersonal or intrapersonal pressure. In strong evaluation, by contrast, Taylor suggests that "good" is more than the desirable or that which results from an analysis of possible consequences. "It is also defined by a qualitative characterization of desires as higher and lower, noble or base, and so on" (23).

The re-active poles of aggression and passivity are defined by one prevailing value or desire—self-protection. Nothing rises above this priority. The center of the continuum however suggests a better developed perspective because it coincides with a view of self and other that is more reflective, more objective, and potentially more accurate. One might say that self-biases are less prominent, so freedom of choice is expanded. Taylor (1985) suggests that "One is a bigger person, with a broader, more serene vision, when one acts out of this higher standpoint" (67).

The collective evaluations of a person, either strong or weak, compose a sort of *moral map* (Taylor 1985), or his later term, *framework* (1989). He defines this cognitive and affective schema as "an intrinsic part of . . . discerning the good or higher life, or the shape of our aspirations, or the shape of our life. . . . It involves defining what it is we are really about, what is really important to us; it involves entering the problematic area of self-understanding and self-interpretation" (Taylor 1985, 68). Such schemata motivate and direct human action in the relational world.

As a working model lies at the heart of attachment and self-development, this internal map lies at the heart of agency and self-movement. Assertiveness suggests a strategic moral map where outer action in the relational world is linked to better awareness of self and other. From this perspective, relational movement is a willed act, a free choice that accounts for self and other. To the extent that it makes such an account, it creates the conditions for love. Aggressiveness and passivity suggest a map where outer action is linked to less developed reflection, and the goal is self-focused and therefore less likely to create the conditions for love.

SELF-GENERATED COVERINGS VERSUS SELF-GIVING LOVE

The *attachment continuum* speaks to centered and off-center selfhood. It is foundational in understanding how persons engage the purposes for which they are created. The *agency continuum* addresses communal actions and re-actions. It assists in understanding how and why human agents move within the relational world. When these two continuums depicting self-structure (Who am I?) and self-movement (Where am I going?) are joined, their interaction depicts a two-dimensional model that illuminates emergent conditions for love to be present and active.

Figure 3 illustrates the relationship of the attachment continuum and the agency continuum. The central area represented by joining the dynamic *position* of a securely attached self and the dynamic *movement* of assertive communal agency in the world creates the conditions for well-developed personhood. Intentionally willed relational actions are initiated out of a working model of self and other rooted in security. Dominating fears are minimized, so subjectivity and intersubjectivity move in dynamic equilibrium. Self-awareness and an outward orientation are more compatible. Self and communion are complementary functions in which each serves the other. The personhood that emerges from the synergy of the dynamic center frees people to choose intimacy when it is wise to do so. The balance of task and relationship is practically re-conceptualized so that living is not based in rigid rules. Truth is perceived relationally. Moreover, the stage is set for love, and the conditions emerge for the Triune God to move without barriers.

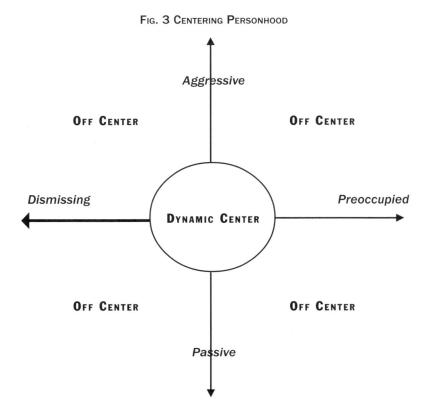

FIG. 3 CENTERING PERSONHOOD

The peripheral area alternatively represents self-generated coverings. They are off-center strategies that reflect self-protective re-actions and restrict mature personhood. Self and communion in this area are not complementary; instead communion becomes the tool of self. Others are objectified and used for self-purposes. Consequently, relational movement is a means to an end, namely felt security. Self must be consistently guarded against threat from the outside. Intimacy is untrustworthy. Choice is limited by the defensive nature of this process. Freedom is relinquished for safety. Love is hindered under these conditions, and self-protective barriers impede the movement of the triune God.

The Basic Coverings: Four Off-Center Strategies. Coverings by their nature are barriers to God's movement; yet, they are chosen as in the garden to protect a self that feels naked and vulnerable. There are four basic relational coverings represented by the four off- center quadrants of this two-dimensional model (Fig. 4). Quadrant 1 represents aggressive self-separation. This self-protective strategy can be called controlling. Those who move in a controlling manner protect self by never surrendering to others. They are extremely independent to the point of being lone rangers. They emphasize task ahead of relationships. They pursue their own protective agenda through these tasks, and others must participate with them or get out of the way. Relational conflicts are win-lose propositions, and they cannot lose.

Quadrant 2 represents aggressive self-dispersion. This self-protective strategy can be called *pursuing*. Those who pursue relationships in this manner protect self by recruiting valued others to follow their vision. Self is most protected when it is not concealed in relationships but openly expressed and recognized. They refrain from demanding that others follow their agenda, as in Quadrant 1, because they are preoccupied with relationships and do not want to risk losing a source of security. However, they will persuade, manipulate, and even coerce others to follow them in their pursuits. They are often "nicely" pushy when the pressure is on.

Quadrant 3 represents passive self-separation. This self-protective strategy can be called *withdrawing*. Those who move in a withdrawing manner protect self by avoiding self-revelation. They feel safest when self is concealed and hidden in relations with others. Tasks are over-emphasized since relationships are full of demands for self-disclosures. They function best when others let them do what they want to do. Relational conflicts are avoided at all costs.

Quadrant 4 represents passive self-dispersion. This self-protective strategy might be called *complying*. Those who move in relationships in a complying manner protect self by following others and relinquishing their own agenda. Self is protected best when it takes on the agenda of others. Protective self-denial becomes the means to security. The greatest fear for someone moving in relationships in this manner is that persons might be burdened by their wants or desire and leave the relationship. Relational conflict is the context for more self-sacrifice.

The commonality of all of these off-center strategies is that they create conditions for self to be protected without regard for, and usually at the expense of, others. Personhood is diminished as self is elevated in status above communion, and the foundation for love is dismantled. Indeed, the intent of each off-center strategy is to induce persons with whom they relate to respond from the opposite off-center diagonal. Control rigidly wants compliance. Compliance desperately seeks control. Pursuing evokes withdrawal, and withdrawal solicits pursuit. Off-center strategies beget off-center responses.

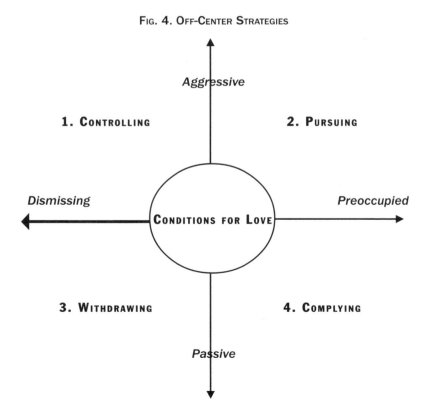

FIG. 4. OFF-CENTER STRATEGIES

The central dynamic area in this two-dimensional model on the other hand creates the emergent conditions for love of God, others, and the nonpersonal world. Figure 5 shows that this area is not static but dynamic and responsive to whatever relational conditions persons are facing. The conditions always look different based on the other and the circumstances of the other. Conditions must adjust for that which creates the opportunity for God to be realized. Love, therefore, takes many forms and is often indefinable without some awareness of the context. Yet in the highest form it is always characterized by assertive relational actions for the benefit of others, initiated by a self who chooses such an approach. It rightly reflects the concept of self-emptying (*kenosis*), in which self-giving actions and self-limiting actions are chosen for reasons that transcend self-protection. Love is the emergent quality of centered personhood.

It is understandable that when facing the enormity of this challenge to choose love, it is usually perceived as idealistic. What Christian thought calls sanctification looks like the most unrealistic standard, beyond that which could be expected of any normal individual. It seems beyond the scope of practical living. Realistically, it is and it is not. Laporte (1997) explains:

> The Christian recognizes that the only power in which we are able to fully achieve a love which affirms the mystery of the other as other is God's love. Our loving relationship with God enables us to counter our sinful proneness to invest in a created reality, human or less than human, a significance for our fulfillment which only God deserves. Though we fail, through God's grace we can repent, learn from our failures, and continue on the right path. (233)

What then creates the conditions for God's loving presence and movement? When dismissing of attachment moves toward the center on the attachment continuum, persons can demonstrate the choice to be *separate from others* when such a choice creates the conditions for love. In love persons can stand alone, when the situation calls for it, without disengaging. One makes space for others to be themselves. When preoccupied with attachment moves toward the center, the choice to be *connected with others* is exhibited, but only as it creates the conditions for love. In love persons must, as a situation dictates, be able to stand with others without taking over or carrying their responsibilities. Depending on the circumstances, mature persons are capable of separate love, connected love, or any degree in between the two. There is always an irresolvable dynamic tension between how separate and how connected to be. The determining question remains, "What gives God (and others) the best conditions to be present?"

FIG. 5. CENTERED CONTINUUM

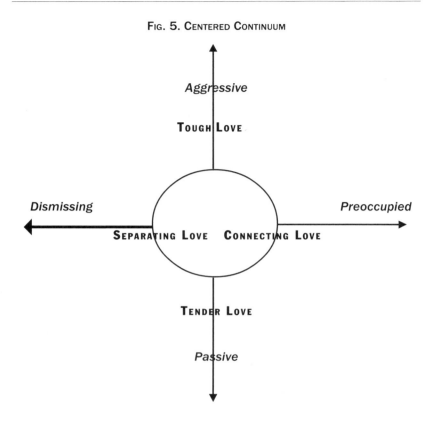

On the agency continuum when aggressiveness attenuates and moves toward the center, persons can choose to express what has come to be called "tough love." In love persons can say no to others and set limits with others without usurping their freedom of choice or movement. When passivity moves toward the center, the choice to express tender love is possible without giving up freedom of choice or movement. In love persons can choose to nurture and care for others without obligation. Mature persons are capable of tough love, tender love, or any degree in between the two. Again, a dynamic tension exists between how tough and tender to be from one situation to the next. The determining question remains, "What gives God (and others) the best conditions to move?"

The most conducive conditions for love are realized when a person is able to relate from the dynamic part of center that is needed for the relational circumstances. The area of the center is chosen because it invites the other into communion in the manner that can most easily be heard at that time. Centered relating speaks to the underlying fear that motivates protective off-center strategies. Maturing persons become better and better at discerning how to invite persons into the center through authentic loving communion.

The Second Person of the Trinity as the Model of Love

Where does one turn to begin to see the dynamic and centered living described in this two-dimensional model? How might this theory be operationalized? Trinitarian theology again provides a practical answer. Through the operation of the Third Person of the Trinity, the incarnated Second Person of the Trinity is the tangible model of human personhood and love. Swoebel (1991) explains:

> [T]hough the eternal Son assumed human nature into personal union with himself, the Word of God does not act directly and immediately on the human nature, but only leaves Christ's human nature intact so that it can serve as the paradigm of our humanity. . . . [T]he divine image in human beings, lost in the Fall, is first renewed in Christ's human nature so that Christ becomes the prototype of a new humanity where the divine image is restored. . . .[C]onformity with Christ [in human beings is] affected by the agency of the Holy Spirit, just as the Holy Spirit creates in the humanity of Christ the divine image by energizing, sanctifying, and perfecting it. The operation of the Holy Spirit is in this way seen as constitutive both for the renewal of the divine image in Christ and for the transformation of the Christian life into conformity with Christ and thus into the likeness of the divine image. (21)

In Jesus, one sees a human person in balance—the image of God, re-imaged. Self and communion are viewed in perfect complementarity from one situation to the next. The outcome, love, looks different from one situation to the next as it dynamically adjusts from one context to the next. Jesus never seems to have a formulaic approach to others. That may be why love remains so difficult to define behaviorally. There is no static definition. It is living and breathing, like the Person.

When the Second Person of the Trinity was asked what was the secret to the life he lived, he reported that he simply created the best conditions for the Father to be present and moving in every circumstance (John 5:19, 8:28, 12:49). Every person when meeting Jesus was invited into the balance of the Trinity. They were invited into love. Jesus' actions created the conditions for God to be present and moving in every situation. He navigated a life without barriers to the Father's presence. In this lies his perfection. He never succumbed to the temptation to cover himself self-protectively and use communion as a tool for self. Indeed, those who met the Second Person of the Trinity always met the First Person of the Trinity as well.

We come back around then to the point where this discussion started—with the Trinity. Human personhood, as communing selfhood, reflects its prototype. As we participate in loving relationships we discover our goal as persons, and that goal, whether we realize it or not, is to reflect the Second Person of the Trinity.

15

The Trinitarian Nature of the Transmodern Person

Mark Lowery

The important questions of modern and postmodern thought are not inimical to Christianity.[1] Rather they invite Christian theology to retrieve and extend its heritage, particularly its rich heritage of meditation on the concept of person. Trinitarian theology represents a particularly insightful part of that meditation. It is precisely within the developments of trinitarian theology that the mature notion of person gained currency, a notion that includes the unique, embodied particularity of each subject, and at the same time the relational nature of each subject. It is just such a notion of person, as relational substance, that can both meet the demands of modern and postmodern inquiry and propel our notion of personhood to the new "transmodern" frontiers described by Paul Vitz in this volume's introductory essay.

THE CHALLENGES OF MODERNITY AND POSTMODERNITY

Enlightenment modernity reacted against the capriciousness of various manifestations of the Christian faith, manifestations that betrayed a heteronomous belief system wherein truth is extrinsically imposed on the individual, violating the dignity of the person (Ashley 1985, 60, 61, 87, 90, 159).[2] While modernity upheld the rational pursuit of the truth, it left the self unmoored to the Transcendent, and also unmoored to the community. Without transcendence and communality, the modern autonomous self emerges. (John Bechtold's essay in this volume notes how technology exaggerates our autonomy, leading to a kind of "hyperautonomy.") In this autonomous reaction to heteronomy, paradoxically, modernity points in the direction of another form of arbitrariness. The autonomous self is just as arbitrary and voluntaristic as the heteronomous God. Heteronomy and autonomy are flip sides of the same voluntaristic/nominalist coin.

Postmodernism does us a great favor in pointing to these gaps, and then in showing us exactly where we end up if we try to fill those gaps without transcendence and communality. We end up with a self not worth saving and so the "essential self" is abandoned altogether. In a study done on postmodern artists, one notes the shocking anger they displayed when asked about anything having to do with essences (Hunter, Nolan, and Eck, 79–94). There is a "neurotic fear" of faith in God—"it is the fear of being 'duped'; the fear of losing one's personal autonomy; the fear of intimacy; the fear of giving oneself in love to anyone or anything; the fear of losing one's pathological defenses" (Vitz 1995, 39–40). The desire for autonomy is so powerful that any sense of being "created" strikes fear into the postmodern heart. As the Orthodox theologian, John Zizioulas (1985) comments:

> This is "the most tragic side of the person's quest: the transcendence of the "necessity" of existence, the possibility of affirming his existence not as a recognition of a given fact, of a "reality," but as the product of his free consent and self affirmation. This and nothing less than this is what man seeks in being a person. But in man's case this quest comes into conflict with his createdness: as a creature he cannot escape the "necessity" of his existence. (40–41)

Absent a "doctrine of creation," postmodernism has abandoned any semblance of an essential self. With this emptiness, the impetus is toward community. As Norris Clarke (1994) has noted:

> [R]eal being tends to be reduced to nothing more than a pattern of relations with no subjects grounding them, or as a pattern of events with no agents enacting them. The fundamental polarity within real being between the "in-itself" and the "toward others," the self-immanence and the self-transcendence of being, collapses into the one pole of pure relatedness to others. (102–3).

The community that is discovered, however, turns out to be highly fragmented, fleeting, and illusory, precisely because there can be no genuine community unless there are genuine selves to make it up. In sum, postmodernity poignantly marks our need for both a substantial, embodied self and for genuine relationality. "Substantiality and relationality are here equally primordial and necessary dimensions of being itself at its highest intensity," Clarke (1992, 607) notes and then adds:

> [I]f the substance, or *in-itself*, pole of being is dropped out, the unique interiority and privacy of person are wiped out also and

the person turns out to be an entirely extroverted bundle of relations, with no inner self to share with others. But there is no need
for this either/or dichotomy between substance and relation, once
the notion of substance as center of activity—and receptivity—
has been retrieved. *To be* is to be substance-in-relation. (609)

The dynamic polarity between substance and relation was nearly lost
in the modern age. Gil Bailie, in his contribution to this volume, notes the
desperate self-referentiality of the modern self. Descartes, Locke, and Hume
worked with "emasculated versions of substance" and in reaction, as Clarke
(1992) notes "a large number of modern and contemporary thinkers have
simply rejected substance entirely as a nonviable mode of being. . . . As a
result, the person tended to be reduced to nothing but a relation or set of
relations" (608). The search for balance is exemplified in the life and work
of Mikhail Bakhtin, as noted in Caryl Emerson's contribution to the present
volume. The "carnival self" lacked relationality, the "dialogic self" lacked
substance, and the "architectonic self" headed toward more integration.

This interconnection of relation and substance, avoiding an imbal-
ance toward one or the other, is precisely what is needed in order to avoid a
heteronomous answer to modernity and postmodernity. Interestingly, the
quest for this interconnectedness is the dynamic that drove the trinitarian
controversies of the first millennium and which remain with us in the ecu-
menical discussions between East and West. We might say that modernism
and postmodernism are not new constructs of ideas, but variations on a
perennial theme, that of the balance between substance and relationality in
the quest to grasp the full meaning of person.

When faced with the morbidity of modernism/postmodernism, it is
always tempting to revert back to the tradition as it was instantiated in
some past age—a "paleomorphic" tendency. The varied fundamentalisms
in the present cultural context are instances of such paleomorphism. However tempting such comfortable reversion can be, it disallows the growth
and development that can come from taking the *questions* of modernity/
postmodernity seriously. When such questions are confronted, humanity
remains on a positive trajectory that recovers the tradition creatively—and
that is the trajectory of transmodernity which this volume limns.

A Trajectory toward Transmodernity

If the questions raised by postmodernity are valuable, so too is its own
tacit admission that the answers lie beyond itself. (Bailie speaks of discovering a lost mystery right within postmodernism.) Claiming that there is

no transcendent "metanarrative," but only partial, ambiguous, fragmented narratives, it has—surprise!—provided a metanarrative. We cannot escape a transcendent frame of reference—the only question will be about the nature of that transcendent reference. So, postmodernity not only points at the holes in modernity, it also cancels itself out, but in a way that points beyond itself. It does not point back to modernity, nor back behind modernity.

As Paul Vitz (1995) has noted:

> [M]ost relativistic systems of morality are absolutist about something—typically about moral relativity itself, and about those psychological processes that support moral relativism. Thus, for example, "getting in touch with your feelings" is an absolute value in the thinking of Carl Rogers because it supports that development of a self that will choose its own values. The point is that the absolutism of such systems is at the service of relativism. (28)

Charles Taylor (1989) concurs:

> We may sharply shift the balance in our definition of identity, dethrone the given historic community as a pole of identity, and relate only to the community defined by adherence to the good (or the saved, or the true believers, or the wise). But this doesn't sever our dependence on webs of interlocution. It only changes the webs, and the nature of our dependence. (39)

Postmodernity's search for something beyond itself suggests that a transmodern perspective will be one rooted in the person as *agent*, the "acting person." As Ulric Neisser (1997) has put it, "[T]heories of the self have usually looked inward, trying to find the self in the head. The results have been disturbing: the harder they look, the less they find" (19). Neisser notes that fortunately there is another place to look for the self:

> Each of us is an active agent in a real environment, and we can directly see that this is the case. Thus we are—and know that we are—*ecological selves.* . . . [Studies show] that babies have a realistic grasp on the environment. Their experience is no meaningless blur; on the contrary, they are ecologically located selves. . . . Encounters with persons . . . are special. We do not entirely control them. They occur irregularly, in ways that depend on the presence and attitude of an essentially mysterious other. Only by the grace of that other can we reach the heights of joy that human contact may bring—or for that matter, the corresponding depths of de-

spair . . . for most of us, interpersonal relations remain more than a little mysterious throughout life. (19; 25; 28–29)

Bailie, in this volume, notes how we receive truth more richly when we receive it from others.

We can look at the actual experience of "ecological selves" and at least take seriously what we find: people actually think transcendence is important. A phenomenology of the "acting person" is at work here, which takes seriously the actual experience of agents finding meaning. Even those who claim to find no meaning are on a trajectory toward meaning! The phenomenological turn to "the appearances" refuses to reduce such experiences to mere epiphenomena (Linker 2000, 6–9). Vitz (1995) notes that secular theories of personality and counseling, assuming religious motivations irrelevant or pathological, run contrary to people's actual beliefs:

> To ignore this obviously important psychological reality is an egregious example of bad clinical practice. It would be like doing a physical examination on someone by testing only functions that exist above the neck and below the waist. . . . A Christian theory of personality is, then, psychologically realistic. But it is not realistic in a merely psychological sense; it is based on reality, on what exists outside the self. To be a person is to respect external realities. By making the individual self the center of personality, all modern theories of personality remove people from reality. (25, 33)

In sum, to be ecologically located is to have an orientation that transcends the self, an argument Stephen Stratton develops in this volume.

Participatory Theonomy and the Trinity: A Revolutionary View of Personhood

Avoiding the extremes of autonomy and heteronomy, we can navigate through modernity and postmodernity to a new transmodern plane. The fresh theonomy we retrieve could be called a "participatory theonomy" in that the self genuinely participates in truth, rather than truth being extrinsically imposed on the self on the one hand (a voluntaristic God) or entirely arbitrated by the self on the other hand (the voluntaristic self) (John Paul II 1993). To put it in other words, the truth must be friendly to our being.

More often than not in the postmodern age, the very notion of transcendence appears as a heteronomous imposition, alien to personal uniqueness and dignity. But a trinitarian understanding of transcendence reveals that our very notion of the person, unique and relational, comes from the philosophic and theological explorations about the nature of the Trinity. Far from a foreign and mysterious imposition, the Trinity signals to us the constitutive elements of our own personhood—God properly understood is friendly to our being. And, with special potential to respond to the deepest yearnings of postmodernity, a trinitarian view of personhood resonates with the deep need to be communal, coming full circle to a view of communality that does not eclipse the unique identity of the person.

The concept of "person" has a history or a "career" (Schmitz 1986). Pre-Christian thinkers foreshadowed the concept of person, capturing certain aspects of the whole truth that remained hidden without special revelation. While "person" can in principle be understood by reason, in fact it remains partially hidden until revelation sheds light on it—afterwards, it suddenly becomes clear how reasonable such truths are. As Clarke (1992) puts it:

> It is one of those not infrequent cases in Western thought (also found in most Eastern traditions in an analogous way) of a basic metaphysical concept that as a historical fact received its first stimulus and illumination from a theological source, but once 'unveiled' can become a self-sustaining philosophical insight, recommending itself by its superior explanatory power. (617–18).

An essential feature of participatory theonomy is its intrinsic reasonableness.

It is interesting to note in passing that Christians, in their struggles with working out the trinitarian and christological conflicts, were not looking for the insight about person that they found. The concept of person was the perfect solution to key christological and trinitarian heresies, but it proved to be much more. It was the unveiling, a revelation and a discovery simultaneously, of the richly textured reality, namely "person." We might say that "person" is the final cause of history, the transmodern magnet toward which humanity is headed .

TRINITARIAN UNVEILING: SUBSTANCE AND RELATIONALITY ARE SIMULTANEOUS

Ratzinger (1970) outlines the central features of just what treasures were unveiled. In the relational notion of person developed within the theology of the Trinity lies concealed a revolution in man's view of the world: the undivided sway of thinking in terms of substance is ended; relation is discovered as an equally valid primordial mode of reality . . . and it is made apparent how being that truly understands itself grasps at the same time that *in* its self-being it does not belong to itself; that it only comes to itself by moving away from itself and finding its way back as relatedness to its true primordial state. (455–64)

The trinitarian perfection of personhood means that to be a person is to be in communion, to be in relation. "Thus there is an immense innate dynamism in the very nature of actual being as such," says Clarke (1992), "wherever an act of existing is found . . . to pour over into self-expression, self-communication of its own inner perfection of goodness" (604). The person is an *acting* person, as Clarke (1992) goes on to explain:

[F]inite being pours over naturally into action for *two* reasons: (1) because it is *poor*, i.e., lacking the fullness of existence, and so strives to enrich itself as much as its nature allows from the richness of those around it; but (2) even more profoundly because it is *rich*, endowed with its own richness of existence, however slight this may be, which it tends naturally to communicate and share with others. (605)

Relation is coextensive with being, solidarity is coextensive with subjectivity. "To be" is not to be autonomous, but to be persons in pure relation. Nor is relation a heteronomous extrinsic addition to person; it is intrinsic to personhood, both for the Trinitarian God and likewise for human beings made in God's image. Here we are at the heart of participatory theonomy: the truth about God is friendly to our being, not a capricious imposition. The truth imposes itself only by virtue of its own truth.

Relation is the activity constitutive of the trinitarian God, an activity that is dynamic self-gift: "To be a person, in a word, is to be a *lover*, to live a life of *inter*personal self-giving and receiving" (Clarke 1992, 610). Western theology saw essence or substance as the trinitarian starting point, conceptually prior to relation, the Eastern starting point. But the Father cannot be the primal lover except in relation to the Son in the Spirit—hence relationality is not conceptually subsequent to essence, but *simultaneous to it*. As Clarke notes, to posit as "unexpressed *some reality* . . . over and above those relationships" would be to immediately subordinate God to an exterior *super*reality. Therefore the trinitarian "*relationship* is really the same thing as God's *substance*" (601). Substance and relational personhood in the Trinity are intrinsically interconnected.

RELATION AND PERSON, EAST AND WEST

While Ratzinger correctly notes that in trinitarian theology "the undivided sway of thinking in terms of substance is ended," the fresh emphasis on relationality must not eclipse the importance of substance. This was the tendency in the East, evidenced in the commentary of John Zizioulas:

> [A] person cannot be imagined in himself but only within his relationships. . . . [T]rue knowledge is not a knowledge of the essence or the nature of things, but of how they are connected within the communion-event. . . . The mystery of being a person lies in the fact that here otherness and communion are not in contradiction but coincide. Truth in communion does not lead to the dissolving of the diversity of beings into one vast ocean of being, but to the affirmation of otherness in and through love. The difference between this truth and that of 'nature in itself' lies in the following: while the latter is subject to fragmentation, individualization, conceptualization, comprehension, etc., the person is not. So in the context of personhood, *otherness* is incompatible with *division*. (1985, 105–7)

The same difficulty is inherent in postmodernism, as noted earlier: reacting against the essentialist, rationalist structure imposed by modernity, postmoderns turn to relation but with nothing substantial left that can be in relation. As Josef Pieper has put it, "Relating-to, conforming-with, being-oriented-toward—all these notions presuppose an inside starting point" (Clarke 1992, 608). And Clarke (1993) also adds:

> For the very meaning of relation implies that it is *between* two terms that it is connecting, between two relat*eds*. A relation cannot relate nothing.
>   . . . No relation can be self-supporting by itself. If what it relates is itself a relation, then we must look further for a grounding of that. . . . There must be an *in-itself* somewhere along the line to ground the betweenness. This is the ontological role of substance in a being: to provide the abiding unifying center for all the being's relations and other attributes. . . . This is too often forgotten by phenomenologists and personalists who tend to stress so exclusively the person as constituted by its relations to others that the inner depth and interiority of the person tend to get swallowed up in its extraverted relationships. The inseparable complementarity of *in-itself* and *towards-others* must be maintained: to be is to be *substance-in-relation* (16–17).

Western trinitarian theology tended to emphasize the substantial, as opposed to relational, aspect of the Trinity. The West sees substance/nature as conceptually prior to the relationality of the three. The West starts with the one substance, the one divine nature that is the foundation of the Trinity. The East, on the other hand, saw relationality as conceptually prior. It is right in the midst of the conversation between East and West—however polemically charged it often was—that we see a tremendous "growth spurt" in the "career" of the notion of "person."

To appreciate this growth spurt, we must unravel some challenging terminology (Kasper 1997, 257–63; Bettenson 1963, 29–52). We start with two words, *hypostasis* and *ousia*, which were originally synonymous, but which (together) had dual meanings. They could refer (1) to the essence of a thing—e.g., all men share the essence of man-ness (a general meaning)—or they could refer (2) to the essence of the individual, what we would call "person" (particularlized meaning). Note that there was no clear ontological category for the distinct persons in the one Godhead. At the Council of Nicea in 325, *hypostasis* and *ousia* remained undistinguished, and although the oneness of God was affirmed against Arianism, a positive articulation of the dynamic tri-personal relations within that oneness was lacking. It was because of Athanasius (at the Council of Alexandria in 362, poised between Nicea and Constantinople), and then the work of the Cappadocian fathers (Basil, Gregory of Nazianzus, and Basil's younger brother Gregory of Nyssa) that they were distinguished, so that *hypostasis* refers to the particularized meaning, and *ousia* refers to the more general meaning, an "essence."

But the word *hypostasis* (literally, "that which stands under or supports") was typically translated into Latin—relying on that literal meaning—with *substantia* (also "that which stands under or supports"), and the difficulty then is that the Trinity devolves into a tritheism—three *hypostases* is taken to mean *three substances*. It is clear why the West recoiled and emphasized a single substance underlying the relations. (This is especially understandable in light of the West's sensitivity to the danger of adoptionism, that Christ is an adopted son of the Father, one who "entered into relation" with the Father, not one who was consubstantial with the Father.)

Ideally, *substantia* would have been used to translate *hypostasis*, namely, person; and *essentia* would have been used to translate *ousia*, namely, the general essence of a thing. The latter never gained currency, leading to unfortunate confusion of a major sort. Instead, the Greek *ousia* becomes the Latin *substantia* (general being). So, how will the West express the notion of "individualized person" that the East expressed with *hypostasis*?

The West, alongside using "one substance," also used "three persons" (from *persona*). Here, *persona* would refer to the "particularized" meaning (no. 2, above). But just as *hypostasis* was somewhat repulsive to the West, *persona* was somewhat repulsive to the East. Why?

The East recoiled at the typical Western formulation of "one substance, three persons." *Persona* meant for them the Greek *prosopon*, which indicated "mask" or "mere appearance." So, they chose *hypostasis* instead. For, if *prosopon* understood as "appearance" were used, then the Trinity would devolve into "modalism" (also "monarchianism")—God is strictly one substance, who "appears" in a variety of modes or masks. And in point of fact, Sabellianism had used *prosopon* to do just that, to convey the notion of "temporary role" (they used the analogy of the sun: it has three *prosopa* [in the sense of three manifestations], light, heat, and the orb itself.) Likewise, the "Patripassianism" of Praxea refuted by Tertullian could not distinguish the members of the Trinity as distinct persons, holding that the Father entered the Virgin and suffered and died. (Unitarianism is a modern form of modalism.) In sum: against these unfortunate uses of *prosopon* the East opposed using that word to describe the Trinity.

Basil, at the Council of Constantinople in 381, fighting Sabellianism, was the Cappadocian father most responsible for clarifying matters for the East. He noted that the *prosopa* in God, rather than being mere masks, exist as *hypostases*—*hypostases* now understood in the new sense as persons, not in the misunderstood-by-the-West sense as substances, but as persons-in-relation. A person is a subject or principle, a "who," who exercises or instantiates a more general principle of being. (Also, recall that the East was sensitive to the error of Arianism, which makes the Son an inferior deity, or a creature, not a divine person, so that those related to the Father are not quite caught up into, truly related to, the Father, the one divine substance.) As Bailie notes in his contribution to this volume, *hypostasis* is the central contribution Christianity made to the discovery of "person." A person is not one who "comes in his own name" (substance only) but one grounded in another (relational substance).

There is much more to the "career" of the reality "person," but as a result of the complex intellectual history surrounding the councils of Nicea, Constantinople, Ephesus, and Chalcedon, the distinction and interrelation of person and nature had begun to emerge. The formulations from these councils helped solve the question of the Son's relation to the Father, and the solution set in motion the further solution to the question of the two natures of Christ (which were, no surprise, "hypostatically united"). The concept of person as substance-in-relation emerges as the perfect solution, and "behind our backs" as it were emerges a concept that will have immense anthropological impact as well: made to the image of a Trinitarian God, we understand who we are as persons in a fresh way, dimly foreshadowed by many thinkers in the past, but now bathed in fresh light.

THE ANTHROPOLOGICAL IMPLICATION: CHRIST REVEALS MAN'S AUTHENTIC FREEDOM

The profound freedom that the indwelling of the Trinity allows is the exact opposite of a "necessitated" structure heteronomously imposed on man. Unfortunately, throughout the tradition this "freedom of the gift" has often been muted, and it is this lost freedom that secular modernity (and in its turn postmodernity) reacted against.

The moment that humans sense themselves as necessitated partners for God, God becomes alien, for humans are then not loved freely and graciously (there is no "freedom of the gift"), but rather God's love becomes "a need of God and a completion of God" (Kasper 1997, 243). The Old Testament shows that this cannot be the nature of God's love—it must be free. But the Old Testament does not answer the question of God's vis-à-vis. This is left to the New Testament revelation that Jesus is the eternal "Thou" of the Father. How does this revelation affect us? In the Spirit we are accepted into this free communion of love (Kasper 1997, 243–44). Only if God is eternally in himself the exchange of absolute love between paternal (active/receptive) and filial (receptive/active) modes of infinite freedom can the "divinization" of human freedom find its sufficient ground and prototype: the Son's manner of being-God before the Father (Turek 2000). In a word, "Christ reveals man to himself" (*Gaudium et Spes*, 1984, no. 22). Humans long for absolute freedom, but it must be in the manner of receiving it from the Father, through the Son, in the Spirit—not the absolutizing of free will and political freedom, but the ordering of those capacities toward the truth, resulting in authentic freedom.

Christ's personhood, in which the divine and human are both included, is not an exceptional kind of personhood but is a precise indicator of what our personhood is. If we emphasize only the divine nature of the Word, the Word's personal and filial mode is neglected. Christ then becomes an essentialist divine being over and against us, in whom we believe because "that's the essence of things" and because authority tells us to. (Note the link here between essentialism and institutional authority, against which the Eastern tradition has steadfastly reacted, and against which postmodernity has likewise reacted.) Christ then, instead of revealing humans to themselves, becomes a *theological exception* to the philosophical view of the person, and thus the real contribution of Christian faith to human thought is not realized. "The exception shows us that we have built our closets too small, as it were, and that we must break them open and go on in order to see the whole" (Ratzinger 1990, 450). We must see Christ as the "true fulfillment of the idea of the human person." This has always acted as a "spark in intellectual history" though often it was at a standstill.

To say that Christ is one (divine) person has often been seen as a subtraction from Christ's humanity. We end up seeing person as absent in Jesus. Rather, nothing is lacking in his humanity—his humanity is the full flowing of the human person on the trajectory toward the divine. As Ratzinger (1990) says, "I believe that if one follows this struggle in which human reality had to be brought in, as it were, and affirmed for Jesus, one sees what tremendous effort and intellectual transformation lay behind the working out of this concept of person" (448). Contrary to the Greek and Latin mind, person is not conceived in substantialist terms but in existential terms.

In Christ, being with the other is realized radically—this is the meaning of his having two natures in one person. It does not cancel his being-with-himself but brings it fully to itself. In Christ, human existence is not canceled but comes to its highest possibility. Christ is the "directional arrow" that indicates what being human tends toward. Christ reveals man to himself (Ratzinger 1990, 452; *Gaudium et Spes*, 1984, no. 22).

RELATIONAL SUBSTANCE AND THE EAST/WEST CONTROVERSY

A tragic "muting" of "person" appeared as the differences between East and West manifested themselves in the *filioque* controversy. The Latin formula, that the Spirit proceeds from the Father "and the Son" meant to indicate the common, substantial principle unifying the Trinity. The Eastern formula, that the Spirit proceeds "from the Father *through* the Son," focuses more on relationality.

The East starts with the Father-as-person, who is conceptually prior to the trinitarian substance. The Trinity is explained dynamically, with the Son and the Spirit originating in the Father. This seemingly more biblical approach emphasizes the economic Trinity, that is, the Trinity as experienced in the history of salvation. God does not act as an undifferentiated essence. The Son and Spirit act in a personal way, in personal modes related to their ultimate origin in the Father.

The East wants to avoid any sense of "necessity" in the free self-communication of God, and senses that the Western model succumbs to a kind of structured, hierarchical, necessitated "emanationism." The East is horrified at the idea that we could grasp the "nature" of creation as a necessary emanation from the Father, through the Son, to the Spirit, down to creation. This destroys freedom and destroys wholeness. Humans end up captured in a kind of "biological necessity" (Zizioulas 1985, 50)—"stuck," determined, with a "nature" and its immutable laws. Baptism, adoption as a Son, frees us from this fallen, created state:

> The Christian through baptism stands over against the world, he exists as a relationship with the world, as a person, in a manner free from the relationship created by his biological identity. . . . As an ecclesial hypostasis man thus proves that what is valid for God can also be valid for man: the nature does not determine the person; the person enables the nature to exist; freedom is identified with the being of man. (Zizioulas 1985, 57)

The East would place Pneumatology on an equal plane with Christology, suspecting that Christology dominated in the West, yielding a hierarchical pattern that focuses too heavily on human history and therefore on human institutions. The Western *filioque*, for the East, minimizes Pneumatology, linking the Spirit to Christ and therefore to history and its institutions. Indeed, the East suspects a lurking heteronomous authoritarianism associated with this emphasis on history and institutions (Zizioulas 1985, 101–3). For the East, in contrast, the Holy Spirit points rather to an eschatological element: "The liturgical ethos of Orthodoxy will probably never make it possible for her to be fully involved in history" (Zizioulas 1985, 140).

The way out of the East/West quagmire is the same as the way out of the quagmire of modernity/postmodernity: the notion of person as "substance-in-relation." I would take one further step, though, in light of the East's caveat regarding substance: instead of "substance-in-relation," we might speak of relational substance to capture the simultaneity of substance and relation that inheres in the notion of person.

AN APPLICATION: THE "THEOLOGY OF THE BODY"

Thus far, we have traced various aspects of the "career" of the reality "person." We have discovered that in and through the discovery/revelation of the nature of the Trinity and the nature of Christ, the notion of person as relational substance has emerged. It is precisely this notion of person that can answer the questions of modernity and postmodernity, but to do so a new transmodern step must be taken that shows the *embodied nature* of trinitarian anthropology. I would like to suggest one specific way in which this anthropology is adequate to the enormous tasks confronting us. It helps us understand the nature of the body which has become "raw material" for our manipulation.

The "theology of the body" so creatively developed by Karol Woytyla—Pope John Paul II (1997)—shows how the phenomenon of relational substance is literally *written into the body*. His exegesis of Gen. 1–3 shows the original solitude of Adam (substance) transformed into the "original unity" (relationality) between man and woman. "It is precisely the experience of solitude that leads man and woman to recognize their uniqueness as persons and to reach out to one another to form a communion of persons (*communio personarum*) that is an image of God's own communion in the three persons of the Blessed Trinity" (Schu 2003, 80). It is precisely this profound transcendent meaning about communion that is written into the body itself.

> Man became "the image and likeness" of God not only through his own humanity, but also through the communion of persons which [was] man and woman right from the beginning. . . . Man becomes the image of God not so much in the moment of solitude as in the moment of communion. Right "from the beginning," he is not only an image in which the solitude of a person who rules the world is reflected, but also, and essentially, an image of an inscrutable divine communion of persons. . . . Obviously, that is not without significance for the theology of the body. (John Paul II 1997, 46–47)

Our biological dynamisms, while not yielding complete answers to moral questions, nonetheless exist as basic starting points for the moral life: "The person...discovers in the body the anticipatory signs, the expression and the promise of the gift of self, in conformity with the wise plan of the creator" (John Paul II 1993, no. 48). Hence, the body "speaks a language," a language of anticipatory signs, providing parameters within which we live the moral life. It is not as if the body were mere raw material "out there," over and against us, upon which we exercise our moral decisions. Rather, the body is integral to us as persons, and its language contributes to those decisions.

The fundamental language that the body speaks is the language of self-gift. Rather than using the body to treat ourselves and others as objects—think of rape and slavery as quintessential examples—the actual giving of self occurs in and through the body. Hence, the body carries or manifests "the call to give oneself in love to another person, and to receive in turn his or her gift of self" (Schu 2003, 82). As John Paul II (1997) notes, "The human body, with its sex, and its masculinity and femininity . . . includes right from the beginning the nuptial attribute, that is, the capacity of expressing love, that love in which the person becomes a gift and—by means of this gift—fulfills the meaning of his being and existence" (63). John Paul II gives a name to this language of dyadic self-giving that is infused into the body: the nuptial meaning of the body. He goes so far as to claim that "The awareness of the meaning of the body . . .—in particular its nuptial meaning—is the fundamental element of existence in the world" (John Paul II 1997, 66).

In a word, the opening toward transmodernity—person as relational substance—pulsates right within the dynamism of the body. Truth is not a foreign extrinsic imposition, but is a reality we participate in *as* embodied beings.

FROM THE DYADIC TO THE TRIADIC NATURE OF THE PERSON

True relationality is dyadic, imaged after the trinitarian persons. When the Father loves the Son, He also desires for the beloved to become the lover. This dyadic dimension of giving is an essential feature of participatory theonomy: "If one contends that loving (*agape*) is the noblest . . . loving act, since the lover wishes only (and all) the best for the beloved, then it stands to reason that the lover would likewise desire the beloved to have the same joyful experience as he, the lover, already possesses" (Murr 2001, 14). Otherwise, self-giving turns into a heteronomous form of self-aggrandizement, whereby the giver enjoys a sense of superiority over the passive receiver. Instead, giving must be dyadic, with the giver receiving the receptor's own self-gift. As Clark (1992) writes:

> the radical dynamism of being as *self-communicative* evokes as its necessary complement the active, welcoming *receptivity* of the receiving end of its self-communication. Authentic love is not complete unless it is both actively given and actively—gratefully—received. And both giving and receiving at their purest are of equal dignity and perfection. The perfection of being—and therefore of the person—is essentially dyadic, culminating in *communion*. (613)

From the dyadic nature of the person (substance-in-relation) we are poised to take a further step to a "triadic" plane (Schindler and Clarke 1994; Clarke 1992, 613; Clarke 1994, 119–20; Clarke 1993, 580–98). In every finite (created) substance—which is intrinsically relational—there is a more primordial relation of receptivity constitutive of its very being, before it can pour over into relation/action. It (each substantial person) has already received its very act of existence from another, and ultimately from

God, the source of all existence. A fundamental outlook of *gratitude* results from this part of the triadic notion of person. Stephen Stratton's essay in this volume discusses "balanced selfhood," "balanced agency," and the four deviations from such balance by which agents express their insecurity. It is a lack of gratitude to a higher source that contributes to such insecurity. Precisely to include gratitude in our understanding of person (the move from dyadic to triadic), the term "relational substance" (with "relational" as both receptive and active) may be preferable to "substance-in-relation."

Returning for a moment to the "theology of the body," we discover that the "nuptial meaning of the body" is best explained with not just the dyadic but the triadic notion of person. The very triadic structure of creation is the transcendent meaning infused in the body. We receive creation as a gift from the Creator, who is pure self-giving love, and made in his image we are capable of self-gift, a self-gift that includes the way we live and give with our bodies. Such giving is "an echo of the gift that is all of creation" (Schu 2003, 83). To give one central example, the dyadic self-giving of spouses opens outward to a "third," to a potential child, with the recognition that the creator enables this possibility in and through the biological gifts of fertility and coition. Fertility and coition are not biological raw material over which we arbitrate, but are infused with a profound triadic personal meaning that is reflective of the triadic giving in the inner-trinitarian life (John Paul II 1997, 81–82).

The emphasis on gratitude as a central meaning inscribed in the person helps solve a thorny problem with the "theology of the body": how can there be a profound personal meaning inscribed in a body wracked by pain or in a psyche with damaged raw materials? The damaged bodily or psychological raw material invites a person to a profound sense of sheer dependence, a radical kind of gratitude, which in turn is what allows the person (as substance) to give the self over to another (relation).

THE ECCLESIAL DIMENSION: "IN THE UNITY OF THE HOLY SPIRIT."

It is the sense of gratitude that best defines the nature of the church. Those who step away from the "crowd" that is caught in the downward spiral of self-assuredness do so because they realize there is a higher source to which they can become connected. Here, caught up in a new community of those who gratefully recognize a higher source of their being, they can find freedom from misdirected desire. Or, the couple steps away from the usual cultural pattern of treating the body as a means to an end and recognizes that their very biological dynamism partakes in the triadic life of a higher source. They are part of a new community wherein they can find freedom from misdirected passions, from concupiscence.

Let us trace this idea of gratitude among the persons of the Trinity on our way to understanding the ecclesial dimension of the person. When the Father loves, he would not want this love to be accepted as a matter of duty, as an inferior accepting the extrinsic imposition of the superior. Rather, given that self-donation is essential to being (being as relation) he would want his beloved to have the fulfilling experience of self-donation also. This is precisely what happens in the relation between the Father and the Son. This is the model for the dyadic dimension of self-giving. Clarke notes:

> The proof that this welcoming, active receptivity is a mode of actuality and perfection, not of potentiality and imperfection, is seen clearly when we turn to the intra-trinitarian life of God. Here it is of the essence of the personal being of the Son as such that it be totally and gratefully receptive to the gift of the divine nature from the Father; the personality of the Son might well be called "subsistent gratitude." (613)

The role of the Spirit is brilliantly noted by Hans Urs von Balthasar (1998):

> Only in holding-onto-nothing-for-himself is God Father at all; he pours forth his substance and generates the Son; and only in holding-onto-nothing-for-himself of what has been received does the Son show himself to be of the same essence of the Father, and in this shared holding-onto-nothing-for-themselves are they one in Spirit, who is, after all, the expression and personification of this holding-onto-nothing-for-himself of God, and the eternal product of this ceaselessly flowing movement. (519)

Note the triadic dimension: only after receptivity is self-gift possible. "So too with the Holy Spirit as the love image of both Father and Son, receiving its whole being from them as gift and reflecting that back as the pure essence of actively receptive love" (Clarke 1993, 613).

In connecting this triadic feature of the Trinity to human persons, we find the quintessential moment of participatory theonomy: God allows us to be caught up in the Son, collected as it were into the Son's space, and this is precisely what it means to be "in the unity of the Holy Spirit," a unity that allows us access to the Father "through, with and in Christ." As Ratzinger has put it, "Christ, the one, is here the 'we' into which Love, namely the Holy Spirit, gathers us and which means simultaneously being bound to each other and being directed toward the common 'you' of the one Father" (Ratzinger 1990, 453). The very idea of "person" expresses the idea of dialogue by referring to God as I, you, and we. In light of this knowledge of God, the nature of humanity is illumined (Ratzinger 1990, 443). And Ratzinger (1990) concludes that "The Christian concept of God has as a matter of principle given the same dignity to multiplicity as to unity. While antiquity considered multiplicity the corruption of unity, Christian faith, which is a Trinitarian faith, considers multiplicity as belonging to unity with the same dignity" (453.) The Trinity, far from a foreign heteronomous imposition on humanity, reveals to us our very selves as relational beings:

> The Lord Jesus, when he prayed to the Father "that all may be one
> . . . as we are one" (Jn 17:21–22), opened up vistas closed to human
> reason. For he implied a *certain likeness* [emphasis added] between
> the union of the divine persons and the union of God's children in
> truth and charity. This likeness reveals that man, who is the only
> creature on earth which God willed for its own sake, cannot fully
> find himself except through a sincere gift of self. (*Gaudium et Spes*,
> no. 24)

NOTES

1. Several portions of this chapter appear in different form in Mark Lowery, "Trinitarian Foundations for Subjectivity, Solidarity and Subsidiarity," *Catholic Social Science Review* (2002), 95–106.
2. Heteronomy, a state of being in which an individual is subject to the imposition of external laws and rules, is contrasted throughout this chapter to autonomy, in which an individual operates without external constraints.

Works Cited

INTRODUCTION: FROM THE MODERN AND POSTMODERN SELVES TO THE TRANSMODERN SELF

Bellah, R., et al. 1985. *Habits of the heart: Individualism and commitment in American life.* New York: Harper & Row.

Clarke. W. N. 1993. *Person and being.* Milwaukee, WI: Marquette University Press.

Conner, R. 1992. The person as resonating existential. *American Catholic Philosophical Quarterly* 66: 39–56.

Cushman, P. 1990. Why the self is empty: Toward a historically situated psychology. *American Psychologist* 45: 599–611.

———. 1995. *Constructing the self, constructing America: A cultural history of psychotherapy.* New York: Addison Wesley.

Gergen, K. J. 1991. *The saturated self: Dilemmas of identity in modern life.* New York: Basic Books.

———. 1998. *The self: Death by technology.* Charlottesville, VA: University of Virginia Press.

Landy, R. J. 1993. *Persona and performance: The meaning of role in drama, therapy and everyday life.* New York: Guilford.

Lasch, C. 1978. *The culture of narcissism.* New York: W. W. Norton.

Ratzinger, J. 1970. *Introduction to Christianity.* Translated by J. R. Foster. New York: Herder and Herder.

———. 1990. Retrieving the Tradition: Concerning the Notion of Person in Theology. *Communio* 17: 438–54.

Taylor, C. 1989. *Sources of the self: The making of modern identity.* Cambridge, MA: Harvard University Press.

Torrance, T. 1983. *The mediation of Christ.* Grand Rapids, MI: Eerdmans.

———. 1985. *Reality and scientific theology.* Edinburgh: Scottish Academic Press.

Vitz, P. C. 1994. *Psychology as religion: The cult of self-worship* (2nd ed.). Grand Rapids, MI: Eerdmans.

————. 1995a. A Christian theory of personality: Interpersonal and transmodern. In *The nature and tasks of a personalist psychology*, edited by J. M. Dubois, 23–26. Lanham, MD: University Press of America.

————. 1995b. The trans-modern church. *Crisis* 13 no. 11: 40–42.

————. 1998. The future of the university: From postmodern to transmodern. In *Rethinking the future of the university*, edited by D. Jeffrey and D. Manganiello, 105–16. Ottawa: University of Ottawa Press.

Ziziolas, J. D. 1985. *Being as communion*. Crestwood, NY: St. Vladimir's Seminary Press.

CHAPTER 1: THE IMITATIVE SELF: THE CONTRIBUTION OF RENÉ GIRARD

Augustine 1991. *Confessions*. Translated by H. Chadwick. Oxford: Oxford University Press.

Braudy, L. 1986. *The frenzy of renown: Fame and its history*. New York: Oxford University Press.

Cary, P. 2000. *Augustine's invention of the inner self*. Oxford: Oxford University Press.

Cervantes, M. de. 1970. *The adventures of Don Quixote*. Translated by J. M. Cohen. Baltimore: Penguin Books.

Descartes, R. 1968. *Discourse on method and the meditations*. Translated by F. E. Sutcliffe. Harmondsworth, UK: Penguin Books.

Edwards, D. 1997. Personal symbol of communion. In *The spirituality of the diocesan priest*, edited by D. B. Cozzens, 73–84. Collegeville, MN: The Liturgical Press.

Evdokimov, P. 1985. *The sacrament of love: The nuptial mystery in the light of the Orthodox tradition*. Crestwood, NY: St. Vladimir's Seminary Press.

Gergen, K. J. 1991. *The saturated self: Dilemmas of identity in contemporary life*. New York: Basic Books.

Gillespie, M. A. 1996. *Nihilism before Nietzsche*. Chicago: University of Chicago Press.

Girard, R. 1965. *Deceit, desire, and the novel: self and other in literary structure*. Translated by Y. Freccero. Baltimore: Johns Hopkins University Press.

————. 1993. Introduction to *On the way of freedom*, by R. Kaptein. Dublin: Columbia Press.

————. 1996. The Question of anti-Semitism in the Gospels. In *The Girard Reader*, edited by J. Williams, 211–24. New York: Crossroad Publishing.

Gregorios, P. M. 1992. *The light too bright: The enlightenment today.* Albany, NY: State University of New York Press.

Lubac, H. de. 1958. *Catholicism: A study of dogma in relation to the corporate destiny of mankind.* Translated by L. C. Sheppard. New York: Sheed and Ward.

———. 1986. *The Christian faith: An essay on the structure of the Apostles' creed.* Translated by R. Arnandez. San Francisco: Ignatius Press.

Rahner, K. 1962. *On the theology of death.* Translated by C. H. Henkey. New York: Herder and Herder.

Richard, L. 1997. *Christ: The self-emptying of God.* New York: Paulist Press.

Rousseau, J. 1953. *The confessions.* Translated by J. M. Cohen. London: Penguin.

Saulny, S. 2001. Into the groove, and proving their love. *New York Times* (July 26): 6.

Schmitz, K. L. 1986. The geography of the human person. *Communio* 13 (Spring): 27–48.

Shakespeare, W. 1997. Antony and Cleopatra. In *The Complete Works of Shakespeare,* 4th ed., edited by D. Bevington, 1293–1344. New York: Longman.

Taylor, C. 1989. *Sources of the self: The making of the modern identity.* Cambridge, MA: Harvard University Press.

Temple, W. 1940. *Nature, Man and God.* London: Macmillan.

von Balthasar, H. U. 1986. *Prayer.* Translated by G. Harrison. San Francisco: Ignatius Press.

———. 1988. *Theo-Drama: Theological dramatic theory, vol. I: Prologomena.* Translated by G. Harrison. San Francisco: Ignatius Press.

Woolf, V. 1959. *The waves.* San Diego: Harcourt Brace Jovanovich.

Zizioulas, J. D. 1985. *Being as communion.* Crestwood, NY: St. Vladimir's Seminary Press.

Zweig, P. 1968. *The heresy of self-love: A study in subversive individualism.* New York: Basic Books.

Chapter 2: Building a Responsive Self in a Post-Relativistic World: The Contribution of Mikhail Bakhtin

Bakhtin, M. 1981. *The dialogic imagination: Four essays by M. M. Bakhtin.* Edited by M. Holquist. Translated by C. Emerson, and M. Holquist. Austin, TX: University of Texas Press.

———. 1984. *Problems of Dostoevsky's poetics.* Edited and translated by C. Emerson. Minneapolis: University of Minnesota Press.

———. 1984. *Rabelais and his world.* Translated by H. Iswolsky. Bloomington, IN: Indiana University Press.

————. 1986. *Speech genres and other late essays.* Edited by C. Emerson and M. Holquist. Translated by V. W. McGee. Austin, TX: University of Texas Press.

————. 1990. *Art and answerability: Early philosophical essays by M. M. Bakhtin.* Edited by M. Holquist and V. Liapunov. Translated by V. Liapunov. Austin, TX: University of Texas Press.

————. 1993. *Toward a philosophy of the act.* Edited by V. Liapunov and M. Holquist. Translated by V. Liapunov. Austin, TX: University of Texas Press.

Bell, M. M. and M. Gardiner, eds. 1998. *Bakhtin and the human sciences.* London: Sage Publications.

Coates, R. 1998. *Christianity in Bakhtin: God and the exiled author.* Cambridge: Cambridge University Press.

Emerson, C. 1997. *The first hundred years of Mikhail Bakhtin.* Princeton, NJ: Princeton University Press.

————, ed. 1999. *Critical essays on Mikhail Bakhtin.* New York: G. K. Hall.

Felch, S. M. and P. J. Contino, eds. 2001. *Bakhtin and religion: A feeling for faith.* Evanston, IL: Northwestern University Press.

Hirschkop, K. and D. Shepherd, eds. 2001. *Bakhtin and cultural theory.* 2nd ed. Manchester, UK: Manchester University Press.

Nielsen, G. M. 2002. *The norms of answerability: Social theory between Bakhtin and Habermas.* Albany, NY: State University of New York Press.

CHAPTER 3: THE ROLE OF LOVE IN THE DEVELOPMENT OF THE SELF: FROM FREUD AND LACAN TO CHILDREN'S STORIES

Butler, J. 1993. *Bodies that matter: On the discursive limits of "sex."* New York: Routledge.

Butler, J. 1997. *The psychic life of power: Theories in subjection.* Stanford, CA: Stanford University Press.

Fairbairn, W. R. D. 1986. A revised psychopathology of the psychoses and psychoneuroses. In *Essential papers on object-relations,* edited by P. Buckley, 74–82. New York: New York University Press.

Foucault, M. 1970. *The order of things: An archaeology of the human sciences.* New York: Pantheon.

Freud, S. 1961. The ego and the id. In *The standard edition of the complete psychological works of Sigmund Freud,* vol. 19, edited and translated by J. Strachey, 3–66. London: Hogarth Press.

Kristeva, J. 1987. *Tales of love.* Translated by L. S. Roudiez. New York: Columbia University Press.

Lacan, J. 1977. *Ecrits: A selection.* Translated by A. Sheridan. New York: W. W. Norton.

Lear, J. 1990. *Love and its place in nature: A philosophical interpretation of Freudian psychoanalysis*. New Haven, CT: Yale University Press.

Lewis, T., F. Amini, and R. Lannon. 2000. *A general theory of love*. New York: Random House.

Nygrens, A. 1957. *Agape and eros*. Translated by P. S. Watson. London: SPCK.

Rhodes, C. 1972. *The necessity for love: The history of interpersonal relations*. London: Constable.

Sendak, M. 1963. *Where the wild things are*. New York: Harper and Row.

Taylor, C. 1989. *Sources of the self: The making of the modern identity*. Cambridge, MA: Harvard University Press.

Tillich, P. 1954. *Love, power, and justice: Ontological analyses and ethical applications*. London: Oxford University Press.

Van Haute, P. 2002. *Against adaptation: Lacan's "subversive" of the subject*. Translated by P. Crowe and M. Vankerk. New York: Other Press.

Verhaeghe, P. 1999. *Love in a time of loneliness: Three essays on drive and desire*. Translated by P. Peters and T. Langham. New York: Other Press.

White, E. B. 1954. *Charlotte's web*. New York: Harper and Row.

CHAPTER 4: PERSONS AS OBLIGATED: A VALUES-REALIZING PSYCHOLOGY IN LIGHT OF BAKHTIN, MACMURRAY, AND LEVINAS

Asch, S. E. 1951. Effects of group pressure upon the modification and distortion of judgments. In *Groups, Leadership, and Men*, edited by H. Guetzkow, 177–90. Pittsburgh: Carnegie Press.

———. 1952. *Social psychology*. Englewood Cliffs, NJ: Prentice-Hall.

———. 1956. Studies of independence and submission to group pressure: I. A minority of one against a unanimous majority. *Psychological Monographs* 70, no. 9.

———. 1990. Comments on D. T. Campbell's chapter. In *The legacy of Solomon Asch: Essays in cognition and social psychology*, edited by I. Rock, 53–55. Hillsdale, NJ: Lawrence Erlbaum Associates.

Bakhtin, M. M. (1984). *Problems of Dostoevsky's poetics*. Edited and translated by C. Emerson. Minneapolis: University of Minnesota Press.

———. 1986. *Speech genres and other late essays*. Edited by C. Emerson and M. Holquist. Translated by V. W. McGee. Austin: University of Texas Press.

———. 1993. *Toward a philosophy of the act*. Edited by V. Liapunov and M. Holquist. Translated by V. Liapunov. Austin: University of Texas Press.

Baumeister, R. F. 1995. Self and identity: An introduction. In *Advanced social psychology*, edited by A. Tesser, 51–97. New York: McGraw-Hill.

Beek, P. J., M. T. Turvey, and R. C. Schmidt. 1992. Autonomous and nonautonomous dynamics of coordinated rhythmic movements. *Ecological Psychology* 4: 65–95.

Brown, T. 1996. Values, knowledge, and Piaget. In *Values and knowledge*, edited by E. Reed, E. Turiel, and T. Brown, 137–70. Mahwah, NJ: Lawrence Erlbaum Associates.

Buss, D. M. 1999. *Evolutionary psychology: The new science of mind*. Needham Heights, MA: Allyn and Bacon.

Caird, J. K. and P. A. Hancock. 1994. The perception of arrival time for different oncoming vehicles at an intersection. *Ecological Psychology* 6: 83–109.

Campbell, D. T. 1990. Asch's moral epistemology for social shared knowledge. In *The legacy of Solomon Asch: Essays in cognition and social psychology*, edited by I. Rock, 39–52. Hillsdale, NJ: Lawrence Erlbaum Associates.

Cialdini, R. B. and M. Trost. 1998. Social influence: Social norms, conformity and compliance. In *The Handbook of Social Psychology*, vol. 2, edited by D. Gilbert, S. Fiske, and G. Lindzey, 151–92. 4th ed. Boston: McGraw-Hill.

Costall, A. 1995. Socializing affordances. *Theory and Psychology* 5: 467–81.

Cushman, P. 1990. Why the self is empty: Toward a historically situated psychology. *American Psychologist* 45: 599–611.

———. 1993. Psychotherapy and moral discourse. *Theoretical and Philosophical Psychology* 13: 103–13.

Davis, T. B. 1995. Deconstructing prejudice: A Levinasian alternative. *Journal of Theoretical and Philosophical Psychology* 15: 72–83.

deRivera, J. 1989. Choice of emotion and ideal development. In *Emotions in ideal human development*, edited by L. Cirillo, B. Kaplan, and S. Wapner, 7–34. Hillsdale, NJ: Lawrence Erlbaum.

Dollard, J., L. W. Doob, N. G. Miller, O. H. Mowrer, and R. R. Sears (1939). *Frustration and aggression*. New Haven, CT: Yale University Press.

Feather, N. T. 1999. *Values, achievement, and justice: Studies in the psychology of deservingness*. New York: Kluwer Academic/Plenum Publishers.

Flach, J. M. and M. R. H. Smith. 2000. Right strategy, wrong tactic. *Ecological Psychology* 12: 43–51.

Friend, R., Y. Rafferty, and D. Bramel. 1990. A puzzling misinterpretation of the Asch "conformity" study. *European Journal of Social Psychology* 20: 29–44.

Gergen, K. J. 1991. *The saturated self: Dilemmas of identity in contemporary life*. New York: Basic Books.

———. 1994. Exploring the postmodern: Perils or potentials? *American Psychologist* 49: 412–16.

Gibson, J. J. 1979. *The ecological approach to visual perception*. Boston: Houghton Mifflin.

Givón, T. 1989. *Mind, code and context: Essays in pragmatics.* Hillsdale, NJ: Lawrence Erlbaum Associates.

Grice, H. P. (1975). Logic and conversation. In *Syntax and semantics, vol. 3: Speech acts,* edited by P. Cole and J. Morgan, 41–58. New York: Academic.

Grice, Paul. (1991). *The conception of value.* Oxford: Clarendon Press.

Harré, R. and P. R. Secord. 1972. *The explanation of social behaviour.* Oxford: Basil Blackwell.

Harris, P. 1985. Asch's data and the "Asch effect": A critical note. *British Journal of Social Psychology* 24: 229–30.

Heschel, A. J. 1965. *Who is Man?* Stanford, CA: Stanford University Press.

Hodges, B. H. 1983. Love is more than a feeling. *His* 43 (January): 13–15.

———. 1985. Human identity and the values of learning: The seven C's. In *Christian approaches to learning theory: Vol. 2. The nature of the learner,* edited by N. DeJong, 93–111. Lanham, MD: University Press of America.

———. 1987. Perception is relative and veridical: Ecological and biblical perspectives on knowing and doing the truth. In *The reality of Christian learning,* edited by H. Heie and D. Wolfe, 103–39. Grand Rapids, MI: Eerdmans.

———. 1995. *Beyond goals: The place of values in a world of postmodern affordances.* Paper presented at Eighth International Conference on Perception and Action, July, Marseilles.

———. 1997. *The importance and inadequacy of consciousness.* Paper presented at the Ninth International Conference on Perception and Action, July, Toronto.

———. 2000. Remapping psychology: A new look at values in scientific ontology. *Christian Scholar's Review* 29: 471–97.

———. 2004. *Values in perception, action, cognition, and emotion.* Manuscript in preparation. Gordon College, Wenham, MA.

Hodges, B. H., and R. M. Baron. 1992. Values as constraints on affordances: Perceiving and acting properly. *Journal for the Theory of Social Behaviour* 22: 263–94.

Hodges, B. H., and A. Geyer. 2002. *A nonconformist account of the Asch experiments: Values, pragmatics, and moral dilemmas.* Manuscript under review. Gordon College, Wenham, MA.

Katz, S. 1987. Why there is no error in the direct theory of perception. *Perception* 16: 537–42.

Kendler, H. H. 1999. The role of value in the world of psychology. *American Psychologist* 54: 828–35.

Kugler, P. N., R. E. Shaw, K. J. Vicente, and J. Kinsella-Shaw. 1991. The role of attractors in the self-organization of intentional systems. In *Cognition and the symbolic processes: Applied and ecological perspectives,* edited by R. R. Hoffman and D. S. Palermo, 387–431. Hillsdale, NJ: Lawrence Erlbaum Associates.

Lakoff, G. and M. Johnson. 1980. *Metaphors we live by.* Chicago, IL: University of Chicago Press.

———. 1999. *Philosophy in the flesh: The embodied mind and its challenge to western thought.* New York: Basic Books.

Laudan, L. 1984. *Science and values: The aims of science and their role in scientific debate.* Berkeley, CA: University of California Press.

Lazarus, R. S. and B. N. Lazarus, B. N. (1994). *Passion and reason: Making sense of our emotions.* Oxford: Oxford University Press.

Levinas, E. (1989). Ethics as first philosophy. In *The Levinas reader,* edited by S. Hand, 75–87. Cambridge, MA: Basil Blackwell.

MacIntyre, A. 1981. *After virtue.* South Bend, IN: University of Notre Dame Press.

Macmurray, J. 1957. *The self as agent.* London: Faber and Faber.

———. 1961. *Persons in relation.* London: Faber and Faber.

Maio, G. R. and J. M. Olson, 1998. Values as truisms: Evidence and implications. *Journal of Personality and Social Psychology* 74: 294–311.

Martin, J. E. 1989. Aesthetic constraints on theory selection: A critique of Laudan. *British Journal of Philosophy of Science* 40: 357–64.

Martin, J. E. and B. H. Hodges. 1987. Learning, values, imagination, and responsibility: Appropriate ambiguity. In *Christian approaches to learning theory: Vol. 3. Freedom and discipline,* edited by N. DeJong, 85–99. Lanham, MD: University Press of America.

Martin, J. E., G. B. Kleindorfer, and W. R. Brashers. 1987. The theory of bounded rationality and the problem of legitimation. *Journal for the Theory of Social Behaviour* 17: 63–82.

Martin, J. E., G. B. Kleindorfer, and J. H. Buchanan. 1986. Piagetian reflections on legitimacy, justificationism, and learning theory. *The Genetic Epistemologist* 14: 1–13.

Michaels, C. F. and C. Carello. 1981. *Direct perception.* Englewood Cliffs, NJ: Prentice-Hall.

Midgley, M. 1991. *Why can't we make moral judgements?* New York: St. Martin's Press.

Milgram, S. 1974. *Obedience to authority: An experimental view.* New York: Harper and Row.

Morson, G. S. and C. Emerson. 1990. *Mikhail Bakhtin: Creation of a prosaics.* Stanford, CA: Stanford University Press.

Moscovici, S. 1985. Social influence and conformity. In *Handbook of social psychology,* vol. 2, edited by G. Lindzey and E. Aronson, 347–412. 3rd ed. New York: Random House.

Murdoch, I. 1970. *The sovereignty of the good.* London: Routledge & Kegan Paul.

———. 1992. *Metaphysics as a guide to morals.* London: Penguin.

Palmer, C. 1989. Mapping musical thought to musical performance. *Journal of Experimental Psychology: Human Perception and Performance* 15: 331–46.

Peperzak, A. T. 1997. *Beyond: The philosophy of Emmanuel Levinas.* Evanston, IL: Northwestern University Press.

Pyszczynski, T., J. Greenberg, and S. Solomon. 2000. Why do we need what we need? A terror mangagement perspective on the roots of human social motivation. In *Motivational science: Social and personality perspectives,* edited by E. T. Higgins and A. W. Kruglanski, 76–99. Philadephia: Psychology Press/Taylor and Francis.

Reed, E. S. 1988. *James J. Gibson and the psychology of perception.* New Haven, CT: Yale University Press.

———. 1996. *Encountering the world: Toward an ecological psychology.* New York: Oxford University Press.

Rokeach, M. 1973. *The nature of human values.* New York: Free Press.

Sabini, J. and M. Silver. 1982. *Moralities of everyday life.* Oxford: Oxford University Press.

Schwartz, B. 1986. *The battle for human nature.* New York: W. W. Norton.

———. 1990. The creation and destruction of value. *American Psychologist* 45: 7–15.

Schwartz. S. H. 1994. Are there universal aspects in the structure and contents of human values. *Journal of Social Issues* 50: 19–45.

Sedikides, C. 1993. Assessment, enhancement, and verfication determinants of the self-evaluation process. *Journal of Personality and Social Psychology* 65: 317–38.

Seligman, C., J. M. Olson, and M. P. Zanna. 1996. *The psychology of values: The Ontario symposium,* vol. 8. Mahwah, NJ: Lawrence Erlbaum Associates.

Shanon, B. 1993. *The representational and the presentational: An essay on cognition and the study of the mind.* New York: Harvester Wheatsheaf.

Shotter, J. 1984. *Social accountability and selfhood.* London: Basil Blackwell.

———. 1993. *Cultural politics of everyday life.* Buckingham, UK: Open University Press.

Skinner, B. F. 1953. *Science and human behavior.* New York: Free Press.

Steiner, G. 1989. *Real presences.* Chicago: University of Chicago Press.

Still, A. and A. Costall. 1991. *Against cognitivism: Alternative foundations for cognitive psychology.* London: Harvester Wheatsheaf.

Taylor, C. 1989. *Sources of the self: The making of the modern identity.* Cambridge, MA: Harvard University Press.

Todd, Z. 1993. *Metaphorical activity in communicative context—a dialogic analysis of figurative language.* Primacy of Action Conference, December, University of Manchester, UK.

Trevarthen, C. 1993. The self born in intersubjectivity: The psychology of an infant communicating. In *The perceived self: Ecological and interpersonal sources of self-knowledge,* edited by U. Neisser, 121–73. New York: Cambridge University Press.

Turvey, M. T. 1990. Coordination. *American Psychologist* 45: 938–53.

———. 1996. Dynamic touch. *American Psychologist* 51: 1134–52.

Uzgiris, I. C. 1996. Together and apart: The enactment of values in infancy. In *Values and knowledge,* edited by E. Reed, E. Turiel, and T. Brown, 17–39. Mahwah, NJ: Lawrence Erlbaum Associates.

Valsiner, J. 1987. *Culture and the development of children's action.* Chichester, UK: Wiley.

Varela, F. J., E. Thompson, and E. Rosch. 1993. *The embodied mind: Cognitive science and human experience.* Cambridge, MA: MIT Press.

Warren, W. H. and R. E. Shaw. 1985. *Persistence and change.* Hillsdale, NJ: Lawrence Erlbaum Associates.

Williams, R. N. 1994. The modern, the post-modern, and the question of truth: Perspectives on the problem of agency. *Journal of Theoretical and Philosophical Psychology* 14: 25–39.

Winold, H., E. Thelen, and B. D. Ulrich. 1994. Coordination and control in the bow arm movements of highly skilled cellists. *Ecological Psychology* 6: 1–31.

Zebrowitz, L. A. 1990. *Social perception.* Belmont, CA: Brooks-Cole.

CHAPTER 5: FINDING A SELF TO LOVE: AN EVALUATION OF THERAPEUTIC SELF-LOVE

Adams, R. 1998. Self-love and the vices of self-preference. *Faith and Philosophy* 15: 500–513.

Annas, J. 1992. The good life and the good lives of others. In *The good life and the human good,* edited by E. Paul, F. Miller, and J. Paul, 133–48. Cambridge: Cambridge University Press.

Aristotle. 1941. *The basic works of Aristotle.* Edited by R. McKeon. New York: Random House.

Bird, O. 1964. The complexity of love. *Thought* 39: 210–20.

Browning, D. 1987. *Religious thought and the modern psychologies: A critical conversation in the theology of culture.* Philadelphia: Fortress Press.

Butler, J. 1950. *Five sermons preached at rolls chapel; and, A dissertation upon the nature of virtue.* Indianapolis: Bobbs-Merrill.

Charry, E. 2001. Theology After Psychology. In *Care for the soul: Exploring the intersection of psychology and theology,* edited by M. McMinn and T. Phillips, 118–33. Downers Grove, IL: InterVarsity Press.

Chazan, P. 1998. *The moral self.* New York: Routledge.

Colby, A. and W. Damon. 1992. *Some do care: Contemporary lives of moral commitment.* New York: Free Press.

Hampton, J. 1993. Selflessness and the loss of self. In *Altruism,* edited by E. Paul, F. Miller, and J. Paul, 135–65. Cambridge: Cambridge University Press.

Hanfling, O. 1993. Loving my neighbor, loving myself. *Philosophy* 68: 145–57.

Harrison, B. 1989. Morality and interest. *Philosophy* 64: 303–22.

Holley, D. 1999. *Self-Interest and beyond.* St. Paul, MN: Paragon House.

————. 2002. Self-Interest and integrity. *International Philosophical Quarterly* 42: 5–22.

Lewis, C. S. 1952. *The screwtape letters.* New York: MacMillan.

Lomas, Peter. 1999. *Doing good? Psychotherapy out of its depth.* Oxford: Oxford University Press.

Rieff, P. 1966. *The triumph of the therapeutic: Uses of faith after Freud.* Chicago: University of Chicago Press.

Schmidtz, D. 1995. *Rational choice and moral agency.* Princeton, NJ: Princeton University Press.

Sidgwick, H. 1962. *The methods of ethics.* 7th ed. Chicago: University of Chicago Press.

Taylor, C. 1989. *Sources of the self: The making of the modern identity.* Cambridge, MA: Harvard University Press.

Vitz, P. 1994. *Psychology as religion: The cult of self-worship.* 2nd ed. Grand Rapids, MI: Eerdmans.

Wallach, M. and L. Wallach. 1983. *Psychology's sanction for selfishness: The error of egoism in theory and therapy.* San Francisco: W. H. Freeman and Company.

Chapter 6: The Meaning of Embodiment: Neuroscience, Cognitive Psychology, and Spiritual Anthropology

Brown, D. E. 1991. *Human universals.* New York: McGraw-Hill.

Damasio, A. R. 1994. *Descartes' error.* New York: Grosset/Putnam.

Cavalli-Sforza, L. 2004. Personal communication with author, July.

John Paul II. 1987. *Development and Solidarity: Two Keys to Peace.* Message in celebration of the World Day of Peace, January, Vatican City.

Jonas, H. 1966. *The phenomenon of life: Toward a philosophical biology.* New York: Harper and Row.

Kagan, J. 1998. *Three seductive ideas.* Cambridge, MA: Harvard University Press.

Kass, L. R. 1994. *The hungry soul: Eating and the perfecting of our nature.* New York: Free Press.

Lakoff, G. and M. Johnson. 1999. *Philosophy in the flesh: The embodied mind and its challenge to western thought.* New York: Basic Books.

Pascal, B. 1965. *Pensées.* Translated by H. F. Stewart. New York: Pantheon Books.

Stern, D. 1985. *The interpersonal world of the infant: A view from psychoanalysis and developmental psychology.* New York: Basic Books.

Tattersall, I. 2000. Once we were not alone. *Scientific American* 282 (January): 56–62.

Taylor, C. 1991. *The ethics of authenticity.* Cambridge, MA: Harvard University Press.

Zahn-Waxler, C. and M. Radke-Yarrow. 1990. The origins of empathic concern. *Motivation and emotion* 14, no. 2: 107–30.

CHAPTER 7: THE EMBODIED SELF: EVIDENCE FROM COGNITIVE PSYCHOLOGY AND NEUROPSYCHOLOGY

Aronson, E. and S. Rosenbloom. 1971. Space perception in early infancy: Perception within a common auditory-visual space. *Science* 172: 1161–63.

Ainsworth, M. 1989. Attachment beyond infancy. *American Psychologist* 44: 709–16.

Bermúdez, J. L. 1998. *The paradox of self-consciousness.* Cambridge, MA: MIT Press.

Bower, T. G. R. 1972. Object perception in infants. *Perception* 1: 15–30.

Bremner, J.G. 1988. *Infancy.* Oxford: Basil Blackwell.

Bruner, J. 1986. *Actual minds, possible worlds.* Cambridge, MA: Harvard University Press.

———. 1977. Early social interaction and language acquisition. In *Studies in mother-infant interactions,* edited by H. R. Schaffer, 271–89. New York: Academic Press.

Butterworth, G. 1981. The origins of auditory-visual perception and visual proprioception in human development. In *Intersensory perception and sensory integration,* edited by J. D. Walk and H. L. Pick, 37–70. New York: Plenum Press.

Cheour-Luhtanen, M., K. Alho, L. Saino, T. Rinne, K. Reinikainen, M. Pohjavouri, M. Renlund, O. Aaltonen, O. Eerola, and R. Näätänen. 1996. The ontogenetically earliest discriminative response of the human brain. *Psychophysiology* 33: 478–81.

Clarkson, M. G., I. V. Swain, R. K. Clifton, and K. Cohen. 1991. Newborns' hear orientation toward trains of brief sounds. *Journal of the acoustical society of America* 89: 2411–20.

Collins, N. and A. Read. 1990. Adult attachment, working models, and relationship quality in dating couples. *Journal of Personality and Social Psychology* 58: 644–63.

Condon, W. S. and L. W. Sander. 1974. Neonate movement is synchronized with adult speech: Interactional participation and language acquisition. *Science* 183: 99–101.

Coren, S., L. M. Ward, and J. T. Enns. 1999. *Sensation and perception.* 5th ed. Fort Worth, TX: Harcourt Brace.

Davidson, R. J. and K. Hugdahl, K., eds. 1995. *Brain asymmetry.* Cambridge, MA: MIT Press.

Davis, J. E. 2000. Not dead yet: Psychotherapy, morality and the question of identity dissolution. In *Identity and social change,* edited by J. E. Davis, 155–78. New Brunswick, NJ: Transaction Publishers.

DeCasper, A. J. and W. Fifer. 1980. Of human bonding: Newborns prefer their mothers' voices. *Science* 208: 1174–76.

Dunkeld, J. and T. G. R. Bower. 1980. Infant response to impending optical collision. *Perception* 9: 549–554.

Eimas, P. D., E. R. Siqueland, P. Jusczyk, and J. Vigorito. 1971. Speech perception in infants. *Science* 171: 303–6.

Feeney, J. and P. Noller. 1991. Attachment style and verbal descriptions of romantic partners. *Journal of Personal and Social Relationships* 8: 87–215.

Field, T. M., R. Woodson, R. Greenburg, and D. Cohen. 1982. Discrimination and imitation of facial expression in neonates. *Science* 218: 179–81.

Frager, R. and J. Fadiman. 1998. *Personality and personal growth.* 4th ed. New York: Longman.

Gibson, J. J. 1979. *The ecological approach to visual perception.* Boston: Houghton Mifflin.

Greenberg, J. R. and S. A. Mitchell. 1983. *Object relations in psychoanalytic theory.* Cambridge, MA: Harvard University Press.

Hazan, C. and P. Shaver. 1987. Attachment as an organizational framework for research for close relationships. *Psychological Inquiry* 5: 1–22.

Jusczyk, P. W. 1986. Toward a model of the development of speech perception. In *Invariance and variability in speech processes,* edited by J. S. Perkell and D. H. Klatt, 1–19. Hillsdale, NJ: Erlbaum.

Kellogg, R. 1970. *Analyzing children's art.* Palo Alto, CA: National Press Books.

Kilpatrick, L. and K. Davis. 1994. Attachment style, gender, and relationship stability: A longitudinal analysis. *Journal of Personality and Social Psychology* 66: 502–12.

Kuhl, P. K. and A. N. Meltzoff. 1982. The bimodal perception of speech in infancy. *Science* 218: 1138–41.

Kuhl, P. K. 1987. Perception of speech and sound in early infancy. In *Handbook of infant perception, vol. 2: From perception to cognition,* edited by P. Salapatek and I. Cohen, 275–382. Orlando, FL: Academic Press.

Lennebert, E. H. 1967. *Biological foundations of language.* New York: Wiley.

Locke, J. L. 1983. *Phonological acquisition and change.* New York: Academic Press.

MacKain, K., M. Studdert-Kennedy, S. Spieker, and D. Stern. 1983. Infant intermodal speech perception is a left hemisphere function. *Science* 219: 3147–49.

Martin, G. B. and R. D. Clark. 1982. Distress crying in neonates: Species and peer specificity. *Developmental Psychology* 18: 39.

Meltzoff, A. N. and M. K. Moore. 1977. Imitation of facial and manual gestures by human neonates. *Science* 198: 75–78.

———. 1983. Newborn infants imitate adult facial gestures. *Child Development* 54: 702–9.

Monte, C. F. and R. N. Sollod. 2003. *Beneath the mask: An introduction to theories of personality.* 7th ed. Hoboken, NJ: Wiley.

Muir, D. and J. Field. 1979. Newborn infants orient to sounds. *Child Development* 50: 431–36.

Murray, L. and C. Trevarthen. 1985. Emotional regulation of interactions between two-month-olds and their mothers. In *Social perception in infants,* edited by T. M. Field and N. A. Fox, 177–97. Norwood, NJ: Ablex.

Nanez, J. 1988. Perception of impending collision in 3-to-6 week-old infants. *Infant Behavior and Development* 11: 447–63.

Neisser, U. 1988. Five kinds of self-knowledge. *Philosophical Psychology* 1: 35–59.

Petitto, L. A. and P. E. Marentette. 1991. Babbling in the manual mode: Evidence for the ontogeny of language. *Science* 251: 1493–96.

Schmitz, K. 1986. The geography of the human person. *Communio* 13 (spring): 27–49.

Schmuckler, M. A. and H. Y. Tsang-Tong. 2002. The role of visual and body movement information in infant search. *Developmental Psychology* 36: 499–510.

Simner, M. L. 1971. Newborn's response to the cry of another infant. *Developmental Psychology* 5: 136–50.

Simpson, J. 1990. Influence of attachment styles on romantic relationships. *Journal of Personality and Social Psychology* 59: 571–80.

Solomon, J. and C. George. 1999. *Attachment disorganization.* New York: Guilford.

Summers, F. 1994. *Object relations theories and psychopathology.* Hillsdale, NJ: Analytic Press.

Trevarthen, C. 1993. The self born in intersubjectivity: The psychology of an infant communicating. In *The perceived self: Ecological and interpersonal sources of self-knowledge,* edited by U. Neisser, 121–73. New York: Cambridge University Press.

Tulving, E. 1983. *Elements of episodic memory.* New York: Oxford University Press.

Vitz, P. C. 1990. The use of stories in moral development: New psychological reasons for an old education method. *American Psychologist* 45: 709–20.

Von Hosten, C. 1982. Foundations for perceptual development. *Advances in infancy research* 2: 241–61.

Wertheimer, M. 1961. Psychomotor coordination of auditory and visual space at birth. *Science* 134: 1692.

Chapter 8: Losing Our Memories and Gaining Our Souls: The Scandal of Alzheimer's Dementia for the Modern or Postmodern Self

Allen, D. (1990). Natural evil and the love of God. In *The problem of evil,* edited by M. Adams and R. Adams, 189–208. Oxford: Oxford University Press.

Anderson, W. T. 1998. *The future of the self: Inventing the postmodern person.* New York: Putnam.

Bayley, J. 1999. *Elegy for Iris.* New York: Picador.

Brown, M. F. 1997. *The channeling zone: American spirituality in an anxious age.* Cambridge, MA: Harvard University Press.

Brown, W., N. Murphy, and H. N. Malony. 1998. *Whatever happened to the soul?* Minneapolis: Fortress Press.

Damasio, A. 1999. *The feeling of what happens: Body and emotion in the making of consciousness.* New York: Harcourt Brace.

Davis, J. 2000. Not dead yet: Psychotherapy, morality, and the question of identity dissolution. In *Identity and social change,* edited by J. Davis, 155–78. New Brunswick, NJ: Transaction Publishers.

DeBaggio, T. 2002. Losing my mind: An intimate look at life with Alzheimer's. New York: Free Press.

Gergen, K. J. 1991. *The saturated self: Dilemmas of identity in contemporary life.* New York: Basic Books.

Gunton, C. 1997. *The promise of Trinitarian theology.* Edinburgh: T & T Clark.

Jeeves, M. 1997. *Human nature at the millennium.* Grand Rapids, MI: Baker Books.

Kitwood. T. 1990. The dialectics of dementia: With particular reference to Alzheimer's disease. *Aging and Society* 10: 177–96.

———. 1996. A dialectical framework for dementia. In *Handbook of the clinical psychology of aging*, edited by R. J. Woods, 267–72. Oxford: John Wiley and Sons.

Lehmann, H. 1982. Affective disorders in the aged. *Psychiatric Clinics of North America* 5: 27–44.

Lewis, C. S. 1949. *The weight of glory.* Grand Rapids, MI: Eerdmans.

Lifton, R. J. 1993. *The protean self.* New York: Basic Books.

Lyotard, J-F. 1993. *The postmodern explained.* Translated by D. Barry. Edited by J. Pefanis and M. Thomas. Minneapolis: University of Minnesota Press.

Moltmann, J. 1985. *God in creation: A new theology of creation and the Spirit of God.* San Francisco: Harper and Row.

Plantinga, C. 1989. Social Trinity and tritheism. In *Trinity, incarnation and atonement: Philosophical and theological essays,* edited by R. Feenstra and C. Plantinga, 21–47. Notre Dame, IN: University of Notre Dame Press.

Plantinga, C. 2002. *Engaging God's world: A Christian vision of faith, learning and living.* Grand Rapids, MI: Eerdmans.

Rice, J. S. 1999. Romantic modernism and the self. *The Hedgehog Review* 1: 17–24.

Rokeach, A., M. Moye, T. Orzeck, and F. Esposito. 2001. Loneliness in North America and Spain. *Social Behavior and Personality* 29: 477–89.

Sabat, S. 2001. *The experience of Alzheimer's disease: Life through a tangled veil.* Oxford: Blackwell.

Shenk, D. 2001. *The forgetting: Alzheimer's, portrait of an epidemic.* New York: Doubleday.

Snowden, D. 1997. Aging and Alzheimer's disease: Lessons from the Nun Study. *Gerontologist* 37: 150–56.

———. 2002. *Aging with grace: What the Nun Study teaches us about leading longer, healthier and more meaningful lives.* New York: Bantam Books.

Taylor, C. 1989. *Sources of the self: The making of modern identity.* Cambridge, MA: Harvard University Press.

Wilson, B. and D. Wearing. 1995. Prisoner of consciousness: A state of just awakening following herpes simplex encephalitis. In *Broken memories,* edited by R. Campbell and M. Conway, 14–30. Oxford: Blackwell.

CHAPTER 9: SELF-CONSTRUCTION THROUGH CONSUMPTION ACTIVITIES: AN ANALYSIS AND REVIEW OF ALTERNATIVES

Alwitt, L. 1995. Marketing and the poor. *American Behavioral Scientist* 38: 564–77.

Anwal, M. A. 1994. *Reframing subaltran organizational praxis in transmodernity: A study of the Gramen Bank*. Ph.D. diss., Ohio University.

Argyle, M. 1987. *The psychology of happiness*. London: Methuen.

Baudrillard, J. 1988. Consumer society. In *Jean Baudrillard: Selected Writings*, edited by M. Poster, 29–56. Cambridge: Polity Press.

Baumeister, R. F. 1986. *Identity: Cultural change and the struggle for self*. New York: Oxford University Press.

Baumeister, R. F. 1997. The self and society: Changes, problems, and opportunities. In *Self and identity*, edited by R. D. Ashmore and L. Jussim, 191–217. New York: Oxford University Press.

Beck, U. 1992. *Risk society: Towards a new modernity*. London: Sage.

Belk, R. W. 1988. Possessions and the extended self. *Journal of Consumer Research* 15: 139–68.

Belk, R. W. and R. W. Pollay. 1985. Materialism and magazine advertising during the twentieth century. In *Advances in consumer research*, edited by E. Hirschman and M. Holbrook, 394–98. Provo, UT: Association for Consumer Research.

Benton, R., Jr. 1987. Work, consumption, and the joyless consumer. In *Philosophical and radical thought in marketing*, edited by A. F. Firat, N. Dholakia, and R. P. Bagozzi, 235–50. Lexington MA: Lexington Books.

Berger, P. L. 1990. *A rumor of angels: Modern society and the rediscovery of the supernational*. New York: Doubleday Books.

Bocock, R. 1993. *Consumption*. New York: Routledge.

Brownlie, D., M. Saren, R. Wensley, and R. Whittington. 1999. Marketing disequilibrium: On redress and restoration. In *Rethinking marketing: Toward critical marketing accounting*, edited by D. Brownlie, M. Saren, R. Wensley, and R. Whittington, 1–22. Thousand Oaks, CA: Sage.

Burns, D. J. 2001. Non-market need pairing: A review and analysis. In *Enhancing knowledge development in marketing*, edited by G. W. Marshall and S. J. Grove, 118–19. Chicago: American Marketing Association.

Burroughs, W. J., D. R. Drews, and W. K. Hallman. 1991. Predicting personality from personal possessions: A self-presentational analysis. In *A handbook on ownership and property*, edited by F. W. Rudmin. Special issue of *Journal of Social Behavior and Personality* 6: 147–64.

Castro, J. 1991. The simple life. *Time*, April 18, 58–63.

Clammer, J. 1992. Aesthetics of the self: Shopping and social being in contemporary Japan. In *Lifestyle shopping: The subject of consumption*, edited by R. Shields, 195–215. London: Routledge.

Cooley, C. H. 1902. *Human values and social order*. New York: Charles Scribner's Sons.

———. 1908. A study of the early use of self-words by a child. *Psychological Review* 15: 339–57.

Cova, B. 1996. What postmodernism means to marketing managers. *European Management Journal* 14: 494–99.

———. 1997. Community and consumption: Towards a definition of the "linking value" of product or services. *European Journal of Marketing* 31: 297–316.

Crocker, D. A. 1998. Consumption, well-being, and capability. In *Ethics in consumption: The good life, justice and global stewardship,* edited by D. A. Crocker and T. Linden, 366–90. Lanham, MD: Rowman and Littlefield.

Cross, G. 1993. *Time and money: The making of consumer culture.* New York: Routledge.

Csikszentmihalyi, M. 1982. The symbolic function of possessions: Towards a psychology of materialism. In *Proceedings of the 90th annual convention of the American Psychological Association.* Washington, DC: American Psychological Association.

Csikszentmihalyi, M. and E. Rochberg-Halton. 1981. *The meaning of things: Domestic symbols and the self.* Cambridge: Cambridge University Press.

Cummins, W. 1996. Love and liqueur: Modernism and postmodernism in advertising and fiction. In *Advertising and culture: Theoretical perspectives,* edited by M. Cross, 61–74. Westpoint, CT: Praeger.

Cushman, P. 1990. Why the self is empty: Toward a historically situated psychology. *American Psychologist* 45: 599–611.

———. 1995. *Constructing the self, constructing America: A cultural history of psychotherapy.* Reading, MA: Addison-Wesley.

Dass, R. 1981. Introduction. In *Voluntary simplicity: Toward a way of life that is outwardly simple and inwardly rich,* edited by D. Elgin, 13–19. New York: William Morrow and Company.

DeGeorge, R. T. 1990. *Business ethics.* New York: Macmillan.

Dellinger, R. W. 1977. Keeping tabs on the Joneses. *Human Behaviour,* 20–30.

Dholakia, N., A. F. Firat, and R. P. Bagozzi. 1987. Rethinking marketing. In *Philosophical and radical thought in marketing,* edited by A. F. Firat, N. Dholakia, and R. P. Bagozzi, 373–84. Lexington, MA: Lexington Books.

Diener, E., E. Sandvik, L. Seidlitz, and M. Diener. 1993. The relationship between income and subjective well-being: Relative or absolute? *Social Indicators Research* 28: 195–223.

Dittmar, H. 1992. *The social psychology of material possessions: To have is to be.* New York: St. Martin's Press.

Dittmar, H. and J. Drury. 2000. Self-image—Is it in the bag? A qualitative comparison between "ordinary" and "excessive" consumers. *Journal of Economic Psychology* 21: 109–42.

Donner, D. 1985. Bike thieves take more than just metal: They steal a big part of someone's life. *Daily Utah Chronicle,* October 30, 11.

Douglas, M. and B. Isherwood. 1978. *The world of goods: Towards an anthropology of consumption.* London: Allen Lane.

du Gay, P., S. Hall, L. Janes, H. Mackay, and K. Negus. 1997. *Doing cultural studies: The story of the Sony Walkman.* London: Sage.

Duval, T. S., V. H. Duval, and J. P. Mulilis. 1992. Effects of self-focus, discrepancy between self and standard, and outcome expectancy favorability on the tendency to match self to standard or to withdraw. *Journal of Personality and Social Psychology* 62: 340–48.

Elgin, D. 1993. *Voluntary simplicity: Toward a way of life that is outwardly simple, inwardly rich.* New York: William Morrow and Company.

Elliott, R. 1997. Existential consumption and irrational desire. *European Journal of Marketing* 31: 285–96.

Elliott, R. and K. Wattanasuwan. 1998. Brands as symbolic resources for the construction of identity. *International Journal of Advertising* 17: 131–44.

Erikson, K, T. 1976. *Everything in its path: Destruction of community in the Buffalo Creek flood.* New York: Simon and Schuster.

Ewen, S. 1989. Advertising and the development of consumer culture. In *Cultural politics in contemporary America,* edited by I. Angus and S. Jhally, 82–95. New York: Routledge.

Ferguson, H. (1992). Watching the world go round: Atrium culture and the psychology of shopping. In *Lifestyle shopping: The subject of consumption,* edited by R. Shields, 21–39. London: Routledge.

———. 1996. *The lure of dreams: Sigmund Freud and the construction of modernity.* London: Routledge.

Festinger, L. 1954. A theory of social comparison processes. *Human Relations* 7: 117–40.

Fowles, J. 1996. *Advertising and popular culture.* Thousand Oaks, CA: Sage.

Fromm, E. 1976. *To have or to be?* New York: Harper and Row.

Frow, J. 1997. *Time and commodity culture: Essays in cultural theory and postmodernity.* Oxford: Clarendon Press.

Fullerton, G. L. 1998. The marketing concept in a post-modern era. In *Enhancing knowledge development in marketing,* edited by P. J. Gordon and B. J. Kellerman, 198–203. Chicago: American Marketing Association.

Gabriel, Y. and T. Lang. 1995. *The unmanageable consumer: Contemporary consumption and its fragmentation.* Thousand Oaks, CA: Sage.

Gay, C. M. 1998. *The way of the (modern) world.* Grand Rapids, MI: William B. Eerdmans.

Gergen, K. J. 1991. *The saturated self: Dilemmas of identity in contemporary life.* New York: Basic Books.

Giddens A. 1991. *Modernity and self-identity: Self and society in the later modern age.* Cambridge: Polity Press.

Goffman, E. 1961. *Asylums*. New York: Doubleday.

Grodlin, D. and T. R. Lindlof. 1996. The self and mediated communication. In *Constructing the self in a mediated world*, edited by D. Grodlin and T. R. Lindlof, 3–12. Thousand Oaks, CA: Sage.

Hammerslough, J. 2001. *Dematerializing*. Cambridge: Perseus Publishing.

Hargrove, T. 2000. Study: Religion will thrive. *Youngstown Vindicator*, March 11, B9.

Hartley, J. 1999. *Uses of Television*. London: Routledge.

Hoch, S. J. and G. F. Loewenstein. 1991. Time-inconsistent preferences and consumer self-control. *Journal of Consumer Research* 17: 492–507.

Holley, D. M. 1999. *Self-interest and beyond*. St. Paul, MN: Paragon House.

Holstein, J. A. and J. F. Gubrium. 2000. *The self we live by*. New York: Oxford University Press.

Holt, D. B. 1997. Post-structuralist lifestyle analysis: Conceptualizing the social patterning of consumption in postmodernity. *Journal of Consumer Research* 23: 325–50.

Ingram, J. A. 1997. Modern and postmodern issues in Christian psychology: An integrative transmodern proposal. *Journal of Psychology and Theology* 25: 315–28.

James, W. 1890. *The principles of psychology*. Vol. 1. New York: Henry Holt.

Jameson, F. 1991. *Postmodernism, or, the cultural logic of late capitalism*. Durham, NC: Duke University Press.

Kasser, T. 2002. *The high price of materialism*. Cambridge, MA: MIT Press.

Kotler, P. 1987. Humanistic marketing: Beyond the marketing concept. In *Philosophical and radical thought in marketing*, edited by A. F. Firat, N. Dholakia, and R. P. Bagozzi, 271–88. Lexington, MA: Lexington Books.

———. 2000. *Marketing management*. Upper Saddle River, NJ: Prentice Hall.

Kottler, J. A. 1999. *Exploring and treating acquisitive desire: Living in the material world*. Thousand Oaks, CA: Sage.

Kubey, R. and M. Csikszentmihalyi. 1990. *Television and the quality of life: How viewing shapes everyday experience*. Hillsdale, NJ: Lawrence Erlbaum Associates.

Laing, J. R. 1992. The new ghost towns: A vicious shakeout takes its toll on shopping malls. *Barron's* (March 16): 8–9, 20, 22, 24, 26.

Landy, R. J. 1993. *Persona and performance: The meaning of role in drama, therapy, and everyday life*. New York: Guilford Press.

Lane, R. E. 1998. The road not taken: Friendship, consumerism and happiness. In *Ethics in consumption: The good life, justice and global stewardship*, edited by D. A. Crocker and T. Linden, 218–48. Lanham, MD: Rowman and Littlefield.

Langman, L. 1992. Neon cages: Shopping for subjectivity. In *Lifestyle shopping: The subject of consumption*, edited by R. Shields, 40–82. New York: Routledge.

Lessnoff, M. H. 1994. *The spirit of capitalism and the Protestant ethic: An enquiry in the Weber thesis.* Aldershot, UK: Edward Elgar.

Levi-Strauss, C. 1965. The principle of reciprocity. In *Sociological Theory*, edited by L. A. Coser and B. Rosenberg, 84–94. New York: Macmillan.

Lewis, P. V. 1985. Defining "business ethics" is like nailing Jell-o to a wall. *Journal of Business Ethics* 4: 377–83.

Luyckx, M. 1999. The transmodern hypothesis: Towards a dialogue of cultures. *Futures* 31: 971–82.

Lyon, D. 1999. *Postmodernity*. Minneapolis: University of Minnesota Press.

Magnet, M. 1987. The money society. *Fortune* (July 6): 26–31.

Martin, J. and J. Sugarman. 2000. Between the modern and the postmodern: The possibility of self progressive understanding in psychology. *American Psychologist* 55: 397–406

Marsden, G. M. 1994. *The soul of the American university: From Protestant establishment to established nonbelief.* New York: Oxford University Press.

Massnick, F. 1997. *The culture is CEO: How to measure what your customers want—and make sure they get it.* New York: AMACOM.

McLeod, B. 1984. In the wake of disaster. *Psychology Today* 18: 54–57.

Miller, B. 1997. Mall shoppers with a mission, *American Demographics* 19: 26–27.

Miller, D. 1987. *Material culture and mass consumption.* Oxford: Blackwell.

Myers, D. G. 1992. *The pursuit of happiness: Who is happy and why.* New York: William Morrow and Company.

———. 2000. *The American paradox: Spiritual hunger in an age of plenty.* New Haven, CT: Yale University Press.

Needleman, J. 1991. *Money and the meaning of life.* New York: Doubleday.

Ornstein, R. and L. Carstengen. 1991. *Psychology: The study of human experience.* San Diego: Harcourt, Brace and Jovanovich.

Packard, V. O. 1980. *The hidden persuaders.* New York: Pocket Books.

Pollay, R. W. 1986a. The distorted mirror: Reflections of the unintended consequences of advertising. *Journal of Marketing* 50: 18–36.

———. 1986b. Quality of life in the padded sell: Common criticisms of advertising's cultural character and international public policies. *Current Issues and Research in Advertising* 9: 173–250.

Rassuli, K. M. and S. C. Hollander. 1986. Desire—Induced, innate, insatiable? *Journal of Macromarketing* 6: 4–24.

Reekie, G. 1992. Changes in the Adamless Eden: The spatial and sexual transformation of a Brisbane department store 1930–1990. In *Lifestyle shopping: The subject of consumption*, edited by R. Shields, 170–94. London: Routledge.

Richins, M. L. 1995. Social comparison advertising, and consumer discontent. *American Behavioral Scientist* 38: 593–607.

———. 1996. Materialism, desire, and discontent: Contributions of idealized advertising images and social comparison. In *Marketing and consumer research in the public interest*, edited by R. P. Hill, 109–32. Thousand Oaks, CA: Sage.

Rosenblatt, P. C., R. P. Walsh, and D. A. Jackson. 1976. *Grief and mourning in a cross-cultural perspective*. New Haven, CT: HRAF Press.

Rushing, J. H. and T. S. Frentz. 1995. *Projecting the shadow: The cyborg hero in American film*. Chicago: University of Chicago Press.

Rutherford, J. 1990. A place called home: Identity and the culture politics of difference. In *Identity: Community, culture, difference*, edited by J. Rutherford, 1–20. London: Lawrence and Wishart.

Sarup. M. 1996. *Identity, culture and the postmodern world*. Athens, GA: University of Georgia Press.

Schor, J. B. 1991. *The overworked American: The unexpected decline of leisure*. New York: Basic Books.

———. 1998. *The overspent American: Upscaling, downshifting, and the new consumer*. New York: Basic Books.

Schwartz, B. 1994. *The costs of living: How market freedom erodes the best things in life*. New York: W. W. Norton and Company.

Shields, R. 1992. Spaces for the subject of consumption. In *Lifestyle shopping: The subject of consumption*, edited by R. Shields, 1–20. New York: Routledge.

Shoulberg, W. 1998. Mall-igned. *Home Textiles Today* (August 10): 16.

Shweder, R. A. and E. J. Bourne. 1988. Does the concept of the person vary? In *Culture theory*, edited by R. A. Shweder and R. DeVine, 158–99. Cambridge: Cambridge University Press.

Sirgy, M. J., D. Cole, R. Kosenko, H. L. Meadow, D. Rahtz, M. Cicic, G. X. Jin, D. Yarsuvat, D. L. Blenkhorn, and N. Nagpal. 1995. Developing a life satisfaction measure based on need hierarchy theory. In *New dimensions in marketing/quality of life interface*, edited by M. J. Sirgy and A. C. Samli, 3–25. Westpoint, CT: Quorum Books.

Slater, D. 1997. *Consumer culture and modernity*. Cambridge: Polity Press.

Smith, R. H., E. Diener, and R. Garonzik. 1990. The roles of outcome satisfaction and comparison alternatives in envy. *British Journal of Social Psychology* 29: 247–55.

Snyder, C. R. and H. L. Fromkin. 1980. *Uniqueness: The human pursuit of difference*. New York: Plenum Press.

Solomon, M. R. 1983. The role of products as social stimuli: A symbolic interactionism approach. *Journal of Consumer Research* 10: 319–29.

Thompson, J. B. 1995. *The media and modernity: A social theory of the media.* Cambridge: Polity Press.

Toronto School of Theology. 1972. *Truth in advertising: A symposium.* New York: Harper and Row.

Twitchell, J. B. 1996. "But first, A word from our sponsor": Advertising and the carnivalization of culture. In *Dumbing down: Essays on the strip mining of American culture,* edited by K. Washburn and J. F. Thornton, 197–208. New York: W.W. Norton and Company.

———. 1999. *Lead us into temptation: The triumph of American materialism.* New York: Columbia University Press.

Veenhoven, R. 1991. Is happiness relative? *Social Indicators Research* 24: 1–34.

Vitz, P. C. 1994. *Psychology as religion: The cult of self-worship.* 2nd ed. Grand Rapids, MI: William B. Eerdmans.

———. 1995. Trans-modern church. *Crises* (December), 40–42.

———. 1998. The future of the university: From postmodern to transmodern. In *Rethinking the future of the university,* edited by D. L. Jeffrey and D. Manganiello, 105–16. Ottawa: University of Ottawa Press.

Wachtel, P. L. 1989. *The poverty of affluence: A psychological portrait of the American way of life.* Philadelphia: New Society Publishers.

Warde, A. 1994. Consumption, identity-formation and uncertainty. *Journal of the British Sociological Association* 28: 877–98.

Warren, H. B. and D. J. Burns. 2002. The atmospheric matrix: A mental model for decision making. In *Enhancing knowledge development in marketing,* edited by W. Kehoe and J. H. Lindgren, 85–86. Chicago: American Marketing Association.

Weber, M. 1958. *The Protestant ethic and the spirit of capitalism.* New York: Scribner.

Wirtz, J. and J. E. G. Bateson. 1999. Customer satisfaction with services: Integrating the environment perspective in services marketing into the traditional disconfirmation paradigm. *Journal of Business Research* 44: 55–66.

Xiaoming, H. 1994. Television viewing among American adults in the 1990s. *Journal of Broadcasting and Electronic Media* 38: 353–60.

Young, N. 1992. Postmodern self-psychology mirrored in science and the arts. In *Psychology and postmodernism,* edited by S. Kvale, 135–145. Thousand Oaks, CA: Sage.

Yount, D. 1997. *Spiritual simplicity: Simplify your life and enrich your soul.* New York: Simon and Schuster.

CHAPTER 10: THE SELF AT THE HUMAN/COMPUTER INTERFACE: A POSTMODERN ARTIFACT IN A DIFFERENT WORLD

Baumeister, R. F. 1987. How the self became a problem: A psychological review of historical research. *Journal of Personality and Social Psychology* 52: 163–76.

Bermúdez, J. L. 1998. *The Paradox of self-consciousness.* Cambridge, MA: MIT Press.

Card, S. K., T. P. Moran, and A. Newell. 1983. *The psychology of human-computer interaction.* Hillsdale, NJ: Lawrence Erlbaum Associates.

Cushman, P. 1990. Why the self is empty: Toward a historically situated psychology. *American Psychologist* 45: 599–611.

Flavell, J. H. 1979. Metacognition and cognitive monitoring: A new area of cognitive-development inquiry. *American Psychologist* 34: 906–11.

Hassan, I. 1987. Toward a concept of postmodernism. In *The postmodern turn: Essays in postmodern theory and culture,* 84–96. Columbus: Ohio State University Press.

Kurzweil, R. 1999. *The age of spiritual machines.* New York: Penguin.

Licklider, J. C. R. 1960. Man-computer symbiosis. *IRE Transactions on Human Factors in Electronics HFE-1,* 4–11.

Natoli, J. and L. Hutcheon. 1998. *A postmodern reader.* Albany, NY: State University of New York Press.

Norman, D. and S. W. Draper, eds. 1986. *User centered system design.* Hillsdale, NJ: Erlbaum.

Norman, K. L. 1991a. Models of the mind and machine: Information flow and control between humans and computers. In *Advances in computers,* edited by M. C. Yovits, vol. 32, 201–54. New York: Academic Press.

———. 1991b. *The psychology of menu selection: Designing cognitive control of the human/computer interface.* Norwood, NJ: Ablex Publishing Corp.

———. 2001. *A Modern/Postmodern framework for trends in Human/Computer interaction.* LAP-2001–03. Laboratory for Automation Psychology, University of Maryland, College Park, MD. http://lap.umd.edu/lapfolder/papers/LAP2001TR03/.

Powell, J. N. 1998. *Postmodernism for beginners.* London: Writers and Readers Limited.

Shiffrin R. M. and R. C. Atkinson. 1969. Storage and retrieval processing in long-term memory. *Psychological Review* 76: 179–93.

Shneiderman, B. 1998. *Designing the user interface: Strategies for effective human-computer interaction.* 3rd ed. Reading, MA: Addison-Wesley.

———. 2002. *Leonardo's Laptop.* Cambridge, MA: MIT Press.

Snodgrass, J. G. and R. L. Thompson, eds. 1997. *The self across psychology: Self-recognition.* New York: New York Academy of Sciences.

Stalder, F. 2001. The age of spiritual machines: When computers exceed human intelligence. *Computers & Society* 31: 23–35.

Suler, J. 1996. *The psychology of cyberspace.* Rider University. http://www.rider.edu/user/suler/psycyber/psycyber.html.

Taylor, C. 1989. *Sources of the self: The making of modern identity.* Cambridge, MA: Harvard University Press.

Chapter 11: Technology and the Self: Approaching the Transmodern

Benjamin, L. T., Jr. 1988. A history of teaching machines. *American Psychologist* 43: 703–12.

Birkerts, S. 1994. *The Gutenberg elegies: The fate of reading in an electronic age.* Boston: Faber and Faber.

Brooks, D. 2001. The organization kid. *Atlantic Monthly,* April, 40–54.

Gergen, K. J. 1991. *The saturated self: Dilemmas of identity in contemporary life.* New York: Basic Books.

Ginsberg-Klemmt, E. 2001. Bringing the world with us—virtually. *Newsweek,* May 28, 15.

Harrison, M. and L. Klein, L., directors. 1995. *Visions of heaven and hell: Selling the future* [Videorecording]. Available from Films for the Humanities & Sciences, Princeton, NJ.

Heim, M. 1993. *The metaphysics of virtual reality.* New York: Oxford University Press.

Keyes, R. 1992. The idol factory. In *No God but God: Breaking with the idols of our age,* edited by O. Guinness and J. Seel, 29–48. Chicago: Moody Press.

Mazlish, B. 1993. *The fourth discontinuity.* New Haven, CT: Yale University Press.

McLuhan, M. 1964. *Understanding media: The extensions of man.* New York: Signet Books.

Noble, D. F. 1999. *The religion of technology: The divinity of mankind and the spirit of invention.* New York: Penguin.

Postman, N. 1992. *Technopoly.* New York: Vintage Books.

Rawlins, G. J. E. 1996. *Moths to the flame: The seductions of computer technology.* Cambridge, MA: MIT Press.

Schuurman, E. 1995. *Perspectives on technology and culture.* Translated by J. H. Kok. Sioux Center, IA: Dordt College Press.

Slouka, M. 1995. *War of the mind: Cyberspace and the high-tech assault on reality.* New York: Basic Books.

Swenson, R. A. 1992. *Margin: Restoring emotional, physical, financial, and time reserves to overloaded lives.* Colorado Springs, CO: NavPress.

Turkle, S. 1995. *Life on the screen: Identity in the age of the internet.* New York: Simon and Schuster.

Winner, L. 1986. *The whale and the reactor.* Chicago: University of Chicago Press.

Wurman, R. S. 1989. *Information anxiety.* New York: Bantam Books.

Chapter 12: Personal Identity: Postmodern or Transmodern? A Study of College and University Undergraduates at the Turn of the Millennium

Aay, H. and S. Griffioen. 1998. *Geography and worldview.* Lanham, MD: University Press of America.

Anwal, M. A. 1994. *Reframing subaltran organizational praxis in transmodernity: A study of the Bank Gramen.* Doctoral dissertation, Ohio University, Athens, Ohio.

Ashley, B. M. 1985. *Theologies of the flesh: Humanist and Christian.* Braintree, MA: Pope John XXIII Medical Moral Research and Education Center.

Bailie, G. 1995. *Violence unveiled: Humanity at the crossroads.* New York: Crossroad.

Bermúdez, J. L. 1998. *The paradox of self-consciousness.* Cambridge, MA: Massachusetts Institute of Technology Press.

Bruner, M., M. Preda, J. Norwine, and A. Ketcham. 1994. The meaning of meaning in a post-meaning age. *International Social Science Journal* 46, no. 2: 285–93.

Clemens, S. L. 1977. *Adventures of Huckleberry Finn.* New York: W. W. Norton.

Coats, K. 2001. Personal communication with author, July 12, 2001.

Cushman, P. 1990. Why the self is empty: Toward a historically situated psychology. *American Psychologist* 45: 599–611.

Davis, J. E. 2000. *Identity and social change.* New Brunswick, NJ: Transaction.

Edge, H. L. 1994. *A constructive postmodern perspective on self and community: From Atomism to Holism.* Lewiston, NY: Edwin Mellen Press.

Felch, S. 2001. Personal communication with author, July 13, 2001.

Gergen, K. J. 1991. *The saturated self: Dilemmas of identity in contemporary life.* New York: Basic Books.

Heerman. J. 1941. *O Christ: The Lutheran Hymnal.* [hymn]. Chicago: Concordia, No. 512.

Heim, S. M. 2001. God's diversity. *Christian Century,* January 24: 14–18.

Hodges, B. 2001. *Hopeful, suffering selves: A proper postmodernism?* Grand Rapids, MI, July 5, Pew/Calvin College Summer Seminar on Restoring the Self.

Hume, D. 1965. *A treatise of human nature.* Hamden, CN: Archon Books.

Huntington, S. P. 1996. *The clash of civilizations and the remaking of world order.* New York: Simon and Schuster.

Inglehart, R. 1990. *Culture shift in advanced industrial society.* Princeton, NJ: Princeton University Press.

————. 2000. Culture and democracy. In *Culture matters: How values shape human progress,* edited by L. E. Harrison and S. P. Huntington, 80–97. New York: Basic Books.

Ingram, J. A. 1997. Modern and postmodern issues in Christian psychology: An integrative transmodern proposal. *Journal of Psychology and Theology* 25: 315–28.

John Paul II 1990. *Redemptoris Missio.* December 7, 1990, encyclical. http://www.vatican.va/edocs/ENG0219.

Kerr, P. 1992. *A philosophical investigation.* New York: Plume.

Kierkegaard, S. 1954. *The sickness unto death.* Garden City, NJ: Doubleday.

Kinlaw, D. F. 2001. *Elohim.* Unpublished manuscript. Wilmore, KY: Francis Asbury Society.

Kuhn, T. 1962. *The structure of scientific revolutions.* Chicago: University of Chicago Press.

Kundera, M. 1984. *The unbearable lightness of being.* New York: Harper and Row.

Lakoff, G. and M. Johnson. 1999. *Philosophy in the flesh: The embodied mind and its challenge to western thought.* New York: Basic Books

Landes, D. 2000. Culture makes almost all the difference. In *Culture matters: How values shape human progress,* edited by L. E. Harrison and S. P. Huntington, 2–13. New York: Basic Books.

Larner, G. 1998. Through a glass darkly: Narrative as destiny. *Theory and Psychology* 8: 549–72.

Lewis, C. S. 1964. *The discarded image.* Cambridge: Cambridge University Press.

Licklider, J. C. R. 1960. Man-computer symbiosis. *IRE Transactions on Human Factors in Electronics HFE-1,* 4–11.

Luyckx, M. 1999. The transmodern hypothesis: Towards a dialogue of cultures. *Futures* 31: 971–82.

Mahoney, D. J. 2002. Whittaker Chambers: Witness to the crisis of the modern soul. *Intercollegiate Review* 37: 41–48.

McLaren, B. 2001. *A new kind of Christian.* San Francisco: Jossey-Bass.

Milosz, C. 2001. *Milosz's ABC's.* New York: Farrar, Straus and Giroux.

Mirzoeff, N. 1999. *An introduction to visual culture.* New York: Routledge.

Murdoch, I. 1978. *The sea, the sea.* New York: Viking.

Murr, C. T. 2001. A psychology of personalism: The phenomenology of Maurice Nedoncelle. Unpublished Master's thesis. New York University, New York.

Natoli, J. and L. Hutcheon. 1993. *A postmodern reader.* Albany, NY: State University of New York Press.

Nedoncelle, M. 1984. *The Personalist challenge: Intersubjectivity and ontology.* Translated by F. Gerard with Fr. Burch. Allison Park, PA: Pickwick.

Neuhaus, R. J. 2001. *The second one thousand years: Ten people who defined a millennium.* Grand Rapids, MI: Eerdmans.

Nooteboom, C. 1987. *In the Dutch Mountains.* Baton Rouge, LA: Louisiana State University Press.

Norman, K. L. 2001. The postmodern self at the human/computer interface. Presented at the Pew/Calvin College Seminar on Rediscovering the Postmodern Self, Grand Rapids, MI, July 24.

Norwine, J. and J. M. Smith. 2000. *Worldview flux.* Lanham, MD: Lexington.

Odajnyk, W. 1965. *Marxism and Existentialism.* Garden City, NY: Doubleday.

Oden, T. 1991. Then and now: The recovery of patristic wisdom. In *How my mind has changed,* edited by J. Wall and D. Heim, 123–34. Grand Rapids, MI: Eerdmans.

Ortega y Gasset, J. 1968. In search of Goethe from within. In *The dehumanization of art and other essays on art, culture and literature,* 131–74. Princeton, NJ: Princeton University Press.

Percy, W. 1983. *Lost in the cosmos: The last self-help book.* New York: Pocket Books.

Pierce, C. P. 2001. A journey to the beginning of time. *Esquire* (August): 80.

Rushing, J. H. and T. S. Frentz. 1995. *Projecting the shadow: The cyborg hero in American film.* Chicago: University of Chicago Press.

Schneewind, J. B. 1998. *The invention of autonomy.* Cambridge: Cambridge University Press.

Stoeltje, M. F. 2002. Kids should come first, regardless of parents' marital state. *San Antonio Express-News* (May 9): 1F.

Stratton, S. 2001. Personal communication with author, July 12, 2001.

Sweeney, S. E. 2001a. "It's nothing personal": Investigating postmodernist selfhood in Memento. Presented at the Pew/Calvin College Summer Seminar on Rediscovering the Self. Grand Rapids, MI, July 25.

Sweeney, S. E. 2001b. Personal communication with author. July 26, 2001.

Taylor, C. (1989). *Sources of the self: The making of the modern identity.* Cambridge, MA: Harvard University Press

Tuan, Yi-Fu. 1982. *Segmented worlds and self.* Minneapolis, MN: University of Minnesota Press.

Vitz, P. C. 1994. *Psychology as religion: The cult of self-worship.* 2nd ed. Grand Rapids, MI: Eerdmans.

———. 1995. A Christian theory of personality. In *Limning the psyche: Explorations in Christian psychology,* edited by R. C. Roberts and M. R. Talbot, 20–40. Grand Rapids, MI: Eerdmans.

———. 1995b. Trans-modern church. *Crisis,* December, 40–42.

———. 1998. The future of the university: From postmodern to transmodern. In *Rethinking the future of the university,* edited by D. L. Jeffrey and D. Manganiello, 105–16. Ottawa: University of Ottawa Press

———. 2001a. The self: From a postmodern crisis to a transmodern solution. Public Lecture, Spoelhof Center, Calvin College, Grand Rapids, MI, July 20.

———. 2001b. Comments made during a discussion at the Pew Charitable Trust/ Calvin College Seminar on "Rediscovering the Postmodern Self." Grand Rapids, MI: Calvin College.

von Balthasar, H. U. 1986. On the concept of person. *Communio* 13: 18–26.

Williams, J. G., ed. 1996. *The Girard reader.* New York: Crossroads/Herder.

Zizioulas, J. D. 1995. The doctrine of the Holy Trinity: The significance of the Cappadocian contribution. In *Trinitarian theology today: Essays on divine being and acting,* ed. C. Schwobel, 44–60. Edinburgh: T&T Clark.

CHAPTER 13: SOCIAL PSYCHOLOGY AND THE SELF: TEACHING AND RESEARCH

Bailie, G. 1995. *Violence unveiled: Humanity at the crossroads.* New York: Crossroad.

Baumeister, R. F. 1987. How the self became a problem: A psychological review of historical research. *Journal of Personality and Social Psychology* 52: 163–76.

Cushman, P. 1990. Why the self is empty: Toward a historically situated psychology. *American Psychologist* 45: 599–611.

DeLoach, J. S. and A. Gottlieb. 2000. *A world of babies: Imagined childcare guides for seven societies.* Cambridge, MA: Cambridge University Press.

Deutsch, M. and H. B. Gerard. 1955. A study of normative and informational social influence upon individual judgment. *Journal of Abnormal and Social Psychology* 51: 629–36.

Gergen, K. J. 1991. *The saturated self: Dilemmas of identity in contemporary life.* New York: Basic Books.

Gunton, C. 2001. Relational being in the image of God. Paper presented at Trinity Institute's 32nd National Conference, May, New York.

Jackson, S. 1968. *Come along with me: Part of a novel, sixteen stories, and three lectures.* New York: Viking.

Kenrick, D. T., S. L. Neuberg, and R. B. Cialdini. 2002. *Social psychology: Unraveling the mystery.* 2nd ed. Boston: Allyn & Bacon.

Latane, B. and J. M. Darley. 1968. Group inhibition of bystander intervention in emergencies. *Journal of Personality and Social Psychology* 10: 215–21.

Martin, J. and J. Sugarman. 2000. Between the modern and the postmodern: The possibility of self and progressive understanding in psychology. *American Psychologist* 55: 397–406.

Milgram, S. 1974. *Obedience to authority: An experimental view.* New York: Harper.

Murr, C. T. 2001. *A psychology of personalism: The phenomenology of Marice Nedoncelle.* Unpublished Master's thesis. New York University, New York.

Pipher, M. 1997. *The shelter of each other: Rebuilding our families.* New York: Ballantine.

Plantinga, C., Jr. 1995. *Not the way it's supposed to be: A breviary of sin.* Grand Rapids, MI: Eerdmans.

Ross, L. 1977. The intuitive psychologist and his shortcomings: Distortions in the attribution process. In *Advances in experimental social psychology,* edited by L. Berkowitz, vol. 10, 174–221. New York: Academic Press.

Ross, L. and R. E. Nisbett. 1991. *The person and the situation: Perspectives of social psychology.* Philadelphia: Temple University Press.

Taylor, S. E., L. A. Peplau, and D. O. Sears. 2003. *Social psychology.* 11th ed. Upper Saddle River, NJ: Prentice Hall.

Van Leeuwen, M. S. 1982. The unfulfilled apprenticeship of North American psychology. *Christian Scholar's Review* 11: 291–315.

Vitz, P. 1995. A Christian theory of personality. In *Limning the psyche: Explorations in Christian psychology,* edited by R. C. Roberts and M. R. Talbot, 20–40. Grand Rapids, MI: Eerdmans.

Weiner, B. 1996. *Judgments of responsibility.* New York: Guilford.

Weiner, B., R. P. Perry, and J. Magnusson. 1988. An attributional analysis of reactions to stigmas. *Journal of Personality and Social Psychology* 55: 738–48.

Wolters, A. M. 1985. *Creation regained: Biblical basics for a reformational worldview.* Grand Rapids, MI: Eerdmans.

CHAPTER 14: SELF, ATTACHMENT, AND AGENCY: LOVE AND THE TRINITARIAN CONCEPT OF PERSONHOOD

Ainsworth, M. D. S., M. C. Blehar, E. Waters, and S. Wall. 1978. *Patterns of attachment: A psychological study of the strange situation.* Hillsdale, NJ: Erlbaum.

Alberti, R. E. and M. L. Emmons. 1990. *Your perfect right: A guide to assertive living.* 6th ed. San Luis Obispo, CA: Impact Publishers.

Bermúdez, J. L. 1998. *The paradox of self-consciousness*. Cambridge, MA: MIT Press.

Bowlby, J. 1988. *A secure base: Parent-child attachment and healthy human development*. New York: Basic Books.

Brunner, E. 1939. *Man in revolt*. Philadelphia: Westminster Press.

Clarke, W. N. 1993. *Person and being*. Milwaukee: Marquette University Press.

Cooley, C. H. 1968. The social self: On the meanings of "I." In *The self in social interaction*, edited by C. Gordon and K. Gergen, 87–91. New York: John Wiley and Sons.

Damasio, A. 1999. *The feeling of what happens: Body and emotion in the making of consciousness*. San Diego: Harcourt, Inc.

Gunton, C. 1991. Trinity, ontology and anthropology: Towards a renewal of the doctrine of the Imago Dei. In *Persons, divine and human: King's College essays in theological anthropology*, edited by C. Schwobel and C. Gunton, 47–61. Edinburgh: T. & T. Clark.

———. 1993. *The One, the Three, and the Many: God, creation, and the culture of modernity*. Cambridge: Cambridge University Press.

———. 1997. *The promise of Trinitarian theology*. Edinburgh: T. & T. Clark.

Hagberg, J. O. 1994. *Real power: Stages of personal power in organizations*. Salem, WI: Sheffield Publishing Co.

Hogan, R. M. and J. LeVoir. 1985. *Covenant of love: Pope John Paul II on sexuality, marriage, and family in the modern world*. Ft. Collins, CO: Ignatius Press.

Johnson, S. 1997. The biology of love. *Networker*, September/October, 36–41.

Kasper, W. 1996. *The God of Jesus Christ*. New York: Crossroad.

Kegan, R. 1994. *In over our heads: The mental demands of modern life*. Cambridge, MA: Harvard University Press.

Kinlaw, D. 2001. *Elohim*. Unpublished manuscript. Wilmore, KY. Francis Asbury Society.

Kirkpatrick, L. A. 1999. Attachment and religious representations and behavior. In *Handbook of attachment: Theory, research, and clinical applications*, edited by J. Cassidy and P. R. Shaver, 803–22. New York: Guilford Press.

Laporte, J. 1997. Kenosis as a key to maturity of personality. In *Limning the psyche: Explorations in Christian psychology*, edited by R. C. Roberts and M. R. Talbot, 229–44. Grand Rapids, MI: Wm. B. Eerdmans.

LeDoux, J. 1996. *The emotional brain: The mysterious underpinnings of emotional life*. New York: Simon and Schuster.

Lewis, T., F. Amini, and R. Lannon. 2000. *A general theory of love*. New York: Vintage Books.

Lopez, F. G. and K. A. Brennan. 2000. Dynamic processes underlying adult attachment organization: Toward an attachment theoretical perspective on the healthy and effective self. *Journal of Counseling Psychology* 47: 283–300.

Macmurray, J. 1991. *The self as agent.* 2nd ed. Atlantic Highlands, NJ: Humanities Press.

Markus, H. and E. Wurf. 1987. The dynamic self-concept: A social psychological perspective. *Annual Review of Psychology* 38: 299–337.

Mead, G. H. 1962. *Mind, self, and society.* Chicago: University of Chicago Press.

Mikulincer, M. 1995. Attachment style and the mental representation of the self. *Journal of Personality and Social Psychology* 69: 1205–15.

Moltmann, J. 2001. God's kenosis in the creation and consummation of the world. In *The work of love: Creation as kenosis,* edited by J. Polkinghorne, 137–151. Grand Rapids, MI: William B. Eerdmans.

———. 2001. *The Spirit of life: A universal affirmation.* Minneapolis: Fortress Press.

Neisser, U. 1997. The roots of self-knowledge: Perceiving self, it, thou. In *The self across psychology: Self-recognition, self-awareness, and the self concept,* edited by J. G. Snodgrass and R. L. Thompson, 19–33. New York: New York Academy of Science.

Nelson, K. 1997. Finding one's self in time. In *The self across psychology: Self-recognition, self-awareness, and the self concept,* edited by J. G. Snodgrass and R. L. Thompson, 102–16. New York: New York Academy of Science.

Palmer, P. 1990. *The active life: A spirituality of work, creativity, and caring.* San Francisco: Jossey-Bass Publishers.

Ratzinger, J. 1990. Retrieving the Tradition: Concerning the Notion of Person in Theology, *Communio* 17: 438–54.

Roland, A. 1988. *In search of self in India and Japan: Toward a cross-cultural psychology.* Princeton, NJ: Princeton University Press.

Rothbard, J. C. and P. Shaver. 1994. Continuity of attachment across the life span. In *Attachment in adults: Clinical and developmental perspectives,* edited by M. B. Sperling and W. H. Berman, 31–71. New York: Guilford Press.

Schore, A. N. 2003a. *Affect dysregulation and the disorders of self.* New York: W. W. Norton and Company.

———. 2003b. *Affect regulation and the repair of the self.* New York: W. W. Norton and Company.

Stratton, S. P. 1991. Intensive case studies of attachment utilizing a naturally-occurring separation in marital relationships. Ph.D. diss., Auburn University.

Swoebel, C. 1991. Introduction. In *Persons, divine and human: King's College essays in theological anthropology,* edited by C. Schwobel and C. Gunton, 1–29. Edinburgh: T. & T. Clark.

Taylor, C. 1985. *Human agency and language: Philosophical papers.* Cambridge: Cambridge University Press.

———. 1989. *Sources of the self: The making of modern identity*. Cambridge, MA: Harvard University Press.

Tiryakian, E. A. 1968. Existential self and the person. In *The self in social interaction*, edited by C. Gordon and K. Gergen, 75–86. New York: John Wiley and Sons.

Vitz, P. 1995. A Christian theory of personality. In *Limning the psyche: Explorations in Christian psychology*, edited by R. C. Roberts and M. R. Talbot, 20–40. Grand Rapids, MI: Eerdmans.

———. 2001. The self: From a postmodern crisis to a transmodern solution. Paper read at Calvin College, July 20, Grand Rapids, MI.

Zizioulas, J. 1985. *Being as communion*. Crestwood, NY: St. Vladimir's Seminary Press.

Chapter 15: The Trinitarian Nature of the Transmodern Person

Ashley, B. (1985) *Theologies of the Body: Humanist and Christian*. Braintree, MA: Pope John Center.

Bettenson, H., ed. 1963. *Documents of the Christian church*. London: Oxford University Press.

Clarke, W. N. 1992. Person, Being, and St. Thomas. *Communio* 19: 600–618.

———. 1993. *Person and being*. Milwaukee: Marquette University Press.

———. 1994. To be is to be substance-in-relation. In *Explorations in Metaphysics*, edited by W. N. Clarke, 102–22. Notre Dame, IN: University of Notre Dame Press.

Gaudium et Spes. 1984. In *Vatican Council II: The Conciliar and Post Conciliar Documents*, edited by A. Flannery, O.P., 903–1000. Collegeville, MN: The Liturgical Press.

John Paul II. 1993. *Veritatis Splendor*. Boston: Pauline Press.

———. 1997. *The Theology of the Body*. Boston: Pauline Press.

Kasper, W. 1997. *The God of Jesus Christ*. New York: Crossroad.

Linker, D. 2000. John Paul II, Intellectual. *Policy Review* (October/November): 3–18

Murr, C. T. 2001. *A psychology of personalism: The phenomenology of Marice Nedoncelle*. M.A. thesis, New York University, New York.

Neisser, U. 1997. The roots of self knowledge: Perceiving self, it, and thou. In *The self across psychology: Self-recognition, self-awareness, and the self concept*, edited by J. G. Snodgrass and R. L. Thompson, 19–33. New York: New York Academy of Science.

Ratzinger, J. 1970. *Introduction to Christianity.* New York: Herder and Herder.

———. 1990. Retrieving the Tradition: Concerning the Notion of Person in Theology, *Communio* 17: 438–54.

Schindler, D. and N. C. Clarke. 1993. *Communio* 20: 580–98.

Schmitz, K. L. 1986. The geography of the human person. *Communio* 13 (Spring): 203–4.

Schu, W. J. 2003. *The splendor of love.* New Hope, KY: New Hope Publications.

Siskind, A. 1994. Is "nothing" sacred? "Sacred" cosmology among the avant-garde. In *Between sacred and secular: Research and theory on quasi-religion,* edited by A. Greil and T. Robbins. Religion and the Social Order, vol. 4. Greenwich, CN: JAI Press.

Taylor, C. 1989. *Sources of the self: The making of the modern identity.* Cambridge, MA: Harvard University Press.

Turek, M. 2000. Systematic Theology. Course materials, University of Dallas, Irving, TX.

von Balthasar, H. U. 1998. *Theodrama.* Vol. 3. Translated by G. Harrison. San Francisco: Ignatius.

Vitz, P. 1995. A Christian theory of personality. In *Limning the psyche: Explorations in Christian psychology,* edited by R. C. Roberts and M. R. Talbot, 20–40. Grand Rapids, MI: Eerdmans.

Zizioulas, J. 1985. *Being as communion.* London: Darton, Longman and Todd.

Abstracts

1. The Imitative Self: The Contribution of René Girard

GIL BAILIE

Is it true that we can only become our true selves by learning to imitate someone else? Gil Bailie answers "yes" to this question and, in the face of modern attempts to define selfhood in terms of autonomy, reconsiders the role of models in developing an authentic sense of self. Drawing on René Girard's notion of mimetic desire—that we inevitably desire what we see another desiring—Bailie illuminates our human compulsion to imitate. And in illustrations drawn from Augustine, Rousseau, Cervantes, Shakespeare, Virginia Woolf, Madonna, and pop culture he demonstrates the devastating consequences of following shoddy models and the vital importance of choosing models who will help us grow into mature selves.

Bailie also traces the devolution of the term "person," with its iconic sense of imitation, into the modern notion of the "self," with its self-reflective—and idolatrous—autonomy. Authentic personhood, developed through mimetic desire, is linked with a nuptial, covenantal understanding of truth, Bailie suggests. Discovering truth consists not so much in locating an abstract ideal "out there" in the world as it does in pledging oneself, with unwavering fidelity, to the One who is the author and exemplar of truth.

2. Building a Responsive Self in a Post-Relativistic World:

The Contribution of Mikhail Bakhtin

CARYL EMERSON

The writings of Mikhail Bakhtin, the twentieth-century Russian thinker, have often been pressed into service in the West to support the postmodern notion of a transgressive, libertarian, "carnival" self that flouts tradition and promotes autonomy. In this chapter, Caryl Emerson extracts Bakhtin from this comfortable niche and reasserts one of his fundamental questions: "How might I *not* comfortably belong, how might I remain on the outside, but always in a creative way?"

Emerson examines three intersecting models of personality, devised and revised by Bakhtin throughout his life—the *dialogic*, the *carnival*, and the *architectonic* self, all of which are theologically inflected but not therapeutic. That is, none are designed to make us feel better by enhancing our self-confidence or by bringing us immediate relief, but rather each imposes obligations to those who are other than ourselves. Emerson argues that Bakhtin's selves do not follow the model of Cartesian unmediated self-reflection and integration but instead devote themselves faithfully to dynamic relationships where they learn the validity—indeed the necessity—of other people's perspectives and gain the wisdom to make moral judgments and to act responsibly in this world.

3. The Role of Love in the Development of the Self:

From Freud and Lacan to Children's Stories

KAREN COATS

"I think, therefore I am." This Cartesian dictum has governed thinking about the self for nearly three hundred years. But the crises of the last century have put that formulation into question. With its notion of a disembodied self, "I think, therefore I am" leaves the self lost and in disarray. In this chapter, Karen Coats explores the role played by love in the development of the self and suggests that we revise Descartes to read, "I love, therefore I am." This redefinition turns on a refreshed understanding of love and the way it works to construct the relations of self and other.

In our everyday experience, this emphasis on love hardly seems to need explaining; we know that children have the best chance to thrive and develop capacious, self-giving egos in loving environments, and often fail to do so where love is lacking or somehow dysfunctional. Working at the intersections of continental psychoanalysis and contemporary views of the self as an embodied person who develops in relation with specific others and as a response to Otherness itself, Coats looks at the ways in which love mediates human growth. Using examples from children's literature, she describes how love, through the psychic processes of idealization and identification, characterizes the self's growth.

4. Persons as Obligated: A Values-Realizing Psychology in Light of Bakhtin, Macmurray, and Levinas

BERT H. HODGES

Descartes' *cogito*—"I think, therefore I am"—divided the modern self into two realms: the moral and the mechanical. As a moral, disembodied, thinking agent, the self was autonomous. But this thinker was imprisoned in a body that belonged to the meaningless, mechanistic world. This separation of the moral from the mechanical in Cartesian psychology all but guaranteed the loss of a meaningful self and the impoverishment of psychology as a science. In particular, values were seen merely as external impositions upon an autonomous self, rather than as deeply motivating goals intrinsic to human personhood.

Bert Hodges utilizes psychological research on perception and action in this chapter to illustrate and argue that values are fundamental to reality and to our knowledge, action, and concern in it. Persons are embodied, ecologically situated, responsible agents who perceive and act prospectively to realize epistemic and moral values such as truth and justice. Hodges argues that research suggests this values-realizing motivation often yields frustration and suffering, a situation resonant with postmodern understandings of the self. He uses insights from Bakhtin, Macmurray, and Levinas to explore how hope and integrity might emerge from our frustration, if we are willing to endure our overwhelming obligation "to the Other" and the "unfinalizability" of existence.

5. Finding a Self to Love:

An Evaluation of Therapeutic Self-Love

DAVID M. HOLLEY

The injunction to "love ourselves" has become such a commonplace in contemporary society that we are scarcely conscious of its power to shape the way we think about selves. But its very status as received wisdom suggests the need to reexamine its main assumptions. The key questions to ask, David Holley suggests, are "Who is this self we are to love?" and "What does it mean to love ourselves?" A self that thinks of itself as an autonomous and isolated entity will be too "thin" to sustain an adequate love; it may replace genuine love with indulgence or myopic self-absorption. Similarly, such a self will tend to think of the action of love merely as the satisfaction of desires. In contrast, Holley argues that "loving myself is bound up with cherishing ideals that are central to my identity."

Drawing on contemporary psychological theory as well as Aristotle's *Nichomachean Ethics*, Holley describes the need for proper moral development to a self who would learn to value the long-term good of both the individual and the community. In the absence of such moral development, the self who is loved and who loves may become defective and cause more harm than good. Indeed, if we take the command to "love ourselves" as a therapeutic model, we may be tempted to replace the primary goal of loving neighbors *as we love ourselves* with the self-centered and ultimately self-defeating goal of promoting our own goods over those of others. But by affirming the value of other selves and acquiring "extended personal interests," proper self-love can unite the project of loving the self with the project of loving others within a broader communal context.

6. The Meaning of Embodiment: Neuroscience,

Cognitive Psychology, and Spiritual Anthropology

WILLIAM B. HURLBUT

The emerging discipline of cognitive neuroscience is making us increasingly aware of the extent to which all humans share a common neurophysiology that leads to basic similarities in our modes of consciousness and sociality. In perceptual interpretation, conceptual categorization, and cognitive strategies there are remarkable similarities in individuals across cultures. In this chapter, William Hurlbut argues that these scientific developments provide a basis for re-imagining humanity in a way that preserves the strengths both of diversity and unity, and on that basis offers hope for genuine intercultural communication, understanding, and moral consensus.

Hurlbut examines facial recognition, early responsiveness between infants and mothers, and other scientific evidence to argue that the whole of the material world may be seen as an intelligible "language" of being and the foundation for personal and social existence.

7. The Embodied Self: Evidence from
Cognitive Psychology and Neuropsychology

Paul C. Vitz

The postmodern self is often construed as an arbitrary social- or self-constructed identity. In this chapter, Paul Vitz argues that the evidence from cognitive psychology and neuropsychology points to universal characteristics of the human nervous system—including higher cognition and experiences that contribute to the concept of the self—that put severe limits on such notions of autonomy.

Vitz examines universal forms of infant sensory and perceptual experience, invariant early interpersonal interactions, common early language learning, childhood interpersonal relationships, and other universal cultural factors, all of which are solidified and particularized for each self through the action of memory. This understanding of the embodied self frees us from the constructions of both the autonomous self-reflective modern self and the de-centered pastiche postmodern self while allowing for a trajectory of transcendence. As human beings grow and become interpersonally and intellectually more developed, they come to understand that they have over time transcended—moved beyond and above—their previous self-understandings. It is in choosing the goal of transcendence that freedom enters into self-development—a freedom that exists in the context of the earlier body-based and interpersonal self.

8. Losing Our Memories and Gaining Our Souls: The Scandal of Alzheimer's Dementia for the Modern or Postmodern Self

GLENN WEAVER

The common core of the self, developed through the universal factors described in the preceding chapter by Paul Vitz, is also de-developed under the impact of Alzheimer's dementia. Yet, as Glenn Weaver argues in this chapter, the loss of memory by persons affected by Alzheimer's dementia does not mean the total loss of the self. A relatively enduring core of self-identity remains, despite the breakdown of narrative unity.

Weaver examines the impact of Alzheimer's dementia through scientific, literary, and personal accounts of the disease, but he also contends that modern and postmodern definitions of the self offer little hope to those suffering from Alzheimer's or to their families. In contrast, Weaver suggests that we reclaim more substantial anchors to the human self, namely physical embodiment, significant relationships with others, and the experience of love, all of which are incorporated in the biblical understanding of the nature of persons.

9. Self-Construction through Consumption Activities: An Analysis and Review of Alternatives

DAVID J. BURNS

Few people would argue with the charge that contemporary Western society is dominated by consumerism, but less attention has been paid to the ways in which such consumerism shapes notions of the self. When consumption activities play a major role in the construction of the self, particularly as people define themselves through the products they buy in a mall-based culture, a number of problems emerge. David Burns examines four of these in some depth: the impossible-to-obtain ideal images presented by advertising; the lack of adequate resources for appropriate self-construction; the quandary of being rich in things and poor in time; and the risk of losing the self when shopping becomes "not merely the acquisition of things . . . [but] the buying of identity."

Burns also examines three solutions to the problem of the consumption-construction self and points out their inadequacies in our market-based economy: redefining work to meet the needs of self-fulfillment; redefining marketing to appeal to better values; and regulating advertising. As an alternative, he suggests a return to and reestablishment of the historical bases for forming a more sturdy conception of the self, namely the family, community, and religion.

10. The Self at the Human/Computer Interface:

A Postmodern Artifact in a Different World

KENT L. NORMAN

As we spend significantly more time interacting with and through machines, we invest and embody more of ourselves at the human/computer interface with and through digital artifacts. These artifacts take the form of electronic records and journals of our lives and encode aspects and preferences in terms of digital codes. In this chapter, Kent Norman discusses the self as a set of conceptualizations relative to the human/computer interface. The transition from the modern to the postmodern world witnesses a change in these conceptualizations and the imprint they have left on the interface. While the trend has superficially been toward personalization, the real effect has been one of creating disembodied selves.

Norman argues that in the face of our increasing utilization of computers, we must resist the tendency to deify or even to humanize the computer. No matter how useful, a machine is still a machine. He also insists that we must view the self as more than a mere symbol-processing agent and recover the analogical conception of the person as a mind/body/spirit unit that is inherently incongruent with digital code.

11. Technology and the Self: Approaching the Transmodern

JOHN BECHTOLD

Humans have always tended to put their faith in their own accomplishments. In our technological age, this means we are in danger of turning technology into an idol, substituting it for a transcendent God. John Bechtold argues that we are lured into this idolatry because technology so closely mimics the classical attributes of God: technology's pervasiveness can pass for omnipresence; its efficiency and autonomy for omnipotence; and its vast amount of data for omniscience.

When we succumb to the temptation to possess these pseudo-qualities, we lose our sense of self, Bechtold argues. The cyberworld distances us from contact with the physical world and other people; we become tethered to technology and wearied by its incessant demands; data gathering replaces genuine knowledge; and relational numbing sets in when too many people want instant access to our time and energy. As antidote, he suggests a considered return to the embodied and relational self that recognizes its own, and technology's, limitations.

12. Personal Identity: Postmodern or Transmodern?

A Study of College and University Undergraduates

at the Turn of the Millennium

JIM NORWINE ET AL.

Jim Norwine and his associates begin with the thesis that we are now all postmoderns, albeit ranging widely in degree. This chapter explores what "to be postmodern" may say about personal identity at the start of the third millennium. The authors report on the results of a survey designed to explore worldviews and values, with particular emphasis on the self, which was administered in winter 2001–2 at eight American colleges and universities.

In their analysis of the data, Norwine and his associates note that far from being "slain," traditional and modern values often remain quite robust, yet the condition of postmodernity inclines students toward a major cultural paradigm shift, one which favors two related yet competing worldviews, which they characterize as "radical postmodern" and "transmodern."

13. Social Psychology and the Self: Teaching and Research

SHERRI B. LANTINGA

The discipline of social psychology focuses on how other people power-fully influence our everyday behavior. Social psychological research is usu-ally conducted in a modernist frame, but important research outcomes are then often synthesized into textbooks undergirded by postmodern perspec-tives. Sherri Lantinga argues that the challenge in the classroom is to teach about the fundamentally relational and responsible self to students who are convinced believers in radical individuality, and also in a discipline where the researchers themselves are confused about whether radical individual-ism or social embeddedness better describes the nature of people.

Lantinga describes her research on undergraduates' perspectives of what constitutes the self. Using the prompt "Write an essay on what you mean by the word 'self,'" she discovered that while students have a difficult time defining the self, they are generally convinced that they individually control these elusive "selves," independent of their social or physical con-texts. She concludes with a number of concrete recommendations for in-class demonstrations or assignments that help clarify the nature of the self and reinforce the virtues of relationality and responsibility.

14. Self, Attachment, and Agency: Love
and the Trinitarian Concept of Personhood

STEPHEN P. STRATTON

The term *person* originated in Christian theology's developmental struggle to comprehend the nature and experience of a triune God. Thus, the Trin-ity provides the appropriate analogy for understanding human personhood. Stephen Stratton argues that, by extrapolating from this fundamental theo-logical doctrine, the building blocks for an understanding of healthy and unhealthy human personhood can be realized. In particular, the concepts of selfhood and communion may be integrated into a larger whole.

Stratton looks at healthy selfhood through the lens of human attach-ment, and at healthy communion through the lens of human agency. In so doing, what it means to be a human person—a communing self—becomes clearer. Moreover, this dynamic relationship of particularity (self) and process (communion) transcends the modern and postmodern to establish a transmodern notion of how love is applied to any human relationship. A two-dimensional model is hypothesized that illustrates love-in-action and uses the Second Person of the Trinity as its incarnation.

15. The Trinitarian Nature of the Transmodern Person

MARK LOWERY

In this chapter, Mark Lowery argues that modernism and postmodernism are not new constructs but rather are variations on a perennial theme: the balance between substance and relationality in the quest to grasp the full meaning of what it means to be a person. Lowery wends his way through the early theological debates on the nature of the Trinity and the nature of Christ to show how discussions of both substance, particularly in the West, and relationality, particularly in the East, produced as a by-product a robust view of human personhood, namely a concept of persons as "substance-in-relation."

Rather than simply reverting to tradition, however—what Lowery calls a paleomorphic tendency—he uses the questions of postmodernity and the resources of the Christian theological tradition to continue a positive trajectory of describing and promoting the human person. For Lowery, "relational substance" captures the simultaneity of substance and relation that inheres in the notion of person, as well as the freedom to be and become that is central to our experience.

Notes on Contributors

Gil Bailie is the president and founder of the Cornerstone Forum and the author of *Violence Unveiled: Humanity at the Crossroads* (Crossroad, 1995).

John Bechtold is Professor of Psychology at Messiah College. He teaches and has developed courses around the topic of technology and its psychological effects.

David J. Burns is Associate Professor of Marketing at Xavier University. He is co-author of *Retailing* (Dame Publications, 1998) and *Retail Management: Strategies, Tactics, and Practices* (Macmillan, 1994). His research has appeared in a number of journals, including *Psychology and Marketing, Journal of Marketing Theory and Practice, Journal of Social Psychology, Journal of Business Ethics,* and *Journal of Consumer Satisfaction, Dissatisfaction and Complaining Behavior.* He has also authored several book chapters and video segments.

Karen Coats is Associate Professor of English at Illinois State University. She is the author of *Looking Glasses and Neverlands: Lacan, Desire, and Subjectivity in Children's Literature* (University of Iowa Press, 2004) and various articles on children's and young adult literature.

Caryl Emerson is the A. Watson Armour III University Professor of Slavic languages and Literatures at Princeton University. She is the author of numerous works on Bakhtin, including *Mikhail Bakhtin: Creation of a Prosaics*, with Gary Saul Morson (Stanford University Press, 1990) and *The*

First Hundred Years of Mikhail Bakhtin (Princeton University Press, 1997), and is a primary translator of Bakhtin into English.

Susan M. Felch is Professor of English at Calvin College and past director of the Seminars in Christian Scholarship program. She is the author/editor of numerous books including *The Collected Works of Anne Vaughan Lock* (Arizona, 1999); *Bakhtin and Religion: A Feeling for Faith* (Northwestern University Press, 2001); and a series of four books on the seasons, each of which is subtitled *A Spiritual Biography of the Season* (Skylight Paths Press, 2002–6). She has published articles on sixteenth-century British writers, Mikhail Bakhtin, and literary criticism.

Bert H. Hodges is Professor of Psychology at Gordon College. He is the author of articles in social, cognitive, and theoretical psychology and is working on a book on values and cognition.

David M. Holley is Professor of Philosophy and Chair of the Department of Philosophy and Religion at The University of Southern Mississippi. He is the author of *Self-Interest and Beyond* (Paragon House, 1999) and numerous articles in philosophical journals on philosophy of religion, ethics, and moral psychology.

William B. Hurlbut, M.D. is a consulting professor in the Program in Human Biology at Stanford University and a member of the President's Council on Bioethics. He is the co-editor of *Altruism and Altruistic Love: Science, Philosophy and Religion in Dialogue* (Oxford, 2002) as well as numerous articles on bioethics and the biology of moral awareness.

Sherri B. Lantinga is Associate Professor of Psychology at Dordt College. She has presented her work on the self at conferences for psychology instructors and for Christian grade school teachers.

Mark Lowery is Associate Professor of Theology at the University of Dallas. He is the author of *Living the Good Life* (St. Anthony Messenger Press, 2003) and articles on moral theology and Catholic social thought.

Kent L. Norman is an Associate Professor of Cognitive Psychology at the University of Maryland. He is the author of *The Psychology of Menu Selection: Designing Cognitive Control at the Human/Computer Interface* (Ablex Press, 1991), and *Teaching in the Switched On Classroom: An Introduction to Electronic Education and HyperCourseware, Laboratory for*

Automation Psychology (lap.umd.edu, 1997), He has authored articles on the psychology of human/computer interaction and interface design.

Jim Norwine is Regents Professor of Physics/Geosciences at Texas A&M University-Kingsville. He is the author of numerous scholarly articles, such as "The Meaning of Meaning in a Post-Meaning Age" (*International Social Science Journal*, Paris, 1994) and the author/editor of six books, including *A Postmodern Tao* (UPA, 1993); *The New Third World* (Westview, 1998); *Worldview Flux* (Lexington Books, 2000); and *Water for Texas* (Texas A&M University Press, 2004).

Stephen P. Stratton is Director of the Center for Counseling at Asbury College. His primary areas of interest include attachment dysfunctions in adults and the integration of psychology, theology and neuroscience.

Paul C. Vitz is Senior Scholar at the Institute for the Psychological Sciences in northern Virginia and Professor of Psychology Emeritus at New York University. He is the author of some half-dozen books, the most recent being *Faith of the Fatherless: The Psychology of Atheism* (Spence, 1999), and of many articles and essays, primarily dealing with the relationship between psychology and Christianity.

Glenn Weaver is Professor of Psychology at Calvin College. He is the author of several recent chapters on the nature of scientific psychological explanation and Christian understandings of human persons in the book: *Science of the Soul: Christian Perspectives on Psychological Research* (University Press of America, 2003) and a chapter "Embodied Spirituality: Spiritual and Self-Identity Experiences Among Persons with Alzheimer's Dementia" in the book: *From Cells to Souls and Beyond* (Eerdmans, 2004).

Index